ANTONIONI

Antonioni

OR, THE SURFACE OF THE WORLD

Seymour Chatman

UNIVERSITY OF CALIFORNIA PRESS
Berkeley   Los Angeles   London

University of California Press
Berkeley and Los Angeles
University of California Press, Ltd.
London, England
© 1985 by
The Regents of the University of California

Library of Congress Cataloging in Publication Data

Chatman, Seymour Benjamin, 1928–
Antonioni, or, The Surface of the world.

Filmography: p.
Bibliography: p.
Includes index.
1. Antonioni, Michelangelo.   I. Title.   II. Title:
Antonioni.   III. Title: Surface of the world.
PN1998.A3A654   1985   791.43′0233′0924   85-1025
ISBN 0-520-05205-6
ISBN 0-520-05341-9 (pbk.)

Printed in the United States of America

2   3   4   5   6   7   8   9

The mere exposure to the visible surface of the world will not arouse ideas unless the spectacle is approached with ideas ready to be stirred up.

—Rudolf Arnheim

Images are mute, yet presently the silent cinema begins to talk, and I recognize its language.

—Vladimir Nabokov (in his last interview)

A movie has meaning in the same way that a thing does: neither of them speaks to an isolated understanding; rather, both appeal to our power tacitly to decipher the world of men and to coexist with them. It is true that in our ordinary lives we lose sight of this aesthetic value of the tiniest perceived thing. It is also true that the perceived form is never perfect in real life, that it always has blurs, smudges, and superfluous matter, as it were. Cinematographic drama is, so to speak, finer-grained than real-life dramas: it takes place in a world that is more exact than the real world. But in the last analysis, perception permits us to understand the meaning of the cinema. A movie is not thought; it is perceived.

—Maurice Merleau-Ponty

Not to speak does not mean that one has nothing to say. Those who do not speak may be brimming over with emotions, which can be expressed only in forms and pictures, in gesture and play of feature. The man of visual culture uses these not as substitutes for words, as a deaf-mute uses his fingers. He does not think in words, the syllables of which he sketches in the air like the dots and dashes of the Morse code. The gestures of visual man are not intended to convey concepts, which can be expressed in words, but such inner experiences, such nonrational emotions as would still remain unexpressed when everything that can be told has been told.

—Béla Balázs

It was precisely by photographing and enlarging the surface of the things around me that I sought to discover what was behind those things.

—Michelangelo Antonioni

Contents

Acknowledgments

I would like to thank the following persons who helped me, one way or another, in writing this book: Lucilla Albano, Bertrand Augst, Michael Billingsley, Yvette Biró, Michel and Claudia Bodmer, Ernest Callenbach, Guido Carboni, Carlo di Carlo, Francesco Casetti, Elaine Chekich, David Cohen, Furio Colombo, Sophie Consagra, Walter Cini, David Degener, Anthony Dubovsky, Ray Durgnat, Umberto Eco, Paul Ekman, Linus Eukel, Marilyn Fabe, Guido Fink, Nancy Goldman, Jennifer Hammett, Steve Hawes, Beverle Houston, George Huega, Peter Hughes, Ann Juell, Bruce Kawin, Marsha Kinder, Edith Kramer, David Littlejohn, Lars Lerup, Sam Levin, Ronald Levaco, Tom Luddy, Patrizia Magli, Enzo and Franca Mancini, Gianni Massironi, Mark McFadden, Lino Miccichè, Fiorenza Möller, Gavriel Moses, Laura Mulvey, William Nestrick, Pino Paioni, Constance Penley, Patrizio Rossi, Tsurumi Rumberger, Thomas Schmidt, Marilyn Schwartz, Peter Selz, Kaja Silverman, Michael Silverman, Bill Smith, Patrick Smith, Aldo Tassone, Laura Thielen, Peter Wollen, and Robin Wood. Special thanks are due the director and staff of the Centro Sperimentale di Cinematografia in Rome for helping me view rare Antonioni films and to the director and staff of the Ufficio Cinema of the Comuni di Ferrara for inviting me to participate in their conference on Antonioni in autumn 1983.

To the National Endowment for the Humanities I wish to express my appreciation for support that enabled me to work in Rome. To my wife, Barbara Blomer, and to my daughter, Mariel, thanks are due (more than words can express) for making the trip memorable beyond the merely professional level. To the American Academy in Rome we owe our gratitude for housing and other support during our stay.

To Michelangelo Antonioni I want to express my deep gratitude for various kindnesses, in particular a long and no doubt for him exhausting interview and the loan of films that I could not find elsewhere.

A Note on Photographic Reproductions

It has become a rueful tradition in film books with photographic illustrations to apologize for their quality, especially that of frame reproductions as opposed to photographs taken by still photographers on the set. (For the sake of simplicity I shall refer to all the reproduced photographs as frames.) Images that look clear and sharp on the screen in the theater often turn out blurred and muddy even when reproduced with the best equipment. Perhaps that is one more artifact of the persistence-of-vision phenomenon. One feels a special sorrow, in the case of a visual artist like Antonioni, not to be able to provide photographs that do justice to the wonderful images on the cinema screen. I ask my reader to consider these illustrations as the merest of sketches, as rough indexes to the frames and shots they are meant to recall. The problem is especially acute when reproducing frames from color films like *Il deserto rosso.*

Beyond that apology there lies a more implicit one—for presuming to capture within the covers of a book anything like what passes before us at twenty-four frames per second. As my friend Leo Braudy put it in his book *Jean Renoir,* that is like trying to characterize a literary career with a list of the poet's ten favorite words.

Introduction

What is impressive about Antonioni's films is not only that they are good but that they have been made at all. Films depend directly on mass public support in the form of ticket purchases. Antonioni's films do not appeal to large audiences, and like many another artist he has had to be tenacious, tough-minded, and resilient to pursue his exacting goals through many difficult years. In a 1980 television interview on RAI with Lino Miccichè he said: "I always had to fight like crazy to make cinema, because my films . . . have always been tremendous commercial failures. . . . The producers consider me a cold director, a sophistic director, an intellectual director."[1]

Why do average moviegoers find Antonioni difficult? Perhaps because his subtleties of form make the content seem more abstruse than it really is. The slow editing pace, the careful, subtle, measured camera movements, and the long holds on faces and details of location violate their expectations and elicit the question that producers most dread—What's this movie about anyway? Yet the preoccupations of the films do not differ markedly from those of network television's daily fare—the difficulty of sustaining a love relationship, of finding work that is meaningful, of weathering the stormy conflict between our own drive and others' expectations of us. It is not the first time that the form of a work has obscured its meaning—though economic exigencies make that phenomenon rarer in film than it is in the other arts. Of course, it may attest to a film's power that some viewers walk out. As Roland Barthes put it in a tribute to Antonioni:

The activity of the artist is suspect because it disturbs the comfort, the security of the established senses, because it is at once expensive and free, and because the new society which seeks to find itself through diverse regimens has not yet decided what to think.[2]

The discomfort felt by average moviegoers was felt even more acutely by nervous producers. For years Antonioni has been *regista maledetto,* doomed to be unpopular because he was too private. Antonioni recalls one of the blunter of these rejections, made in the fifties by a producer named Amato: "You, Antonioni, are a great director, but we've got to kill you . . . because you're dangerous to cinema, because it's such a pain to see your films."[3] The producers who have risked their

1

energy and capital on Antonioni's projects will be remembered with gratitude for their vision and contribution to the art of cinema.

Antonioni has to some extent been vindicated by time. Hooted and derided by audiences at the Cannes film festival in 1959, *L'avventura* was a few years later judged to be one of the ten best films of all time. Far from being dated, it is more accessible than ever; what was opaque twenty years ago seems translucent today. (The same fate befell other great filmmakers, the Fellini of *8½* and the Bergman of *Persona*.) Antonioni's films have even anticipated issues of widespread public concern. *La notte, L'eclisse,* and *Il deserto rosso,* for instance, touched on the unnerving collapse of normal assumptions about the safety and stability of the environment at a time when few people thought about such matters. It is not hard to see in them implications for the lives of residents of Three Mile Island or Love Canal. Although environmental anxieties have come to be exploited by pop films and television programs (microwave bombardments by the Russians, all manner of UFOs, shootouts in space), Antonioni's art has disdained such popularizations precisely because they remove us, through comforting fictions, from our real plight. Here his superior vision and control show their power. For all their hysteria and manipulativeness, commercial films cannot evoke the chilly truths of the final sequence of *L'eclisse.* Of course, artists are not spokespersons, and still less opinion managers. They are concerned not to exploit a public predicament but to show us its implications in an honest and beautiful way. With an artist's prescience, Antonioni perceived signs years before most of us had ever heard the word *ecology,* but his exacting and original vision was not easy to read. The films provided few clues, and practically none of the clues were verbal.

The central and distinguishing characteristic of Antonioni's mature films (so goes the argument of this book) is narration by a kind of visual minimalism, by an intense concentration on the sheer appearance of things—the surface of the world as he sees it—and a minimization of explanatory dialogue. The rendered surface is eloquent once one has learned to read it, and, even more, to accept its esthetic and narrative self-sufficiency. To the viewer familiar with minimalism in the other arts, especially in literature (as in the work of Hemingway and Robbe-Grillet), the demand is not outlandish. But to traditional audiences, for whom story is paramount, the films have seemed troublingly opaque.

To say that Antonioni is obsessed with the surface of the world is not to say that his films are unconcerned with the depths of personality—motives, perceptions, the vicissitudes of the emotional life. On the contrary, he emphasizes these precisely by leaving to the viewer the task of inferring them from (often enigmatic) signs. The very effort demanded of the audience ensures a heavy psychological accent. As in the modern novel, the omission of explicit text paradoxically adds implicit meanings. *We* fill in what is missing, to the limits of our imagination and experience. The demand placed on viewers is even more challenging than that placed on readers of a novel precisely because of the constraints of the medium. Films do not allow us to stop and reflect on what we have read: the projector, not our eyes, controls the pace. So reflection is deferred, and visual attention and memory are exercised by the deferral.

Antonioni took a long time to learn how to render the effect of surface—fifteen or more years and no fewer than five feature films. Though his early work showed promise, his later artistry is very clearly the result of effort and experimentation. He is a made, not a born, artist. He had to free himself of conventional cinematic means of rendering narrative, especially in respect to dialogue, conventional sound effects, and commentative music. We can see this development beginning in the first films (Chapter 1). Flawed as they are, they show an acute sensibility struggling to master the medium. The first unqualified success is *Il grido* (Chapter 2), which serves as a bridge to the great films of the late 1950s and the 1960s—*L'avventura, La notte, L'eclisse,* and *Il deserto rosso* (Chapters 3–6). With *Blow-Up* (Chapter 7) Antonioni enters a new, international phase. His style secure, he takes up new themes—the problem of the visual perception of reality, especially as it touches the artist (*Blow-Up*), political revolution (*Zabriskie Point,* Chapter 8), and personal identity and death (*The Passenger,* Chapter 9). His last two films (*Il mistero di Oberwald,* Chapter 9, and *Identificazione di una donna,* Chapter 10) also show movement into new realms, both thematic and technical.

In describing this development, my focus is primarily on the films. I introduce few biographical details—only those that directly pertain to Antonioni's evolving art.[4] But I do quote extensively from Antonioni's highly articulate writings and interviews, since they provide an excellent and revealing commentary on his intentions and method—one that the English-speaking reader may not know.

The amount of space devoted to each film in the following account only partly reflects my feeling of its importance in cinema history. I have discussed at length several lesser films that cannot readily be seen by American filmgoers—the "Prefazione" to *I tre volti* entitled "Il provino," *Il mistero di Oberwald,* and *Identificazione di una donna.* The discussion is proportionately shorter concerning films like *Blow-Up* that have been widely seen and discussed in America.

1

Early Films

DOCUMENTARIES

Although he had written screenplays for feature films as early as 1939, Antonioni started his career with short documentaries. The experience was decisive: *L'avventura* is inconceivable without its shots of ordinary Sicilian life, as is *La notte* without those of the Milan suburbs or *L'eclisse* without those of the EUR section of Rome.

Antonioni's first documentary was *Gente del Po* (People of the Po), begun in 1943 at the time and near the place where Visconti was shooting *Ossessione,* a film that influenced at least two of Antonioni's own films. Only parts of the original footage escaped the war, and Antonioni was not able to finish the film until 1947. In 1948, he made another documentary, *N.U.* (short for *Netteza urbana*), about the street cleaners of Rome. He made several more documentaries— *L'amorosa menzogna* (The Amorous Lie, 1948–1949), on the *fumetti,* the comic strip–like photoromances popular in Italy; *Superstizione* (Superstition, 1949), on superstitious practices in the Italian countryside; *Sette canne, un vestito* (Seven Reeds, One Suit, 1950), on the manufacture of rayon thread; *La villa dei mostri* (The Villa of the Monsters, 1950), on the statuary in the Villa Orsini in Bomarzo; and *La funivia del Faloria* (The Funicular of Mount Faloria, 1950), on the funicular railway near the town of Cortina d'Ampezzo.[1]

Gente del Po and *N.U.* provide dazzling early evidence of Antonioni's powers. Though they do not experiment with narrative structure, they evoke an unmistakably Antonionian mood. The explanatory voice-over is used with restraint; the images more or less speak for themselves. Each film beats to the rhythm of the life that it portrays. In *Gente del Po,* the camera follows the slow movement of the river down to its wide mouth at the Adriatic, and the very images are regulated by that irrepressible current. The river is broad, opaque with silt, "as flat as a span of asphalt."[2] It dominates not only the vistas but also the quality of everyday life in "an impoverished country, where everything flows slowly like the seasons, like the river." Antonioni's camera captures that movement with broad, slow sweeps

Frame 1

and countersweeps or holds on slowly drifting boats. Every image is referred
back to the river's blank, noncommittal dominance—bargemen loading their
boats, field hands threshing and reaping, couples courting, housewives washing,
cooking, nursing, shopping, or just standing. The whole life of the river vibrates
and pulsates in clear though flatly lit tones. Preferring the visual image to the
soundtrack, *Gente del Po* shows the first evidence of Antonioni's lifelong effort to
uncover the meanings of things beneath the mystery of their appearances.

 N.U. also finds a rhythm in its subject—a day in the life of Rome's sanitation
workers, who sweep away as the busy city whirls around them. The film emphasizes their "invisible" omnipresence. Antonioni asks us to take a slow, steady
look at the world around us, to forget our ordinary preoccupations, and to contemplate that which lies slightly athwart them. Though the film begins at dawn
and ends at dusk, its principle of arrangement is geographic as well as chronological. First we see a worker alone in the Piazza del Popolo, then one in the Piazza
del Quirinale, then one against San Pietro, another against the bells of Trinità dei
Monti, and so on. The film reverses ordinary travelogue interests: however variegated the brilliant Eternal City may be, the street cleaner is everywhere, invisible
to the populace and indifferent to the landmarks yet ironically essential to them,
to Rome's *nettezza,* its propriety. We see him, humble, modest, even docile,
working alone or with a fellow worker, behind a broom, followed by a truck. We
see him eating against a wall or taking a postprandial nap. We see his efficacy and
modest technology. We see him feeding garbage to the pigs.

 Gente del Po and *N.U.* already convey the tensions of Antonioni's later career.
Only hasty readings of these films interpret them as criticisms of the social system. True, there are sad images: mothers and babies endure the elements; workers drink milk out of metal pails, fetch morsels from a garbage can, or eat their

Frame 2

lunches in the bleak street against a stone wall. We know that mothers and babies need better conditions and that workers deserve the sausages that hang temptingly in shop windows before their eyes. But that does not seem to be the message—nor does there seem to be any message at all. The films offer more than easy appeals to sympathy or social reform. We are shown the awesome Po with the humble architecture of its inhabitants and the light irony with which a sanitation worker sweeps up the scraps of a letter discarded in an argument between a middle-aged husband and wife, reminding us that the garbage man always has the last word. The camera eye refuses to simplify, to reduce the heterogeneous complexity of the world to a few motifs merely in order to validate some ideology. (Several early critics erred in stressing Antonioni's "Marxism.") In this earliest evidence, we see Antonioni's primary allegiance to a *vision* of the world in its plastic particularity. His vision of the street cleaners is cool: we are not asked in any direct way to sympathize with their lot. The wall and their placement against it form an interesting design, the kind of pattern that we would expect to find in art photographs. The carefully articulated scale and distribution of the figures, the textures and lighting, the very beauty of the imagery discourage easy social judgments. Antonioni's most valuable contribution to the cinema can already be seen—his unrelenting insistence on the value of the pure visual given. The theme of *N.U.* is "That is the way they look, the sanitation workers; that is the way our streets get cleaned; here is one part of the banal urban scene made visible; what do you make of it?" Few filmmakers had asked such a question before 1948, and it seemed a particularly odd question to ask in Rome three short years after German soldiers and partisan guerillas had fought in its streets. Even in the thick of war-oriented neorealism, Antonioni's viewfinder was beginning to track a kind of film that was different from any that cinema audiences had ever seen.

The look of these short films is not unfamiliar to the fan of Antonioni's later work. After the credits appear against a wall, the very first shot of *Gente del Po*, the first film of his career, is already moving: a pan to the left on peasants unloading sacks of flour from a truck. The word used by the screenplay to describe the shot is *scoprire*, which can mean "uncover" or "reveal" in a relatively conventional theatrical sense, as when we say, "The curtain rises, revealing the interior of a lavish Manhattan apartment." But it also means "discover." This movement of almost surprised discovery calls immediate attention to the existence of the camera, the medium of registration, and the eye behind it. Here begins Antonioni's lifelong attack on cinematic illusion, on the myth that the visual images should be somehow secondary, working only in the service of the story. With increasing subtlety, he would come to challenge the traditional dominance of story over imagery and over the activity of the camera that photographs it.

The words of *Gente del Po*'s title apply literally. These are real *gente*, people, and this is the real Po River, the flowing sheet of gray behind, in front of, and around them. We speak of the human images in a landscape painting as *figures*—meaning the main objects of our attention—and of landscapes, buildings, and so on as *ground*. Here we are prompted to ask, Is this film primarily about the people or about the Po? Which is the figure, and which is the ground? Has the river made the people what they are, or do the people live there because of the kind of people they are? At the very outset of his career, we see the birth of one of Antonioni's chief preoccupations, the tension between figure and ground. The buds in these short documentaries would ultimately bear elegant fruit in *L'eclisse*, which raises the ground of a banal streetcorner in the EUR section of Rome to blinding figure by literally erasing the characters in its last minutes.

The technique of *Gente del Po* is relatively conventional—mostly static setups punctuated by traditional pans and cutaways. The strategy is familiar: first the human situation is shown, then the same old river, which "just keeps rollin' along," or vice versa. The overwhelming monotone of the river—moving but always the same—is invoked by simply reverting to it. The river's indifference to human fate is signaled by its juxtaposition with human situations of different emotional charge: a woman feeding her man, a field worker looking wistfully at the passing boat, a *ragazzo* wooing a *ragazza*, a mother giving medicine to her sick child. The incessant reference back to the river is quite natural. Indeed, it is a little too easy, reflecting something of an apprentice stage of work.

N.U. is subtler. Consider one small but telling example. Whereas in *Gente* the camera movements or editing cuts always reinforce our sense of the Po's importance (regardless of the nature of that importance), *N.U.* offers a camera movement so strikingly arbitrary as to prefigure *Il deserto rosso* or *The Passenger*. The film is ostensibly about how we overlook workers and tasks in the urban scene in our everyday obsession with our own affairs. Usual textual logic would suggest a regular foregrounding of the street cleaner, precisely to make him visible. And indeed, foregrounding is Antonioni's modus operandi in the first, establishing part of the film: the patient and humble form of the street cleaner is placed against various landmarks of Rome so that it emerges as the figure to be noted simply by the code of repetition. But roughly halfway into the film, we encounter a street cleaner asleep at the foot of some steps. Then the camera pans to the facade of a tiny church. The unidentified church appears nowhere else in the film: the very next shot is of another street cleaner sleeping in a quite different place, on a wall of the Gianicolo hill overlooking a panoramic view of Rome. The ordinary reading of this pair of shots would be this: Street cleaners sleep wherever they can, indifferent to their surroundings, whether these are a modest church or a wall overlooking the splendor of Rome. At a certain level, that is the meaning. But the way in which the camera lingers on the church hints at something more. In that delay, that hesitation or contemplative suspension of the camera, the tiny church ceases to be a background for the street cleaner's nap and becomes an object of independent interest, suggesting—but not supplying—its own story. It is like *The Passenger*'s camel and rider, which have no relevance to Locke's search for the rebels but which the camera follows for ever so long and inexplicable a minute. Suddenly, the reading becomes problematic. Does the film say that the church is picturesque? Does it say that the street cleaner and the church are alike in their modest serviceability? Does it implicate this church and thereby the Church in the plight of the working class? Who knows? With the enigma comes enrichment of a peculiarly modern, open sort. This is the first instance, I think, of Antonioni's commitment to the open text. Who else would have dared in so brief a film to allow his camera to be "distracted" from its "normal" task?

These documentaries resemble Antonioni's later films in other ways as well. The tonality tends to be muted, a mixture of greys, rather than the usual high contrast that we associate with films made under the bright sun or studio lights of Hollywood. The lighting effects of *Gente del Po* remind us of *Il grido* (1956), and *N.U.*'s tonality resembles that of the cityscapes of *Cronaca di un amore* (Story of a Love Affair, 1950) and *La signora senza camelie* (The Lady Without Camelias, 1952–1953). Already, too, we get a sense of Antonioni's compositional ability, particularly in his placement of figures against their grounds. He shows his preference for long and medium shots over close-ups, although *Gente del Po* is burdened with a number of rather sentimental close-ups. In that film, the surfaces and lines of the river, the fields, the houses, and the boats permit him to divide up the frame in ways that he was to develop in the gorgeous cinematography of his films of the 1960s. In the Rome of *N.U.*, too, he finds plenty of lines to manipulate, especially when they permit him to emphasize the depth of field.

As for sound, Antonioni still had much to learn. The relation between the visual and auditory tracks of *Gente del Po* is conventionally redundant: the voice says, " At this hour, people are on the banks," and immediately there appears a shot of people on the banks. *N.U.* shows a bit more subtlety: the invisibility of the *spazzini* is made clearly evident before we are told that they are invisible. And some of the more delightful bits are unaccompanied by voice-over, for instance, the elderly street cleaner who swoops down on the scraps of the torn letter or the amorous young street cleaner who drags his broom behind him. Antonioni seems

Frame 3

to treat the voice-over only as a necessary evil: he uses some in the first quarter of the film to reinforce the themes of the street cleaner's invisibility and the necessity of the sanitation service, but then it ceases. Antonioni's distrust of words manifests itself early, but he will only act on that distrust after four relatively talkative feature films.

L'amorosa menzogna and *Superstizione* are lesser documentaries, though they have their own sorts of charm. *L'amorosa menzogna* is about the making of a *fumetto*, or photoromance, of that title in a shabby little studio in Rome. It features the models who play the lovers in the actual photoromance, an auto mechanic named Sergio Raimondi and a shopgirl named Annie O'Hara, along with the "director," photographer, and lighting technician who worked on the "production." One places these words between smiling quotation marks because *L'amorosa menzogna* shows humorously that the creation of a fumetto resembles in a modest way the creation of a film, though at the critical moment the histrionically posed models

Frame 4   *Frame 5*

freeze instead of act. In place of a cinematographer and an imposing Mitchell, there is a funny little photographer and an old twin-lens Rolleicord. The film is not visually striking, except for one sequence that anticipates later work in some interesting ways. It is Antonioni's first mirror shot. A pan shows Annie O'Hara's reflection in a big vanity mirror, then repeats it in a small mirror to her right, then moves across a fumetto cover to the real Annie. Antonioni uses mirrors elaborately in *L'avventura* and *L'eclisse* to reflect critical moments when the heroine's sense of identity is questioned. *L'amorosa menzogna*, which is amusing in a light satirical way, reflects an aspect of Antonioni that the broad public does not know well but that is amply evident in his interviews and writings. He is a man of wit as well as intelligence. Indeed, he used the experience of this film to draft a scenario that became Fellini's *Lo sceicco bianco* (The White Sheik).[3]

Superstizione locates its case histories in a simple village in the Marche. Its interest is mostly anthropological. The film shows villagers making charms, casting spells, and exorcizing ills in the most unself-conscious way. A girl breaks her mirror. A warlock helps another girl find out why her fiancé has not written in three months. An old woman kills a snake, burns it, and scatters its ashes in front of an enemy's door. Another old woman puts money into the pocket of a dead man who is carried by on a wooden sled. There is no particular logic to the order in which these practices are displayed, but they are so odd that organization does not seem to be a problem. The film is interesting, but anyone could have made it.[4]

It was not films about curiosities but documentary films in which Antonioni evoked real places—the Po River or the *piazze* of Rome—that helped him to achieve his mature narrative style. Such evocation was to prove more than a mere record: he was training himself in a textual method that would ultimately prevail in his fiction movies (after a relatively false start that was to stretch through two films). As the most recent Italian book on Antonioni says, the first of Antonioni's labors with the movie camera was the ability

to interrogate things, the external worlds, people, and to make them reveal, through their external semblances, their internal truths, their innermost sense, that which Antonioni himself was to call their mystery.[5]

CRONACA DI UN AMORE (1950):
Genre and the Long Take

Cronaca di un amore (Story of a Love Affair, 1950), Antonioni's first feature film, recounts the story of Paola Fontana (Lucia Bosè), the young wife of Enrico Fontana (Ferdinando Sarmi), a wealthy Milanese industrialist who becomes unaccountably jealous of her life before they were married. He hires a detective to make inquiries and thus unwittingly brings Guido Garroni (Massimo Girotti), a high school sweetheart, back into Paola's life. Garroni warns her about the detective's inquiries but assures her that they need not worry about the death of Guido's previous girlfriend. (Paola and Guido did not actually kill her, but they failed to warn her about stepping into an open elevator shaft.) Their old infatuation, heightened by guilt and fear of discovery, rises to fever pitch, and Paola persuades Guido to murder her husband. He waits on a road at dusk at a spot that Enrico is sure to pass, but he does not have to act: upset by the detective's report, Enrico loses control of the car and dies in the resulting accident. Paola is thrown into a panic by the arrival of the police, who come to notify her of her husband's death. She rushes to Guido, who promises to join her the next day but instead leaves for the railroad station.

As this plot summary suggests, *Cronaca di un amore* moves very much within the limits of genre. Since Antonioni had been a film critic and historian before starting to make films, it is not surprising that his first film should owe something to the film noir—or *giallo* in Italian, since in Italy the covers of mystery stories are yellow, rather than black as they are in France. But in *Cronaca di un amore,* the conventions of the genre become a pretext for themes and concerns that are quite different from those of Hollywood. (During much of his career, we find Antonioni playing against genres rather than observing their dictates.) Hollywood film noir focuses on plot rather than character, on such questions as, Who did it? and Will they get away with it? In contrast, *Cronaca di un amore* emphasizes, rather, the mental state of the protagonists, especially the guilt, fear, and anxiety that seem to persist whether the danger that they are facing is real or not. Their free-floating anxiety leads the lovers into a strange lassitude that critics likened to existential malaise. The heavy psychological emphasis subtilizes the issues, unlike early Hollywood film noir, where truth, however deeply concealed, is ultimately comprehensible. In *The Maltese Falcon,* for example, Brigid O'Shaughnessy (Mary Astor) is unmasked as a member of the gang, and Sam Spade (Bogart), resisting her blandishments, sends her off to the penitentiary. Spade's commitment to a monolithic justice is never less than arrow straight. The morality of *Cronaca,* like that of the subtler Hollywood films noirs, is less clear-cut: the couple do not actually cause the two deaths; they only wish for them. It is not even clear that Paola is going to be arrested at the end, though it is obvious that she fears she will be. Probably the police are just coming to inform her of her husband's death. The moral questions are muddy, like the river behind them as they stand on the bridge in a memorable scene, planning Enrico's murder.

More interesting, though somewhat difficult for foreign audiences to under-stand, is how the conventions of film noir are adapted to the Italian scene. It owes much to Visconti's *Ossessione,* whose themes of lust, jealousy, and greed move easily from the Southern California of *The Postman Always Rings Twice* to the Po Valley. But the thematic of *Cronaca di un amore* is more complex. Antonioni uses the film noir genre as the basis of an inquiry into the morals and psychology of the class enriched by Italy's postwar "economic miracle." Critics often argue that *Cronaca di un amore,* like other films of the fifties (for instance, Rossellini's *Viaggio in Italia,* 1953), represents a second, or psychological, stage of Italian neorealism. Antonioni himself said that the only useful way of prolonging neo-realism was by turning it inside out. Naturally, this new emphasis presupposes a considerable knowledge of recent Italian history, which serves to make these films less directly accessible to foreign audiences than rawly immediate films like *Paisà.* Even when we read the explanations of Italian critics, we may well feel that we have missed something. For instance, a critic of 1954 explains the film in terms of Paola's and Guido's dissatisfaction with themselves and with the con-formist society that surrounds them.[6] They cannot relate to others, to work, to the problems of society. So they feel a fatigue, a Sartrean nausea. For example, Paola says while lying in Guido's bed, "Now the worst moment arrives: getting dressed. I can't do it." An implacable destiny makes them weary and apathetic. Thus the psychological and artistic justification of the film: "And now?" asks Paola, plaintively, after the death of her husband. "Now we can't continue, don't you see?" responds Guido. The energetic American tradition would demand, But why not? Why would Guido not want to stay on, now that the coast is clear, since he is guilty of nothing, and his sweetheart is rich and free? His sudden antipathy for Paola is even more unaccountable than his acquiescence in her murder scheme. It is hard to understand in what sense Paola is dissatisfied with herself: she enjoys the clothes, the social activity, the fancy restaurants enough to refuse Guido's suggestion that she elope without the money. And surely, what Guido is overtly and justifiably dissatisfied with is his poverty: he seems more envious than contemptuous of the circles in which Paola travels.

Most problematic of all to American taste is what makes the lovers submit to the implacable destiny that prescribes Guido's abandonment of Paola. The de-nouement seems less existential than operatic. By not accounting for Guido's cryptic decision, the film makes us wonder which narrative convention to apply. Not that of the Hays Office version of film noir, which would insist that if the couple were guilty they must get caught, but if they were not guilty they must go free together. Nor would neorealism insist on an arbitrary decision like Guido's. Only in melodrama or opera are we apt to encounter such inexplicable tragic endings, and it is hard not to feel that our emotions are somewhat manipulated by the final shot of Paola standing before her doorway in a white evening dress, "canceled" by a black diagonal line.

Though the film conveys the protagonists' defeat, apathy, and fatigue, it does not tell us why they feel that way. True, such feelings resemble those of later characters—Aldo in *Il grido,* Sandro in *L'avventura,* Lidia and Giovanni in *La*

Frame 6

notte. But the later films do not operate within generic constraints, so they do not
need to acknowledge traditional causality. Of course, existential anguish, *nausée,*
is authentically matched with causelessness. But the conventional film noir elements in *Cronaca di un amore* offer traditional claims to narrativity. If this were
an ordinary American film noir, the haunting sense of defeat would be justified.
The couple on the run would have to get caught. Crime did not pay, and they and

the audience knew it. The ethic of *Cronaca di un amore* is subtler and more ambiguous. It is neither fear nor puritanic guilt that torments the couple. But what does torment them is something of an Italian secret. Critics often distinguish between the national Antonioni of the fifties and the international Antonioni of the late sixties and seventies. My own difficulty with motivation in *Cronaca* argues the justice of that distinction. Though it is interesting to be told by Italian critics that Paola and Guido are social products of an economic miracle that somehow causes their moral disintegration, foreign audiences must cast about for other, more universal explanations of their fate. Difficulty in doing so tends to limit the film's appeal.

The dependence on genre also has some formal repercussions. Film noir demands full and complicated plot development firmly rooted in suspense and surprise; these concerns are alien to Antonioni's early temperament and style. True, *Cronaca di un amore* presents a recognizable sequence of events—the couple fall in love, Paola convinces Guido to murder Enrico, Enrico dies by accident, Guido leaves Paola, and so forth. There is not yet the irresolution (like "life itself") that characterizes the plots of the later films. But Antonioni is no Hitchcock; indeed, one critic sees him as Hitchcock's "antipode." He ignores the prescriptions of suspense and surprise whenever it suits his thematic or visual purpose, which is practically all the time. When surprise does occur, as in Enrico's accidental death, the impact is strangely muted, especially by film noir standards: instead of a dramatic close-up on the crash—screeching brakes, spinning wheels, fiery explosion, and so on—Antonioni shoots the accident from Guido's point of view a mile down the road. The fire is so far away that we do not quite understand why he should be interested in it; it does not occur to us at first that the burning car is Enrico's.

In the later films, other values compensate for and even validate unexpected quirks of the characters' behavior. Where these are not made manifest, the resultant ellipses of motive and behavior, like ellipses of plot, coincide formally with Antonioni's growing laconic view of life. But here, ellipsis deprives the narrative of whatever coherence the genre might afford, so the impact of the whole, including the brilliant cinematography, is somewhat weakened.

The characters seem to want to be Antonionian, that is, possessed of a depth to which their surface appearance provides the only key, but the conventions of genre do not allow it. The conflict between generic melodrama and documentary realism—the realism of sheer chronicle—is most pointed in the dialogue: "When I saw you dancing with her . . . it was more than I could handle [*è stato più forte di me*]" or "As soon as I saw you, I knew everything was the same between us . . . I was waiting for you all these years, and I didn't even know it." These lines do not sit well with the bleak objective view of such people, the moral coldness, puzzling weakness, selfish capriciousness and insensitivity that the camera is trying to render. Only in *Il grido* and the tetralogy would Antonioni develop a spare dialogue that did not detract from his splendid images.

Doubtless it was Antonioni's very desire to escape the limits of genre that gave rise to these inconsistencies in *Cronaca di un amore.* The problem is that he could not yet go far enough; he could not turn the film into what *L'avventura* was to become, "a *giallo* in reverse" (his own phrase). One can imagine such a film: Enrico could mysteriously have disappeared before Paola even thought about the murder; then, after a few delicious weeks together, the couple could discover that more than an irate husband was keeping them apart. I do not seriously offer this as a revision, but it does suggest the kind of openness of plot that would inform his later masterpieces.

Cronaca's dialogue also demonstrates a false start toward the achievement of psychological motivation. Not observation of life itself, which characterizes the documentaries and the great tetralogy, but imitation of movies of the thirties produced such lines as "Love is a destructive, inescapable magnet." The motivation is simplistic, naive, and, above all, overarticulated. As the torch song has it, "Can't help lovin' that man of mine." Paola can't get over Guido; Guido can't get over Paola; Joy, the model, can't get over Valerio, the shady car dealer; and so on. The film presents a relatively conventional version of the emotional "fragility" that *L'avventura* evokes so unconventionally. It would take Antonioni nine years to find his characteristic if harshly lit vantage on the emotions and to learn to display them with the laconic objectivity that he is only able in *Cronaca* to apply to buildings, landscapes, and the ordinary life of the city. He had to learn to transform the words "Can't help lovin' that man of mine" into "I can't decide whether I love him or not" (Anna to Claudia at the opening of *L'avventura*) or "I can't explain to you why I don't love you anymore" (Vittoria to Riccardo at the beginning of *L'eclisse*).

Backgrounds traditionally support story, rendering action believable, verisimilar, and corroborative of our sense of the characters' moods or situations. The background behind the Ringo Kid in our first glimpse of John Wayne in *Stagecoach* is the Western country around Monument Valley. Metonymy makes him big as all outdoors. Similarly, at the end of *Citizen Kane,* Charles Foster Kane is pictured as a large, imposing, but empty shell of a man made to seem more alone and lonely by the echoing grandeur of the vast corridors of Xanadu. Traditionally, locale functions not only as an arena of action but as a connotator of mood. One remembers, for example, the cold office building that entraps the murderer in Lang's *M* as a wholly different kind of place from the building bright with social promise that gives birth to Arizona Jim in *Le crime de M. Lange.* But both buildings valorize the action, so one can justifiably call them theatrical. Just as stage backdrops and props are immediately readable in the context of a play, those created for the studio or found in the real world by the director are traditionally subservient to—that is, redundant with—the plot, character, and themes of the film.

The point is important because it was Antonioni's later achievement to question the inevitability of such redundancy. In *L'avventura, L'eclisse,* and *Il deserto rosso,* the backgrounds are obdurately and even aggressively autonomous; they make powerful, obliquely independent contributions to the films. In his early features, however, Antonioni employs more recognizably traditional theatrical

Frame 7

conventions and symbolism. In *Cronaca di un amore,* the streets, buildings, rooms, and landscapes of Ferrara and Milan are easy to read as signs of the events and situations that transpire against them. We first see Paola in furs in front of an opulent gallery of La Scala opera house, as Guido in the countershot stands in his worn overcoat in front of a huge, gaudy signboard advertising the fabrics manufactured by Paola's husband. However brilliantly photographed, the two backdrops are as immediately accessible as the backdrops in the films of Griffith and Lang. Both characters are enveloped by the banality of quotidian life—Paola by a meaningless luxury and Guido by a no less meaningless poverty. The meaninglessness of social difference and sexual jealousy are two mainsprings of the plot.

Still, the traditional iconography of *Cronaca* is not without formal subtlety. Two sequences stand out in this respect. They both emphasize vanishing point perspective and hence deep space. In the first, a distant prospect is formed by the lines of a hydroplane landing basin. The couple discuss the disquieting news of the private detective's investigation, but the lines seem to imply a limitless future together if they can only muster the energy and courage to break away from the past (a continual theme in Antonioni's work, as we shall see).[7] The second arresting perspective shot occurs toward the end of the film, as the lovers plan the murder of Enrico. The shot is a single take around four minutes long. The back-

Frame 8

drop is formed by a canal that recedes toward the horizon of the Po Valley. But this time the vanishing point backdrop suggests not promise but the pointlessness of everything. The irony of empty directionality is conveyed by a complete 360-degree pan, which shows the canal extending off in both directions and hence meaninglessly, since there is no more reason for going off in one direction than there is in the other. The hydroplane basin had suggested an ultramodern, magically immediate escape route. It stretched out, vectorlike, into a sunny future, once they escaped their tricky but not tragic predicament, for after all they had not killed Giovanna. But now, on the bridge, they are plotting Enrico's murder, and they know that nothing can extenuate their guilt. Like Lady Macbeth, Paola suddenly understands the enormity of her plan. The empty distance behind her on one side of the bridge exactly balances the empty distance on the other. She is unsure of her bearings in a moral wasteland, and the landscape points up her predicament.

As for the interior scenes, Antonioni ingeniously found props that enabled him to "paint" his frame with black lines, behind, around, and seemingly even on top of his characters. In the *pensione* scene, Paola is crisscrossed by such lines, which emanate from the window and the bed frame. The lines clearly suggest the web of a spider. Later, in the famous elevator shaft sequence, when Paola first raises the idea of murdering her husband, she appears again clearly at the center

Frame 9

of a web formed by the lines of wrought-iron railings, elevator cables, and so on. The imagery is connotative in a creative though rather literary way. The use of black lines, of course, was very popular in Hollywood films noirs, where its effects were promoted by low-key, chiaroscuro lighting filtered by beams, shutters, slats, wires, and grillwork. The establishment of mood was the sole task of such constructions. One recalls, for example, the sinister mood of the first shots of *Mildred Pierce* inside the beach house where the Zachary Scott character lies murdered. The imagery is often symbolic: in a shot at the end of the film, a line cuts the frame diagonally, symbolically "canceling" Paola, in the way that a diagonal line through the name of a town on a signpost means in the European traffic code that the town is now behind the driver (see Frame 6, p. 14).

    Cronaca di un amore relies to an unprecedented degree on the use of the long take—the single, extended shot of long duration that records an elaborate complex of movements—its own, the actors', or both. The total number of shots in this film has been estimated at 160, about one fourth of the usual number for a ninety-minute feature film of the 1930s. The long-take style was practiced by von Stroheim, Renoir, Welles, and others but never to this extent and never with quite this elaborate degree of choreography.[8] Indeed, argues Noël Burch, the film's composition is virtually balletic, a ballet by disjunction. Since the storytelling is handled allusively by the sound track, there is no need for explanatory on-screen action. And since the

Frame 10

shots proceed by elaborate and sweeping tracks into and through the location, there is a profound sense of depth, of mingling with the characters and the objects in their world. Traditional categories like close-up and long shot lose their meaning in this kind of film, since the camera moves back and forth with unrestrained fluidity, approaching or distancing itself from the setup or being suddenly approached or left by actors who enter and exit the frame from the sides. As Burch puts it, the viewer's sense is of a constant recomposition of frame.[9]

Yet, for all its intrinsic interest, Antonioni's long-take deep-focus style of filmmaking seems at odds with the film noir genre. It extends the visual field in all its axes and rejects shock close-ups on faces and significant objects. It avoids Hitchcock's favorite shot: the cut to the sinister object that a sudden close-up makes enormous—a cup of poisoned coffee, a spy's missing finger, a woman's name traced in the steam on a railroad car window. In Antonioni's hands, the long-take camera style tends to brood, to prowl slowly, and never to be quite satisfied with the objects that it finds. His long-take style enhances realism in the documentaries, but in a fictional context it strongly implies narrative subjectivity, the subjectivity of a directorial point of view.[10]

Thus arises an unresolved if interesting tension between the content and the formal structure of the film. Content offers the traditional crime melodrama— woman as lure, detectives, surveillance, planned murder, police pounding on the door. But the camera's slow inquiry and the elaborately studied composition undermine the suspense and continually raise the question, What is this movie really about? So we turn to other aspects of the characters' situation—social, economic, psychological;[11] unfortunately, our ignorance of the Italian scene prevents us from doing much with them. The camera's movements and pauses are attractive, it seems, precisely at the expense of the story, which is thereby dedramatized (an expression popular with Antonioni's French critics). That makes the film all the more difficult for the foreign viewer to grasp. We come to wish that the camera had indeed recorded another kind of story, like L'avventura's. Antonioni had to learn to avoid the constraints of formula and to modernize his narrative structure before the true beauties of his long-take style could emerge.

I VINTI (1952) AND *TENTATO SUICIDIO* (1953): The Episode Film and the Hazards of Moralism

I vinti (The Defeated, 1952) is Antonioni's least successful film, as he has acknowledged.[12] Made for a production company of Catholic persuasion, it tries to link topical documentary with popular sentimental drama for the moral edification of the masses. The result is unsatisfactory by the standards of either genre. There is little excitement in the action, and the efforts at portraying ordinary life in Paris and Rome are weakened by the irrelevance of the locations to the stories. Though the film's thesis is that the problem of juvenile delinquency is international, it is not clear how that purpose was served by the scrupulous location shooting. One suspects that Antonioni soon washed his hands of the plot and concentrated on what interested him most—how streets, houses, and rooms look to the documentarist. Unfortunately, even the cinematography is inferior to that of the documentaries and *Cronaca di un amore*.

The film begins with a voice-over accompanying shots of newspapers in various languages. It characterizes youth today as burned-out by passive experience of the war during infancy. Sensational headlines are shown: "He Killed for Twenty Cigarettes"; "Gangster, Aged 8, Goes to Court"; and even "What's Wrong with British University Women?"

Three stories illustrate this thesis. Each story is placed in a different country.[13] In the first story, a group of Parisian teenagers takes a trip to the country. Georges gets his friend André to steal his father's gun. A lively fellow, Pierre (Jean-Pierre Mocky), who leads them to believe he is a rich racketeer, joins them at the last moment. He flashes a roll of foreign banknotes and talks nonchalantly about going to Panama. The others plan to go to Algeria. In the country, Pierre strolls off with Simone (Etchika Choureau), who is supposed to be André's girlfriend. She asks him to take her along with him to Panama. He confesses that he has been bluffing, that he isn't rich, but she refuses to believe him and persuades him to write a letter, ostensibly to make her parents believe that she and André have broken up but really to create an alibi for murdering him. He agrees, writes the note, then takes a walk with André, who shoots him. His body is found. The police call Georges's father about the body, and when Georges and André return, the father marches André off to the police, telling his son to return home because he had nothing to do with the shooting. So much is made to happen and so many characters appear on the screen in so little time that it is impossible to attribute genuine motivation to any of them, especially within the narrow thematic limits set by the introduction. The act of murder manages to seem gratuitous, even silly, not the necessary consequence of widespread social ills.

Antonioni's original version of the second, or Italian, story was to have recounted the fate of a young neo-Fascist, Arturo Botta, who feels compelled to perpetrate heroic acts of violence in support of his cause.[14] After bombing a public building and distributing pamphlets, his gang is captured, though he escapes. He demands a meeting with a party leader, who is furious with the gang for taking independent action and declares its members ousted from the party. In utter frustration, Arturo goes out on the Tiber in a boat, ties a small Italian flag around his face, and shoots himself in the back of the neck in order to portray himself as a political martyr and "to rouse the lazy bastards" to the fervor of the struggle.

This version ran afoul of the Italian censor, and it was scrapped. One wonders exactly why. Did the Christian Democrats not want to admit that a young man could become a Fascist in 1952? Or that he would be prepared to die for his beliefs? Or that someone would want to kill himself for any other reason than romance (as in *Tentato suicidio*)? But quite apart from the censor's concerns, we can ask how this sequence relates to the film's thesis—that young people (as the voice-over narrator puts it) are "joyous, almost sportive in their violence," that they are nihilistic, resembling the American gangster, "triumphantly audacious" in their individualism, "cynical and deprived of remorse." Botta seems selfless and dedicated, though his behavior is eccentric. Indeed, much of the scenario portrays the neo-Fascists as a well-ordered group (that may be what bothered the censors) gravitating around the cool, determined Antonio, who was trained during the war in the counterresistance corps. The political commitment of these young people, however deplorable their goals, makes it difficult to discount them as mere juvenile delinquents.

The second version of the Italian episode, the one that appears in the film, is even worse. It concerns a young man from a rich family, Claudio (Franco Interlenghi), who wants more than his father will give him. So he gets involved in a contraband cigarette business on the Tiber. Caught in the act, he escapes, but he is injured severely. Bleeding internally, he manages to get to the house of his girlfriend Mariana (Anna Maria Ferrero), with whom he begins a wistful, operatic, but inconclusive discussion. She takes him to the doctor, but when she comes back to the car, where she has left him, he is gone. He staggers home and dies in his bed, just as the police arrive to arrest him. His parents, of course, had no knowledge of his criminal activities.

Fans of Antonioni can only be embarrassed by the first two episodes of this film, whose moralizing is heavy-handed even by Hollywood standards of the thirties. The voice-over sounds not like a narrator but like a preacher mouthing comfortable truisms. Not only does the voice-over assert its thesis, but it also offers simplistic explanations. As babies, the voice-over tells us, these individuals were passive witnesses to violence, which was part of the natural order of things. So their obsession with gangster movies is only natural. The reasoning is so insubstantial that one could just as easily imagine the voice arguing the opposite with the same equanimity, say, that peace leads to boredom, and so adolescents are attracted to the fictional violence purveyed by the media. Adding insult to injury, the exemplary episodes refuse to exemplify. Nothing in the personalities or backgrounds of the characters shows them to be burned-out. On the contrary, they seem to be pleasant, decent kids, so it is difficult to attribute their crimes to character disorders.

Not only do the concerns of the film seem profoundly un-Antonionian, but they are presented in a format that is uncharacteristically clumsy and obtrusive. In the French episode, each of the main adolescent characters is shown saying goodbye to his or her parents in precisely the same disrespectful way. The Italian episode takes the form of a relatively monotonous peregrination through Rome by the fatally injured hero. The actor who plays him is not accomplished, and he looks all too healthy as he wanders about and finally dies in his own bed.

Nor is there much else in the film that is interesting. Giovanni Fusco, whose solo saxophone score was appropriate to the film noir atmosphere of *Cronaca*, failed Antonioni completely in *I vinti*. The music has nothing to do with the thesis, serving only to affix trite national labels to the three episodes: accordians wheeze that Parisian street tune you know so well, mandolins strum Neapolitan and Italian countryside music, and a piano tinkles "Oh Johnny Boy" in the third, British episode. The music is more suitable for a travelogue. The camera continues its long-take sweeps, but they have distinctly less impact here than they did in *Cronaca di un amore*. There, genre supplied at least a core of motivation for the shots. But no technical ingenuity can relieve the monotony of *I vinti*'s content. Indeed, it seems to increase the monotony. The frame compositions are inferior in quality to those of the earlier film. In the first two episodes of *I vinti*, the actors are deployed woodenly and obviously, particularly when they must strike romantic poses. The crowding into the frame of people who have no particular reason for being there is a major compositional problem—one that plagues Antonioni's style until the arrival of the wide-screen format in the late fifties and sixties. The banality of the imagery seems to reflect the confusion between genres, between screen magazine sensationalism and sentimental romance, that undermines the French and Italian episodes.

The British episode of *I vinti* escapes the trap set by the thesis by ignoring it. True, the hero, Aubrey Hallan, is in his twenties, but his personal eccentricity has nothing to do with his youth, juvenile delinquency, or the war. A would-be poet who dislikes work, he sees a chance to win fame and fortune by murdering a middle-aged woman and then "discovering" her body. He persuades a London newspaper to allow him to write up the story. But he is not satisfied with the temporary public interest and wants to earn more money from the newspaper, so he offers to confess to the crime, confident that he carried it out so well that the police will not be able to get a conviction in court. He goes on trial; his confession is read in voice-over by the prosecution, and the events described are shown in flashback (the last time Antonioni would use this device until *The Passenger*). Of course, Aubrey loses his case, but he shows no remorse for his deed.

This episode seems more successful than the others not because it exemplifies the juvenile delinquency motif but because it finds support in the sturdy British genre of the reclusive, eccentric killer. Hallan reminds us of Hitchcock's villains in *Strangers on a Train, Shadow of a Doubt,* and *Frenzy* rather than of André, or Claudio, or indeed anyone before or after in Antonioni's films. His eccentricity (well portrayed by Peter Reynolds) motivates the camera's distanced view.

Antonioni was very inspired by the British scene: some location photographs in the published screenplay show his appreciation of the English landscape. In the visual beauty with which they depict the chilly gray climate, the photographs remind us of *Gente del Po*. At the same time, they prefigure *Blow-Up*. Perhaps because the plot of this episode is less sentimental and moralistic than are the French and Italian episodes, the backgrounds achieve a greater degree of autonomy. Here, we see the beginnings of the detached photographic brilliance that proves so startling in Antonioni's later films.

Not only did Antonioni clearly take pleasure in choosing locations for the English episode, but he imbued them with something of the independent surface realism of his later mise-en-scène. In one scene, the camera starts on the telephone booth from which Hallan speaks to the reporter, then moves to a lady with a dog, and ends on a police car rushing to the scene—as if it were interested more in its own eccentric trajectory and the space evoked than in recording the plot. The squat row houses and streets of the village seem strikingly real, like the later sights and sounds of London. As Hallan takes the newspaper reporter to the dog

Frame 11

Frame 12

Frame 13

track, the camera makes greater visual capital of the dogs and their handlers than
the story requires. At the moment when Hallan announces his guilt to the reporter, the camera refuses to linger on his face, occupying itself instead with a
child playing with a ball (shades of Lang's *M*). At the end of the film, as the
reporter confirms the guilty verdict over the phone to his editor, the camera
moves to shots of tennis players in white and of the tranquil roofs of Hallan's
home town in the quiet evening light. Something of the mere contingency, the
mere presence of the world so characteristic of the later style is beginning to
show. The buildings, streets, and people behind Hallan sustain their own intransi-
gent character as he walks past them. The British episode was considered good
enough to be included in a compilation film called *Il fiore e la violenza* (The
Flower and the Violence); the other segments were by Jean Renoir and François
Reichenbach.

Although *Tentato suicidio* (Suicide Attempt, 1953) was filmed after *La signora
senza camelie,* it is useful to include here, because it is another of Antonioni's
efforts in the episode film format. It is part of a film organized by Cesare Zavattini, Riccardo Ghione, and Marco Ferreri called *Amore in città* (Love in the City).
Antonioni shot the twenty-minute film in gratitude to Marco Ferreri, who had
helped him to finance *Cronaca di un amore*. Originally much longer, it had to be
cut drastically to fit into *Amore in città*.

Dozens of attempted suicides stand around in a white studio. Three are selected to tell their stories. As in *I vinti,* the selection lacks variety: all three are
young women who were driven to their desperate acts by frustration in love af-

Frame 14

fairs. In each case, an unsmiling young man dressed in a long overcoat bears silent witness that the ending was "happy" and that the young lady's problem has been solved. Irony is strongly implied, though it is not motivated by the narration. The only variable seems to be the means: one woman threw herself in front of a car, another jumped into the Tiber, and the third slashed her wrists. Some interesting compositions foreshadow *L'avventura* and *Il deserto rosso.* But the women are suspiciously photogenic, especially the third, who admits that she wants to become a movie actress. (One could perversely imagine her attempting suicide just to get into Antonioni's movie.)

No real effort is made to find out what lies under the surface. Perhaps the implication is that there is nothing there, that these people are all surface, that they do not know how they feel. Technique is reduced to simple interviews: the would-be suicides just face the camera and tell their stories. The voice-over asks what happened, then the camera recreates it on the actual scene. Antonioni was committed to Zavattini's formula for the *film-inchiesta*, the inquest film, which portrays case histories in their actual settings. After the story, the voice-over asks whether everything is all right now; the would-be suicide says that it is. The results are banal—but not interestingly banal, not banal in the mysterious way of the last minutes of *L'eclisse*. Nothing, of course, is really explained: "I was expecting a baby." "I had seen my husband a few days before in a car with a woman." "Nothing is important to me." And everything, inexplicably, is fine now: "I left my lover . . . .I still care for him but with time I have come to realize that he is a real egotist." "Now you're happy, no?"—"Now, I am, yes." "Now I see everything more clearly . . . I'd like to become an actress." It's not even good cinéma vérité, because the voice-over is too audible, too manipulative, and, worst of all, too moralizing. As the last girl waits to tell her story, the judgmental voice says: "She's a typical example of that dissatisfied youth which offers so much material to the chronicles of our daily life." The format has been called "situation-testimonial."[15] However we label it, it was a dead end that Antonioni promptly and appropriately dropped.

I vinti and *Tentato suicidio* are so different from Antonioni's films of the sixties and seventies that we may wonder how the same man could have made them. After all, Antonioni has said that it was not in his nature to make programmatic or thesis films. The only precedent for these films is his documentaries. But *I vinti* and *Tentato suicidio* represent, I think, an unprofitable extension of Antonioni's early realism. His commitment to visual actuality, however, remained strong, and he had only to figure a way out of the impasse of story, at least of the kind of sentimental story that compromised the authenticity of surface that he so determinedly sought with his camera.

LA SIGNORA SENZA CAMELIE
(1952–1953):
Melodrama Inadequately
Self-Interrogated

Unfortunately, he did not progress very far in *La signora senza camelie* (The Lady Without Camelias, 1952–1953). Sentimentality is commonly defined as unearned pathos. The pathos that we are supposed to feel at the end of the film about the fate of Clara Manni has not been earned. Clara (Lucia Bosè), a shopgirl, is discovered by the successful producer Gianni Franchi (Andrea Checchi), who admires her looks, not her acting ability. Gianni falls in love with her and becomes jealous about seeing her in intimate poses with actors. He marries her quickly and, in an attempt to change her image, casts her as Joan of Arc. The film is a failure at Venice, and in despair he takes an overdose of sleeping pills. Gianni survives, but Clara, dissatisfied with Gianni and her forced retirement, starts an

Frame 15

affair with Nardo (Ivan Desny), a handsome playboy diplomat. But Nardo has no intentions of spoiling his career by marrying her. Clara leaves him, turning for advice to the kindly actor Lodi (Alain Cuny), who recommends plunging into work. Clara sets out to become a really good actress. Though she continues to receive offers for run-of-the-mill films, quality directors do not call on her. Finally, she turns to Gianni, who is producing an epic. Not only does he refuse to hire her, but he warns her that actresses in the film business age quickly. In despair, she accepts a part in a second-rate picture called *Slave of the Pyramids*. Capitulating to "fate," she calls Nardo, to resume their dismal affair.

It is difficult to know what irony was intended by the reference in the title to Dumas (and to the Greta Garbo film). Even taking the story on its own terms, Clara's plight seems trivial in comparison to that of Marguerite Gauthier. All that really bothers her at the movie's end is that her acting roles are not distinguished. But (we want to shout) even the Laurence Oliviers and Bette Davises of the world have played their share of awful roles. Her willful plunge into the worst film possible and the resumption of her tedious love affair is stereotypically masochistic in the best tradition of grand (and soap) opera.

This denouement is based on some highly improbable premises: Gianni will not hire Clara for the role because she is not a good enough actress. Yet he has hired an

American star not for her talent but for her name. We are supposed to feel sorry for
Clara at the end, but it is hard to know why. Since her demands are both muddled
and excessive, pity for her seems unmotivated. It might have been otherwise if
there were independent evidence for her promise as an artist (though the theme of
the artist who suffers because of a refusal to compromise is also threadbare). Further, too much of Clara's sudden interest in serious acting seems to be a consequence of her disappointment in love. She turns to Lodi not because she genuinely
wants to know how to act but because "her life is a mess." The problem seems
suspiciously "female," in an old, discredited sense of that word: the story could
easily have appeared in a 1935 issue of *Cosmopolitan* or *McCall's*.[16]

This is not to say that the confusion of love with work is not a viable theme for
serious fiction. On the contrary, Antonioni would put it to excellent use when
portraying Sandro in *L'avventura*. However, in *La signora senza camelie* the confusion is not examined but only presumed. It is a convention of sentimental romance that a woman's only true interest is love, that a career is only a distraction
from the "real thing," and that a woman will naturally and properly turn to her
lover as a compensation for life's frustrations. Clara (the subtext seems to read)
errs in seeking a serious career, and her punishment is Nardo, that is, a nonserious
lover, who refuses to make a permanent commitment. (This stereotyped treatment, perhaps the fault of the screenwriters,[17] makes Antonioni's pioneering ren-
ditions of such free women as Lidia in *La notte,* Vittoria in *L'eclisse,* and The Girl
in *The Passenger* all the more impressive.) In short, we are invited to extend our
sympathies to the pathetic heroine on faith,[18] just because the camera portrays
her tall, slim, dark figure in languishing postures. "What do you want me to do?"
she asks Gianni. "Do you want me to become an extra? Once perhaps I could, but
now . . . Don't you realize I've changed, too?" It is hard to identify with Clara's
predicament, especially after still another producer appears to ask her to star in a
movie. Why can Clara not pick intelligently among the offers made her and thus
establish her reputation in the hope of securing better parts? Why must she return
masochistically to Nardo? Why must she walk, in the words of the screenplay,
"like an automaton"? These questions should not arise: the fact that they do
suggests that the film relies heavily on sentimental presuppositions. Antonioni
manages in his mature films to universalize his characters' problems so that it is
easy for us to identify with them: with Claudia when she recognizes that loyalty is
quickly forgotten, with Lidia when she realizes that love passes, with Vittoria
when she sees that physical attraction and intellectual affinity need not go hand in
hand. This ability to universalize develops in direct proportion to Antonioni's
growing confidence in the open text. But as long as he felt obliged to deal with a
special emotional situation like Clara's in the ways prescribed by tradition and
genre, his films could not rise much above the emotional level of popular magazine fiction.

La signora senza camelie shows little stylistic development over the preceding
films. Its basic problem is the overabundance of dialogue. Still, Antonioni has
begun to achieve a degree of freedom in plot construction, since he introduces

Frame 16

chronological gaps of considerable duration. However, the elapsed periods tend
to be marked by dissolves, fade-outs, or musical indications or by obtrusive explanatory dialogue. The crisp punctuation provided by the silent straight cut is
still several pictures off. However, the dialogue has a few good moments. It is
particularly effective in the mouths of the haut monde minor characters who hang
out at the swanky town house owned by Nardo's ex-mistress, Simonetta, which is
being used as a location for Gianni's film. In one of the film's few genuine moments, we get a sense of what it was like to shoot a movie in Rome in the 1950s: a
bystander says of Clara, "But I imagined her differently," to which her husband
replies, "It's always like that."

Indeed, one of the disappointments of the film is that Antonioni, unlike the
Fellini of *8½*, was not inspired to come to real terms with the problems of the
filmmaker. The sequences shot in Cinecittà and at the Venice Film Festival and
assorted movie houses in Rome and Milan are, technically speaking, authentic.
But they function as mere backdrops for Clara's forlorn poses. There is no film-
about-film documentary, none of the detail that interests Antonioni in his later
short film on the screen test of Queen Soraya, the "Prefazione" to *I tre volti*
(1965). The screen is too preoccupied with dull two-shots of Nardo wooing Clara.
What is visible behind—a boatdock on the Lido, the Piazza Colonna, the EUR
suburb, a shadowy set in Cinecittà—possesses none of the symbolic weight of the
sets in *Cronaca di un amore*. And, detached from interesting content, the long
tracking shot seems to be a mere mannerism. The gray light that worked well in
the somber moments of *Cronaca di un amore* here seems simply flat. Again, the
screen is too often crowded with people standing around or seated and demonstra-
bly posing, except in the well-orchestrated scene in Simonetta's house and the

Frame 17

interesting sequence in the cinema in Venice. Clara is seen from behind hastily
exiting as her own huge image, in the costume of Joan of Arc, looms on the screen
before a derisive audience.

LE AMICHE (1955):
Adventure in Literary Adaptation

Le amiche (The Girlfriends, 1955) is Antonioni's first film to rely on an important literary source, the novella "Tra donne sole" by the gifted novelist Cesare Pavese.[19] The resulting film is somewhat more realistic than *La signora senza camelie,* but it does not entirely avoid sentimentality. Pavese's novella recounts the adventures of Clelia (played by Eleonora Rossi Drago in the film), a successful young businesswoman from the lower classes of Turin, who returns to her hometown to open a branch of the fashion salon that employs her in Rome. In first-person narrative, she tells how she fell in with a rich young socialite, Momina (Yvonne Furneaux), and her circle of women friends—the frivolous Mariella (Annamaria Pancani); Nene (Valentina Cortese), a potter; and Rosetta (Madeleine Fischer), who at the outset of the story has just attempted suicide. Despite active socializing, Clelia manages to renovate the salon in time for the grand opening. During the course of this effort, she finds herself attracted to Carlo (Ettore Manni), the lower-class foreman of the workers decorating the salon. But when it comes time for her to return to Rome, she does not hesitate to do so. She has simply grown too used to an independent life to conceive of settling down now. Nor does she regret leaving her Turinese friends, especially after Rosetta succeeds in killing herself on a second attempt.

The screenwriters, Suso Cecchi D'Amico and Alba De Cespedes, to whom Antonioni evidently turned as experts in feminine psychology, made some crucial changes in Pavese's story that compromised its cool, even bleak tone. In the novella, Rosetta kills herself out of sheer ennui and disgust for the life that she and her friends live. (Clelia rejects as stupid the explanation offered by others that Rosetta suffered from guilt over a brief lesbian experience with Momina when they were younger.) In the film, however, she kills herself out of unrequited love. Once again, as in *La signora senza camelie,* the implication is that for a woman without a man, life is not worth living. (Perhaps this modification was introduced to counterbalance Clelia's decision to give up her Turinese suitor for business life in Rome, an act that may have seemed incomprehensible to Italian film audiences of 1955.) Indeed, in the novella, the love issue is inconsequential, whereas in the film each woman has to have specific romantic interests, and the geometry of the resulting relationships has to be clear; triangles are favored. Further, in a theatrical but relatively unmotivated scene, Clelia attacks Momina publicly for having "killed" Rosetta with her cynicism. But that confuses the issue of unrequited love—Rosetta, after all, drowns herself, the montage tells us, immediately after Lorenzo rejects her. Again, the film relies on the kind of gossipy plotting that we associate with women's magazines, not with Antonioni. Moreover, the film fails to preserve the interesting decadence of Pavese's novella. Some important events are bowdlerized: for instance, in the novella, the architect (Franco Fabrizi) who hangs out with the group, just after making love to Momina, seduces Clelia, who is too tired and too bored to resist, in the bed that Momina has just left. The film makes no mention of Clelia's sexual activity. Her relationship with Carlo resembles the theoretically erotic but actually platonic affairs that were commonplace as vehicles for American stars of the forties.

Clelia is made more sympathetic in other respects as well. She becomes Rosetta's protectress, taking the train back to Turin from the seaside in order to keep Rosetta from harming herself. However, the ending of the film is excessively emotional: Clelia and Carlo are supposed to say goodbye at the train station, but he hides behind a sign, presumably to make-things-easier-for-her-by-acting-as-if-he-didn't-care-so-that-she-would-think-he-wasn't-worth-it-after-all—an all too familiar convention of melodrama. An issue that Pavese's story never intended to raise is that of divided loyalty. But that seems to be the film's major theme, and it deprives Clelia of the strength she derives from her profession. In Pavese's novella, Clelia leaves Carlo because she prefers her career. In the film, Antonioni and his screenwriters supply a scene which suggests that Clelia's decision is based on a sense of the differences in their levels of culture and sophistication. Whence this sense of "differences"? Carlo proposes furniture for the salon that is completely inappropriate. Thus, their love cannot be.

Though it is clear that Antonioni was attracted to Pavese's realism, especially to Pavese's courage in reporting the inconclusiveness of the emotional life, he seems to have accepted all but two of the D'Amico-Cespedes modifications (one is the scene on the beach discussed below).[20] The film seems to have been the last that he produced in this manner. Beginning with *Il grido,* improvisation on the set—using the scenario as notes rather than as an ironclad contract that had to be fulfilled—was to become his normal working practice.

Still, the theme of what Antonioni came to call *la freddezza morale*—moral coldness—is at least partly communicated in this film, in the figure of Momina, who bitchily dominates the group scenes; in Mariella; in the architect, well played by Franco Fabrizi, the cowardly Fausto in Fellini's *I vitelloni;* and in Nene's husband, the painter Lorenzo, played by Gabriele Ferzetti, soon to be Sandro in *L'avventura.* But the acting is not up to the level of the later films. The women are difficult to distinguish: they dress too much alike and resemble each other physically. Antonioni seems to overemphasize the homogeneity of the group of friends; perhaps he wanted to show that a decadent society is also a homogenizing one. But the tough appearance of the women is at odds with the film's plot and theme. The visuals are ahead of the story, looking forward as they do to the more persuasive evocation of the Italian *alta borghesia* in *L'avventura.*

Whatever its problems of content, the style of *Le amiche* shows considerable development over *La signora senza camelie.* With a gifted new cinematographer, Gianni di Venanzo, who was to work with him on his next four films,[21] Antonioni made rapid strides toward the visual perfection of the films of the sixties. *Le amiche* simply looks better than any of his films since *Cronaca di un amore* and *N.U.* The resolution of the images is sharper, and the compositions are more

Frame 18

interesting. Though an occasional group shot is awkward, the major sequences
place and displace characters deftly and even ingeniously. The long-take style
achieves an almost baroque complexity—as in the sequence in the art gallery
when Lorenzo and the girlfriends hotly discuss Rosetta as her portrait slides into
and out of the frame behind them. And Antonioni now more habitually frames his

Frame 19

actors with vertical and horizontal lines (so characteristic of the later films), using
doors, doorframes and moldings, hallways, and so on to do so. In Clelia's hotel
room, for example, the lines traced by such objects seem to circumscribe her life.
In a later scene in a *rosticceria,* horizontal glass shelves and verticals provided by
such homey objects as wine bottles and salamis place Clelia and Carlo in a cozy,
intimate area, although the restaurant has no other customers. The sequence is
very effective in communicating in a purely visual way the pull that her old,
simple lower-class life exerts on the sophisticated Clelia. Suddenly, the equilibrium is disturbed as Mariella and the architect enter: oblique shadows pour across
the room, and as they leave (the architect telling Mariella that Carlo is not important enough to meet), the couple is shot in a cramped corner down the full length
of the room, with no soft intervening lines to mediate their isolation. What looked
cozy and intimate now seems squalid and vulnerable.

The scene on the beach is visually the best in the film, and it anticipates *L'avventura* in the subtlety of its spatial disposition. Antonioni assembles his cast of characters and orchestrates their movements in the same confident way in which he handles the search on the island for Anna in *L'avventura,* the party at the industrialist's
house in *La notte,* and the cozy "orgy" in Max's *baracca* in *Il deserto rosso.* Unlike
the group shots in *La signora senza camelie,* the scene on the beach communicates
meaning by careful arrangements and rearrangements of the characters. The scene
opens with one of Antonioni's characteristic pans from empty to occupied space.
The girlfriends stand on a kind of platform, and because of the distance at his
disposal, Antonioni can get all the characters into the frame without crowding. The
camera follows them down the steps, against the background of dark trees and then

Frame 20

over to the beach, only incidentally picking up Lorenzo, who is leaning against a pillar at a separate, higher level. The shot visually embodies the separateness of the women's world, which ultimately is closed to men. The beach, sky, and water provide a vast arena within which the characters can at once disport and reveal themselves. The empty ambience nakedly demonstrates the power of the little clique both to embrace and to ostracize. As Mariella callously remarks that Rosetta might as well kill herself since she does not have a man, the group parts to form a kind of aisle or passageway through which Rosetta passes, uncomforted in her despair. The beach offers no resistance to cruelty: its very openness facilitates the creation of this parody of a wedding archway.

The beach seemed to have had an important liberating effect on Antonioni's sense of composition. He found in sky, sand, and water just the expanse to prepare his camera for the freewheeling independence that is the stylistic hallmark of

L'avventura. However, for all its anticipation of the techniques of the later film, *Le amiche* is by no means its equal. Some shots are unnecessarily explicit, as in a telephone conversation that is no less tedious than the one in *La signora senza camelie* between Clara and her mother. The stunning ellipsis of the later films has yet to develop: too many scenes in *Le amiche* are connected by old-fashioned dissolves. And there are still a few of those awkward middle-distance shots in which you can see everyone's shoes. The music is not good; Antonioni was not yet able to shake Fusco's stranglehold on the soundtrack, which is filled with inane airs for saxophone, for solo piano, for mechanical piano, for electric guitar, and for an ungodly duo of electric organ and harp. At its worst, as in a sequence set in the fashion salon, it sounds like the Hawaiian tunes played on supermarket Muzak.

2

Il grido

Il grido (1957) marks a turning point for Antonioni. It is the first film to show his
mature style and preoccupations. A rendition of ordinary life in the Po Valley, its
surface approximates documentary authenticity. Unlike his earlier feature films,
its dialogue cannot be faulted; in particular, the hero's lines seem to these non-
Italian ears genuinely to capture the laconic, often inarticulate, but always deeply
felt emotions of the workingman. The photography evokes the lines and masses
of the river in a myriad of middle-range gray tones, perfecting the nuances of
Gente del Po. And most important of all, the film's narrative structure departs
from genre, thereby marking the beginning of Antonioni's inquiry into the se-
crets of the open text.

Openness derives primarily from the loose, picaresque plot with its single
basic motif: the hero's restless need to move on, always in reaction to the psychological blow leveled at him by his woman in the opening moments of the film.
Aldo (Steve Cochran), a sugar refinery worker from the town of Goriano, is suddenly told by Irma (Alida Valli), the woman with whom he has lived for eight
years and by whom he has had a daughter, that she no longer loves him and wants
to marry another man. Humiliated and ostracized, he leaves with his daughter,
Rosina, for parts unknown. Wandering down the river, he visits an old girlfriend,
Elvira (Betsy Blair), a seamstress who lives with her younger sister, Edera (Gabriella Pallotta). Elvira understands that she will always be second-best to Irma in
Aldo's heart. When Edera, drunk after a dance, tries to seduce Aldo, he decides
that Elvira's home is not the place for him. He and Rosina move on into the country, where they stop at a gas station owned by tough, sexy Virginia (Dorian Gray).
Aldo and Virginia become lovers, and he stays on as her helper. Rosina spends
most of her time with Virginia's father, an eccentric old anarchist who is trying to
recover the farm that Virginia sold in order to buy the gas station. Virginia finally
takes him to the old people's home. Rosina is estranged from the couple after she
sees them making love in a deserted field, and she is sent back to Irma. But after
her departure, Aldo feels too dispirited to stay with Virginia, so he drifts off
again, this time to a symbolic end of the line, the sandy estuary of the Po (east of

Porto Tolle, the region photographed in *Gente del Po*). He finds a deserted hut on
the flats and takes up with Andreina, a fragile prostitute. The annual floods are
beginning, rain pours through the roof, and there is no food. Andreina goes off to
town to trade herself to a cafe owner in exchange for a meal. Aldo follows her,
calls her names, and finally leaves in disgust. He hitches a ride on a truck, which
takes him past Virginia's station. Mail has arrived from Irma, but Virginia has lost
it. Arriving at Goriano, Aldo makes his way through a crowd protesting the use of
farmland for an American airfield. Through a window, he sees Irma with her new
baby. She follows him to the blast furnace where he used to work. "In a state of
complete exhaustion," the screenplay says, he climbs the tower. Irma calls out to
him. Then, in the words of the screenplay:

> Aldo hears her voice and he looks down. Irma calls again.
> *Irma*: Aldo! . . .
> That call is the only thing in the world that could pull him out of his depression. He
> leans over the railing and reels for a moment as if to resist [*tentandi di resistere*] a sudden
> vertigo.
> Irma looks up from below. Her eyes are wide open. Her face becomes twisted with
> sudden, tremendous fright. She emits a bloodcurdling scream.
> In the silence, her loud, long outcry [*grido*] accompanies Aldo's fall, covering the
> sound that his body makes as it strikes the ground [*E nel silenzio, il suo grido è lungo, come
> accompagnasse la caduta di Aldo e ne coprisse il tonfo*].

I quote the screenplay because many critics have interpreted Aldo's death as
suicide.[1] Whatever one may think of Steve Cochran's success in communicating
Aldo's vertigo, which apparently is brought on by his "state of complete exhaustion" and the sudden appearance of Irma, neither his movements nor the context
suggests that his conscious intention is suicide. Aldo does not jump, however
strong his unconscious death wish may be. True, he has little to live for, and true,
we cannot know the exact thoughts in his mind the moment before he falls. But
suicide does not suit the context. The original film treatment makes Antonioni's
intention clear:

> It's a building of three floors, he's on the scaffold of the third. He's working well, with
> assurance, not a wasted movement, he's always been a great bricklayer [in the film, Aldo is
> a mechanic]. The woman has a lump in her throat, and moist eyes. Then she calls him.
> The bricklayer leans over to look. For a long time he doesn't hear the sound of her
> voice, his name pronounced by her. There she is down there, making signs of greeting to
> him, just to him. But why does he see her so badly? He is not conscious of his body's
> shaking, he continues to gaze at her with a heart that seems to burst in his chest, and to
> shake like a drunkard.
> Below, the woman keeps looking at him, but she's no longer smiling. She calls him, she
> calls him again to tell him to be careful, and then her voice becomes a strangled scream.
> Perhaps the bricklayer heard it as he fell, and was glad to hear it, before he smashed
> into the ground, a few feet from her.[2]

When the film is run in slow motion, one can clearly see Aldo rock on his heels
and topple over. He does not jump. There is no voice-over: his thoughts cannot be

Frame 21

heard on the sound track. Antonioni had come to that critical point in his art where he was willing to risk everything on the viewer's ability to read the film's meaning in the context, the actor's faces, and other aspects of the visual surface. That this was his conscious intention is clear from an interview of 1958:

The technique I use (which is an instinctive one, for I do not decide a priori to shoot in any given way) seems to me to be directly tied up with my desire to follow the characters in order to unveil their most hidden thoughts. I may perhaps be deceiving myself in thinking that one can make them speak by following them with the camera. But I believe it is much more cinematographic to try to catch a character's thoughts by showing his reactions, whatever they may be, than to wrap the whole thing up in a speech, than to resort to what practically amounts to an explanation.[3]

Antonioni doubtless overestimated the capacity of an audience to "catch a character's thoughts" from nonlinguistic behavioral clues alone. (Even an important English commentator, Ian Cameron, missed the point: "It looks like vertigo, but that seems a pointless ending, so presumably it's suicide."[4]) The expectations raised by the conventions of story apparently have overridden the sensory evidence for many viewers. The innovative film director, Antonioni was discovering, must strengthen his audience's capacity to respond to purely visual clues. The narrative requirements of *Il grido* probably were too exacting to trust to the visuals alone, but in later films Antonioni did succeed in preparing the audience to meet his new visual challenge.

What does Aldo's death mean? The last sentence of the original treatment— "Perhaps the bricklayer heard it as he fell, and was glad to hear it"—reflects the intention of the ending: Aldo does not climb the tower in order to commit suicide but simply to recapture something of the pleasure that he once took in surveying the landscape and seeing his family's place in it. As he nostalgically reminisces to Andreina in a rare moment of talkativeness: "When I was working at the sugar refinery, don't think that I was just sitting around watching the sugar beets . . . I was one of the few people who worked there steady; I was in charge of the blast furnace. From up there, I could see my house . . . and even my little daughter playing in the backyard."

Of course, people do return to well-loved places to commit suicide. But that is not what is happening here. Aldo's fall is rather the accidental consequence of a movement of yearning toward Irma, the only woman who could ever satisfy him. Having caused his earlier spiritual death, she now inadvertently causes his physical death, and her cry of horror responds not just to that calamity but to her sense of responsibility for it.

Aldo's romantic but self-destructive monogamy, Antonioni felt, was an example of the male's emotional plight in the mid 1950s. In the face of incredible scientific advances, man, he felt, was saddled with

a rigid and stereotyped morality, which all of us recognize as such and yet sustain out of cowardice or sheer laziness . . . a heavy baggage of emotional traits, which cannot exactly be called old and outmoded but rather unsuited and inadequate. They condition us without offering us any help; they create problems without suggesting any possible solutions. And yet it seems that man will not rid himself of this baggage. He reacts, he loves, he hates, he suffers under the sway of moral forces and myths, which today, when we are at the threshold of reaching the moon, should not be the same as those that prevailed at the time of Homer but nevertheless are.[5]

Antonioni made this remark of Sandro in *L'avventura,* but Aldo is an important precursor of Sandro—not as an artist, intellectual, or *altoborghese* but as a victim of outmoded emotional assumptions. As Philip Strick puts it, "the emphasis of the film is upon emotional, not economic, poverty."[6] The real tragedy in *Il grido* is not Aldo's death but his inability to adjust to the vicissitudes of the emotional life, his inability to give Irma up gracefully and go on to another woman. God may have said that we should stick to one mate, but God is dead, whatever they think down in the Po Valley, and we had better patch up our lives as best we can.

Antonioni was taken to task by some class-conscious critics for endowing a mere worker with such advanced existential problems. Here is a typical comment:

Aldo by rights should have hammered Irma into the ground before dragging her off to the altar. Yet after a slap or two he gives up, because *she* says everything is over. That she should be concerned about abstract matters like losing face and that he should put her feelings higher than his own at such a time implies a sentimentality very alien to rustic common sense.[7]

But it is hard to believe that the Italian working class is as neanderthal as all that. Antonioni's view is worth quoting:

It's not true that workers have coarser emotions than ours: all that's different is their way of *dealing* with them, of expressing them . . . We bourgeois are used to complicating our emotions, to fantasizing about them; then at a certain point we stop and find a way of resolving even the most dramatic situation. They, on the other hand, go back to the source of the emotions, live them in their true, immediate substance; in short, they go more to the heart of things.[8]

But going back to the source of their emotions does not mean that they are in greater control of them. It is just as believable that Aldo senses the ineffectuality of his blows as it is that Giovanni senses the ineffectuality of his forced embrace of Lidia on the golf course in *La notte*.

The romantic interpretation that reads the film as an instance of the power of love is no less erroneous. Indeed, Antonioni has explicitly denied this interpretation: "*Il grido* is not, as many like to say, a film glorifying eternal love, but plainly and simply a critical film, in which the hero is neither weak nor impotent but merely alienated. *Il grido* is a film about the alienation of the feelings."[9] *Il grido* shows how limited the emotional resources are—even of working people—and how inflexible and outmoded our traditional reactions to the crises of life.

Critics who faulted the film for not providing a clear social commentary mistook its intention and thrust. It is misleading to speak of a "personal-political linkage which is intended between the destruction of Aldo and the destruction of Goriano's whole way of life."[10] Nothing in the context suggests it. We infer that Aldo does not join the striking workers and farmers precisely because he is too obsessed with his own problems even to see them, just as Giuliana cannot make sense of the strike at the opening of *Il deserto rosso*. Obsessions block whatever energy one might have for community action. And though Aldo perishes, there is no reason to believe that Goriano will perish. On the contrary, its vigorous political action seems exactly appropriate to the situation, and thus indicative of community health, not of neurosis. Antonioni sets Aldo's uxorious mania very clearly apart from the norms of his community.

Indeed, the use of nonprofessional extras for the townspeople underlines the point that Aldo and Irma represent special cases. Only critics who misread the film in their search for a standard social commentary on the working classes have difficulty recognizing the homogeneity of the acting. Certainly it was Steve Cochran's best performance in an otherwise undistinguished career. Yet strangely enough, Antonioni was criticized publicly for his way of working with actors. Some critics went so far as to question his ethics. John Russell Taylor called it a "curious mode of direction" to require actors "not to act in the ordinary

sense of the term but simply to do what they are told without understanding."[11]
Antonioni explained his method of directing actors with his usual incisiveness:

The film actor need not understand but simply be. One might reason that in order to be it is
necessary to understand. That's not so. If it were, then the most intelligent actor would
also be the best actor. Reality often indicates the opposite . . . His reflections on the character he is playing, which according to popular theory should bring him closer to an exact
characterization, end up by thwarting his efforts and depriving him of naturalness. The
film actor should arrive for shooting in a state of virginity. The more intuitive his work, the
more spontaneous it will be.[12]

In asking the actor to show up on the set in a "virginal" state, Antonioni makes
the same demand that he makes of himself: "Sometimes I arrive at the place
where the work is to be done, and I do not even know what I am going to shoot.
This is the system I prefer: to arrive at the moment when shooting is about to
begin absolutely unprepared, virgin."[13] When directing actors (like Betsy Blair)
who insist on knowing exactly what he has in mind, Antonioni feels forced to use
what he calls a "hidden method . . . to stimulate in the actor certain of his innate
qualities of whose existence he is not himself unaware—to excite not his intelligence but his instinct—to give not justifications but illuminations. One can almost trick an actor by demanding one thing and obtaining another." To accuse a
director who practices such trickery of being unethical is to miss a crucial technical point: an actor who signs a contract to make a film does not reserve the right to
make the final cut. If something displeases the actor about the performance, he or
she must recognize the occupational hazard. The relationship between actor and
director in a film can be no more egalitarian than that between the musicians and
the conductor of an orchestra, as Fellini wittily points out in his *Orchestra Rehearsal*. This is especially true if the director is an *auteur*, if it is his film from the
very inception. Why? Because only he can decide how the meanings conveyed by
the actor's appearance and voice fit the other signifiers that compose the film,
how they all blend to communicate his intention:

The first quality of a director is to see. This quality is also valuable in dealing with actors.
The actor is one of the elements of the image. A modification of his pose or gestures
modifies the image itself. A line spoken by an actor in profile does not have the same
meaning as one given full-face. A phrase addressed to the camera placed above the actor
does not have the same meaning it would if the camera were placed below him.
    These few simple observations prove that it is the director—that is to say, whoever
composes the shot—who should decide the pose, gestures, and movements of the actor.[14]

When Antonioni calls the actor merely one more plastic component of the film,
of the same order of importance as the lighting, the music, and the props, he is
not guilty of dehumanizing the profession. He is simply arguing that what the
director finally delivers is a sequence of images and sounds. The situation in the
cinema is quite different from that in the theater, where the actor remains a palpable human being throughout the entire play, embodying the character not only
during the brief instant of a shot but for hours on end. The stage director cannot
control the details of the actor's appearance once the play has begun. The actor

must become something of a director. The distance between the stage actor and the audience is constant, a permanent long shot, because the angle of vision is always the same; there are no cuts to other perspectives. The stage actor is not subject to the control of an intervening registering device: he shows himself to the audience in a completely unmediated way. As Susan Sontag puts it, "cinema is an *object* (a *product,* even), while theatre is a performance."[15]

Antonioni's oblique relation to his actors, his insistence on unrehearsed natural-ness, and his desire to photograph them virtually unawares express the documen-tary spirit, in which images are allowed to speak for themselves to the exclusion of dialogue, commentative music, and heavily explanatory context. *Il grido* is the first feature film in which Antonioni allows the visuals to carry the narrative burden to a degree practically unknown since *Der letzte Mann.* That his experiment failed to capture some plot-relevant details of his characters' states of mind is perhaps less important than that it blazed a vital new stylistic path. The film helped him to make a highly innovative discovery about cinematic characterization: that the very un-readability of motive and feeling in a character's facial and bodily expression could itself become the sign of a certain important emotional climate.

Il grido shows advances in other respects as well. Its narrative structure is almost as sophisticated as that of *L'avventura.* For instance, it handles the passage of time no less deftly. Bartolini, the coscenarist, in interesting notes on the film that were published with the screenplay, writes that two fundamental problems preoccupied Antonioni during the rewrite of the treatment: how to communicate the "weight of the years" of Aldo's relationship with Irma, which alone could justify his misery in losing her, and how to emphasize the persistence of Irma's influence on Aldo.[16] Antonioni first thought that flashbacks could best express the continuity and duration of the action but finally decided against them, preferring to match the long, slow, straight river with a loose, picaresque series of events that conveyed the sense of an unrelieved flow of time. Unlike his other films, *Il grido* suggests a lengthy period—months certainly, perhaps even a year—as Aldo wanders down to the mouth of the Po and back. And it does so with a minimum of cinematic trickery, at the most a dissolve or two. Leprohon correctly praises the "classic spareness" of *Il grido.*[17]

Perhaps even more significant for the evolution of Antonioni's narrative style is the importance that he assigns in *Il grido* to incidents that appear not to be connected with the main lines of the plot. It is precisely the irrelevance of the motorboat race, of the working-class dance, of the visit of Elvia's client, of the discussion with the dredgers about animal life in South America, and so on to Aldo's obsession with Irma that isolates him increasingly from the life about him. We are repeatedly made to feel that only half his mind is on what is happening; the other half is back in Goriano. This use of irrelevance illustrates another important development in Antonioni's style: the plot develops no longer explicitly through major events but implicitly in silent interstices between minor events. Beginning with *Il grido,* his films, like certain modern novels, come to demand more infer-ential ability from the audience than cinema had dared yet ask.

Frame 22

Antonioni's return to the Po Valley had a magical effect on his cinematography. The reaching out into the spaces of nature that was only episodic in previous films—in the bridge scene in *Cronaca* and the beach scene in *Le amiche*—here becomes the very principle of continuity. The low regular horizon dominates the compositions, as it does in Dutch landscape painting. But the effect is quite different. As in Visconti's *Ossessione,* the line does not exalt but rather dwarfs; it refuses to support Aldo's lonely figure, which moves aimlessly along. And the other verticals are also stumpy: utility poles and pollarded trees serve as metonyms of his bafflement. However beautiful the pruned trees will become, spring is far off, and their present amputation only underlines the bleakness of Aldo's predicament. When in his first blind reaction Aldo tries to beat Irma into submission, she holds onto a tree for support. The fight takes place at an elevation above the river, made irrelevantly beautiful at this distance by the framing trees. But Aldo's efforts fail, and he moves down to the mud and squalor of the river, becoming himself a moving stump along its bank, his future lopped off like so many branches. His hands—which once performed skilled labor at the sugar refinery—are now stuck dismally in his pockets. Aldo, cut off from his roots, is and looks a spiritual amputee. Yet Antonioni's treatment of the setting is still relatively traditional in its symbolism. The landscape is still largely illustrative. It

Frame 23

remains for *L'avventura* and the later films to evoke the neutral, contingent environment, the surface of the world for its own sake.

In rare flashes of hope, we feel that Aldo's restless migration may lead to a better life. For a few moments, the bright El Dorado of Australia seems a possibility, but it ends when he tosses the torn pieces of the recruiting brochure to the wind. The closest that Aldo comes to stability is the prospect that Virginia offers at her gas station. As Aldo and Rosina approach, the camera appropriately abandons its customary lateral view of them framed against the cold horizon for a shot down the highway, which is given direction and purpose by the solid white pentagon of Virginia's building.

But this is only a momentary respite. The predominant appearance is flat, not only in terrain but also in dimensionality. Anticipating a later style, the shots of Aldo against flat nothingness cancel depth of field to create a sense of entrapment, like that of T. S. Eliot's Prufrock "pinned and wriggling on a wall." That Aldo's

Frame 24

Frame 25

entrapment is depicted not against a wall indoors but against all outdoors makes it the more poignant and ironic. He cannot move into dimension, into depth. Lacking the emotional fortitude to resist the flow of circumstance, he cannot cross or alter the line he must follow. The river carries him to its local end and then returns him to his small death at the feet of his "only" woman.

   Il grido's interior shots also use verticals to suggest entrapment and the barriers between people. In their house, Aldo and Irma are separated by doorframes

Frame 26   *Frame 27*

and the like, and a glass door is used to show how the child, Rosina, is trapped in the impasse between her mother and father. In his final plight, Aldo (like Riccardo in *L'eclisse* after him) finds himself momentarily stopped by a barred gate. As a symbol, the bars would be heavy-handed, but as a metonym their motivation is amply justified.

Of course, Antonioni did not limit himself to vertical lines in his choice of compositional features. In his customary "virginal" way, he found objects whose shapes made fascinating contributions to the rest of the picture. For instance, when Rosina stumbles upon her father and Virginia making love in a ditch, she moves into a space filled by the huge wooden reels used for transporting utility cables, now empty. The reels are not symbolic of anything in particular, but their shapes and size seem just right to mirror the child's shock and consternation. And in the sequence in which Aldo reminisces to Andreina about his life at home, Antonioni places two wooden decoy ducks next to them on the river bank. Again, it would be absurd to find symbolism in the ducks, but at the same time they seem oddly suitable to the situation. Andreina shows childlike interest in them. They seem to represent some absurd parody of the kind of family life that the two could have together; they also evoke the frivolous pleasures of the rich from the perspective of the down-and-out.

Antonioni's camera continues to move prodigiously in this film; he is still committed to the long-take style and to shooting in depth. The distance of the camera from the actors continues to be a function of the locale: for plein air shots, the distances are considerable. The most evocative are the long and extreme long shots of Aldo against an empty landscape. As for interiors, the distance between camera and figure in any one shot seems determined by the contingency of the actors' movements. It would be difficult to label many shots as close-ups or medium shots.

The lighting in the film is perhaps its most striking visual effect. There are no pure whites and only occasional pure blacks—almost everything is gray, though in myriad tones. Clearly, the wintry light has been captured by a visual artist who knows it in his bones, from his own childhood in Ferrara. Some of the loveliest

Frame 28

effects in the film occur at the beginning, when Aldo races home in the fog to find out why Irma has been acting so strangely. The editing is slow and rhythmic; sudden cuts would be wrong in a film where clock time is stretched out and finally irrelevant to the plot. The dissolves do not seem old-fashioned but perfectly appropriate to Aldo's vagabondage.

The music, too, shows a definite improvement over that of the previous films. Fusco wrote a simple, short poignant theme for solo piano that echoes Aldo's sad plight against the bleak visuals. The only other music in the film appears at the beginning and the end, and it, too, is attractive both in melody and in instrumentation—a slightly raucous tragicomic hurdy-gurdy theme played on a xylophone that is not so much a folk tune as it is the kind of music that we would expect to hear in the streets of a place like Goriano.

3

The Great Tetralogy
Plots and Themes

If the films of Antonioni's apprenticeship show diverse and sometimes wayward strands of originality, the four mature films—*L'avventura, La notte, L'eclisse,* and *Il deserto rosso*—constitute a solid core of achievement. Even early on, critics felt that the first three films formed a trilogy. I would extend the group to include *Il deserto rosso,* which differs from the earlier films only in its use of color but not significantly in theme, plot structure, or character type. About the plight of still another middle-class Italian woman, in another difficult relationship, again at odds with her environment, it looks backward rather than forward to the quite different thematic concerns of the later films. I do not claim that Antonioni intended a cycle of four films, only that the themes, style, and worldview are best understood if the films are looked at as a loose unity.

In the tetralogy, the "Antonionian film," as the world understands that expression, was born. The surface of the world was finally captured and then polished with consummate skill. Plots and themes (this chapter), characters (Chapter 4), and settings (Chapter 5) were integrated in a new and brilliant synthesis in a style (Chapter 6) that would be increasingly admired and copied by other filmmakers.

With *L'avventura* (The Adventure, 1959), Antonioni established himself as one of international cinema's great artists. The story, which occurred to him on a cruise among the Aeolian Islands off Sicily, concerns the unexplained disappearance of a young woman, Anna (Lea Massari), from the uninhabited island Lisca Bianca ("White Fishbone"), to which she had sailed on a luxury yacht, and the impact of her disappearance on her lover Sandro (Gabriele Ferzetti) and her friend Claudia (Monica Vitti). Anna's feeling for Sandro is highly ambivalent— she both wants him and rejects him. Claudia seems to be the only one who is genuinely upset by Anna's disappearance. With unseemly haste, Sandro is attracted to Claudia and turns his attention to her. At first shocked, she finally responds to his courting as they wander through Sicily looking for Anna. During the search, Sandro sees a prostitute, Gloria Perkins, cause a riot in Messina; he observes the poisoned marriage of a pharmacist and his wife in Troina; and, in a moment of frustrated spite, he spoils the drawings of an architecture student in Noto. Now lovers, Sandro and Claudia rejoin the group of friends with whom they

51

sailed on the fateful cruise—Patrizia, owner of the yacht, her husband Ettore, for
whom Sandro works as consultant, and another couple, Corrado and Giulia,
whose only pleasure is to torment each other. Arriving at a palatial hotel in Taormina, with Anna seemingly forgotten, Claudia and Sandro are a confirmed couple. But during their very first night there, Sandro betrays Claudia with Gloria
Perkins, whom he meets casually in the hotel lobby. In the final scene, Sandro sits
weeping with remorse in a deserted piazza; Claudia comes up behind him and
puts her hand lightly on his head.

   La notte (The Night, 1960) takes up problems at the other end of the love
spectrum, those of a long-term couple. It concerns the marital difficulties of a
successful Milanese writer, Giovanni Pontano (Marcello Mastroianni), and his
wife Lidia (Jeanne Moreau). As the film opens, the couple visit a friend, Tommaso, who is dying in a hospital. Overcome by tears, Lidia must leave the room.
Giovanni soon follows, but on the way to the elevator he is lured into an embrace
by a hospitalized nymphomaniac. Nurses burst into the room as they are about to
make love. After a hectic drive through traffic, the Pontanos arrive at a cocktail
party in honor of Giovanni's new book. Lidia slips out for a long walk. In the
Milan suburbs, she witnesses some toughs engaged in a brutal, almost ritualistic
fight, and then she sees some more constructive youths launching toy rockets in a
field. She finds herself in the neighborhood where she and Giovanni first lived
together and telephones him to join her. He fails to share her enthusiasm for the
place. That evening, they go to a nightclub and watch a striptease act, then to a
sumptuous party at the house of a business tycoon. The party lasts all night.
During its course, each wanders off, Giovanni to find Valentina, the tycoon's
daughter, and Lidia to be found by Roberto, a handsome man-about-town. Neither adventure comes to anything, and at dawn the couple walk away from the
house across the tycoon's golf course. Sitting in a sand-trap, Lidia tells Giovanni
that Tommaso had been in love with her and had tried to help her develop her
intellect when she was young, but she had been too foolish to appreciate him. She
confesses that she no longer loves Giovanni; all she feels is pity. Refusing to
accept the truth that their relationship is dead, Giovanni forcefully makes love to
her in the sand-trap as the camera drifts away.

   In *L'eclisse* (The Eclipse, 1962) Antonioni continues his examination of the
problem of emotional relationships. In one sense, his view about the very possibility of such relationships has grown bleaker than it was in the two preceding
films, where, for better or for worse, the couples stayed together. This film begins
with the breakup of one relationship and ends with the unexplained disappearance
from the screen of both partners to a second. Vittoria (Monica Vitti), a Roman
woman in her mid twenties, ends her two-year relationship with Riccardo (Francisco Rabal), a morose writer in his thirties. She cannot explain her reasons to
him, though his distraction and apathy provide *us* with adequate reasons. Visiting
her mother, who plays the stock market obsessively, Vittoria meets Piero (Alain
Delon), an energetic young broker. He pursues her vigorously, and she finally
accepts him as a lover, but she refuses to consider marriage or to treat the relationship as anything more than one of physical attraction. She cares for Piero, but she

is put off by his materialistic approach to life. After making love one afternoon in Piero's office, the couple part, their mood changing from playfulness to unexplained gravity. They embrace, promising to see each other that evening, and the day after, and the day after that. But when eight o'clock arrives and the camera awaits them at their usual rendezvous, they do not appear. Instead, we are shown seven minutes of the ordinary life of the EUR suburb of Rome, in a series of shots made strangely tense and even sinister by the absence of the characters. The film ends with a close-up on the blinding light of a streetlamp as the music swells to a harshly discordant climax.

Il deserto rosso (Red Desert, 1964), Antonioni's first color film, concerns the plight of Giuliana (Monica Vitti), the highly neurotic wife of a Ravenna engineer, Ugo (Carlo De Pra), and mother of a young son. Visiting Ugo at the factory one day, she meets Corrado (Richard Harris), another engineer who is trying to collect a group of technicians for a project in Patagonia. Corrado is attracted to Giuliana, visits her at an empty store that she plans in a vague way to turn into a boutique, and invites her to tour the countryside with him as he looks for workers. She tells him indirectly about her mental problems—her attempted suicide and hospitalization. The scene changes to a shack on the river, where Giuliana, Ugo, Corrado, a lecherous friend, Max, his wife, Linda, and Emilia, a woman Max is trying to seduce, have a kind of orgy manqué complete with aphrodisiac quails' eggs. Giuliana is able to relax in the warmth of the place, but when no one will confirm the scream she hears from a passing quarantined ship, she bolts and nearly drives off the pier. One morning, her young son awakens, apparently paralyzed in the legs. She tries to comfort him, telling him the story of a young girl who, playing happily alone on a beach, sees a strange ship approach shore and then leave and then hears sweet music coming from erotic-looking rocks and the sea itself. Giuliana learns that her son has tricked her, presumably in order to stay home from school. Highly upset, she visits Corrado in his hotel room, where they make love. Though that calms her for a moment, she leaves Corrado, presumably for good; on her way home, she stops in front of a docked Turkish freighter and tries to explain her plight to an uncomprehending but sympathetic sailor. In the final sequence, we see her with her son again in front of the factory, as in the opening shot; when the boy asks her whether the birds die when they fly through the poisonous yellow smoke issuing from the smokestacks, she says that the birds have learned to avoid the smoke. The implication is that there is some hope for Giuliana: though not cured, perhaps she is beginning to learn how to avoid whatever it is that sets off her anxiety.

THEMES AND THEMATICS

Instead of themes, one is tempted to speak, stylishly, of the thematics of the middle stage of Antonioni's career. On the model of the French original, I use *thematic* to mean not themes taken singly but something like a coherent network

Edipus

of themes. And the themes of Antonioni's later films do tend to interconnect in complex patterns.

In another sense, the suffix -*ic* means "the study of," as rhetoric is the study of the rhetor, phonetics is the study of the phone, and so on. *Thematic* suggests a clear separation of subject examined from technique of examination. It enables us to see components of texts not as natural objects but as conventions and thereby to avoid the conclusion that it is in the "nature" of narratives to contain themes. For there is such a thing as a themeless or pointless story, even at the level of the art narrative (for example, some texts by the Surrealists). It is important to be able to ask whether there are such things as "Antonionian" themes, not merely to pre-suppose them, especially since Antonioni has said that his films are about "noth-ing." Certain critics, missing the irony, have agreed. Precisely what he means is a principal question for any account of his art.[1]

Clearly, Antonioni's films do mean more then they say, that is, they imply something more than "This is the surface of the world as I choose to exhibit it," although they imply that, too. (Perhaps they imply that all other generalizations derive secondarily from this basic one.) We are made more comfortable about investigating Antonioni's themes after reading interviews in which he articulates them himself. Unlike many visual artists, Antonioni is highly verbal, a brilliant speaker and writer fully capable of expressing his intentions. For instance, he has spoken of his desire to capture the "spiritual aridity . . . and moral coldness" (*freddezza morale*) of the upper classes of postwar Italian society. So it is not the films' thematic meaninglessness but rather their unusual formal demands that make them difficult for the mass audience. Resenting the challenge, many view-ers and reviewers prefer to believe that they are pointless records of modern life, that they are, indeed, about nothing.

Antonioni made his wonderful remark after a visit to Mark Rothko's studio. What he said exactly was, "Your paintings are like my films—they're about noth-ing . . . with precision."[2] The best gloss on "nothing" that I have seen is Richard Gilman's:

Antonioni's films are indeed about nothing, which is not the same thing as being about nothingness.

L'avventura and *La notte* are movies without a traditional subject (we can only think they are "about" the despair of the idle rich or our ill-fated quest for pleasure if we are intent on making old anecdotes out of new essences). They are about nothing we could have known without them, nothing to which we had already attached meanings or sur-veyed in other ways. They are, without being abstract, about nothing *in particular,* being instead, like most recent paintings, self-contained and absolute, an action and not the description of an action.

They are part of that next step in our feelings which art is continually eliciting and recording. We have been taking that step for a long time, most clearly in painting, but also in music, in certain areas of fiction, in anti-theatre. It might be described as accession through reduction, the coming into truer forms through the cutting away of created encum-brances: all the replicas we have made of ourselves, all the misleading because logical or only psychological narratives, the whole apparatus of reflected wisdom, the clichés, the inherited sensations, the received ideas.[3]

What may seem to the casual moviegoer an inconsequential string of happen-
ings is obviously a reflection of what passes for life today. In *La notte,* for example,
the heroine visits a dying friend, attends a tedious reception, takes a walk in the
suburbs, attends a fashionable party, and ends up bleakly confronting her husband with her feeling that their marriage has reached a dead end. Nonoccurrences
these may be, but they are very resonant ones. They reveal what her life and, to a
great extent, our own lives are like—what they are "about." Their very inconclu-
iveness seems to be a profound part of the truth of the representation.

The reduction to "nothing" constitutes a rejection of the comforts of traditional narrative.[4] By *L'avventura* (even by *Il grido*), Antonioni no longer felt the
need to account for behavior, to provide clues to its meanings and consequences.
He has achieved extreme honesty in a medium in which that virtue often seems
unobtainable. Central to his honesty is the acknowledgment that one cannot
know what motivates people, that actions are indeed a mystery. This would seem
virtually fatal to an art that relies on large sums of risk capital. How can a producer
justify investing in a film that he knows will frustrate and baffle the mass audience's need for reassurance? "What do you mean, you don't *know?*" he hears the
crowds roar. "You've *got* to know!"

But Antonioni's texts, while lacking in comfort, provide glorious esthetic re-
wards for those who are able and willing to accept his naked vision:

> The acceptance is made of what we are like: it is impossible not to accept it as this film [*La
> notte*] dies out on its couple shatteringly united in the dust, because everything we are not
> like, but which we have found no other means of shedding, has been stripped away. . . .
> This stripped, mercilessly bare quality of Antonioni's films is what is so new and marvelous
> about them. The island criss-crossed a hundred times with nothing come upon; the conver-
> sations that fall into voids, Jeanne Moreau's head and shoulders traveling microscopically
> along the angle of a building, unfilled distances, a bisected figure gazing from the corner
> of an immense window, the lawn of the rich man across which people eddy like leaves;
> Monica Vitti's hand resting on Ferzetti's head in the most delicate of all acceptances;
> ennui, extremity, anguish, abandoned searches, the event we are looking for never
> happening—as Godot never comes, Beckett and Antonioni being two who enforce our
> relinquishments of the answer, the arrival, two who disillusion us.[5]

EXISTENTIAL ANXIETY:
La malattia dei sentimenti

The central thematic of the tetralogy is the perilous state of our emotional life.
Narcissism, egoism, self-absorption, ennui, distraction, neurosis, existential anxiety: many terms have been proposed for the complex state of mind that was first
defined clearly by Kierkegaard and that has seemed particularly afflicting since
World War II. These terms struggle to characterize a life lacking in purpose, in
passion, in zest, in a sense of community, in ordinary human responsiveness, in
the ability to communicate, in short, a life of spiritual vacuity. Antonioni had
been preoccupied with that state of mind since *Cronaca di un amore*, but, for the

reasons proposed in Chapter 1, he was not able to portray it convincingly until he made his sixth feature film, *L'avventura*. As long as he tried to *account* for it through the conventional rationalizing structures of dialogue, genre, "psychology" (especially "female psychology"), his vision seemed doomed to inauthenticity. Only when his art grew strong enough to reject traditional narrative paraphernalia and to evoke the surface of life with clarity could he genuinely capture the lineaments of the modern mood.

What also helped was his emergent understanding of what he came to call the "fragility" *(fragilità)* of the emotional life—its unstable, shifting, amorphous character, in which one feeling passes without rhyme or reason into another, so that people do not know themselves why or how it is that they behave as they do. Feelings, he claims, are not definitive but "fragile, seductive, reversible." Everywhere there are "symptoms of . . . restlessness in our psychology . . . feelings and . . . morality."[6] A virtual "malady of the emotional life," he calls it, *una malattia dei sentimenti.* If we focus on the analytic rather than the moral overtones of this phrase, it serves very well to name the thematic of the tetralogy.

Naturally, such problems find their most acute expression in love relations. So all four films turn on love: love is the emotion in which restlessness, spiritual aridity, and moral coldness are displayed most revealingly. Women are the main protagonists, not because feminine psychology says that love is their proper domain but because Western civilization, Antonioni thinks, has left to them alone a modicum of the capacity to acknowledge feelings, a capacity virtually lost by men, especially intellectual men. The obsession with the erotic side of life

is a symptom of the emotional sickness of our time. But this preoccupation with the erotic would not become obsessive if Eros were healthy, that is, if it were kept within human proportions. But Eros is sick; man is uneasy, something is bothering him. And whenever something bothers him, man reacts, but he reacts badly, only on erotic impulse, and he is unhappy. The tragedy in *L'avventura* stems directly from an erotic impulse of this type— unhappy, miserable, futile.[7]

One cannot resist comparing Sandro's behavior with that described in Freud's famous essay, "The Most Prevalent Form of Degradation in Erotic Life": "When the original object of an instinctual desire becomes lost in consequence of repression, it is often replaced by an endless series of substitute-objects, none of which ever give full satisfaction. This may explain the lack of stability in object-choice, the 'craving for stimulus,' which is so often a feature of the love of adults."[8] Clearly, Gloria Perkins and, more sadly, Claudia (as *he* treats her) must fail to satisfy Sandro, since they are inappropriate substitutes, anodynes, for the creative and meaningful architectural work that he cannot do.

Work is the other half of Freud's great dyad of life: Sandro, angry and guilty enough to ruin a young architect's sketch "accidentally," rushes back to the hotel and tries to force Claudia to make love (a particularly bad piece of timing; only minutes before, he was too preoccupied to respond to her light-hearted seduction, probably by obsessive architectural thoughts). Claudia senses that it is not herself that he lusts after but Woman, any woman, which is just his name for

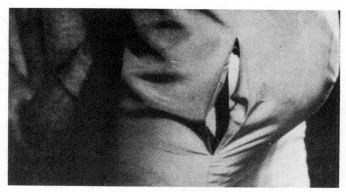

Frame 29

"distraction from meaningful work." She says despairingly that at such moments she feels she does not know him. The remark is more profound than she realizes: in seeking Woman, he reduces himself to simple, instinctual Man, thereby losing whatever identity he has that is worth knowing.

The theme of sick Eros reverberates in the behavior of the minor characters, like the silly Raimondo, the would-be lover of Patrizia, owner of the yacht, a man bored with his useless life, following passively the dictates of a facile society; this year, the fashion is snorkeling. She indulges him, in a kind of ironic maternalism, out of her own moral indolence. Not virtue but boredom keeps her from succumbing. Her response caricatures Claudia's indulgence of Sandro at the end of the film, while another aspect of love, that exemplified by Corrado and Giulia, the couple who have been together too long, caricatures the whole institution of marriage. No wonder Anna has grievous misgivings. And the masses? Sex in the head obsesses the entire male population of Messina. The adventuress and call girl Gloria Perkins splits her overly tight skirt, revealing a few centimeters of begartered skin for publicity purposes. An all-male crowd assembles and begins to howl. A reductio ad absurdum: so many howling for such small reward. It is sex twice removed: not even voyeurism, but the merest report of a voyeuristic possibility. What a superb image of mass anodyne sex as substitute for work: half a city not merely distracted but literally immobilized.

For Giovanni in *La notte*, sex is never far from consciousness. Two steps from the threshold of his dying friend's hospital room, he cannot resist the temptation of a nymphomaniac's "passion." In nymphomania, of course, sexual preoccupation has become pathological. But what is significant is less the nymphomaniac's fate than the test of Giovanni's distractibility. He flunks ingloriously. When Giovanni asks Lidia (of all people) to sympathize, she refuses, remarking: "An experience like that is something you could turn into a nice story. Call it 'The Living and the Dead.'" What does she mean? Superficially, Giovanni and the nymphomaniac, the would-be "lovers," are the living, while poor Tommaso is the dead. But one can envision at least two deeper interpretations: the nymphomaniac is

Frame 30

the living because of the psychotic vitality that arouses her to any man who passes by, while Giovanni is the dead because of the passive and predictable way in which he allows himself to be dragged into a meaningless embrace and to think that it was his charm that prompted it. Or, Giovanni is the living because he responds, even if weakly and absurdly, to the nymphomaniac's compulsive and mechanical cravings, while she is dead because she can only imitate genuine love. The incident is a curious but efficient reflection, in the moral sphere, of Tommaso's illness, which appears to be gastric cancer. Just as in cancer, where a hectic, abnormal life rages among the cells of the body, so in nymphomania a hectic, abnormal love rages among the cells of the spirit. It feeds on the normal, balanced structure of feelings, blocking the possibility of nonsexual sorts of human contact. (The themes of the cancerous body and the cancerous spirit find another parallel in the image of the cancerous city, which feeds on its inhabitants.) At the party, Giovanni thinks he has a chance for a "more meaningful relationship" with Valentina, the beautiful and intelligent daughter of his host. After a difficult night, however, during which nothing much happens between them, she ends up expressing more sympathy for Lidia than for him. She says wryly that the two have exhausted her. Finally, Giovanni's sense of rejection is made complete by his wife's sad, straight talk in the sand-trap. He cannot bear another refusal of his sexual favors and forces himself on his wife. People addicted to sex cannot afford diplomatic abstentions.

Frame 31

In *L'eclisse,* too, eroticism plays an intense role. Piero divides his obsessiveness among women, the stock market, and sports cars. For him, eroticism is simply another outlet for the power drive. In contrast, Riccardo needs a woman for security, as a haven between long and neurotic voyages into himself. Only in Vittoria do we find anything like healthy sexuality.[9] She recognizes and accepts in herself whatever it is that a man excites, even if, like Piero, he is unsuitable in every other way. But in her case, the acceptance argues a downplaying of sex. Because she does not agree with the old mythology that sex is a be-all and end-all, that it should take place only with the "right" person, that it can bind up and resolve, in a single swoon, all life's needs, Vittoria sees the world with rare clarity. She can take pleasure in life's simpler beauties: the sight of rustling trees, billowing clouds, a calm provincial airstrip, flagpoles swaying in the breeze, and even, to Piero's chagrin, a man passing in the street.

In *Il deserto rosso,* sexuality is a palpable mechanism of neurotic relief. At her most desperate moment, not knowing where else to turn, Giuliana goes to Corrado's hotel room. In an ecstasy of ambivalence, she both fights him off and embraces him. And she does experience some relief, however fleeting. The relief is communicated by a celebrated experiment with color. When she enters the hotel, everything is a frigid white—Antonioni even had the plants sprayed with white paint. Afterwards, the walls are blushing pink. The minor characters, as in *L'avventura,* are more exaggerated and obvious in their eroticism. The quasi orgy scene in Max's river shack is perhaps Antonioni's most pointed commentary on the sexual maunderings of the *alta borghesia.* In the heated atmosphere, which

Frame 32

Corrado clearly finds distasteful, the participants discuss sexual practices around the world with great relish. The orgy is curiously unconsummated and for reasons that perhaps go beyond mere concern for the censor. The film suggests that sex in the head does not end in bed. The last word is given to Max's employee's *ragazza*, a matter-of-fact lass who says, a bit disdainfully, that she prefers *doing* "certain things" to talking about them.

Anodyne eroticism wards off the boredom and despair that accompany the unconscious refusal to make one's life meaningful. It does not itself reflect deep passion: on the contrary, it is a rejection, even a flight from passion. And it is not a viable means of communication, only a superficial substitute for it. Only Antonioni's women can honestly confess to the endemic inability to communicate. Anna's frustrated attempts to explain how ambivalent she feels about Sandro are conveyed in two remarkably constructed scenes: one with Claudia in the piazza outside Sandro's studio, and one with Sandro on the island just before she disappears. Equally brilliant is the opening sequence of *L'eclisse*, in which Antonioni uses silence and fragmented dialogue to convey not only the gulf between Vittoria and Riccardo but her painful inability to articulate her feelings. "But why?" he begs. "Surely there is a motive." All she can say is that she does not know why. (Piero, too, comes to complain about her inarticulateness.) By the time of *Il deserto rosso,* not even small children can be counted on to communicate their feelings. Giuliana's son tricks her into believing that he is ill, and he cannot or will not explain why. Giuliana articulates her problems to Corrado in virtually psychotic terms. Only in the language of fairy tale can she describe her true feelings to her son.

It is impossible for these characters to communicate with one another, because they cannot communicate with themselves—an inability that we read in their faces. They are not clear about their real wishes or life goals. They might even deny that one could have any. They are conscious or unconscious escapists, running away from rather than facing up to their problems. The theme of escape appears in some form in virtually every one of Antonioni's films, even his first. In *Gente del Po,* a woman working in the fields watches a barge pass down the river, and the voice-over reads her mind: "She thinks perhaps of happiness. To leave, to

Frame 33

travel, to change her life. The sea is there, at the end of the trip."[10] But the field hand's desire is at least real and justifiable for the quality of her life. Later characters flee—in geographical actuality or into the wilderness of their own minds—for less comprehensible reasons. To ask only about the main characters: What or whom does Aldo hope to find after Irma leaves him? Why does Anna disappear just because she is conflicted about Sandro? Why does Sandro hurl himself into "love"-affairs instead of facing up to his need to go back to architecture? Why is Giovanni so tempted by the life of luxury that he seems ready to hire himself out to a tycoon? What makes Piero run so fast, and what is he running from—or to? What is Corrado trying to prove by going to the wilds of Patagonia? (And in still later films, why is Thomas "off London" this weekend? Where does Mark intend to fly in his stolen airplane? What takes David off to deepest Chad and then even farther, into the mysterious depths of another identity? Why cannot Niccolò find the actress for his film?)

The films clothe the theme of escape in details of imagery and dialogue. *L'avventura* starts with a fast ride by sports car to the easy south and then escapes from land in a luxury yacht. Not satisfied with that, Anna jumps overboard to swim off on her own in a rehearsal of her final disappearance. In *La notte,* Lidia first escapes from the tedium of the publisher's reception by wandering out into the suburbs and later from the tedium of propriety by jumping into the tycoon's swimming pool with her clothes on. She even allows herself to escape for a while with a handsome stranger, but for her own reasons she decides not to go off with him. In *L'eclisse,* we see Vittoria escaping from the oppressive prison that Riccardo has made of her life. Later, she escapes in her imagination to Africa amid the artifacts of Marta's apartment. She also escapes to the Verona airport, a provincial place made exotic by the flight there in a private airplane. A more poignantly definitive escape is made by the drunk who steals Piero's Alfa Romeo and

Frame 34

ends up in the artificial lake of EUR. As the car is pulled out by a crane, we see the drunk's open hand extending over the door in a gesture of farewell. In *Il deserto rosso,* Giuliana escapes Ravenna for a few hours by traveling around the country-side with Corrado as he tries to recruit personnel for his own escape to "meaning-ful work" in Patagonia. There is no evidence that he shall find it. The couple wander around ships and then amid radio astronomy antenna towers; the towers hint at still other voyages, into the reaches of outer space. Clearly, the mysterious boat in the tale that Giuliana tells to her son represents a fantasy of escape. It roars in from nowhere and turns about, without deigning to land: it has "crossed the seas of the world and—who knows?—beyond the world." And at the end of the film, she explains to her son that the birds learn to escape from the poisonous yellow smoke coming out of the factory chimneys by flying around it. The theme of escape continues into the later films, too. If anything, it becomes more insis-tent, as we shall see.[11]

The theme of escape connects with the theme of distraction, a malaise com-mon among Antonioni's characters. One recalls Anna's distracted smile as she looks at Sandro. Or Riccardo's morose pensiveness: for all his concern about Vittoria's departure, he keeps falling into a distracted reverie. Giuliana's distrac-tion amounts to a modus vivendi. Corrado cannot remain attentive to the work-ers' questions about living arrangements on the project in Argentina; his eyes first wander up a meaningless line painted on a wall, then along some empty bottles as he leaves the building.

Distraction is attenuated escapism, a mental gesture of escape; one stays, though reluctantly, on the job.[12] And it is also a kind of inhibited fickleness: the distracted person would like to change the situation, to get out of it, but he or she does not quite dare. So the person "forgets"—even what he or she is looking for. The syndrome is familiar to the psychoanalyst; it is one of the psychopathologies of everyday life: "You go into a room to find something and realize you have forgotten what you were looking for. Then you remember, but perhaps feel some vague sense of dissatisfaction: 'Was that really it?' This sense of bafflement is likely to be keener when you plan a day, a month, a career. The goals and purposes of life, which in youth may have seemed self-evident, in adulthood seem impossible to define."[13] Search is the other side of the coin of escape, its positive name. People who run to are often also running from.[14] That is certainly Sandro's case. To make things worse, he not only defends but rationalizes his behavior, speaking with the deft and dramatic "honesty" of one who needs to persuade himself as much as the other:

CLAUDIA: And when I think you must have said exactly the same things to Anna any number of times . . .
SANDRO: Let's say I did. But I was as sincere with her then as I am right now with you.

But the search need not be escapist; it can be a genuine voyage of self-discovery. In each of these films, the female protagonist is honestly searching for some truth about life more profound than what a mazy, superficial society can offer. In *L'avventura,* Claudia's ostensible quarry is Anna, but she recognizes at a less than conscious level that she is searching for a viable way for herself to be. Despite the hazards of anodyne sex that she sees around her—the eerie voyeurism of the men in the streets of Noto or the blowsy lust of Giulia for young Goffredo (the narcissistic projection of a woman too often rejected by her husband)—and above all despite the promptings of traditional working-class virtues like caution and loyalty, Claudia lets love take its course. It is an honest gesture. And so is the touch she gives to the wretched Sandro at the end; she continues to search, even as she consoles.

Lidia's escape from literary cocktail party chatter into the streets of Milan also turns into a search for meaning, first in the urban space, then in the space of memory, the old neighborhood. But she cannot find meaning among the high rises and side lots and traffic markers of the city, and she cannot induce Giovanni, though he comes to fetch her, to accompany her down memory lane. Only on the golf course, when it is too late, will he be able to really hear how unbreachable a gulf has widened between them over the years.

Vittoria's search seems more successful, if we can find joy (as she does) in the merest sights of life: rustling trees, swaying flagpoles, sprinklers in the sunshine, and the like. Even Giuliana, despite her illness, attempts an honest search. But the fate of the certifiably obsessive is an inability to concentrate. She tries hard to understand what causes Corrado's wanderlust and what it has to do with her own problem; but neurotic fibrillation blocks her, forces her mind onto still another tangent. Even when she stumbles on an uncomprehending but patient Turkish sailor, she cannot stop poring over her symptoms, especially her everlasting need to be helped.

But somehow even Giuliana's vicious circles are better than Sandro's elabo-

Frame 35

rate rationalizations. Antonioni's women are the only ones to understand that the search is essential, for lack of any other viable way to be: "what matters is not the result, which remains in any case uncertain, but the journey itself, the search and the way it is lived out."[15] The model for survival in a desperate age is Vittoria, who, by acknowledging the need to search, manages to remain honest and even cheerful despite the terrors around her.

L'eclisse, as we have seen, continues the thematic of the first two films. But it also extends it. The earlier films limit themselves to the personal impact of the *malattia dei sentimenti*—the uncertainty of emotions, anodyne sex, the problem of communication, escapism. But *L'eclisse* raises the specter of a generalized, over-riding, nameless dread whose grounds are so real, whose possibilities are so genuinely terrifying that it cannot be written off as merely neurotic. It is a fear of the unknown—not only of the atomic bomb, since weapons only top the long list of means by which modern man can destroy himself. The fear is intensified by the fact that few people are willing to articulate it. Not a syllable concerning this brooding anxiety is spoken. Our only hints are commonplace sights: the headline—"Peace Is Weak"—in a newspaper that an anonymous pedestrian is reading, jet vapor trails in the sky, two men watching from a rooftop, a man whose face is taut and unsmiling, and so on. The montage of such shots, which state nothing explicitly, creates a sense of deep foreboding. No one speaks of fear: the ambience makes it hard to say exactly what one is afraid of. Such fear feeds on itself, hanging in the air like the failing light. In an atmosphere of unexpressed and even unconscious apprehension, a love relationship, indeed any relationship, seems impossible to sustain. Surely, it is the trace of fear (the only thing they truly share beyond sexual attraction for each other) that shows in the faces of Piero and Vittoria as they huddle like children together in the last scene in which we see them.

Frame 36

Frame 37

Frame 38

Of all the images in the concluding section of the film, that of the unfinished building veiled in straw matting is the most disquieting. What it seems to say is, "I represent the future, not only its architecture but all its shapeless menace." It reminds us of Yeats' nameless beast slouching towards Bethlehem to be born. There is no turning back to the comfortable, familiar shapes of the past. The only honest thing is to acknowledge our apprehension of the future, a future sparked, for better or for worse, by the incredible energies of science and technology.[16]

EMBODYING THE THEMATIC:
The Rejection of Symbolism

So the films of the tetralogy are indeed "about" something: they are about the anxiety that the world has felt since the fifties. But in a way foreign to commercial movies of the sound era, this condition is shown primarily in images. It is not spelled out in dialogue or connoted by mood music. It is always depicted, never pronounced. It occurs in visual details of plot, behavior, and composition so veiled and subtle that Antonioni risks making the audience impatient and bored. The audience could well protest that there is no action. It would be more accurate to say that the film requires the audience to reconstruct the states of mind that prompted what action there is. Not every moviegoer can or wants to perform such

Frame 39

labor, but the numbers are sufficient to persuade retrospective cinemas, art museums, college film clubs, and the like to keep on screening the films.

The particular kind of interpretation demanded by the tetralogy is that which uncovers significance in the minutiae of appearance. Antonioni's art resembles that of a novelist like Virginia Woolf, except that her medium, in its easy access to the minds of characters, permits explicit psychological interpretations of the text. A Clarissa Dalloway or a Mrs. Ramsay or a Lily Briscoe or the narrator, for that matter, can verbalize the significance of someone's faint grimace or slight hand movement. But those who view a film by Antonioni must do that for themselves: they must learn to read the meanings in appearances—Anna's enigmatic smile, or Lidia's close observation of Valentina as she reads her book at the foot of a long staircase, or the movements of the twig that floats in the cistern at the fatal EUR street corner, or the intense red of the docked freighter in the penultimate sequence of *Il deserto rosso.*

So much is thrown back on the viewer's interpretative ability that it may seem unfair to accuse him or her of overinterpreting. But that is what many critics have done. So it is essential to establish outer as well as inner interpretational limits. The films are open texts, but that does not mean that they are open to *any* interpretation. The problem is particularly acute for viewers disposed to finding symbol or metaphor in the slightest textual uncertainty. For example, the toy rockets launched in a scene in *La notte* were all too quickly labeled phallic, and Antonioni was accused of "heavy-handedly" showing that "sexual restlessness" drove Lidia out into the streets. One critic even argued that the film should have communicated this feeling "directly," that is, unsymbolically. The urge to see symbolism prevented more sensitive interpretations of Lidia's state of mind. To argue that she is looking for sex, that she is "cruising," is to misread her character by falling into the very trap of erotic obsession that, as we have seen, is one of Antonioni's themes. Lidia clearly has other things than men on her mind. In the scenario, she says to Giovanni over the phone: "I'm in front of the Breda plant. In the same old field, there are children playing. I'm sure you'll enjoy that. Imagine, they have rockets. They fly way up. It's beautiful. Don't worry, nothing's happened to me. No, no! I told you nothing happened! Come pick me up, will you?"[17] Then she returns to the field, waiting for him to arrive. The scene is described as follows:

The rockets are very well built. They shoot up quickly into the sky to a considerable altitude, to the children's cries of delight. But the two rockets with which the boys are playing are apparently the last ones, as it is starting to get dark. The children pick up their equipment and leave. Lidia is alone, standing in the field. The sunlight is nearly gone, and the scene again turns squalid and desolate.[18]

Given the context, even the most determined Freudian should find little more than ordinary sublimation of sexuality in a harmless, even creative hobby, especially when rocket launching is compared to the sullen and ugly behavior of the young thugs in the previous scene, who were methodically beating out each other's brains. The youngsters with the rockets have transformed their sexual drives into constructive, quasi-scientific activity. What is important is not the drive but the way it has been made socially useful, even exciting, by the brave new world of technology that Antonioni has celebrated in other contexts, for example, in the colors and shapes of industry in *Il deserto rosso*. Lidia's part here, as elsewhere in her sojourn, is that of silent and objective witness to the sights of the city. To find sexuality so indiscriminately in her behavior is to violate a larger and more important contextual meaning, which is confirmed by the expressions on her face, the movements of her body, the angles and distances from which she is photographed.

Another mistake is to find too precise a tenor in images that bear only a vague or contingent significance. In *L'eclisse*, rustling trees are juxtaposed often enough with Vittoria to suggest an association, but it is, I believe, far too explicit to argue that they symbolize the "agitation of her own thoughts."[19] A symbol or metaphor functions as an independent sign, that is, a something that can stand for another thing when that thing is absent. But when a single rustling tree is seen in the coda portion of *L'eclisse*, the thought that comes to mind is not, "Oh, that stands for Vittoria's agitated thoughts" but rather, "Where's Vittoria?" The appropriate rhetorical figure is not metaphor or symbol but metonymy, the figure of association or contiguity, which, as Roman Jakobson has argued,[20] occupies the semantic pole opposite metaphor.

As we shall see in a later chapter, Antonioni works assiduously on his visual juxtapositions of people with things and of things with other things. Backgrounds are never fortuitous: they provide implicit comment on the characters' actions or vice versa. At the beginning of *L'avventura*, Anna finds her father discussing with a worker the encroachment of the trashy housing development onto his beautiful estate. The restlessly modern Anna is identified with the transitory, noisy new buildings, while her father is matched with the magnificent dome in the distance.

Frame 40

Frame 41

FATHER: I thought you'd already sailed.
ANNA: Not yet, Papa.
FATHER: Don't they still wear sailors' caps with the name of the yacht on them?
ANNA (*frowning*):   No, Papa. Not anymore.

Architecture and dialogue provide co-metonyms of the theme. They do not abstractly symbolize flimsy modernity: they are themselves concrete examples of it.

Similarly, in *La notte*, the graceful old building behind Lidia as she stands at the window of Tommaso's sterile hospital room is metonymic of the waning of old values. It embodies them. Antonioni did not just think up that building, the way Robert Burns thought up the rose or Donne thought up the compasses. Metaphor depends on the sudden and unexpected perception of similarity. Metonymy does not, because it is purely associative, purely tied to the real. The idea of traditional values is reinforced by Lidia's old-fashioned flowered dress, which strikes a quaint and even discrepant garden note in Milan's barren streets. Neither building nor dress is an abstract symbol or concretion taken from another semantic sphere, as are the rose and the compasses. Metonymy is at once a figure for and a literal part of its referent. Hence, it reinforces the actuality of the world of the text. Antonioni's very manner of working, his reliance on the inspiration of actual environments, ensures the supremacy of relational metonymy over substitutive figures like metaphor and symbol.

To argue that Antonioni's images are not usually symbolic in the ordinary sense of the word is not to suggest that they are not motivated by thematic considerations. Motivation is always there, but it is subtle and unassertive (the shot of the exploding desert mansion at the end of *Zabriskie Point* is a rare exception). And it is always rooted firmly in the complex tissue of event and circumstance that constitutes the film. Consider the shot on the train in which Claudia refuses Sandro's overtures and implores him to get off at the next station. The camera cuts to a view of the beach and the surf running alongside. It would be forcing a category to say that the running surf signifies—to Claudia or to us—the mutability of life (or of anything else). The sea, of course, is a traditional symbol of mutability. But this is a particular sea, into which Anna has disappeared and where she still may be. So its connection with Claudia's thinking and situation is basically pragmatic rather than figurative, or it is only incidentally figurative. The film is not "stating" that life and the sea share the property of mutability and that Claudia sees her own fickleness or "fragility of emotion" in it. The association is lighter, more tangential, more allusive. And unlike a genuine symbol, it does not explain the inside by referring to the outside.

In short, Antonioni's images always reverberate with the charge of the whole film, and it is a mistake for interpretation to reduce them to mere symbols. Valentina's floor may resemble a checkerboard and hence suggest the hazard that Giovanni will incur by dallying with her, but it remains obdurately a floor. Whatever there is of phallus or atom bomb in the water tower that looms so visibly outside Riccardo's window must not obscure its own solid weight as an object that is part of modern life. To reduce Antonioni's richly envisioned objects to abstract signs in the interests of discovering what they are "about" would be as much an esthetic desecration as to project his films with a dim bulb.

The titles of the films, however, are verbal, not visual, indices, and they do work in a symbolic way. We see no literal desert in *Il deserto rosso*, no literal eclipse in *L'eclisse*, so efforts to ascertain the meanings of these expressions on symbolic grounds are clearly justified.[21] The words *The Adventure* signify—in the superficial travel bureau sense of the word—an eventful trip on a yacht. At a less superficial level, there is the adventure of Anna's disappearance. Then there is

Frame 42

Frame 43

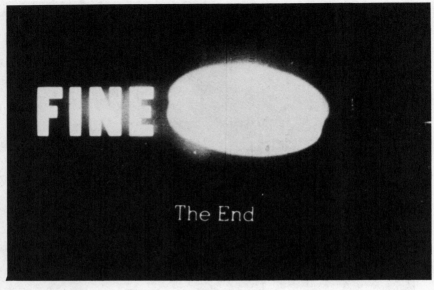

l'avventura

Frame 44

the "sexual adventure," the trivial erotic escapade that Sandro unfairly accuses Claudia of desiring but in which he himself actually indulges with Gloria Perkins. At the deepest level, there is Claudia's painful spiritual adventure of trying to get close to another person in all his psychological complexity.

The night of *La notte* is literally the long night of the party, which ends at dawn on a bleak prospect of marital misery. But it is also a vehicle for the obscurity in our emotional lives that makes marriage so difficult and that darkens our sense of direction in general.

The title *The Eclipse* is more problematic. What or who is overshadowed? How are they affected? What are the global consequences? The film ends, after the disappearance—or, better, the nonreappearance—of hero and heroine, with an illuminational phenomenon: "Sudden close-up of an illuminated street light with a glaringly bright halo encircling the lamp." Is that the eclipse? We tend to think of an eclipse as the darkening of a heavenly body, not as a brightening: the sun is obscured by the moon or the moon by the earth's shadow. But the reverse is at least theoretically possible: a darker body can be eclipsed by a brighter one. Does the bright streetlamp, as metonym for material progress or symbol for the atomic bomb, obliterate the lovers' meeting? Antonioni recalls going to Florence to photograph an eclipse and speculating about the impact on bystanders' emotions. There are two versions of what he said. The English version in the introduction to *The Screenplays of Michelangelo Antonioni* reads: "In that darkness . . . I speculated whether even sentiments [emotions] are arrested during an eclipse. It was an idea that was only vaguely connected with the picture I was making, which was why I didn't retain it. But it could have been the nucleus of another film."[22] But in the 1964 Italian edition of *Sei film* he writes: "During an eclipse emotions, too, are probably arrested. It was an idea that had vaguely to do with the film I was preparing, a sensation more than an idea, but that already defined the film when the film was still far from being defined. All the work that comes after, all the shooting, is always related to that idea or sensation or presentiment."[23] The second version suggests a more interesting account of Antonioni's feelings in the matter. The nonreappearance of the protagonists argues that love is extremely difficult if not impossible in the contemporary world. And since the pair cannot have a "meaningful relationship," Antonioni decides not to show them at all. Their disappearance from the screen seems to be a synecdoche for the suspension of emotional life at a historical moment when civilization pauses to gasp incredulously. At the advent of . . . what? The millennium? Armageddon? The savior (looking perhaps like Albert Einstein)?

The title *Red Desert* is even more enigmatic. Neither industrial Ravenna nor industrial anywhere is written off as a wasteland. The desert seems, rather, to be what Giuliana makes of it. The film is inexorably tied to her point of view. The desert is in her own mind. And, from what Antonioni has said of the "color" of emotions and from what he does with colors in *Il mistero di Oberwald,* red is perhaps the sign of overheated neurosis, of hellish burnout. But paradoxically the heat does not make the colors and shapes of the world less beautiful—it makes them more intense, more saturated and lurid.

Antonioni's themes are only part of his films—and by no means the most important. We should not allow problems of interpretation to obscure the glories of the other parts—the minimalist plot structure, the subtle characterization, and, above all, the unique beauty of the visual surface.

PLOT STRUCTURE:
The Open Text

It has been argued that the key to Antonioni's mature art lies in a kind of "dedramatization" of plot. The term is suggestive, though its implications need careful examination. It is not that the films of the tetralogy are undramatic, for, clearly, they depict conflicts, interpersonal tensions, and the characters' attempts to cope with them. They are dedramatized only in the sense that the conflicts are not shown in a direct and conventionally theatrical way. Drama there is, certainly, but it lies behind the characters' impassive faces. It breaks out at odd moments, for reasons that are not always immediately obvious, as when Vittoria screams at seeing her reflected face trapped between the edge of the mirror and depressed Riccardo in the background.

Frame 45

In another sense, dedramatization can mean denarrativization. Here, the situation becomes more complex. Antonioni's films are denarrativized in the way that much modern fiction is. Critics have exhaustively analyzed the difference between the twentieth century's attitude toward plot and that held by previous centuries (and by unsophisticated audiences today). A common but mistaken view is that writers like Woolf, Joyce, and Proust simply give up plot—or, to use the common phrase, that "nothing happens" in their novels. Of course, those who use that phrase do not mean *literally* that nothing happens but, rather, that nothing "significant" happens. There are no "important" events by the ordinary standards of life—falling in love, marrying, succeeding or failing in business, dying, and so on. Further, modernist novels tend to avoid making events interpretable—*lisible*, readable, is the fashionable term—by clear chains of causality. As we have seen, the older, causative narrative logic prevails in Antonioni's early films. For example, in the first sequence of *Cronaca di un amore*, the detective discusses the case with his boss; in the second, he questions several people in Ferrara about Paola's early life. We conclude that his visit to Ferrara is the consequence of his boss's instructions. Guido appears in Milan and meets with Paola: again, we infer, even before we hear the couple speak, that the meeting is the result of the detective's investigation. *Cronaca di un amore*, like the vast majority of films, moves through a "readable" sequence of cause and effect, in which earlier actions clearly give rise to later ones.[24]

In modernist twentieth-century fiction, the logic of narrative sequence changes. The connection between events becomes less conventionally consequential. It is not always possible to find causation in the plots of *A la recherche du temps perdu*, or *To the Lighthouse*, or *Ulysses*. Sequence, of course, necessarily remains, for narrative must preserve chronology, the march of events, if it is to remain narrative and not become another kind of text—exposition, argument, description, or something else. But in modernist narratives, later events are not self-evidently the consequences of earlier. We may sense a relationship, but it is attenuated, indirect, and it suggests less a particular development of events than a general state of affairs.

It seems useful to have a term for this attenuated narrative logic that avoids suggestions of causation and that still hints at some principle of connexity. In *Story and Discourse* I proposed *contingency:* event B may be said to be contingent on event A if it succeeds it in the chronology of the plot and if both events can be understood to contribute to a more general state of affairs. (Some avant-garde plots depict events as completely random, but that is not Antonioni's way.) In *La notte*, Lidia and Giovanni go from the hospital to a reception for his newly published book—not an obvious causal sequel. Traditional narrative logic would prompt us to look to a later event for an explanation of the connection to the earlier event. But what follows is Lidia's walk in the suburbs, then the nightclub, then the party at the industrialist's mansion, then Giovanni's encounter with Valentina and Lidia's encounter with the handsome bachelor, then the sad scene on the golf course. The causal connections among these events are not clear. For example, there is no particular reason why Giovanni and Lidia should not have gone to the cocktail party first and then to the hospital. The reasons exist only at the level of theme, character, and situation: seeing the dying Tommaso—we infer—makes Giovanni's success seem all the more shallow to Lidia; the cocktail party, the scene of Giovanni's present triumph, makes her anxious to get away by herself; walking alone in the city (an unusual event for a Milanese housewife in 1960) makes her more sensitive to it as a hostile environment; distaste for that environment makes her seek the nostalgia of the old neighborhood; and so on. The critical word here is *infer:* where the connections between events are tenuous, the demands on the audience to interpret, to provide connections, intensify.

Strange as it may seem today, many reviewers felt that *La notte* pushed narrative structure beyond recognizable limits. They said that the story had disappeared, or, if they were more favorably inclined, they described *La notte* as "pure lyric." But it is clear that the film does tell a story, in the familiar sense of that word: it evokes a state of affairs and its consequences. That is, it describes the Pontanos' desultory marriage and Giovanni's discovery of his wife's early attachment to Tommaso, of his own inability to satisfy her deepest emotional needs, and of the shallowness of his own emotional life. Of course, contingent plots can question the very need for events to fit into a pattern in which event B means event A because it is its result. The contingent plot indulges freely in "unnecessary" events, whose relation to an ongoing logical chain is marginal or even nonexistent. Consider two parallel situations, one in the causal plot of *Cronaca di un amore*, the other in the contingent plot of *L'avventura*. In both situations, one person interrogates another about the person whom he is looking for: the detective interrogates one of Paola's old teachers in Ferrara, and Sandro interrogates the old man who is the only resident of the barren island. The teacher's undisguised lechery, whatever independent value it has as a realistic portrayal of the type, remains causally relevant: he remembers Paola's charms *because* it is important to know that she was extremely sexy even as a teenager. But the information provided by the old man of the island is completely gratuitous: the place belongs to Australians; he lived in Australia for thirty years; the people in the photograph are his family; he has just returned from Panarea. None of this information has anything to do with Anna's disappearance or, indeed, with anything else in the movie. The effect is realistic precisely because the information is gratuitous; the old man is not there to advance the plot. He is *simply* there, as one more of Antonioni's stubborn "found objects." His Australian experience and the other details seem to be true because they have no reason not to be. While *Cronaca di un amore* selects details and events that function as signs of the plot, *L'avventura* and its successors undermine this convention by introducing events that are "useless," "pointless" by traditional standards.[25] Not only that: they are played in real time, lasting exactly as long as they would in real life. This is the only justification for what would otherwise be an absurdly long depiction of the search for Anna on the barren island. Not only must Anna's disappearance remain unexplained, but the search for her must be shown to be only a pretext for something else that is going on.

If we look closely at the published shooting script of *L'avventura,* we can see how the plot became more contingent than causal on the set (or in the editing booth), since Antonioni deleted many explanatory passages in the actual process of filming. In one scene, for instance, the idea was that Claudia should yield to Sandro's sexual advances partly because the spectacle of the deserted town had made her feel so lonely and isolated that she needed to cling to him for warmth. The scenario is quite explicit:

> Claudia is . . . silent, somewhat dismayed. Instinctively, she presses up close to Sandro who leads her to a shady spot where the ground is overgrown with weeds . . . Claudia offers no resistance; in fact, she entwines her fingers around his, almost with a sense of desperation. Sandro tries to kiss her. She makes a feeble attempt to resist, looks around, and sees the deserted town, the barren fields, the crumbling, sun-baked walls. She turns and looks at Sandro again, and now it is *she* who kisses *him.*[26]

None of this business occurs in the film. There is no look of dismay, no eye-line matches with the deserted town or the like. We see only the following: a shot of Claudia saying "This isn't a town, it's a cemetery. My God, how dismal. Let's get out of here"; a shot of an alley looking toward the open square, which is dominated by the modernistic church; a shot of Sandro's car starting up and then driving away from the church; the church itself in an extended *temps mort,* as if the town, for the moment, were given the point of view just as it was being abandoned by Claudia and Sandro; and finally a shot of the pair on the hillside in the act of making love.

Frame 46

In transferring the shooting script to film, Antonioni deliberately avoids the easy causative, pregnantly meaningful glance or gesture in favor of depicting things simply as happening. Emotions are "fragile," contingent, and so no more predictable than anything else in this world. Antonioni's practice presupposes a certain audience, one that knows how it feels to offset an attack of loneliness with lovemaking. Audiences that are unwilling or unable to recognize the experience will find Claudia's motivation obscure. But for the proper viewer, the ellipsis will seem just right, more "real" a representation of life than anything that conventional films can offer.

Of course, narratives based on contingent rather than causal logic run the risk of seeming obscure. But the challenge of open texts encourages audiences to participate actively in the interpretive process. The viewer may feel a healthy desire to see the films again. And since the films are very rich, the second viewing is amply rewarded. An event that on first viewing seemed meaningless or capricious or included purely for visual effect is seen on subsequent viewings to fit neatly into the plot. For example, Sandro and the young architect whose drawing he spoils are distracted from their quarrel by the spectacle of a long line of young seminarians dressed in black and shepherded by their teachers. Why that particular spectacle? At the surface level, it may seem to be just a photogenic excuse to get Sandro out of an awkward situation. But a second viewing may recall Sandro's remark to Claudia as they stand on the roof of the church among the bell ropes. Trying to explain why he gave up architecture for cost estimating, he says, "Because . . . once I was asked to draw up an estimate—how much it would cost to build a school. The job took me a day and a half. I earned four million lire for it." The shot of the seminarians going to school recalls that remark, made ironic by the fact that these pupils walk daily to solid architectural triumphs, not shoddy

Frame 47

Frame 48

reinforced concrete boxes. That is not the only meaning of the shot, but it is certainly one of them.

It is obvious that the preference for contingency over causality suggests an epistemology. Since the end of a film never ties up all the threads of its plot, the end is only one more event and no less accidental than any other. So, instead of traditional essences and values, Antonioni's tetralogy emphasizes sheer existence as such. The heroines in these films discover that ideal happiness cannot be found in this world and certainly not in a lover. The best that they can hope for is a modicum of hard-earned freedom. Vittoria, in *L'eclisse,* comes closest to finding it, but only in solitary moments—at a small airport in Verona, on a midnight walk looking for a dog, in a sudden view of wind-tossed trees, in a new friend's apartment as she dances to African drums. The causelessness of these events argues the fortuitousness of life itself. Antonioni's protagonists can achieve nothing more than a positive attitude toward fortuitousness. They can enjoy the exquisite moments when and as they come, even in solitude, without demanding them and without expecting an impossible, all-in-one consummation in love. In that sense, the theme of *L'eclisse* is not only unsentimental but antisentimental: it directly repudiates the ladies' magazine view of life that haunted *La signora senza camelie* and *Le amiche*.

Ellipsis is an important formal property of modernist plots.[27] Ellipsis is not the omission of events but of their mentions; thus it is a matter of narrative discourse, not of narrative story, for the missing events remain necessarily implied. Like novels, commercial films have become more elliptical in recent years. Antonioni's practice was ahead of its time. Still, his plot leaps are never so great as to be incoherent. The theme is always marked strongly enough to account for connections, and at this distance in time it is difficult to understand all the critical fuss that greeted the films.[28]

In most films, especially action films and melodramas, the purpose of ellipsis is to quicken the pace and increase tension. In Antonioni's tetralogy, ellipsis has a different function. It contributes to the sense that motives are unclear, perhaps even inexplicable. Nor does Antonioni use the time saved by ellipsis to add things, to make the plot more intricate; on the contrary, his films seem slow, contemplative, even dreamy. Time saved is more likely than not used ("wasted" in the eyes of conventional critics) for visual effects like *temps morts*, dead holds on the scenery after the actors have departed. This effect, about which I will have more to say, was early related by French critics to the "microrealism" of the *nouveau roman*. They found in it a devotion to what they called the "minute banality of things." In Antonioni's world, however, things are banal only at the superficial level of the traditional, causative plot; at a deeper level, as we shall see, they clamor for our attention. In Antonioni's hands, their individuality and integrity makes them precious, precisely because we cannot explain them away by assigning to them easy background or symbolic meanings. We are forced to see them—truly to entertain them—with the fullest visual attention that we can muster. As Barthes put it, Antonioni has caught their very vibration.[29] Through ellipsis and other manipulations of narrative time, Antonioni insists the way painters do on the sheer wonder of the world's appearance.

That many of the ellipses in *L'avventura* were the idea of Antonioni rather than of his screenwriters emerges clearly from a comparison of the scenario with the finished film. The scenario amply documents the characters' feelings and thoughts. Antonioni could have (and practically every other filmmaker would have) externalized his intentions through conventional means—dialogue, facial expressions, music. Instead, he conveys a few feelings through the scenery, which he uses as a sort of objective correlative, and others he makes no direct effort to express at all, leaving it to viewers to infer them from context as best they can. For example, at the critical moment when Claudia, doubtless feeling rather ambivalent, finds Sandro at the pharmacy in Troina, virtually nothing is said, yet it is not difficult to infer the emotional storm that is raging or the importance of their decision to go off together.

Antonioni often intensifies ellipses by showing them through the straight cut, the shortest instant of film perception. A good example is the ellipsis between the shot of the couple's departure from the deserted village and the shot of the couple making love on the hillside as the train goes by. The straight cut can be made to present information that virtually defies analysis because of the speed at which the viewer's mind must work. Antonioni uses the ellipsis to make it doubly difficult to grasp motives: what is important is not only that the couple have fallen in love, or that they are panic-stricken at the spectacle of the deserted village, or that a woman has been seduced, but that we see an attenuated combination of these events and more: "the whole truth is more complicated and ultimately escapes analysis."[30] The ellipsis is the device par excellence for rendering both the fragility of the emotions *and* the impossibility of accounting for them in any definitive way.

Discarding traditional narrative's obsession with past and future, the films of the tetralogy engage the present event, liberating it from the dictates of conventional story. Antonioni raises to prominence the tangible present by playing against expectations. Audiences must expect Vittoria and Piero to meet again if their not doing so is to have any shock. What happens instead is that story time— the time of the chain of events—stops: the film is denarrativized, and another kind of time, descriptive or expository, takes over. An open-ended ellipsis occurs— the fictional *story* ends, although the movie continues for another seven minutes.

An ellipsis at the very end of a narrative from which the protagonists have disappeared is so unusual that many critics had difficulty interpreting it. Some talked, for example, about Antonioni's excursion into "abstract art." However, he denied that intention point-blank: "The seven minutes have been called abstract, but this is not really so. All of the objects that I show have significance. These are seven minutes where only the objects remain of the adventure; the town, material life, has devoured the living beings."[31]

The final sequence can be considered an establishing shot in reverse, a kind of disestablishing shot. In Hollywood jargon, an establishing shot is a shot at the beginning of a movie whose purpose is to fix the site of the action. There are some good examples at the beginning of *Stagecoach, Psycho,* and *Manhattan.* The logic is this: "If you grant the existence of such and such a place—Monument Valley, downtown Phoenix, the New York City skyline—and how can you deny that it exists when you have it there staring you right in the face?—then it will be easy for you to accept the events that follow as plausible." The convention further argues that all the establishing shots belong to an indefinite time preceding the action itself. Establishing shots function more like travelogues than like documentaries; what they show resembles stage sets more than actual locations of the action. They go little beyond the anticipational, working mostly like a concert overture: "We are beginning," the movie says, "and here are some 'views' to

Frame 49

Frame 50

Frame 51

Frame 52

validate the action and put you in a receptive frame of mind." Unlike documentaries, which invoke places to make statements about them, fiction films show places so that the action can get under way.

In *L'eclisse*, however, the shots of the nondescript Roman suburb come at the end, frustrating the viewer's expectations of a well-formed narrative conclusion. Ordinary movie logic insists that if protagonists are supposed to meet, we either shall see them meet or learn why they do not. The coda of *L'eclisse*, however, accumulates shot after shot of what has until then been only background. Gradually it dawns on us that this is all there is. We are not going to see Vittoria and Piero. But, if all that Antonioni wanted to do was to evoke their parting, he could have ended the film with the shot of Vittoria saying goodbye to Piero or with the high-angle shot of the empty street corner. Why does he embark on a kind of minidocumentary of EUR, showing bus wheels, light towers, skyscrapers jutting into the sky with tiny figures on top? (See photo on p. 65.) And above all, why did he people the landscape with real inhabitants of EUR—total strangers to the fiction? The sequence is a classic example of open text, and any single interpretation, even Antonioni's own, can prove only partial.

As already noted, it has been suggested that the passage leaves the domain of narrative for that of lyric.[32] But what makes the passage lyric (if indeed it is) is not its "poetry" (whatever that word means for cinema). It is rather that narrative time stops and that another textual order takes over. The focus on event becomes a focus on place and on the people and objects that occupy it.[33] Not temporal succession but spatial coexistence becomes the guiding principle. Even the gathering of dusk does not alter the descriptive function. The coda is a portrait of the suburb, not the story of how night falls on it. The substitution of this new, non-narrative text seems to universalize the motif of the going out of the light. The failing light suffuses the street corner where the fictional characters are supposed to meet just at the moment when the street corner ceases to be fictional and resumes its place in the real world. The area of relevance moves beyond the fictional situation of the characters alone: it is a whole society, ultimately a whole civilization, that cannot meet. The end, we cannot help but feel, may be more than just the end of this love affair and this film: hence the power of the final image, the blazing streetlamp (see Frame 44, p. 72).

Though the final sequence is atemporal, it possesses an ordered, descriptive logic, the order of disestablishment, since it moves away from the known particular to the unknown general. The first shots in the sequence show details recalled from Piero's and Vittoria's meetings there—the sprinkling system, the nurse pushing the baby carriage, the pile of bricks outside the building under construction, the barrel standing at the corner of the wooden fence. These peripheral synecdoches invite us to look for the central components, the two characters. Instead, we get a distanced view of the corner from a high angle looking down on the zebra stripes—more of the whole itself, but the critical human parts are still missing. Instead, a stranger (that is, a "real" resident of the "real" EUR) crosses the pedestrian stripes that until then have "belonged" to the fictional protagonists. The stranger suddenly introduces the randomness of real life. Disestablishment has begun. Freezing out whatever measure of warmth we have gathered from our identification with the fictional Piero and Vittoria, the image of a non-fictional pedestrian suffuses the complexion of the street corner with the cold pallor of reality. From now on, we see only indifference in the buildings and vehicles and streets. Or vague anxiety in the faces of bystanders—an anxiety universalized precisely by the fact that we shall never know their stories.

I do not mean to say that the buildings and streets of the EUR suburb are made more important than the characters. It would be too simplistic to insist on a single reading, say, "Things will predominate"—the moral counterpart perhaps of the neutron bomb, which kills people but leaves buildings intact. That would be simply to reinvoke the old convention. No, characters and settings are of equal importance (or nonimportance), since every thing, like every event, is merely contingent. The film asserts nothing; it merely acknowledges the chance coexistence of things and people unrelated, even irrelevant, to one another.

Except in their predilection for ellipsis, the plot structures of the four films do not go beyond the normal ways of handling time. The emphasis on the here-and-now precludes any tampering with time sequence, for example, in flashback or in the summarizing or eliding of long periods of time: the films range from the single day of *La notte* to the indefinite couple of weeks of *L'eclisse* and *Il deserto rosso*. Their tendency to adhere to the classic theatrical unity of time is one more reason for rejecting easy uses of terms like *dedramatization*.

4

The Great Tetralogy
Characters

Four kinds of characters preoccupy Antonioni in the tetralogy: a woman who has been disillusioned by a lover but who continues to muster the courage to seek and speak the truth (Claudia, Lidia, Vittoria); a man, intellectual and/or artist, who is depressed and withdrawn from the world and whose need for a woman is so great that he cannot give up an old relationship or resist the lure of a new one, no matter how inappropriate (Sandro, Giovanni, Riccardo, Corrado); a neurotic who just manages to hold on to sanity (Giuliana); and an apparently well-adjusted person who remains in touch with the world but only through sterile business or technical values (Piero, Ugo).

Like Bergman, Antonioni centered most of his films (up to *Blow-Up*) on the experience of women, explaining in interviews that he found women more in tune with their feelings, more honest, and so more suitable than men as protagonists of films that try to approach the truth about human relations: "*la donna è il filtro più sottile della realtà*" ("woman is the more subtle filter of reality").[1]

In the first three films of the tetralogy, a disillusioned woman and a depressed man are locked in a deadly yet symbiotic relationship. The woman's disillusionment derives (as any feminist would predict) from the man's insensitivity to her needs as a total human being, needs not so different from his: companionship, respect, *her* kind of sex, and simple, ordinary attention. The Antonionian man is desperately unable to supply these, usually as a result of obscure wounds that life has dealt him. *Life* here seems to mean not previous amours but rather the hazards and demands of profession, demands so exacting that he has little time or energy for anything else except appeals for sexual comfort. The appeal is as apparent in the early stages of an affair as it is at the end. Sandro first woos Claudia out of attraction, vanity, and a sense of loss. But no sooner is she comfortably in tow than he begins to use her love as solace for his professional misgivings—not only in the denouement but as early as the stay at the hotel in Noto. Giovanni is unresponsive to Lidia's nostalgia, ignores her as she lies naked in her bath and later during his cool inspection of the striptease act at the night club, and ultimately rejects her for another woman at the party. So oblivious is he to her feelings that he actually expects her to sympathize with him about his little contretemps with the nymphomaniac. By *L'eclisse,* Antonioni has this type of man down so pat that he can evoke Riccardo without supplying any information about his previous life. Under Antonioni's direction, Francisco Rabal oozes need from every pore. The spare dialogue is a masterpiece of smoldering recrimination. We do not have to be told the specifics of the couple's history together, since for any adult the discussion is all too painfully familiar. In Corrado we see the same erotropism. But Giuliana, his love object, is even less stable than he—indeed she is almost a parody of the neurotic, needy lover. Under these circumstances, he does his best to be supportive, but he, too, cannot resist sexual temptation, nor does he bother to ask whether lovemaking is the appropriate response to her writhings, which may be expressions of anguish and not sexual at all. The look on his face seems to say, "Let me take care of your problem: 'masculinity' knows best."[2]

As for Giuliana, Antonioni and Monica Vitti have created a marvel of interpretation—perhaps the most accurate portrayal on film of what Karen Horney calls "the neurotic personality of our time." The film shows with almost clinical precision how to the deeply neurotic mind everything in life is leveled to *the problem:* not only love in its various forms but family responsibility, work, friendship, even simple mechanical tasks like driving a car. The details are perfectly rendered, the metonyms hauntingly real and physical: Giuliana buys a half-eaten sandwich from an astonished worker literally to feed her hunger for contact. And when she describes the floor giving way beneath her feet, what member of the audience feels so secure as not to feel the tremor? The connection between figurative and literal reality is eroded. Antonioni's camera makes us see as she does: the strangely whitened street and hotel lobby, the sinister look of friends in the swirling fog, the saturated colors and incomprehensible shapes of huge machines and equipment. No less palpable to us are her longings—to have everyone and everything she has loved around her to form a wall against the terror. It was only to evoke the intensity of her need that Antonioni broke with strict naturalism to create a fantasy sequence, to use the camera as a direct visual evocation of her "mind screen" (Bruce Kawin's term for the visual projection of the contents of a character's mind).[3] Her only respites from free-floating anxiety are either regressive or bluntly physical: in the retreat to the childish world of the fantasy tale, in the naughty but safe experiment with the aphrodisiac quail's egg, in the sheer physical relief of orgasm in Corrado's room. Yet Antonioni also shows that behind all the fears there are sharply aggressive feelings. What makes Giuliana more apprehensive than anything is how close she feels to violence.

The efficient man seems to be at one with life, but he is no less alienated precisely because he does not realize it. He is ostensibly at home in his world, even master of it. Piero rushes about, pulling "quick turnovers," telephoning other markets long-distance, teasing service people, bullying clients who have trouble meeting their obligations. But he has lost (or never possessed) his soul: he is merely an extension of the larger system that he serves. He understands the fundamentals of capitalism so little that he cannot answer Vittoria's not so silly question, "Where does all that money go when stocks fall?" And despite his external cockiness and confidence with women, he is edgy when he is alone, and he needs a tranquilizer in order to go to sleep. The natural functions are disturbed in those who are programmed. In extreme cases, the individual is so completely absorbed by the program as to forget its purpose. In a treatment for an unmade film called *Il deserto dei soldi* (The Desert of Money), Antonioni wrote: "Once in Las Vegas I saw a woman spend an entire afternoon in front of a slot machine, and when the machine finally gave her back a pile of half-dollars, she walked off without it."[4] The stock market is a more social, more "normal" place than a casino, at least for investors and brokers who have "adjusted" to it. And it is precisely that adjustment, that normalization or acculturation or Lévi-Straussian "cooking" of the raw capitalist motive, that interests Antonioni. Recently he published an amusing account of his research into the life of the stockbroker:

> From the inquiry made years ago for *L'eclisse* the following data emerged:
> There are around two hundred brokers in the Milanese stock market. Their mean age is forty-seven. They have a minimum of two children each. Sixty percent have fishing as a hobby. Often the broker goes fishing with a client. They prefer fishing because it is tranquil and relaxing and offers good conditions for business talk.
> Of the sixty percent who fish, twenty-five percent also like music. Another ten percent like the arts, predominately painting. Fifteen percent go for soccer, and five percent prefer women. Milanese stockbrokers are not Don Juans, according to the survey. They prefer women who give abundantly and quickly. They talk more about shares than about women . . .
> For everybody the stock market is a marvelous habit.
> *A Marvelous Habit* might have been worth using as a title on the screen.[5]

According to the survey that Antonioni reports here, Piero is clearly unrepresentative. Perhaps it is because he is still young and has yet to settle down to his two-plus kids and music or painting or soccer. He is still learning: when he thanks a playboy client for a girl he passed on to him, the client, who has just lost a fortune, warns him to keep his mind on business. Still, in good stockbrokerly form, he prefers women who "give abundantly and quickly" (like hot stocks with "fast turnovers"). Vittoria does give "abundantly and quickly" but for her own reasons. He likes that at first, but, male chauvinist that he is, he ultimately finds her puzzling, and he is genuinely hurt when she refuses his proposal of marriage. Clearly, Piero plays the erotic percentages the same way he plays the market. His whole life jumps to the rhythm of the big board. Ugo is the engineering version of the efficient man, cool and unflappable among his dynamos and steam boilers. And he is passing on to his son his calm if slightly deadly curiosity. Men like Ugo not only understand but come to resemble the gyroscope that can keep even the largest ship stable in the worst of storms. But when it comes to understanding what makes people tick, Ugo is reduced to speechlessness.

Does she like Ugo (or later Corrado?)

ANTONIONI'S THEORY OF CHARACTERIZATION

What characters are like is perhaps less important for an assessment of narrative art than an account of how they are constructed. An author who believes that human feelings are fragile, vague, distracted, and unreliable and who at the same time is committed to an unprecedented use of sheer visual surface will obviously devise special ways of presenting characters. For example, he may show them in clusters of acts that are not only heterogeneous but downright odd, quirky, oblique, and inconsistent. Corrado in *L'avventura* is at once vicious to his wife and kindly and sympathetic to Claudia and Sandro during the hunt for Anna. Riccardo in *L'eclisse* is at once angry, hurt, uncomprehending about Vittoria's decision to leave him and polite, clear, even cool in saying his final *addio* to her.

It is fascinating to see in published treatments of unmade films how Antonioni conceives his characters, even in the formative stage, as quixotic jumbles of isolated traits. In one treatment, he describes his dramatis personae as follows:

An industrialist, chemical branch . . . graduated in chemistry, but who remembers little . . . married for love . . . has told his wife that he wonders if one day they should have children as strange as they are . . . A writer [who] had attended a course in speed reading. Two hundred lines per minute. He is still terribly slow, however, in writing . . . He rereads his published novels, each time with renewed hope, and each time he returns them to the shelf disappointed . . . evenings he reads near a window by candlelight. At midnight, he extinguishes the candle, whether finished or not . . . He was already famous when he met the industrialist and his wife . . . The mistress of the writer. Obsessed with her own height and with death. Recently she wrote to a famous French biologist to ask what death was. "Death is a statistical hypothesis," wrote the biologist, "Yours sincerely . . ." A forty-year-old ex-deputy. Cited as witness in a civil suit, he had gone to the trial with his suitcase a few hours before his departure [on the trip with the industrialist] . . . A middle-aged lady, nubile, attractive. She has just returned from the fair in Rostov, Russia, where she bought one or two rings of the Budennyi family. She paid fifty thousand dollars. On the eve of the trip with her friends, an annoying attack of hypertension made her consult a doctor. The doctor prescribed a laxative. A laxative? . . . The pilot. Complicated, sour, full of anxiety. He awoke that morning discontented with himself. When the maid would bring him the newspapers, he would read them in one breath, angrily. Then he would call everyone to discuss what he had read. If another had a different opinion, he would insult him . . .[6]

The point about these sharply delineated characters seems to be that there *is* no point. They all die instantly in the plane crash that occurs as the pilot tries to fly through a storm. Only the diary of the writer's mistress remains intact. Death is a great leveler; in its grip all that serves to differentiate people comes to naught. And there is no evidence that these traits mean anything at all—except how oddly and incomprehensibly complex people are. The industrialist's preoccupation with the eccentricity of his prospective children can have nothing to do with the writer's speed reading, his mistress's obsession with death, the middle-aged lady's nubility or hypertension, the ex-deputy's court experience, or the pilot's discontentment—and vice versa.

Antonioni's way of displaying these random arrays of traits is also random:

instead of tending to create a balanced and compact structure within which the individual characters emerge dramatically through the concise development of plot situations, the camera follows significant small nuances of behavior that have no relation to the actualization of the story line and frames material that, from the strict story point of view, would be considered dispersive and gratuitous. The whole film is a flow of images, minutely and implacably scrutinized by the eye of the camera, in which the dramatic situations are scattered and even buried, and the behavior of the characters appears not to be selected or modeled in dramatic function but to be recorded and observed in more strictly ordinary quotidian and apparently insignificant gestures.[7]

These "insignificant" gestures subtly heighten the tension for the viewer precisely because he or she expects that something more eventful should be happening. We expect Claudia to look for Anna, but she spends her time trying on wigs or watching the foolish Giulia flirt with Goffredo. We expect some important encounter between Giovanni and Lidia when they leave the hospital, but they only get stuck in traffic. Giuliana hears a terrifying noise in her child's room, but it is only a toy robot that he forgot to turn off.

THE SURFACE OF BEHAVIOR

Whether the traits are important or odd or inconsequent, the privileged means of portraying them is always the visual image, not dialogue, commentative music, or the like. As early as 1939, when he was still a critic and not yet a filmmaker, Antonioni made his credo clear: "There exists a psychological law which says that to each motion of the soul there corresponds an external motion; to discover these motions is the first task of film authors. And it is clear that the more numerous the motions discovered, the greater the emotion that will be aroused [in the audience]."[8]

Whether or not there is such a "law," the idea has shaped Antonioni's theory of characterization. The clearest of the soul's "motions" is facial expression. As he came to see behavior as fragile, uncertain, opaque, his attitude toward what to show in the face changed: "For me now looking back at them, these [early] films were, rather, too warm; they showed the feelings which I was concerned with in too direct a way, and if I had to do them over again, I would make them a little more controlled."[9]

Even if, as Robbe-Grillet has said, everyone is a realist, it is useful to establish Antonioni's particular brand. Geoffrey Nowell-Smith has put it well:

Antonioni's realism is not naturalism or *verismo*. It is too finely wrought, pared down too sharply to the essentials of what has to be said. It is also too interior, as much concerned to chart the movements of the mind, however objectively regarded, as it is to observe physical emotions and things. But—and this is why Antonioni, like Flaubert, remains basically a realist—movements below the surface are generally left to be deduced from surface reactions. They are not artificially exteriorised in terms of convenient symbols, as in expressionism, nor are they supposed to inhabit a metaphysical world of their own . . . It is also very much a pictorial style, which communicates through the image and uses the sound track as a complement to the image, and rarely as an independent vehicle for the ideas. As a result it makes rather special demands on the sensibility of the spectator *moyen intellectuel,* who is the only type who normally gets round to seeing the films.[10]

DIALOGUE

The Antonioni of the great tetralogy dislikes textual redundancy. He rarely uses more than one track—dialogue, music, imagery, lighting—to express an effect. And he is disposed to allow discrepancies between the visible appearance and the import of what is happening. Conventional movies make a strict and simple correlation between a change of setup and dialogue. Typically, the change to a new place is established in the preceding shot: *Interior: day: police station:* Detective: "We'd better get over there before it's too late." The dialogue explains the new place, both going and coming: *Interior: day: a shabby apartment:* Detective: "What did I tell you? The killer didn't wait; there's her body." In Antonioni's films, the scene changes, but the characters' preoccupations remain the same. Since little dialogue is wasted on establishing place, what is spoken conveys a sense that characters are obsessed by their own thoughts, only a few of which emerge in the dialogue and then only obliquely, as a subtext. Dialogue is the tip of the iceberg of buried consciousness. Anna's ambivalence about her love for Sandro and about life in general is communicated by fragments of her mental fugue spoken at times and in places to which they are totally unrelated: in a parking lot in front of Sandro's apartment or on a cliff with a breathtaking view. The randomness of her remarks argues that they are genuine—if we believe that people cannot disguise their obsessions. Similarly, the nonutterance of thoughts takes on important meanings. We are increasingly sensitized to the discrepancy between words and thoughts, between the facade and the inner reality.

It is clear not only from Antonioni's own pronouncements but also from a comparison of his finished films with their scenarios that locations inspire him to improvise action and dialogue. Yet his improvisatory adjustment to local conditions is restricted essentially to the visual fleshing out of the main lines of the argument. What lies behind the characters' pensiveness is often spelled out in the scenario in elaborate verbal descriptions. The ambivalence of his characters is not accidental. It results from his rejection of standard cinematic methods of communicating emotions—through dialogue, strongly marked facial expressions, pointed editing, and so on. And in that rejection, he accepts the risk that the characters' thoughts may not be evident. When that happens, the movie may falter for a moment. But, the style argues, the ensuing lapse in communication and the enigma that it presents are themselves important aspects of life. They are partly what the films are about. So the loss of detail is compensated for by an overall gain in realism. We know no more about what a character is thinking than does the character standing next to him. But for that very reason, we feel closer, more deeply engaged in the scene. The verisimilitude is completely different from that in traditional works, where—thinking being verbal by convention—

nothing seems easier than to dip into the characters' minds when it suits the author's purpose.

Even when there is dialogue in Antonioni's films, there is no guarantee that it will ensure communication. On the contrary. Consider the non sequitur discussion between Vittoria and Riccardo at the beginning of *L'eclisse*. Vittoria tells him that she is sorry that she cannot work for him any longer. He asks if that is all she has to say to him. She says she is leaving. He panics. And so on: what we sense is elaborate game playing. The only faithfulness is to feelings, not to the audience's traditional need for explication.

The importance of Antonioni's spare dialogue cannot be overstressed. He has virtually returned to the cinema the predominance of the visual that it lost with the advent of sound.

CHARACTERIZATION BY OBJECTIVE CORRELATIVE

Antonioni insistently prefers images to dialogue for communicating a character's feelings. Among the bell towers of Noto, Claudia finds that words cannot convey her feeling about Sandro's offer of marriage; she pulls a bell cord by accident, and she is answered, as if miraculously, by a bell from another church. The answer seems to come from a great distance in space and from a time when life was

Frame 53

calmer, easier to contemplate and to make plans about. The bell ringing, an event *trouvé*, reaffirms what Sandro has just said better than mere words can: "Once they [the buildings] had centuries of life before them. Now—ten, twenty years at the most . . ."

If one had to select Antonioni's leading contribution to the art of cinema, it would have to be his way of relating character to environment. Refusing in these films to treat background as mere decor there solely to "establish" locale, he uses settings to represent characters' states of mind. Reserving setting per se for the next chapter, let us limit the discussion here to its uses in characterization.

The case of "setting-as-state-of-soul" is the most familiar of the possibilities. *Il grido* concerns a journey, so it provides opportunities for plein air shots of great natural and compositional beauty. But Aldo's emotional plight necessarily creates a gulf between what he sees and what Antonioni wants us to see. So the camera remains a neutral observer, a narrator manqué. Beset with troubles as he is, Aldo has no leisure to view his surroundings in any but a mundane, practical way. But to us the lugubrious vast river churning across the plain under a lowering gray sky clearly reflects something of Aldo's own bleak feelings of loss, loneliness, and rootlessness. So it qualifies as an objective correlative in Eliot's classic sense: "a set of objects, a situation, a chain of events which shall be the formula of that *particular* emotion; such that when the external facts, which must terminate in sensory experience, are given, the emotion is immediately evoked."[11]

Antonioni was not the first filmmaker to photograph ambient sets of objects to evoke characters' moods and situations, but he was the first in the sound era to do so on a sustained and calculated basis and to the partial exclusion of verbal means. The device suits an art that is at once intensely psychological and deeply committed to visual realism. A character like Aldo—a reticent worker—cannot be expected to show much emotion on his face or in his body. Eschewing artificial signs, like commentative music, and wanting to restrict himself to the visual field, Antonioni relied on the technique of "landscape-as-state-of-soul" (*paysage-état-de-l' âme*). Aldo remains a narrative object among the other objects along the Po, and those other objects serve as metonymic signs of his inner life.

Similarly, the buildings and engines in *Il deserto rosso* whose sinuous shapes and brilliant colors supply the camera with such beautiful compositional material seem to assail Giuliana's sanity. Yet at a deeper level they function as metonyms of the energy inside her, which neurosis has bottled up and which spills out only in self-destructive ways. Here again, early critics confused metaphor with metonymy, symbol with objective correlative:

All through the film there are the most superb cinematic metaphors for Giuliana's neurosis: the factory dump, strewn with papers and ominous refuse like a battlefield, in which she wanders; the stertorous panting rhythm, like a laboring heart, of a smokestack which emits regular jets of flame and steam; the huge ships that keep appearing in extreme close-up like ominous monsters—there is one amazing scene when Giuliana, tense and hysterical, is standing by a window across which moves with extreme slowness an enormous black prow, blotting out the view inch by inch. But these images seem much too powerful for what they express, as the scene in the fog when Giuliana stands confronting four figures—

Frame 54

her husband, her lover, and two friends—who are one by one blotted out by the thickening mist, as her neurosis separates her from them and erases them from her consciousness. Eisenstein never did anything more baroque, and yet all that is going on is that Giuliana wants to go back to get her handbag and they are offering to do so instead.[12]

If the images were in fact metaphors, they *would* be too powerful—hyperbolic and even bathetic. But they are not. The dump, the pulsing smokestack, the ship—these do not stand for Giuliana's feelings; they are there, and they exacerbate them, but they remain stubbornly themselves, brute realities of our powerful world. In the scale of things, Giuliana's anxiety counts for very little, but to her it is a matter of life and death, and the filmmaker evokes the intensity of her anxiety by any means he can. It is his great innovative talent to do so, powerfully, not through clichés like sturm und drang musical commentary but through cinema's most basic yet most often overlooked means, the visual image.

Antonioni uses the objective correlative to convey not only a character's emotional state but also the character's general situation. Piero's programmed life is annotated by shots of the machinery that capitalism so adores—the big stock exchange board, with its white letters and numbers whose random changes control the lives of those whom it has hypnotized, the battery-operated fan that can cool you in a hot public place, the fountain pen that dresses or undresses the photograph of a girl on its barrel, depending on how you hold it. And even the minor characters have their metonymic apparatus. The nymphomaniac is surrounded by dolls and stuffed animals. Riccardo's claustrophobic irritability is communicated by droning fans, heavy drapes, abstract paintings, the dry noise of an electric razor,

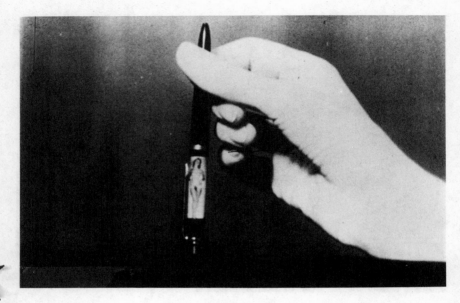

Frame 55

a water tower that resembles an atomic mushroom cloud. Ugo has his boilers and turbines, and his son has a toy mechanical man. It is not that other directors do not use such devices for characterization, but that they do not use them to the exclu- exclusion of more traditional devices. Antonioni is unique in his confidence in the ability of an audience to plumb the depths of surface information.

NARRATIVE SUBJECTS:
TÉMOIGNAGE

Even more innovative is the reverse interaction, in which the character's stance mutely comments on the environment. The possibility of such silent commentary rests on a standard cinema convention, that of the look (glance, gaze, French *re-gard*). Antonioni makes the look a virtual statement in and of itself. Ordinarily, when a character looks at X, the viewer is told, "Look at that X" or "There is an X." But what is merely citational for other filmmakers becomes something like mute pronouncement in a film of Antonioni's middle period. The person looking be- comes a surrogate narrator, a telling-subject, no longer merely one of the told- objects. In narratological terms, the person is an instrument or instance of the discourse, not just a component of the story.[13] But unlike their novelistic counter- parts, the film characters say nothing. Insisting on their purely visual experience, Antonioni makes of them simple but intense witnesses—*témoins*—endowed with some of the moral and legal powers of the French word. Since they say nothing, a heavy interpretational responsibility is thrust on the audience. (The closest literary parallel that I can think of is the task of inferring the thoughts of Nick Adams from the description of what he sees in Hemingway's early short stories.)

The objective correlative or landscape-as-state-of-soul effect and this witness's-perception-as-comment effect differ because they entail different kinds of point of view. *Point of view,* an important and often misused narrative term, can mean three different things: perceptual vantage, conceptual grasp, or personal stake or interest.[14] Here are some examples: Perceptual vantage: "From the Golden Gate Bridge, Henry could see San Francisco burning"—perception and nothing more, the perceiver located so as to see the thing perceived. Conceptual grasp: "Henry knew that the destruction of his home would mean a profound change in his life"—physical location is indifferent; what counts is that the conceiver cognitively focuses (note metaphor) on an issue, circumstance, situation. Personal stake or interest: "Off on assignment in New Delhi, Henry could not know that the destruction of his home would have a profound effect on his life"— since Henry neither sees nor knows about the event, there is no perception or conception; still, it makes sense to speak of the event as taking place from Henry's point of view, since as protagonist of the narrative he is the object of our empathy. Given these distinctions, it is clear that landscape-as-state-of-soul effects entail only the third kind of point of view, that of personal stake or interest. The Po Valley scenery is an objective correlate for Aldo's misery, though he is unconscious of the fact. Conversely, the witness or perception-as-comment technique primarily entails perceptual and conceptual points of view, and personal stake or interest is only secondary. In the first three films of the tetralogy, the witness's act of visualizing not only enables us to focus on what she sees but to infer her unspoken judgments. Independently of that judgment, we can infer the relevance of the spectacle to her own life. Thus, Claudia in the piazza of Noto, Lidia in the suburbs of Milan, and Vittoria in the EUR section of Rome assume the additional narrative task of mediating our vision, freighting it with the unspoken values of the implied author.

Claudia is the first of Antonioni's genuine witnesses. None of the earlier protagonists—Paola, Guido, Clara, Clelia, Aldo—play that role to any extent. If we see things from their point of view, it is only fleetingly and for conventional reasons of plot.[15] (In the case of Aldo, what he sees is always extraneous to his point of view, because all he really wants to see is Irma and his home again.) The scenario suggests that Antonioni conceived of Claudia as a witness right from the very beginning. For instance, the scene in which Claudia watches the torn scraps of Sandro's magazine disappear into the ship's wake is described carefully and even poetically: "The pages come apart in the water. Some of them are quickly swept under by the waves, while others float and slowly drift away: white specks upon which a few sea gulls converge emitting their guttural cries."[16]

This sounds like a note by Antonioni of something he observed sitting aft on a yacht in the Aeolian Sea, where the plot of *L'avventura* first came to him. Though the editors of the film book, who worked from the finished film, hypothesize that her gesture is "as if in protest,"[17] the gesture—a wave of the left arm as she turns

Frame 56

slightly to the left—seems intentionally vague, perhaps nothing more than a witness's astonished response to the *spectacle* of the patterns made by fluttering
pages over ocean spray, like Vittoria's wonder at the spectacle of the flagpoles
jingling in the midnight breeze. This is a role that Claudia clearly plays on many
occasions. As the scenario insists: "Of the entire group, Claudia is perhaps the
only one who really has the desire to explore, to see, and generally to take advantage of whatever the cruise has to offer."[18]

When the protagonists of the tetralogy appear in the witness function, they are
typically framed with their backs to the camera in near foreground.[19] Of course,
other directors use back shots routinely. What is unusual in Antonioni is the fre-
quency with which he uses the shot: in certain sequences, the audience sees more
of the protagonist's back than of her front. The effect is not that of a mere reaction shot[20] but a textual sign that the things or events she sees are intensely absorbing. Further, the back shot avoids giving us any direct information about her
reactions. Here, too, we must form our own opinions about the significance of
what the protagonist has seen. Again, the technique resembles Hemingway's: by
making the audience focus on the neutral, uncharacterized perceptions of a sympathetic protagonist, Antonioni guides us to psychological and moral inferences
about the meanings of what we see her seeing.

We should not confuse the objective correlative or witness effects with other
means of conveying a character's inner life, for instance, interior monologue or
stream of consciousness. I asked Antonioni if he had ever been tempted by voice-

Frame 57

over interior monologue. He said that he had not, for the simple reason that it was "too easy." For him the film medium demands the ingenuity of visual, not trick auditory, solutions to the problem of rendering a character's unspoken thoughts and feelings. Yet critics have used the term loosely to describe his style, one calling Lidia's walk "a long continuous interior monologue" and relating it to Eisenstein's "intellectual cinema" and to Bresson.[21] It is true that Eisenstein planned to use voice-over interior monologue in his projected version of Theodore Dreiser's *An American Tragedy* and that Bresson used voice-over in *Diary of a Country Priest* and other films. But it is hard to see how Antonioni fits into this tradition. Not a syllable is heard from Lidia during her stroll, so the sequence can hardly be called a monologue in any literal sense of the word. Of course, her very act of looking about at the Milan scene as if for the first time communicates some of her feelings about urban appearances—but only by implication. Antonioni stands less in the tradition of Joyce than in that of Hemingway and Robbe-Grillet. In that tradition, what a character sees is described in exhaustive but neutral detail. But the contents of the character's mind are not verbalized; the character's thoughts must be inferred from the descriptions. In "Big Two-Hearted River," for example, the hero's trauma is embodied in the dark parts of the river, and in *La jalousie*, in the stain left by a crushed centipede.[22] In a similar way, Lidia's estrangement from her husband and more generally from the Milanese *alta borghesia* is tracked not by a record of her inner speech but solely by what is shown of the stark and unrelieved concrete buildings and streets of Milan and its *periferia*.

Of course, correlated objects cannot achieve the exactitude of verbal stream of consciousness, nor are Lidia's facial reactions easy to read. Often she appears in long shot and occupies only a small part of the screen. In closer shots, Moreau's face is relatively impassive. Nonetheless, Antonioni achieves a considerable richness of meaning, not in statements of a propositional order but in visual notes on "how things are." The realism is of an unusually pure, almost documentary order. Lidia's walk constructs a little *Gente di Milano* in its own right.

We feel that Lidia, even more than Claudia, is Antonioni's visual surrogate, the instrument of his cool look at the urban scene. She is not a designer or planner or architect, but she inspects people as if she were. She sizes them up against the environment in some important way, to see how they fit, how the whole thing works, or rather how it does not. We feel her coming to understand that her disturbed relationship with her husband is not unrelated to the arid, empty, abstract space in which they live. She sees the same problem in the faces of a parking attendant (a miserable job necessitated by the presence of all those cars), a man exposed by his all-glass office to the gaze of any passerby, a hostile woman high above the street in her apartment. She sees it, in its extreme state, in the murderous battle between the young men in the vacant lot.

Vittoria, too, is a powerful witness of the urban scene. However, she shows a breathless wonder at the sheer beauty of things: the fountain of spray from a powerful water sprinkler, the seeming solidity of cumulus clouds, the soothing sound of small aircraft at the far end of a runway, the face of a passing young man. That attitude makes *L'eclisse* a more joyous film than any other in the tetralogy despite its tense ending. An important emotional correlate is the rustling trees that we see at no less than four critical moments. Clearly, the trees imply a sense of restlessness, of transience—not only that of her own youthful, seeking personality but that of the world as she knows it. The trees are neither ominous nor comforting: they suggest, rather, the profound changes that face us all. We cannot know whether the changes are for the good or the bad, but we do know that they will be—to use one of Henry James' favorite, fraught words—"tremendous."

Frame 58

The most complex point-of-view structure in the tetralogy occurs in *Il deserto rosso*. Pasolini describes it in terms familiar to literary stylistics:

> In *Red Desert,* Antonioni looks at the world at one with his neurotic heroine, re-living it through the "look" of this woman . . . Thanks to this stylistic mechanism, Antonioni has given us his most authentic work. He has finally succeeded in representing the world seen through *his* own eyes because he has substituted, wholly, the world-view of a sick woman for his own vision, which is delirious with estheticism: a substitution justified by the possible analogy of the two visions. But even if some part of arbitrariness entered into this substitution, one could make no objection. It is clear that the "free indirect subjective" is a pretext which Antonioni has, perhaps quite arbitrarily, used in order to obtain the greatest poetic liberty—a liberty which, precisely, borders (and this is why it is intoxicating) upon the arbitrary.[23]

To me, Antonioni does not represent the world through "deliriously esthetic" eyes but rather constructs a remarkable double vision through which we see alternately from Giuliana's point of view and from the camera's own. One means is change of focus. The camera uses a telephoto lens to achieve a very shallow focus; then it refocuses on the background, thereby bringing it into close-up. In the first stage, everything in the background is fuzzy; in the second stage, everything is clear. The first stage of the shot corresponds to Giuliana's vision: the peddler looks unclear and distant. But the second stage conveys the camera's own more neutral reality: the peddler is simply one more thing in the street to be seen. Putting him into focus reestablishes a correct, unneurotic, unintense perspective. Other shots in the film are arbitrary, as Pasolini uses the word, but clearly it is a mistake to make Giuliana the sole witness of the industrial scene. That could not explain why the world rendered is so often gloriously beautiful in color, shape, and abstract design. Only the neutral camera's point of view could make it so.[24]

Frame 59   *Frame 60*

The camera identifies sympathetically with Giuliana's own sense of her plight as often as it likes, always without giving up its prerogative as an independent agent. The situation is very much like the sympathetic use of indirect free style in such novels as *Mrs. Dalloway*[25]—hence the aptness of Pasolini's preempted literary critical term *free indirect subjective*.

5

The Great Tetralogy
Settings and Environments

Setting is so important to Antonioni's mature style that it needs a chapter of its own. By Antonioni's own account, his ideas for films are born of visual epiphanies, fleeting but revealing glimpses of the world around him. He is struck by the sight of two nine-year-old girls playing under the rotunda of the Grand Hotel at Rimini, one of them singing "Oh, such love, oh, such suffering" as she circles around on her bicycle. Or of two thousand garbagemen meeting silently in the Baths of Caracalla as Rome stands "flooded with rubbish, piles of colored filth on the street corners, an orgy of abstract images, extraordinary pictorial fury."[1] Such glimpses are to Antonioni seeds of visual reality—concentrated, pregnant, difficult to explain or paraphrase. They might or might not find their way into a film, but if they do, they preserve their integrity against the absorbing pressures of narrative. Hence the unforgettable flagpoles creaking in the breeze in *L'eclisse,* or the church bells in Noto in *L'avventura,* or the humming radio astronomy towers in *Il deserto rosso.*

OBJETS TROUVÉS

Antonioni has described his process of discovering photographable objects with great explicitness. For Piero's ancestral home, the scenario of *L'eclisse* had asked for

a typical house of the Roman bourgeoisie. The entrance hall is dark, large and cool. Vittoria, coming in from the brilliant light outside, hesitates as though the inside of the house, a presentiment of it—those high ceilings, rooms leading to other rooms, the black heavy furniture, the profusion of knick-knacks on it—repelled her. She even sits down on a chest next to a vase with two umbrellas, her hands between her knees . . .

In the actual house that Antonioni found:

Vittoria goes in, pauses to look at an old painting on the wall, continues toward the inner rooms, stops before a window to look at the wall beyond the courtyard, where a woman appeared in the black frame of another window. The woman disappears almost immedi-

99

Frame 61

ately as though swallowed by the shadows. Vittoria turns back toward the chest. Piero is standing next to the door leading into the living room.

    Why did I change it? Why, because when the scene was composed we had no idea what Piero's house would have been like, so that the screenplay was of value to me only as a psychological note. And even then, only to a certain point.[2]

The objects found in the actual house not only suggested details of plot and character but caused existing details to be rewritten. Such uncommented visuals attentuate the meaning. The text is opened: the other window offers a glimpse of another life, one rendered mysterious by not being explained. Who is this woman suddenly "swallowed by the shadows"? Is she there to illustrate the kind of traditional, restricted, housebound role to which Vittoria would never agree? We can imagine (though we cannot see) Vittoria shudder as she meditates the fate of the middle-class matron. But it is impossible to know her feelings for sure. We are not supposed to. The contingency of incidental objects photographed with loving care opens a world that we must contemplate, not categorize.[3]

    Sometimes the found object comments on the story in a more lighthearted way, as when we see, from Sandro's point of view, an old master painting in the lobby of the luxury hotel in Taormina. The decadence implicit in that depiction of a patriarch taking refreshment at a lady's breast is ironically mediated by the

Frame 62

jaded, complicitous gaze of the young woman, another guest at the hotel. Her eyes convey both boredom and invitation, and though Sandro refuses her, he is soon to accept the favors of Gloria Perkins.

The *objet trouvé* undeniably guarantees the "thereness" of the real world, not because it is verisimilar but because it really *was* there. Antonioni did not invent anything: he merely uncovered it. One consequence of this new kind of realism is that the universe is demonstrated to be basically meaningless. For if this bit of the world is no less and no more worth photographing than any other, questions of moralistic or psychological commentary cannot arise. "There it is" is all the film is willing to say, "the neutral surface—make of it what you will." The semantic burden is shifted to the viewer's shoulders: that is Antonioni's gift to the cinema.

THE AMBIVALENCES OF ARCHITECTURE

What Antonioni finds in the environment is immensely rich and esthetically coherent. It is obvious that Antonioni is a long-time student of architecture, and all his films show a keen interest in buildings and public and private spaces. Already in *Gente del Po* there is loving treatment of the fishermen's houses along the river. A documentary that never got made was to have centered on a specific architectural component. Called *Scale* (Steps) and published in 1950,[4] the film would have been a collection of brief incidents occurring on a variety of stairways. Like *Dub-liners* or the Wandering Rocks section of *Ulysses,* these incidents would have been epiphanic vignettes of Italian life, everything from youthful professions of love, the chatter of postman and housewives, and the disappointment of an unemployed man who sees a No Help Wanted sign at the top of a steep flight of stairs to a mason carrying a heavy load of cement up a ladder, a crowd with political placards running up a wide expanse of official-looking steps, and an inmate being dragged up the steps of a lunatic asylum by orderlies.

In the early fiction films, architecture was still a traditional feature of verisimilar background. By the time of the tetralogy, it had begun to play a more prominent and innovative role. In his 1965 interview with Godard, Antonioni said, "Whereas in earlier films I was interested in relationships between individuals, I am now concerned with the individual in relation to his surroundings (though not with this alone), which means that I have a very different approach to the story."[5] Indeed, the story becomes secondary, a consequence, not a cause, of his new interest in the environment. The represented environment may evoke some theme or merely convey a sense of how it feels to be alive and perceptive these days. The shots often express nothing more—and nothing less—than the seeable wonder of existence.

It is hard to imagine a movie in which buildings do not appear. We tend to ignore them in most films as mere background. But in the tetralogy we come to *read* buildings as architects, urban planners, and designers do. And though the characters do not lose their individual importance, they also function, especially in certain long shots, like mannequins in architectural models.

L'avventura is full of architectural commentary. The contrast between the beautiful and solid old buildings and the shoddy new condominiums is conveyed in the opening scene between Anna and her father. And the disaster of Fascist architecture and planning is documented by the deserted village, a Cassa del Mezzogiorno town near Caltanisetta, Sicily.[6] The street scene in the deserted village (see Frame 46, p. 77) evokes De Chirico's so-called metaphysical period, except that the paintings suggest that the town was once occupied, that the people have gone away and may even return.[7] In *L'avventura,* however, the town looks as if it has never been lived in, as if some intuition warned the Sicilians to have nothing to do with it.

But the true architectural films are *La notte* and *L'eclisse*. For the first time, Antonioni virtually reverses priorities. For moments on end, it is the cityscape that is the true protagonist, and audiences used to empathizing or identifying with a human character must find their expectations strangely undermined. One learns a more appropriate stance, that of fellow observer of an environment that is subtly inimical. I underline *subtly,* since what Antonioni shows is not cataclysmic or even sordid. It is just mediocre, badly done, ill conceived. But that makes it no less ominous.[8]

The city planning and architecture of Milan in *La notte* or of Rome in *L'eclisse* did not cause Lidia's and Vittoria's problems. But personal problems and bad

Frame 63

buildings and misused public space are all parts of a vaster network of problems facing Western man. Bad architecture is simply one visible, concrete manifestation of the *malattia dei sentimenti.*

La notte is the most intensely architectural of Antonioni's films. As the film opens, the camera descends the glass surface of the Pirelli Building in Milan, of all Italian cities perhaps the most anonymous and international. The movement down this space is at once lonely and perversely beautiful. The beauty is that of pure geometry and the smooth perfection of modern materials; the loneliness issues from the lack of human relevance. The absolute and meaninglessly straight lines of the building never reappear in the film, and they are never alluded to by the characters, but they dominate its atmosphere. Since nothing else in Milan is as high, the glass reflects only the city below, from whose business it appears completely divorced. Even the noise of traffic cannot rise high enough to disturb its impersonal and useless tranquility. As Rudolf Arnheim puts it, in a passage that could almost be put forth as a commentary on *La notte:*

Evidently, emptiness is not simply related to the absence of matter. A space on which nothing is built can be pervaded nevertheless by perceptual forces and filled with density, which we might call a visual substance. Conversely the fenestrated wall of a high-rise building . . . may be experienced as empty even though the architect has put something there for us to look at. The effect of emptiness comes about when the surrounding shapes do not impose a structural organization upon the surface in question. The observer's glance finds itself in the same place wherever it tries to anchor, one place being like the next; it feels the lack of spatial coordinates, of a framework for determining distances. In consequence, the viewer experiences a sense of forlornness . . . A prime source for . . . perceptual disorientation is the recent fad of reflecting glass walls, which create a surrealistic contradiction between incompatible images. The wall is destroyed, and the reflection shows a space that is not there.[9]

The slowly descending camera dwells on the interminable monotony of geometric form. Parallel lines will always be parallel: that is their destiny. The shot af-

Frame 64

fords no Chirican perspectives, no shadows, no bugle calls echoing down long colonnades or deserted streets with pennants flapping in the breeze, no ambience of past empires; only the sterile bleakness of outer space, not Star Wars space with its comforting robots but empty lonely zero-degree space. The building, all surface, bears only the most abstract relation to the events of *La notte,* but it does that uncompromisingly.

Consider Frame 64, a production still. The scenario reads: "Lidia . . . reaches a spot where there is an open space between the tall, glass-covered buildings. The sun beats down on the narrow space. She looks at the patch of sky above the buildings as though longing to flee those oppressive walls." The composition of the frame is at once beautiful and oppressive—a paradox characteristic of Antonioni. The tiny human figure, sharply foreshortened by the camera's high angle, amounts to no more than an eighth of the picture. The figure is the center of convergent straight lines (echoed and emphasized by parallels and perpendiculars) that bound perfect oblongs in various tones of white and gray. The textures of these masses are also relatively homogeneous—all this makes Lidia at once the center of and yet, strangely, irrelevant to the composition. The human being is the purpose for which the buildings have been constructed, yet among them she is not only dwarfed but alien, unassimilable. Lidia poses and points her right foot outward like a model, but somehow she does not fit. She is the center, but of what? Do the lines radiate from her, as from a dynamic source? No, the lines target her, transfix her, nail her into place. The huge white block seems to hang there for no other purpose than to crush her. The building pays tribute to the tensile strength of modern materials. It is solid beyond its looks. But it is precisely the look of a building that gives us our sense of security. What good is technology if it only causes unease? The lines are bare and clean; there is no capital, no pediment; concrete sprouts from concrete; it is hard to tell where the building stops and the ground begins. The unwillingness of this building to mark its own limits dooms it to ambiguity. Concrete from concrete? Is there really earth underfoot? Or is the tiny plot of grass an ironic subterfuge? For all his theoretical functionalism, the architect seems to have forgotten whose functions were being accommodated. Nor has he remembered that people need privacy. There is a fine shot of Lidia unwittingly disturbing a man at work who is separated from the street only by glass.

Poor Tommaso has some respite from the architectural sterility of his hospital room. Through his window, he can see a comfortable old building with round arched windows in a vaguely Venetian style (see Frame 41 above). It is no accident that Lidia comes to stand in the window facing that building in her traditional print summer frock. It is the same Lidia who later is to experience nostalgia when she finds herself in the old neighborhood where she and Giovanni first lived together and who ends the film with her reminiscences of Tommaso's youthful love for her. The yoking together of Lidia with architectural tradition is one of the major motifs of the film.

Frame 65

Frame 66

After *L'avventura* there is no comment, no word of architectural judgment, only images. Perhaps the most powerful is that of the mysterious unfinished building at the end of *L'eclisse.* Wrapped in straw it looks as if it had been packed for future use. Next to it, there is a pile of bricks waiting to be set in place. The bricks "remind one of a view of a large city, with skyscrapers and houses crowded

Frame 67

together one on top of the other."[10] The future is already with us, whether or not
we are ready. Its advance is "implacable," in Antonioni's word. Hide our heads in
the sand, fantasize like Giuliana about childhood retreats—beaches and azure
lagoons—as much as we like, we always come back to the city, to science and
industry, if we wish to stay in the world—that is, to stay sane.

By the time of *Il deserto rosso,* Antonioni's attitude seems to have changed.
The images argue that if we look steadily at modern structures—pumps, valves,
boilers, machines, silos—we can see that they have their own beauty, a beauty
not anthropomorphic but nonetheless real and valuable. Giuliana is not an implicit critic of this architecture but a would-be refugee from it. Yet she manages
only to escape into fantasy. Her other attempt, the little boutique on the via
Alighieri, is plainly doomed to failure. The camera takes a wholly different perspective on the industrial structures. Its clear focus and sensitive composition and
framing reveal hidden beauties of color and form. No longer does a character
judge her surroundings, but the surroundings judge her ability to cope. Like
Leger, Antonioni in *Il deserto rosso* tracks complex forms, clean lines, pure colors, fascinating volumes. Never mind that they carry noxious liquids and gas;
pipes become beautiful when their pure colors and bold curves fit so beautifully
into the frame. *Their* adjustment—whatever human beings achieve—is perfect.
The match of form and function is pure, independently esthetic, essentially separate from, even at odds with narrative considerations. Even as we sympathize
with Giuliana's inability to cope with this environment, we marvel at its boiling
energy. We see, perhaps, a way in which one *could* live in such an environment.

CITY PLANNING:
Whatever Happened to the Piazza?

Bars to communication are formed not only by buildings or parts of buildings. The whole layout of a city can thwart communication and community. Consider the street corner rendezvous sequences of *L'eclisse*. A traditionalist novel or film would have had Vittoria and Piero meet in a romantic café. Why this anonymous street corner in EUR? The drab intersection is not mere scenery. It is the sign of a general predicament. It is not only a place where a representative couple fail to meet but a culprit for that failure. It exemplifies, both as instance and as reason, the general incapacity of the modern city to facilitate meeting.

How different is a motor intersection from a square or piazza, the traditional meeting place of lovers! The intersection evokes what is most transitory, casual, and ephemeral in our society: mere encounters, not genuine meetings, among jittery moderns like Piero, who live on the edge of things. The art of making appointments in congenial places is lost to the hurry-up generation, to their fast sports cars and their breezy approach to life. In earlier times, the standard architectural solution to the problem of intersecting streets was the square—the *piazza* (*place, Platz,* from Latin *platea,* a broad street), the *locus classicus* of community, where business during the day yields organically to socializing during the night. In Rome of all places one would expect that graceful alternative to the drab suburban street corner. In the old sections, even the most modest neighborhood boasts its piazza and fountain or at least a spigot.[11]

Frame 68

But in the EUR quarter, no such relief has been planned. A vital tradition has been forgotten in the general amnesia of modernism. The characters, Piero in particular, desperately need esthetic relief (though he probably thinks the only kind that he needs is sexual). His work is appallingly stressful, and he takes sleeping pills and flies off the handle at callers who do not identify themselves quickly enough over the telephone. Ironically, his workplace, the Borsa, fronts on one of the most beautiful squares in Rome, the Piazza di Pietra. But the place has become so crowded and befouled by traffic that socializing, though intensive, is a parody of the refreshing human contact that the great Roman architect intended.

Frame 69

Frame 70

It was Antonioni's original intention to shoot Vittoria and Piero's rendezvous sequence in a tiny modern piazza in EUR.[12] But in the actual film, there is only the intersection marked by zebra pedestrian stripes. Piero says that he will kiss Vittoria when they get to the other side of the street. In the middle, Vittoria stops and says portentously, "*Siamo a metà*" ("We are halfway across"). Clearly, Antonioni's decision to change the site from a square (no matter how shabby) to a mere intersection reflects a feeling that the latter is even more forlorn. In the age of the sports car, people go through lovers like water through sand on a beach. The beginning of a relationship (the very word suggests preprogrammed triviality) is already the middle, and the end is clearly in sight. We do not need to be shown how things end. Like celestial bodies (as the title has it), modern lovers converge only for a few moments, since they are traveling at high speeds in different directions.

Why is this suburban corner so undistinguished and undistinguishable from the thousands like it? What surrounds it is so amorphous that it hardly constitutes a place. The hallowed European square, from Danzig to Lisbon, possesses visual properties that no mere traffic intersection can enjoy. For one thing, the space of a square is autonomous, sui generis. It is not simply the absence of something. It is not merely what remains after buildings are erected around it. It must be planned, and its very existence depends on the limits of impinging structures. They give it what Arnheim calls a "figure character."[13] But the intersection in *L'eclisse* has no such character. It is a void, not an intended place. The buildings that encompass it are without character. On one corner stands a low wall between nondescript houses and the street. On another there are a few randomly placed four-story apartments. On the third lies a low, vague stadium complex of some sort, impossible to read from street level. The fourth corner is dominated by the shapeless building under construction. Not only are these structures nondescript, but their spatial orientation to the crossing is too distant and weak to frame it properly. No, the intersection cannot be considered a humanly relevant place. It has no closure: "Straight-line boundaries do not close a square compellingly. They stop at the corners, but their straightness impels them to continue, not to terminate,"[14] especially when that straightness is at the service of cars. The pavement shared by the two streets was not designed for human feet. Lingering becomes a crime, an obstruction of traffic. Unlike the cobblestones of a piazza, the asphalt of an intersection is not a "floor" for the sky above. The intersection is only a mechanical product, the simplest, cheapest, least humane solution to the problem of automobile circulation. It reflects the needs of cars, not of people. Instead of strollers, they have become "pedestrians," mere pawns in the game of traffic chess. Vittoria and Piero's affair is in a sense already doomed simply by their meeting there. It is not a place for meeting and lingering but only for going separate ways.

Pedestrians crossing intersections are always at the periphery, never the center. Aliens to the place, they need special marks—a zebra-striped zone (*passaggio zebrato* in Italian)—set parallel to the curb like long hyphens to show them where it is safe to cross. These strange marks suggest that the pedestrian is an endangered species (remember the zebra skins in Marta's apartment and the pho-

Frame 71

tograph of zebras in *Il deserto rosso*). The streets are the natural habitat of the automobile; it is people who now have to be guided across them. So accustomed are we to the authority of cars that we concur without a murmur to such street painting. The stripes point with relentless and foolish dynamism. They keep us moving. If we take them at their own logic, we keep going around and around. Their sole concern is to get us off to other business—even if that business is itself endless and pointless.

The zebra-striped intersection is not a genuine place. Its invitation is mechanical, a mere formula. Like the mirror-clad skyscraper, it reflects, in utter redundancy, only its own function, that of crossing. It is a very agony of functionalism. Architectural function achieves significance only when it is matched with human significance. And that is precisely what is being called into question here. How meaningful can lives be that are as regulated as these? The stripes are the blazon of Piero's hectic life, dashing as he does to and fro, around and about, from client to broker, from woman to woman. Perhaps Vittoria does not allow him to kiss her when they reach the other side of the street because she recognizes all this.

I would not dwell on this intersection if Antonioni's camera had not made so much of it. His camera elevations, for example, are not innocent. When the history of the lovers' affair is being followed, the camera rolls along level with them, more or less conventionally immersed in the plot. But after the couple have vanished, the camera moves to a decidedly higher, more objective angle, the angle of scientific inquiry. With the loss of the protagonists, the intersection shifts from object to subject. The new text, which ends the film, is a nonfictional documentary; the intersection is its protagonist. The technique was adumbrated in the scene of the deserted Sicilian town in *L'avventura*. There, the couple left the town behind. Here, the suburb leaves the couple behind. If Antonioni's purpose had been only to show the lovers' breakup, he could have shot Vittoria or Piero returning to the corner alone. The background would then have remained background, unremarkable if verisimilar. But by having both characters disappear, Antonioni insists on the banal intersection, makes us contemplate it with such dreary intensity that we sense, if not completely understand, the ferocious relation between the urban humdrum and the prospect of worldwide technological self-destruction. This intersection in the EUR becomes a harbinger of catastrophe. The banality of the streetlamp makes it an icon of that ultimate banality, push-button atomic war. Antonioni achieves this astonishing effect precisely by frustrating conventional demands for a denouement, transforming the tedium of the ongoing Ordinary into the terror of the End. *L'avventura* and *La notte* tease us into a preoccupation with the characters through a whole battery of modern concerns, especially erotic, and then refocus our attention on the look of things, especially from an architectural perspective. But in *L'eclisse* Antonioni goes much farther, beyond mere appearance. The overexposed streetlight and the overamplified music in the final shot are too much to bear. No other film has left its audience so rudely to ponder the question, Is that all? Is that all there is to this love affair? To our common destiny? To our civilization? To the earth itself?

NATURE AND CULTURE

L'avventura resembles *Il grido* more than the other three films of the tetralogy in favoring natural over urban settings. Most of its significant moments pass under the open sky. Precisely because man did not invent it, nature for Antonioni seems not a subject for man's criticism. Whether savage, as the crags of Lisca Bianca, or soft, as the flowery hills of Sicily, its beauty remains mysterious and neutral, untouched by human quandaries, imperturbably itself, filled with details that have no significance for plot yet that are somehow profoundly meaningful in their own way. In *L'avventura*, the sky—in contrast, say, to the sky above Monument Valley for John Ford—is never there for man, never portending his glories and conquests. It goes its own way: the storm off Lisca Bianca is only a storm—but what a storm! It is not symbolic of the "stormy" emotions of characters or theme.

Lisca Bianca is sufficiently mazy and wild to serve as a backdrop for Sandro's and Claudia's disoriented discovery of their mutual attraction. Antonioni also uses the rugged scenery for compositional purposes. The rocks become a rich source of textures, lines, and masses. For instance, in the sequence in which Sandro first recognizes his passion for Claudia, there are moments when only sky or water separates them and others when the obstacle between them is palpable rock. Antonioni used a curious double-spurred boulder to divide them, to emphasize Claudia's resistance to the idea that she might become Anna's double and replacement. It functions very much like door edges, window bars, and other vertical and oblique framing lines in the other films, effectively separating the couple in a carefully balanced yet provocative way. The boulder is too amorphous to make a good symbol, but it clearly connotes the idea of doubleness (with its cognate duplicity). The rocks of Lisca Bianca not only form a maze, but the maze has no key. They provide a perfect backdrop for characters who are at sea, ethically and psychologically as well as physically. And only stark, flat lighting illuminates their confusion. The effect is completely different from that of the soft hill near Noto where they first make love.

There is little in the way of nature in *La notte,* and what there is—in the *periferia,* on the grounds of the tycoon's estate—bears the marks of man's failures. The final shot on the golf course introduces nature in an almost ironic way: unnerved by his sudden glimpse of the emptiness of his marriage, Giovanni forces himself on his wife in a sand trap (an artificial obstacle created by man to resemble nature, all for the purpose of making the game a bit more difficult).

In *L'eclisse,* nature generally appears as a refuge for the city-weary. But apparently only Vittoria has the serenity to enjoy it; for instance, after she leaves Riccardo, she walks jauntily through the unbuilt areas of the EUR swinging her sweater. We have already noted her happiness at the tranquil airport and her repeated association with the rustle of trees. In *Il deserto rosso,* Giuliana's need for a respite in nature is more desperate, but she is too tied to her neurosis to venture forth except in fantasy. It is interesting to note the textural difference between the beach scenery in the story she tells to her son and the surfaces of her life in Ravenna. Everything near her home is smooth, hard, and cold to the touch, a medley of modern materials—steel, glass, and plastic—whereas the sand and sandstone of the fantasy beach (like the canyons of *Zabriskie Point*) are warm and soft-looking, resembling nothing so much as the limbs and breasts of lovers embracing the sea.

6

The Great Tetralogy
Cinematic Form

As we have seen, Antonioni had been an experimenter from the very start of his career. In his first feature film, he departed from the standard continuity of film since Griffith. Instead of inserts, close-ups for facial reactions, shot-countershots, the 180–degree rule, and other paraphernalia of standard cinematic grammar, Antonioni's camera followed his actors for shots of unprecedented length, which he then spliced together in a relatively conventional way. Still, his early films were not so narratively attenuated as to make them hard to read. In *L'avventura,* however, the problems of an unfamiliar style were compounded by those of an elliptical narrative structure.

THE CAMERA:
Alternatives to Simple Narration

In Antonioni's tetralogy, the camera becomes the subtlest of narrative instruments. Though it can identify with a character's point of view when that suits its purposes, it usually preserves its own identity and distance. As a consequence, some critics have found the films "cold" and "aloof." But that misses the point, which concerns not emotion but function. Unique among feature filmmakers, Antonioni refuses to limit the camera to the simple task of telling the story. Instead, he gives it the independent visual authority that it possesses in photography. Any resulting aloofness is the sign of complex esthetic intention, not of personal temperament. Antonioni is as much concerned with configured lines, volumes, and colors as were, say, Titian and Rubens in their narrative canvases. Like them, he regularly gives as much weight to design as to story elements, though the story is never a mere pretext for the design. Certainly, Antonioni is one of cinema's great visual artists. Many of his frames are worth enlarging and exhibiting as independent works of art. Indeed, they are sometimes beautiful to a fault: they make us want to stop the film so that we can gaze at greater leisure. The ongoing narrative is, I suppose, thereby impaired, but only if we insist on conven-

114

tional ways of watching films. In defense of Antonioni's style, one might argue
that the movie audience can and should develop something of the art lover's capacity to appreciate beautiful visual composition for its own sake.

But it is not really true, on any fair viewing, that his introjection of visual
design considerations weakens plot, character, and theme. Indeed, if anything,
these are enhanced in subtle if unfamiliar ways. It is essential to recognize the
contribution made by the camera's "obsessive framing" (Pasolini's expression)
to the "profound and mysterious intensity"[1] of these films, to the sense they
often create that the narrative is suddenly and inexplicably fraught with resonance
that goes beyond the mere plot.

VARIATIONS ON
DEEP COMPOSITION
AND THE LONG TAKE

We have seen in Antonioni's early films a preoccupation with depth reminiscent of
filmmakers like Renoir and Welles, not to mention Renaissance painters like Piero
della Francesca or moderns like Giorgio De Chirico, whose paintings also suggest a
"strange and memorable foreboding" (a phrase in one of De Chirico's prose po-
ems). While prowling a street of the deserted Mezzogiorno town in *L'avventura,*
the camera uses the dark diagonal lines of structures on each side to enhance the
sense of moving into a deeply shadowed recess. It recalls De Chirico's question:
"Who can deny the troubling connection that exists between perspective and me-
taphysics?"[2] Like De Chirico, Antonioni uses vanishing-point perspective not to
heighten realism (the intention of the Renaissance painters) but for its emotive
value. A prose poem by De Chirico could almost have been written to describe the
crepuscular atmosphere of the finale of *L'eclisse:* "Late in the afternoon, when the
evening light was beginning slowly to obscure the mountains to the east of the
city, and when the cliffs beneath the citadel were turning mauve, one could feel
that SOMETHING WAS GATHERING, as the nurses would say while gossiping on the
benches of the public square."[3] For a man as educated in the arts as Antonioni is,
the resemblance seems hardly accidental, especially in respect to De Chirico's
visual evocation of silence, of emptiness (but *recent* emptiness, with the sounds of
man still echoing just outside the frame), of commonplace objects "surcharged
. . . with a disquieting ambiguity," of an architecture "detached from a near and
present reality," of a presentiment of . . . who knows what?[4]

There are many takes in *L'avventura* that last as long as those characteristic of
Cronaca di un amore or *Le amiche:* for instance, the scene in which Claudia
wakes up in the old man's hut, checks to see whether her dress is dry, and gazes
sadly at the blouse that was Anna's last gift (the first six shots average forty-three
seconds in length). But the panoply of effects has become richer. The long takes
are mixed with many short takes: whereas *Cronaca di un amore* consists of only

160 shots or so, *L'avventura* has 473. Though some last well beyond a minute, many are very brief, sometimes only two or three seconds, and in some cases the brief shots form a considerable series. In the third scene, for example, after Anna's disappearance, Claudia's growing anxiety is depicted in fourteen shots averaging six seconds each. Thus the timing here is not very different from that of Hollywood action footage, and this contributes to the film-noir-in-reverse effect that Antonioni wanted.

What is more typical of *L'avventura* is the use of relatively lengthy shots for the core of a scene, punctuated by relatively brief shots. This arrangement adds a new crispness to the uniquely Antonionian evocation of the surface of the world. The film becomes more absorbing without becoming more conventional. One recalls, for instance, the scene in which Anna goes up to Sandro's room, stares at him ambivalently, then undresses and makes love to him. The sequence contains seventeen shots, three relatively long ones separated by fourteen considerably shorter ones. This pattern is typical of the later films.

Antonioni was also experimenting with ways of increasing pictorial depth. One approach entailed the wide-angle lens, which allows sharp focus at considerable distances from the camera even as it extends the lateral spread. A splendid example is the scene in Tommaso's hospital room in *La notte*. The wide-angle lens creates a kind of space of morbidity: Tommaso lies in his bed, sweating, in pain, yearning to hold on to life just a bit longer, bending toward his friends and his mother. Though the room is small, the lens exaggerates the distance between the occupants, adding to our sense of the strain of the situation. Tommaso's mother seems far away and indistinct as she sits in her chair, and the spaces between the patient and the Pontanos are widened and thus made awkward. The visual effect enhances our feeling that despite all their good intentions, the Pontanos are awed and perhaps slightly repelled by Tommaso's terminal illness. They cannot get too close to it, much as they want to comfort their friend. It is only a matter of inches, but these inches are crucial. Tommaso, an honest man himself, begs them to be no less honest (he reminds one of Tolstoy's Ivan Ilyich). The distance created by the lens belies the slick architecture, the champagne, the pretty nurses, and the whole insistence on seemliness and elegance. One more instance of the muffled sterility of modern life: not even death is allowed its due.

To create effects of depth, Antonioni sometimes uses mirrors. For instance, in a scene of six shots in *L'avventura*, he uses mirrors to establish the theme of the sexual double.[5] Claudia, already identified with Anna by the gift of the blouse, tries on a dark wig under the amused and indulgent gaze of Patrizia, her new instructress in the ways of the leisure class. As the scene opens, we see a blond woman seated at a vanity mirror. We assume that the woman is Claudia, since she is the only blond whom we have seen so far in the movie. But when she turns her head, we discover that it is Patrizia in a blond wig. Patrizia hangs a black wig on the mirror frame. Claudia enters the doorway and then stands observing Patrizia over the top of the mirror. Then, in the mirror's reflection we see, in addition to the frontal image of Patrizia studying her appearance, Claudia's back as she tries

Frame 72

Frame 73

Frame 74

Frame 75

on the black wig. Then she is shown in real life modeling the black wig. There is another mirror whose existence we only discover after the fact, a standing mirror in two parts, like a room screen. We learn about it in a slight visual shock: at a certain point Patrizia pushes one leaf of the mirror and seemingly wipes Claudia off the screen. But Claudia reappears on the other side of Patrizia, just at the moment when Patrizia says, "You look like someone else." The visual confusion about what is surface and what is depth corresponds to the moral and psychological confusion that Claudia must feel as she moves into the aristocratic class.

The camera still prowls through the tetralogy but not to the extent that it did in the earlier films. (The evolution of Antonioni's style reverses that of film history in general, becoming less rather than more systematically mobile.) In a context of general movement, the fixed tripod shot is the exception, enhancing meanings with sudden and unexpected stasis. The most brilliant instance is in the coda of *L'eclisse,* where almost every shot is fixed. The motive is clear: though the camera is supposed to be looking for the vanished lovers, to move while doing so would be unduly to animate the scene and hence belie the flatness and banality that the scene is there to convey. The message to viewers is this: "Do not expect to find our characters in this distressing nonplace. Nothing warm and intimate, perhaps nothing human can happen here."[6]

THE FLAT "ABSTRACT" STYLE

During the period of the tetralogy, another new trend appeared in Antonioni's style. The word that sprang to critics' lips was *abstract*. The word must be properly defined. The films are never abstract in the sense that they abandon plot, character, or theme, even in part. The narrative line continues, though it becomes leaner, less busy, less constrained by having to account for events. It is, rather, the visual framing that becomes more designlike and in that sense more abstract. Actors and settings seem more than ever to have been juxtaposed for visual purposes. The new wide-screen format spreads the actors out and unclutters the mise-en-scène. *L'avventura,* though similar to *Le amiche* in theme, character, and ambience, is less crowded, more rarified in its visual impact. Even as some shots favor deep focus, others stress the surface plane of the screen, minimizing the space between figure and ground. The sense in which this renders the film's style "abstract" is explained in a well-known work by the art historian Wilhelm Worringer.[7] Worringer argues that art derives from two polar impulses, one toward empathy, the other toward abstraction. Empathic art is "organic" and modeled (hence "deep-focused"), like Greek sculpture. In looking at such art objects, our eyes delight in caressing the surfaces and depths and hence in experiencing the objects in the round. Empathic art flourishes in historical periods of psychological harmony, when man feels secure and in tune with the universe and sees himself as its rational center. At the other pole, abstract art "is the outcome of a great inner unrest inspired in man by the phenomena of the outside world."[8] In troubled times, these phenomena become "obscure," "relative," "contingent." The discomfort they cause gets particularized in a widespread "spiritual dread of space . . . of open places." The pure and regular geometry of abstract art then presents an attractive way of controlling, allaying, and sublimating that anxiety.

Tormented by the entangled inter-relationship and flux of the phenomena of the outer world [civilizations like ancient Egypt] were dominated by an immense need for tranquillity. The happiness they sought from art did not consist in the possibility of projecting themselves into the things of the outer world . . . but in the possibility of taking the individual thing of the external world out of its arbitrariness and seeming fortuitousness, of eternalising it by approximation to abstract forms and, in this manner, of finding a point of tranquillity and a refuge from appearances.[9]

Is there a better phrase for describing what Lidia, Vittoria, and especially Giuliana seek than "refuge from appearances"?

Like Egyptian art, modern abstract painting can be seen as a reaction to apprehension induced by the destruction of old notions of space and time. It is hard to take spiritual comfort in the physicist's powerful new explanations of the nature and origin of things. As if to demonstrate Worringer's thesis, artists like Mondrian turned to the ancient regularities of plane geometry. Einstein's theory did not prove Euclid's wrong, only that Euclid's geometry does not apply to the realms of interstellar space. So Mondrian decided to tend our own terrestrial geometric garden. The security and stability of simple geometric shapes became the norm in architecture, too: the gleaming triumphs of Mies van der Rohe and Le

Corbusier testify to man's desire for Euclidian harmony. Where Egyptian art corroborated a cosmogony, modern abstract art tries only to reconcile the old discredited cosmogony with a new and, to most people, incomprehensible one. Even to those few who understand something of this new view of the universe, its implications for politics, morality, and behavior in general remain to be drawn, let alone agreed on. Antonioni wrote a treatment about this very subject. Entitled *Un mucchio di bugie* (A Pack of Lies),[10] it concerns a physicist who lives in a community that surrounds a cyclotron. He knows everything about "nuones," "adrones," and "leptones," but he has not the slightest conception of how to deal with the everyday world of family and community. Workers and peasants who live nearby consider him and his colleagues a strange, incomprehensible breed.

In one way or another, all the films of the tetralogy glory in the lines and masses of plane geometry. Characters are frequently pinned to walls, which are either bare or simply but elegantly divided by a vertical line or two. As we have seen, lines and masses suggest moral or psychological entrapment, unbridgeable alienation, or the like. Love is often literally "barred." But whatever the connotation, the lines and masses remain lines and masses, and to ascribe them entirely to local plot symbolism may be to distort the films' intentions. In the Godard interview, Antonioni explained his view of the complexity of human feelings as well as his retreat from the excessively organic:

It is too easy to say, as some critics have, that I am accusing the world of industry, factories, etc. of turning the people who live there into neurotics. My intention was to point out the beauty in this world, where even the factories have an extraordinary esthetic beauty. A line of factories, with their chimneys silhouetted on the skyline, seem [*sic*] to me much more beautiful than a line of trees which one has seen so often that it has become monotonous, to such an extent that we don't even look any more.[11]

Even more pertinent is his answer to another question:

GODARD: When you begin or end certain shots on more or less abstract shapes, objects or details, do you do it for pictorial reasons?
ANTONIONI: I feel I must express reality in terms that are not completely realistic. Take for instance the abstract white line which comes into the shot at the beginning of the scene in the little grey street [the via Alighieri where Giuliana plans her shop]. This line interests me much more than the car which arrives. It's a way of approaching the character through material objects rather than through her life. Her life basically is only relatively interesting.[12]

Antonioni makes the contours of visible objects speak to the characters' uncertainty about the new order of things. Seeking whatever certainties it can find, all the camera is sure of is the regularity of plane geometry. In such moments, the screen ceases to be a window looking into deep space and becomes a nearby surface of uncertain expanse against which the characters are flattened.[13]

There are several ways in which Antonioni creates flat effects on the screen. One is by posing the character (usually a vulnerable female) flush up against a broad, unrelieved surface. The narrative predicament of characters in this attitude—the nymphomaniac in *La notte*, Vittoria in *L'eclisse*, Giuliana in *Il deserto rosso*—is confirmed by the way they are pinned to the wall. We may be

Frame 76

Frame 77

Frame 79

Frame 78

Frame 80

Frame 81

Frame 82

Red
Desert

Frame 83

reminded of Brecht's dramaturgy of alienation, but Antonioni's inspiration comes from graphic design, not from theater. Why does he do things this way? As one of my friends[14] observes, the cool mise-en-scène may function precisely to keep a lid on things. A Pandora's box of seething emotion lies just behind these overcareful compositions. It is not at all surprising that the films make many in the audience uncomfortable. They may say they are bored, but one suspects that they are uneasy, all the more so because they cannot say why.

The reduction of three dimensions to two, to the plane, also implicates the sense of touch. If we are at a distance from things (and depth implies distance), the eye colludes with the tactile sense to reassure us: "It is upon the certitude of tangible impermeability that . . . the conviction of material individuality also depends."[15] The absence of contour and dimension makes imaginative as well as real touching difficult. To touch is to confirm, and people who are out of touch have a desperate need for tactile reassurance. Giuliana clings to walls, expresses terror that the ground is giving way under her feet, wants to have everyone who has ever cared for her surrounding her like a wall. It is easy to believe that she would grab the sandwich out of the worker's hands just to touch something real and to confirm her touch with her mouth, testing reality the way infants do. Her fright reaches its peak when she sees friends and husband disappearing into and emerging from the billowing fog. Even the eye as surrogate for the hand can no longer be trusted to reach out and touch what to her are life's only supports.

In *La notte*, the nymphomaniac is literally dying to touch someone. Her room is filled with cuddly stuffed animals. She clutches anyone within reach. Giovanni staggers out of her room, repelled by the sight of her wildly kissing the hands of the nurses who restrain her. The need to touch—for the filmmaker himself to stay in touch—makes materiality, "tangible impermeability," central. The touched comes to overshadow the touchers. What interested him in 1964, said Antonioni, was putting the character "in contact with things," because it is material objects that are important.[16] I think he meant *contact* literally, not metaphorically.

The flatness of many scenes in *Il deserto rosso* was effected by using the telephoto lens—not to bring distant objects closer but to reduce depth of field, optically to flatten the distance between foregrounded figures and backgrounded objects. Antonioni told Godard: "I used the telefoto lens a great deal so as not to have any depth of field, which is in itself an indispensable element of realism."[17] He also used strong homogeneous color to promote the flat effect—pure, unshaded, uniform color, unattached to objects.

Though troubled characters like the nymphomaniac and Giuliana want to touch, even to grasp the flat walls behind them, they never succeed. There is nothing to hold on to, no traditional handle that will "give them a hand." Psychologists of perception have shown that an object displayed against a uniform background, even a simple line, does not strike us as lying in the plane of that background but as lying upon it. "The empty environment does not border the line—the way two floor tiles border each other—but continues underneath without interruption."[18]

Antonioni's new concern for the plane was accompanied by a new interest in close-ups, to use a traditional term for an untraditional effect. In *L'avventura,* these shots make no concession to standard Hollywood matching: they do not cue reactions, inserts,[19] or the like. They seem random, as the actors move into and out of frame close by. Often the face of one, then another character appears within the same shot, not in shot-countershot. For Antonioni even the space of intimacy is subject to chance. It is under this justification, perhaps, that he often shows mere fragments of his characters' faces for seconds on end. Sandro is ask-

Frame 84

ing Claudia why she does not want to make love. As she murmurs, "I want every-thing you want," her face dominates the screen. The arrangement seems totally random from the story point of view. It avoids the appearance of a standard shot; it is concerned not with framing for easy readability but with evoking a sense that the camera really shares that diegetic space and that it is trying to keep up with the actors, who swirl around it in impossibly close quarters.[20] When they exit the frame suddenly, the camera seems to lose them altogether.

Antonioni's interest in flat surfaces, which he typically rendered with the tele-photo lens, did not however lead him to neglect depth effects. Indeed, he often established an interesting rhythm by alternating flat and deeply recessed shots in quick succession. Consider the sequence just after that of the pushcart that Antoni-oni had painted white (see frames 59 and 60 above). In this sequence, the two lens extremes are used in quick succession. In the first shot, the telephoto lens plasters Giuliana and the peddler against the wall. The next shots are of Giuliana retreating into the depths of the via Alighieri. The yawing verticals signal the switch to the wide-angle lens. The deep perspective is heightened by the converging horizontals of the bricks, street edges, and roofs. Abruptly, the next shot is of a block of mod-ern working-class flats in Ferrara, where the telephoto lens again flattens Giuliana and Corrado against buildings whose clean functional lines frame them in the per-fect squares and rectangles that characterize this style. Even when the worker's wife opens the door, there is no sense of depth in the apartment behind her. Life is opaque; you do not know what awaits you: the woman is polite but as unreadable as the blank wall behind her. Another deep shot shows a row of immense radio astron-omy antennas that stretch into the distance, and then the camera tilts upward to

Frame 85

Frame 87

suggest vast vertical distances, the dimension of the space age. Finally, reversing
again, the camera suddenly reveals the prow of a ship flattened so that it appears to
sail among the trees. The rhythm of shallow and deep in *Il deserto rosso* is no less
beautiful than its rhythms of color and editing.

THE NEW MONTAGE AND
TEMPS MORT

The flat camera style is accompanied by a new kind of montage. As we have seen, the shots become shorter, less concerned merely to track characters' movements. The process of cutting becomes more prominent, though not in any traditional way. We continue to read the narrative meanings, but they somehow seem not to be the author's fundamental concern. Pasolini was the first to discuss this effect, singling out two operations that make Antonioni's style seem to predominate over his content. They are

(1) the close follow-up of two [camera] viewpoints, scarcely different from each other, upon the same object: that is, the succession of two shots which frame the same portion of reality—first from close in, then from *a little* further away; or else first head-on, then *a little* obliquely; or else, finally, quite simply, on the same alignment but with two different lenses. From this arises an insistence which becomes obsessive, as myth of the pure and anguishing autonomous beauty of things. (2) The technique which consists in having characters enter and leave the frame, so that, in a somewhat obsessive way, the montage is the succession of a series of pictures—which I shall call informal—into which the characters enter . . . so that the world appears as ordered by the myth of a pure pictorial beauty, which the characters invade, it is true, but while submitting to . . . this beauty.[21]

The use of two or more slightly variant shots where a single shot would previously have sufficed, especially where the second shot adds no new information, obviously frustrates traditional narrative expectations. We are forced to *notice,* in an instance of what Russian Formalism calls "highlighting." But we do not understand exactly what it is that we are supposed to notice. We are persuaded to assume that it is the surface of the world—again.

Pasolini's second observation concerns the montage implications of Antonioni's belief that each place is in a way pristine and inviolate, independent of the characters and even of the narrative, and that this presence deserves to be featured, made prominent. Pasolini speaks of the prediegetic importance of the space that characters enter. But Antonioni features postdiegetic space even more prominently, by dwelling on what is left after the characters depart. French critics were quick to label the practice *temps mort,* and it has become popular with other avant-garde directors, like Miklos Jancso. The prediegetic instance can often be conventionally attributed to the familiar conventions of the establishing shot, but the postdiegetic lingering is more immediately provocative because it seems on first viewing to be a mistake, a piece of sloppy editing. In either case, the whole meaning of *establishing* has been radically altered. What is established is not "the same place" but the possibility that it is in reality "another place," perhaps even an extradiegetic place. The scene is made portentous by a delay that challenges the whole tissue of fictionality. The film says not that "this is such-and-such a place, in which plot event X occurs" but rather that "this place is important quite independently of the immediate exigencies of plot, and you will sense (if not understand) its odd value if you scrutinize it carefully. That is why I give you time to do so." This kind of shot does not set the stage for some other shot, but, as Nowell-Smith recognized,[22] it is itself the scene. Not that the simple place as stasis is turned into an event or action. It is rather that the camera's lingering makes the place pregnant with significance. We contemplate intently, in a way parallel to but separate from the characters. We are engaged, even before they arrive or after they leave, in a scrutiny that we do not quite understand but that seems nonetheless urgent.[23]

Temps mort is perhaps the most characteristic of Antonioni's stylistic effects. He has said something about how he originally hit upon it. He was struck by the sense that the characters seemed to appear most profoundly real just at the moment when the actors stopped acting. "When everything has been said, when the scene appears to be finished, there is what comes afterwards. It seems to me important to show the character, back and front, just at that moment—a gesture or an attitude that illuminates all that has happened, and what results from it."[24] The moment of greatest truth is what takes place after the actor's performance ends but before his or her real life resumes. It occurred to Antonioni to let the characters exit the frame and to keep on photographing what was left—to affirm that the background has its own esthetic and thematic autonomy. The effect is that the location is shown to possess an equal but separate reality.

Antonioni fixes or "kills" time on backgrounds that he finds compositionally interesting and leaves to the viewer the task of deciding what meanings the *temps mort* shot evokes. Sometimes this seems relatively easy for us to do, sometimes not. Take the scene in *L'eclisse* where Vittoria goes out into the deserted street at midnight to help find Marta's dog. She seems to disappear into the night, as the camera holds on the scene a few moments afterward. Unlike a conventional effect, say a fade-out, the *temps mort* freezes our vision of the night studded by streetlights. Antonioni had originally planned a similar sequence in an epilogue that the screenplay describes as follows: "The sky is also black. Nothing can be seen except lights and windows: luminous points against a black ground, with the mysterious harmony of an abstract painting."[25] For all the abstraction, the connotation for story is clear: Vittoria is absorbed by the sky. We feel her rushing off in delighted self-abandonment: the *temps mort* asserts the night's softness, its mysterious yielding and enfolding presence.

But some *temps morts* do not fit the plot line so well. They seem more tangential, evocative more of mood than of story, more of poetic connotation than of narrative denotation. One of the most beautiful occurs in *Il deserto rosso* as Corrado and Giuliana's visit to the radio astronomy station in Medicina nears its end. Corrado is surprised that she knew the worker Mario, whose wife and apartment they have just visited. Nothing much has happened; Mario is uninterested in Corrado's offer of a job. The two walk off, but the camera continues for a pungent moment to gaze at the background—an antenna and a nondescript old building— which thereby leaps from background into foreground. The lines of the orange antenna tower move from top left to lower center of the frame; the gray outline of

Frame 88

the building rises vertically slightly right of center and then carries the eye off screen right at a very shallow angle. The composition is exquisite because of the extreme simplicity of the objects, which are made even simpler and more abstract by the flattening of the telephoto lens. The composition means nothing in itself, but even in its abstraction the resulting picture captures a whole mood. It seems there less to comment on a design than to construct one, and whatever our thematic or narrative interpretation, its own stubborn autonomy is fixed in our consciousness. It has nothing to do with the art of the set designer. It constitutes a focused, intentional, and daring abstract painting right in the middle of a commercial feature film.[26]

Like other important filmmakers, Antonioni came in the 1960s to join shots almost exclusively with the straight cut, though *L'avventura* still uses a few dissolves to indicate the passage of time. One particularly effective dissolve occurs just after Anna's disappearance, almost as if to convey it: in the first shot, we see Sandro relaxing on the rocks, with Anna's back to the camera as she watches him. In the second, we see the same rocks but now without characters, at a later time of day. The dissolve clearly means: "Anna was there, but now she is gone."

Antonioni's straight cuts accentuate discontinuities as well as continuities. He saves discontinuity for particularly strong emotional moments, for instance, to highlight the beginning of the love affair between Sandro and Claudia as they search for Anna on the island. Both photography and editing underline their sudden sexual attraction and attendant ambivalence. In a more run-of-the-mill film, the scene would have been edited on shot-countershot principles: first a two-shot of the couple, then anticipation and reaction shots clearly establishing their respective perceptual points of view by projecting their eye-lines to the right or left of frame, then Claudia in close-up, followed by a close-up of Sandro with his eyes

Frame 89

pointed in her direction, and so on. Everything would have been programmed to
make strict, conventional sense. We would always know who was looking at
whom or what, where each stood, where each came from and went to, and there
would be plenty of dialogue to drive the visual points home. The first few shots in
Antonioni's scene do in fact follow that kind of logic. But at two critical moments, the logic is totally undercut, and the whole sequence is thrown into question. The confusion in the way the scene looks corroborates the characters' moral
and emotional confusion. The scene begins with a close-up of the couple, with
the noise of a motor boat over.[27] They turn, and the camera cuts away to a long
panning shot of the sea; we interpret the shot as their scanning of the desolate
seascape. After fixing on a particularly forbidding cliff, the camera pans inland,
with Claudia entering left. As she walks away, the camera turns to Sandro, who
also enters from the left but remains in close-up and then turns, looking down
contemplatively. Though absorbed by the memory of Anna, his expression suddenly suggests an erotic interest in Claudia. He looks offscreen right, and a cut-
away follows to a long shot of the old man. The old man approaches. Sandro
rushes offscreen right, and we expect the next shot to show Sandro and the old
man in middle distance, the old man on the right, Sandro on the left. But what we
get is unexpected: the 180–degree rule is ignored. The old man is now moving
not from background forward but from left to right across the screen, the camera
panning with him.

Frame 90

Frame 91

Frame 92

The shot is in total *faux raccord*. Our orientation is upset, and we are no longer sure of the old man's whereabouts or of Sandro's spatial relation to him. Sandro enters from the right, not the left. We are thrown off balance by the changing directions in this strange environment, all sky and sea and shattered rock.

In the next sequence, Sandro climbs the hill, heading toward the camera as Claudia turns around and goes left offscreen. He blinks his eyes and stares so fixedly that we are set for another eye-line match. We are sure that the next shot will show the object of his gaze. But what follows is a close-up of a hollow in the rocks in which a bowlful of rainwater has collected. Hands appear, draw water, lift it upwards; then we see Claudia rinse her face. From the apparent match with the

Frame 93

Frame 94

Frame 95

Frame 96

previous shot, we assume that Sandro is studying her from the front. But we are wrong. Almost hidden by her head, he approaches unnoticed from behind. Facing us, she wipes her face, as Sandro sits down. She apparently does not know that he is there. Turning one hundred eighty degrees, her back now to us, Claudia is startled to see Sandro's ambivalent expression. She moves left, leaving a screen-length gap between them that is spanned by a peculiar double-spurred rock, very much like an angular modern sculpture. She looks down, and Sandro looks momentarily away, then back at her with something like boyish, complacent defiance. Claudia crosses from frame left to frame right. But she enters the next shot from frame left, in a kind of repetition of the previous movement. Logically, it is simply the same movement continued from another angle, but the editing makes it seem repetitious. In spite of herself, it seems, Claudia has to move past Sandro once more. She stumbles, trying to steady herself by extending her hand. The editing reverses their positions again as Sandro reaches out to help her. Then, in the words of the screenplay, Claudia "stares at him closely, trying to make out his intention," the whole screen separating them again. Shock at his evident romantic interest registers in her face. Antonioni choreographs the actors' positions and movements to emphasize the overlap of their heads and hence, by visual suggestion, the possibility of an overlap of their emotions. The editing makes everything happen very quickly. After the long buildup shot (forty-nine seconds), each of the three shots of the recognition sequence lasts only a few seconds.

The visuals insist on emotional contiguity, even though Claudia's facial expression tells us that she finds his advances unseemly. A superb final composition sums up the whole situation. All the ambiguity of Claudia's plight is caught in Vitti's quizzical expression.[28] The black bulk of Sandro's sweater and head dominates the left half of the screen: her face in the near background is only half the size of his. And the contour of her left shoulder almost exactly parallels that of his right shoulder. His head is slightly tilted to the left. Her face disappears behind his head and then goes offscreen. His head, still seen from behind, sinks for a moment and then rises and exits left. The camera holds on empty space for a brief *temps mort*. All this is accompanied by a low repetitive melody on a solo clarinet that is no less ambiguous: it could be a dirge for Anna, but it could also be a hymn to the mystery of love—which arises when we least expect or wish it.

COLOR

Il deserto rosso was Antonioni's first effort in color, and, as one would expect from an artist of his visual sensitivity, the added dimension both complicated and enriched the film. Critics delighted to inform the public that he had had hotel lobbies, streets in Ravenna, and even part of a forest[29] painted for the film. But the reason was simple: he felt that he could not rely on the laboratory to adjust the colors properly, and incorrect tones would have ruined the effect that he wanted.[30] Thus the act was not that of a crazy perfectionist: a desolate gray was essential, and Eastmancolor requires pure white to simulate gray. Antonioni needed the grays to ensure the contrast with the intensely saturated primary colors of the industrial plant. Antonioni said: "I want to paint the film as one paints a canvas; I want to invent the colour relationships, and not limit myself by photographing only natural colours."[31] And in a later interview he remarked: "Colour is not just a little something extra . . . I wanted to use it to help convey states of mind, and it is realistic colour—at least to the extent that it communicates this kind of reality."[32] "This kind of reality" he defines as "the reality of the moment." The momentary is par excellence the domain of the subjective. But who is the subject? *Subjective* can refer to the psyche of a character, or to that of the camera, the film's mute narrator, or to both concurrently. In *Il deserto rosso*, Antonioni plays with these possibilities richly, joining color with other parameters—camera angle, focus, distance, editing, and sound—to communicate subtle dispositions of point of view. These weave the threads of plot and theme into one of cinema's richest tapestries.

What makes *Il deserto rosso* so chromatically sensitive, such a departure from the standard Hollywood Technicolor film, is Antonioni's sensitivity to all the potential of color. Until recently, Hollywood tended to use only saturated hues. Antonioni combines these with muted, almost monochromatic effects. In the process of exploring the ranges of the three perceptual parameters—hue, value, and saturation—he constructs color rhythms and orchestrations of an intricacy that Eisenstein dreamt of.[33]

In the opening sequences, for example, the colors are very muted, mostly grayish browns and greens. Not even Giuliana's green coat is particularly bright: its color seems somehow muddied by the environment. Her son's tan coat stands out better against the industrial scene that already fascinates him; its brighter color reinforces his distance from his mother, his refusal to share his mother's neurotic neediness, which is concretized in the half-eaten sandwich she buys from one of the strikers.

The world inside Ugo's factory is more chromatically intense. The range of hues is greater, and the colors are purer and more saturated. The metals shine and reflect, and the lines of desks, doors, and window frames provide hard edges for expanses of the strong and uniform colors of our modern era. As Stanley Kauffmann remarks, "The age of plastic and mold-injection and die-stamp is an age of heightened colors."[34] The homogeneity and evenness of the colors contribute strongly to the abstract flatness that we have already noted. When Giuliana descends the steps to the machinery room, her green coat, blue sweater, and auburn hair seem pale against the strong red of the pipes and the myriad metallic shapes behind her. Her colors come from another register, even as the telephoto lens, bringing the intricate background forward, enmeshes her in the tangles of pipes.

The hot reds[35] of the factory scene give way to the cool blues and whites and blacks of Giuliana's home. She wakes up from a nightmare and finds little comfort in Ugo's frosty sexuality (both are dressed in white nightclothes to underline a kind of antiseptic aridity in their relationship). In a motif that we have seen elsewhere (in Sandro's bedroom), the bar to their relationship is literalized by the stair railing, painted the coldest of blues (see Frame 79, page 120). Then a subtle change occurs. During Giuliana's anxiety attack, the walls become white and the blue railing gray, underlining her sense of Ugo's aloofness and the lack of intimacy and contact that clearly exacerbates her problems. The same format is used later in Corrado's hotel room, but there the color of the bar, as one would expect, is red, the color of passion (see Frame 80, page 120).

Throughout the film there is a subtle alternation between color intensity and reticence. We move from the cool grays of the river scenery into the agitated red of Max's shack, then back out again, or from the strange sterile whites of the hotel lobby and corridor—induced, we sense, by Giuliana's chilling realization that her son's ruse has imperilled her slender hold on reality—to the passionate red of the railing on Corrado's bed and then, *postcoitum,* to the suffused warm pink of the walls.[36] Antonioni adds movement to color to suggest a neurotic crisis: just before they make love, Giuliana looks at the wall and ceiling, and the camera peers at them, too, from behind her shoulder. Not only has the wall turned a mottled russet, but the unevennesses in the color seem to move. The effect is as subtle as it is unnerving; one does not so much see as feel the color move. As far as I can tell by studying the shot on the moviola, Antonioni moved the background, not the camera—perhaps he used colored paper or the like on a treadmill. (A similar effect is achieved in *Il mistero di Oberwald* by electronic means.) As we have noted of other aspects of Antonioni's style, color is not so much a symbol of an emotion as a sign of what the emotion has done to the character's perception of the world.[37] Andrew Sarris remarks that the "pipes and railings painted red . . . serve as the architecture of [Giuliana's] anxiety. The reds and blues exclaim as much as they explain."[38] Yes, it is the "exclamatory" property of bright saturated colors that is the most interesting of Antonioni's innovations. His colors are formal elements that stand out against—or, conversely, retreat into—a background. They work like italics in type, precisely because they are so purely visual.

THE SOUND TRACK

In the earliest stages of his career, Antonioni paid great attention to commentative music—music added to evoke or supplement a mood. For *N.U.*, he wrote out precise plans, specifying a chorus of Negro music, a prelude by J. S. Bach, and so on. In the fifties, he relied substantially on Giovanni Fusco's talents, which, as we have seen, did not always stand him in good stead. In *Il grido* and even more so in *L'avventura*, Antonioni began to reduce the use of commentative music, and by the time of *Il deserto rosso*, there is practically none. He was quite explicit about this decision. In 1961, he said:

I am personally very reluctant to use music in my films, for the simple reason that I prefer to work in a dry manner, to say things with the least means possible. And music is an additional means. I have too much faith in the efficacy, the value, the force, the suggestiveness of the image to believe that the image cannot do without music. It is true, however, that I have a need to draw upon sound, which serves an essential "musical" function.[39]

The decision to reduce or eliminate commentative music was a wise one for a director who wanted the audience to look more intently than it was used to. Even as severely reduced as it is in *L'avventura*, commentative music still clearly undermines visual effect and generally seems out of place in the larger context of the emerging style. Consider a sequence whose task is to convey Claudia's preoccupation with Sandro even before she is quite able to admit it to herself. She sits in her room at the Principessa's, in a flourish of petticoats, admiring her rings. She quickly becomes bored: she is not a narcissist. Fusco's music tries hard to catch the subtle mood: it is quixotic, tantalizing, mysterious—an overture of horns then clarinet runs against a dark background of woodwinds. Suddenly she gets up and rushes impetuously to the window, then outdoors onto a veranda to look down into the courtyard. Apparently she hears a car, though no motor noise is audible to us. A more serious, poignant theme against a busy pattern played by clarinets accompanies her movements. The quixotic motif is resumed, first by the flute, then by the clarinet, which now plays an even bouncier tune. This is followed by a very intricate passage played by unison woodwinds, which ends (after she inadvertently sees Giulia and Goffredo going off to his studio) in a rapid upward arpeggio. But the musical interlude seems too charged, too busy for the slight action, too clumsy for her indecisive mood. The paucity of music elsewhere in the film makes this passage seem more important than it really is. That is the trouble with minimizing commentative music—the little music that is played seems unduly emphasized by its rarity. Commentative music functions in an all-or-nothing manner. Once it is reduced, it is difficult not to go the whole way and eliminate it entirely. Films as psychologically complex as Antonioni's do not tolerate its easy semantics.

Increasingly Antonioni limited himself to natural sounds and noises. Despite their apparent banality, it is clear that these sounds were carefully chosen, recorded, and amplified. They function in a way similar to their visual counterparts; they are not only naturalistic components of the situation in which the character finds herself but an auditory objective correlative to her feelings. Take the crucial scene in *L'avventura* where Sandro salves with eroticism the wounds of his failure to live up to his artistic potential. After spoiling the architectural student's drawing, he returns agitatedly to the hotel where Claudia is waiting to go out with him. Previously, he failed to respond to the light-hearted sexiness that prompted her to mouth the words of a rock song blaring from a sound truck. Now, at this inappropriate, and to her inexplicable, moment, he takes her back to their room and tries to make love to her. Environmental sounds have set up an unpleasant and discordant din: the meaningless noise of piano keys being cleaned, the grating voice of the woman who owns the hotel, the noise of a door opening unusually loudly and of their footsteps as he drags her back into their room. Inside the room we hear the loud cry of a street vendor, who sounds almost angry about his message, and the ordinary, irritating noises of traffic. Sandro walks out on the balcony, takes off his jacket, throws his cigarette away in a gesture of distracted irritability typical of urban life. Though he is in romantic Noto, he looks like he is caught in traffic in Milan. Then he closes the shutters, with a last frustrated look at the beautiful church across the street, and turns to seek sexual relief from his problems. The noises of the hotel, the street vendor's cry, the honking and crunching of gears from the automobiles—these are not only the accompaniments of his frustrated desires: they are signs of it, in precisely the way that the rustling trees are signs of Vittoria's restlessness and the strange contorted, colorful pipes are signs of Giuliana's neurosis.

Antonioni introduces abstract commentative noises in *Il deserto rosso* through a repertoire of electronic sounds that resemble those made by the heavy equipment in the actual setting. (Electronic sounds were first used in *La notte* but in a more limited way.) At the opening of the film we hear industrial noises—the heavy pulsing of jets of smoke forced through pipes, the hum of wires carrying enormous voltages, the clamor of factory machines, the roar of a ship's funnel, the hiss of an immense cloud of steam escaping from a boiler. Night falls, and the industrial noises cease, but as Giuliana wakens from a nightmare, breathing heavily, during the first period of silence in the film, an electronic sound begins—a kind of high-pitched whistling. Nothing in the environment explains it, so we conclude that it is there to evoke the unsteadiness of her mind. Antonioni has

substituted commentative noises for commentative music. The association is confirmed by the recurrence of such sounds in the via Alighieri when anxiety forces
her to sit down. The only other commentative sound in the film is the beautiful
soprano voice that sings a wordless song in accompaniment to the idyllic story of
the young girl on the beach that Giuliana recounts to her son. But, interestingly
enough, the song has occurred before, at the very outset of the film. We did not
understand its relation to the grimy industrial scene then, but now in retrospect it
takes on a rich if subliminal resonance. It is the music of Giuliana's longing, even
before we know anything about her.

7

"Il provino" and *Blow-Up*

Antonioni made one more Italian film, or rather one part of an Italian film, in 1965, before going international with *Blow-Up.* The film, *I tre volti* (The Three Faces), was not released outside Italy, and the negative has been destroyed.[1] This is unfortunate, since Antonioni's portion is worth seeing. The producer, Dino De Laurentiis, had the quaint idea of making Soraya, one-time queen of Iran, into a movie star, and he persuaded Antonioni to contribute a "Prefazione" (Preface) called "Il provino" (The Screen-Test) to a three-segment film with Soraya as star of each segment; the second ("Amanti celebri," Celebrated Lovers) was shot by Mauro Bolognini, and the third ("Latin Lover") by Franco Indovina. Unlike the last two segments, which put Soraya's undistinguished talents to fictional use, Antonioni's preface is a small but interesting semidocumentary about how it must feel for a social celebrity to become a movie star. Unlike Bolognini and Indovina, he deals with the real face of Soraya, not the fictional faces that she tries to put on. Though tongue-in-cheek, "Prefazione" is not without some interesting moments, and it is technically excellent, shot by Carlo Di Palma in the same color and manner that he used in *Il deserto rosso* and *Blow-Up.*

A car pulls up under a big neon sign of the letter *A,* and a man is followed into the offices of a big newspaper. The man, a reporter, has learned that a famous but unidentified woman is being readied for a starring part in her first movie. He is determined to get the scoop, and in a very accomplished way he prepares to ambush her that night en route to a secluded studio. (There is a wonderful shot of the car entering a driveway to the studio that is lined with lights like a landing strip on the moon.) But the studio outsmarts him, hustling Soraya through the doors before the photographer can get a good picture of her face.

Once inside, the preparations for her screen test begin, first with makeup tests. Half her face, shown in tight close-up, is covered by a black card, while the other half is made up in various elaborate ways. No one speaks to her as the operation is performed: the technicians discuss the job and prepare her as if she were only a mannequin. The camera studies her face with a similar professional detachment. This inquiry, this searching of the surface, clearly anticipates the central motif of *Blow-Up.* Oddly enough, we sense that there is a real human being

136

behind the modish facade, who has feelings and apprehensions not too different from our own. As she is put through the paces of exploratory beautification, Soraya speaks Persian to her companion, who negotiates in Italian with the technicians but answers the telephone in French, handing it to Soraya, who then begins an animated conversation with her mother in German. There is not even the stability of a single language in the exotic world of film production. She is distressed and asks her mother to come as soon as possible; the voice is flat, and the conversation sounds quite real. Soraya is clearly not enjoying her new experience. Next follows a series of shots of Soraya in different wigs, to appropriate musical accompaniment: a slow blues for the sultry blond wig, a boogie-woogie beat for the pert pageboy bob and the pencil stuck secretarylike in the mouth, a wild gypsy violin to help characterize the long-haired fury who throws a bottle of ink at a mirror. Soraya's companion makes a remark that is typically Antonionian in its out-of-the-blue way: "Do you know what your handicap is? You're always hiding what you feel. Now you must do the opposite." To which poor Soraya responds with genuine if frayed nobility: "I'll do the best I can to succeed."

We move on to the test set, a romantic salon out of the nineteenth century. Soraya walks uncomfortably around its edges in a long gown; she has not yet learned the film actor's superhuman patience. She asks the studio photographer not to take her picture. To underline her disorientation, the camera moves by jump cuts from different angles, distances, and heights among the props (potted palms, a white Renaissance bust of a man). There are close-ups on her hands fiddling with a leaf, picking up a cigarette and lighter, reflected by the mirrorlike surface of the table. An English-speaking functionary finally takes her by the hand. The film cuts to a full shot of her in the salon set in front of the huge terrifying black camera. Her face is tense with apprehension. Someone says, "Take one," the clapper board strikes, and Soraya visibly jumps. The functionary is supposed to talk to her by telephone from the wings to explain the scene and to guide her as she emotes. Amusingly, he cannot find his way to the phone, which is located inside a maze of glass partitions (anticipatory of the backdrop behind Thomas's "bird" models in *Blow-Up*). Antonioni is still taking potshots at architectural absurdity, but he is also experimenting with lines, planes, and transparencies. Finally, Soraya performs, first among the potted palms, then at an open window with "wind" blown in by two ominous long-tubed wind machines that are not unreminiscent of the machinery in Ugo's factory in *Il deserto rosso*. In the final scene, the reporter, who has been plotting all this time to get a photo of Soraya as she exits the studio, is foiled again as she is led through another door and disappears down the road in her limousine.

The film is, of course, a bit of fluff compared to Antonioni's other work of this most productive decade. But it is interesting both thematically and technically. It shows clearly that in 1965 Antonioni had moved beyond his preoccupation with anxiety, neurosis, the *malattia dei sentimenti* into other kinds of investigation. It is not too farfetched to see in the microscopic examination of Soraya's face a new kind of concern with the surfaces of art's materials. Antonioni seems in this short

film to approach the no-man's-land between cinema and metacinema. "Il provino" clearly foreshadows the meditation on the relation between art and reality
that is *Blow-Up*.

BLOW-UP: QUESTIONING THE SCENE, QUESTIONING THE SEEN

> *I always mistrust everything which I see, which an im-
> age shows me, because I imagine what is beyond it.
> And what is beyond an image cannot be known.* (Anto-
> nioni, from the "Introduction" to *Technically Sweet*)

Blow-Up (1967) was Antonioni's first international film, and it was also his most
commercially successful one. It was the first of a three-picture contract with
Carlo Ponti for MGM. That affiliation guaranteed widespread distribution, so
that suddenly thousands of moviegoers who might otherwise never have heard of
Antonioni came to know his name. It is also the only one of his films that can be
described as exciting. That is what made it appealing to the mass audience, to the
great surprise of MGM's management and others in the film industry.[2] The fact
that the murder is not solved, that the body and ultimately the protagonist himself
disappear apparently did not distress as many viewers as the industry had feared.

Thomas (David Hemmings) is a highly successful young London fashion photographer. At the same time, he is working on a book of art photographs about life
in London. As the film begins, we see him leaving a doss house (British for
flophouse), where he has taken some photographs for his book. Driving his Rolls
Royce home, he bumps into a group of mimes, apparently celebrating Rag Week.
At his studio, he begins a normal morning's work, first with the model Verushka
(whom he arouses into a suitably erotic mood), then with a group of models dressed
in outlandish high-fashion costumes. He abandons them in the middle of the ses-
sion and drives to an antique shop, which his agent is negotiating for. The owner is
out, and her elderly assistant refuses to let him buy anything or even to look at the
merchandise. While waiting for the owner to return, he wanders into a nearby park,
where he sees a couple dallying—a young woman and an older, gray-haired man.
The Girl (Vanessa Redgrave) seems to be pulling the Man into a clearing. Thomas
quickly takes a number of photographs. The Girl sees him, rushes over to demand
the roll; he refuses. Later she appears at his studio, still clamoring for the film. He
gives her another roll and develops the film. By making a series of enlargements, he
is able to discern the figure of a man with a gun in a nearby copse. He calls his friend
to tell him that he has saved the Man's life, but he is distracted by two aspiring
teenage models at the door, with whom he has a casual orgy. Returning to his
blowups, he discovers that the Man's head can be seen at the bottom of a tree. He
rushes to the park and sees and touches the body. But he takes no pictures; for the

first time in the film he has forgotten his camera. Back at his studio, he discovers that the prints and negatives have been stolen. When he returns to the park, the body, too, has disappeared. In the last sequence, we see him watching the mimes play a game of tennis without ball or racket. In the very last shot, he, too, disappears from the screen.

Blow-Up was inspired by a short story by the Argentinian writer Julio Cortázar, "Las babas del diablo," translated as "Blow-Up"[3] (though literally it means "devil's drool," a Spanish idiom equivalent to "a close shave"). Narrated alternately and indeterminately in the first and third person, the story recounts an adventure in the life of one Roberto Michel, a Chilean translator and amateur photographer who lives in Paris. Cortázar's story is superficially quite different from the film. One Sunday Michel photographs a weathered blond embracing an adolescent boy. The woman furiously demands the negative. The boy slips off "like a gossamer filament of angel-spit in the morning air. But filaments of angel-spittle are also called devil-spit." At that point, a man in a gray hat appears; he had been sitting in a nearby car reading a newspaper. Several days later, Michel develops the photos and hangs a blowup of the shot of the woman and the boy on the wall, occasionally looking at it as he works. At first he feels satisfied that he helped the boy to escape. But then the images in the blowup start to move: the trees tremble, the woman caresses the boy's cheek, the boy looks suspiciously at the car where the man in the gray hat sits, the man comes up and looks at them "disgusted and demanding." Suddenly Michel realizes that what is about to happen will be worse than he imagined: the woman is seducing the boy only for the man's sake, and the boy is going to agree to a homosexual encounter for money. Michel feels that he himself has begun moving toward them; he enters the picture. The man, who is now looking at him, looms closer and closer until he seems only "a lump that blotted out the island." Michel bursts into tears. In the final paragraph, he lies in his room, looking at the sky through "a very clean, clear rectangle tacked up with pins on the wall of [his] room."

Summarizing the story is not easy, and interpreting it is even more difficult. It is a very open text. My own interpretation is that Michel suffers a schizophrenic episode, probably in response to homosexual conflicts of his own. (Projection, here made literal in the blow-up-become-holographic-movie, is a standard symptom of schizophrenia.)[4] But the problems that Thomas faces seem existential rather than psychiatric. Antonioni has said that the only thing he really borrowed from Cortázar's story was the idea of a crime discovered by making a photographic enlargement. That is not quite true. There are some other similarities: the photograph is taken surreptitiously of a couple meeting illicitly; the partners are of markedly disparate ages; the woman is enraged and tries to prevent the picture or pictures from being developed; the photographer does the developing himself; the photographer discovers that things are worse than he had originally thought or imagined (and they continually get worse); the blowup or blowups finally disappear; and the photographer suffers as a result (Michel is rendered catatonic; Thomas literally disappears).[5]

THEMES, OLD AND NEW

But it is true enough that the thematic preoccupations of the film are different from those of the story. Some are familiarly Antonionian. Distraction is one. In *Blow-Up*, distraction is no longer simply a bad habit: it has become a way of life. Thomas never finishes anything: even at the two most critical moments in the film, when he tries to tell Ron about his grisly discovery, he gets completely sidetracked, first by the sexual romp with the two teenagers, then by an intricate series of events in which distractions interrupt distractions. On his way to persuade Ron to help him photograph the body, he is distracted by a glimpse of the Girl; jumping out of his car, he misses her, hears some muffled rock music, enters a rock music club (in front of the door, a sign bears an amusing pun: Keep Clear).

Inside, he joins an audience watching the Yardbirds, gets caught in a mad scramble for a piece of the guitar that one of the musicians breaks because his amplifier will not work properly. Finally, he arrives at Ron's party, only to find his friend thoroughly stoned. Marijuana is famous for its ability to impair short-term memory. It is not only instrumental to the plot but symptomatic of the prevailing state of mind among the characters. Ron and his friends have found the ultimate—because psychedelically guaranteed—distraction. Looking at Thomas, the befuddled Ron asks, "What's the matter with *him?*" And then, "*What* did you see in that park?" To which Thomas wearily replies, "Nothing." Thomas's response not only indulges Ron's condition, but, more profoundly, it represents the inability of the mod individual, indeed of the whole subculture, to get anything of consequence done. This is not meant in a traditional moral sense: the point is not that Thomas failed to call the police but that he failed to photograph the murder even for his own purposes. He, too, gets stoned. (As Bob Dylan's song puts it, "Everybody must get stoned.")

In Antonioni's earlier films, the characters were unable to convey their feelings to each other at an emotional level, but they could at least communicate superficially. In *Blow-Up*, people cannot do even that; they seem to forget from one moment to the next what has just been said. As a critic commented, "This is a world that cannot negotiate or sustain social interaction."[6] Patricia, wife of the painter Bill, Thomas's neighbor, comes into Thomas's studio just as he discovers that his studio has been rifled. He wants to talk about the murder, and she wants to talk about some kind of trouble she is having, but they cannot stick to either topic. It is as if the ordinary rules of conversation no longer held. The two are so preoccupied that they are unable to respond appropriately to each other's speech acts. The interchange is a tissue of non sequiturs: Patricia asks Thomas if he is looking for something. He answers by skipping to her problem: "Do you ever think of leaving him?" She says she doesn't think so; to which he responds that he saw a man killed that morning. Patricia asks how it happened. He answers, "I don't know. I didn't see." To this blatant self-contradiction, Patricia merely responds,

"You didn't see." The intonation makes it sound not like another question ("What do you mean, you didn't see?") but rather like a sad confirmation of the paradoxical nature of things. She asks, "Shouldn't you call the police?" perhaps trying to be helpful in a world in which things can no longer be taken for granted. But Thomas, riding his own obsessive hobbyhorse, only nods toward the blowup: "That's the body." At this Patricia succumbs to esthetic distraction: "It looks like one of Bill's paintings." Then she returns to her own problem: "Will you help me? I don't know what to do." "What is it?" asks Thomas, a bit irritatedly. But as he waits for her answer, she looks at the photograph again and says, "I wonder why they shot him," and absentmindedly wanders off.[7]

Along with distraction, characters express that familiar Antonionian need to get away from it all. Verushka "goes to Paris" by getting stoned at Ron's party. The woman who owns the antique shop (where Hawaiian music fills the air) longs to escape to Nepal, but when she learns that Nepal is "all antiques," she says she will settle for Morocco. Thomas himself admits to Ron that he wants to get away from London and its "bloody bitches," but the best he can do is to buy a mere synecdoche of flight, an antique wooden propeller. And the mimes represent some ultimate escape: handling the world by treating it as if it were imaginary.

There are also instances of the old-versus-new theme. Thomas's interest in buying an antique shop resembles motifs that we have encountered as far back as *L'avventura:* Raimondo carelessly drops an amphora, a baroque palace houses a police station, and so on. The old man who works at the shop senses the superficiality of Thomas's interest in antiques and refuses to sell him anything. And he is right: Thomas sees the shop only as a way to turn a neat profit on campy nostalgia.

In *Blow-Up,* personal relations have become so attenuated that they have practically vanished. Thomas's wife or girlfriend never appears, has no name; we are not even sure she exists. All we know is that he requests somebody on the pay phone to call him back at his studio in a few minutes. We presume that it is she who calls when he gives the receiver to the Girl. But who can be sure?

So far, I have offered interpretations of Thomas's apparent helplessness that would relate this film to Antonioni's previous concerns. However, the central thematic of *Blow-Up* strikes me as quite new. For the first time, Antonioni directly engages the question of art and in particular its links to illusion and our very capacity to see. As he told Moravia, "To see or not to see is the question." And in the "Preface" to *Technically Sweet,* he says, "In [*Blow-Up*] I said that I do not know what reality is. Reality escapes us, changes constantly; when we believe we have grasped it, the situation is already otherwise. . . . The photographer in *Blow-Up,* who is not a philosopher, wants to see things more closely. But he discovers that, in enlarging too much, the object itself decomposes and disappears. Thus there is an instant in which reality comes forth, but then immediately thereafter it vanishes."[8] It is no longer merely our emotions but now our very perceptions that are called into question. Hence Antonioni's choice of artist as protagonist suggests a clearly a fortiori argument: if even professional eyes cannot master appearances, how can the rest of us assume that seeing is believing?

Antonioni, as we have seen, had in the past always treated surfaces as the only reality. But now even the surfaces have become deceptive. Thomas complains to Ron: "With beautiful girls, you look at them, and that's that." The corpse vanishes, and so does the Girl, under Thomas's very eyes; the last he sees of her is under a shop sign reading *Permutit*. Further, the search for visual truth can be dangerous: the artist risks disorientation, a kind of madness and even death (is the sinister click that Thomas hears in the park after touching the body that of a camera or of a gun?).

When Thomas says to Patricia that he did not see the murder, he is, of course, telling the truth: he only discovered it by artifice, after the fact, through the trace that it left in blackened silver particles. As the plot argues, it is just as easy to erase such marks as it is to put them there in the first place. The blowups are stolen, the body disappears, and it is as if nothing had happened. Thomas comes to lose confidence in his own visual judgment. So distraught is he that he forgets to bring his camera on the only occasion when it is possible to photograph the corpse. Instead of fetching it and returning to the scene, he calls Ron. This highly professional photographer suddenly needs the support of another pair of eyes to do what had before been virtually instinctual. He says desperately to Ron, "I want you to see the corpse. We've got to get a shot of it." To this Ron responds, reasonably if a bit thickly, "I'm not a photographer." Thomas is indeed the photographer and a very gifted one at that. But he is paralyzed by this experience. Why?

It is not too fanciful to see *Blow-Up* as an Antonionian version of the Faust legend.[9] Thomas's mastery of technology lures him into a Mephistophelian bargain. He uses his photographic skills to see more than the naked human eye is supposed to see. And the price he pays for this vision is an intensification of the symptoms that Antonioni's characters know too well: distraction, disorientation, paralysis of the will, perhaps even (to interpret the expression on his face at the end) doubts about one's own sanity.

But, it might be objected, space scientists, police officers, intelligence reconnaissance experts, and other professional investigators use the technology of visual enhancement without jeopardy to their sanity. Why should the fashion and art photographer Thomas be singled out for punishment? The answer seems to have to do with hubris and particularly with artistic hubris. Thomas is both a commercially successful craftsman and a gifted artist. But his manner is overly cocky, and he oversteps the bounds. He is led to believe that he can do literally anything with his camera. He really believes for a while that he has saved a life by taking some pictures. His refusal or inability to give the case to the professionals, the police, argues the artist's claim to private use of what is a public matter. In the public mind, that constitutes a pact with the devil. After all, in many trials, the litigant opposing the accused is named *the people*. But Thomas's hubris leads him to disregard the people's right to what his expertise allows him to see. This theme is anticipated in the brief dialogue between Thomas and the Girl when she first discovers him photographing her in the park. "What are you doing?" she shouts.

"Stop it! Stop it! Give me those pictures. You can't photograph people like that." Thomas replies, "Who said I can't? I'm only doing my job. Some people are . . . bull fighters. Some people are politicians. I'm a photographer." The girl responds, a bit hysterically, "This is a public place. Everyone has the right to be left in peace." Thomas's reply is characteristically beside the point: "It's not my fault if there's no peace. You know, most girls would pay me to photograph them."

To a certain extent, of course, Thomas is right. Photography *is* his job. But it is a certain kind of photography that he is engaged in, rooted in fantasy, not reality, and he gets into trouble when he mixes the two. For fantasy is no less implicit in his documentary of London life than in his fashion work. Photographs are, of course, by definition visual records of the actual. But the use to which Thomas puts his photographs is esthetic, hence fictional. His photographs of the doss house are not genuine social records but elements of an artist's vision of the city. A candid photographer tries to tell a story by catching people at odd moments in odd postures. The formal attractions of line, light, mass, and tone provide motives for pressing the button that are just as strong as those of content. Thomas was as much attracted by the beautiful composition formed by the bodies of the Girl and the Man against the trees as he was by their reason for being there. "The light was very beautiful in the park this morning," he tells the Girl when she comes to his studio for the pictures. Thomas's initial impulse is purely photographic. But he goes astray by not remaining satisfied with the visual surface that he has captured. He wants to discover the "true story" behind it all. And not only that: he wants to *affect* that story. His unwonted interference with reality costs him dearly.

The theme of the Faustian bargain gives *Blow-Up* great force. Perhaps it also explains why the film received not only great popular but also great critical acclaim, even among critics who had reservations about Antonioni's other work. We shall see something like this theme reappear in *The Passenger,* where David Locke strikes another but no less dangerous kind of bargain when he exchanges identities with another human being.

It seems clear that Antonioni is not concerned with the conventional morality of Thomas's actions. Therefore it would be ridiculous to reprehend Thomas for not going to the police like a good citizen or (as some people at MGM seem to have argued) for not solving the murder himself; the film is not a remake of *The Man Who Knew Too Much* but another (this time a philosophical) *giallo* in reverse. Thomas's intention is not to find the murderer but to find the body so that he can complete his photographic narrative. Artists traditionally violate moral norms: decency requires the rest of us to bury corpses, but the art of photography imperiously requires its practitioners to shoot them again.[10] The larger irony, of course, is that Thomas could as easily have used a random cadaver from the morgue to climax the events in the park for his book. His downfall is to demand reality rather than realistic illusion. The artist is doomed to frustration: reality will always elude him, and simulation will not satisfy his demands for perfection.

THE BLOWUPS

Art can never be more than illusion. The ambiguity of visual appearance in *Blow-Up* is illustrated in many details: the transparent plastic panels behind which the models pose; the political placards that read *on* or *no,* depending on how they are held; the random splatter "action" style of Bill's paintings; his wife's peekaboo

Frame 97

Frame 98

fishnet dress; the not quite comprehensible neon sign above the park.[11] In Thomas's own disappearance at the very end, which Antonioni has called his "autograph," the theme of visual ambiguity transcends the mere story and enters the very structure of the discourse.

But it is the blowup sequence itself that most brilliantly advances the theme. We are confronted with no less than three orders of phenomena: the events themselves, that is, our own perception of what occurred out there in the park; the photographic prints and blowups of details of these prints that Thomas makes in his studio; and the crime that he reconstructs from the photographs. These phenomena are worth close inspection, but they are complicated, and we will require labels to keep them straight.

Let us number the actual events that we can see for ourselves:

1. The Man and the Girl climbing a wooded slope;
2. The Girl pulling the Man into a clearing in the park, her back sportively bent and her laughter clearly audible;
3. Another view of the couple, now farther into the clearing;
4. The couple embracing;
5. The couple separating and the Girl walking around looking into various corners of the park;
6. The Girl drawing the Man under a tree opposite the copse where (we later learn) the gunman hides;
7. The couple seen from closer in and laterally, no longer from Thomas's point of view, then the Girl running toward him in the deep background;
8. The Girl, at the top of the stairway, holding her hand in front of her face as if to ward off the photograph and shouting at Thomas to stop;

Frame 99

9. The Girl rushing back to the clearing;
10. The Girl standing momentarily under a tree, then continuing to run away from Thomas and the movie camera until she disappears beyond the copse.[12]

Now if we list the photographs that Thomas develops and hangs while still wet on his studio walls in the order in which they appear in the movie, we have the left-to-right narrative array that Thomas finally constructs (except for one rearrangement). All the photos are enlargements, blowups of the thirty-five millimeter negative taken with Thomas's Nikon. But some are double blowups, that is, they are blowups of certain details of the original blowups, which Thomas photographs again in his studio. In fact, the most crucial photo is a triple blowup. An interesting additional twist is that sometimes what we see has been enlarged not by Thomas but by Antonioni's movie camera closing in on a photo. These enlargements sometimes coincide with Thomas's moving in physically on the blowups, but in a few instances they are not so easy to explain. It is as if the movie camera at times wants to discover the crime on its own, even as it shows us how Thomas did so. It implicates us first in the discovery of the crime, then in Thomas's inability to do anything about it.

Here is the first series of Thomas's blowups. To keep them separate from the actual events, let us use letters:

(a) The Girl pulling the Man, her back bent as if arduously;
(b) The couple kissing, the Man's back to the camera;
(c) A secondary blowup of the couple's faces in (b) confirming that the Girl looks, indeed, very anxious about something she sees in the copse;

Frame 100

Frame 101

Frame 102

(d) A secondary blowup, very grainy in texture, of another sector of (b): the piece of copse at which the Girl is staring; a fence runs along the base, and at first glance there is nothing more discernible above the fence than blotches of black, gray, and white;

(e) The Girl holding her hand in front of her face (corresponding to actual event 8);

(f) A secondary blowup of the Girl's first glimpse of Thomas;

(g) A secondary blowup of the Girl biting her fingernail and the Man looking perturbed, obviously because they now understand what Thomas has been doing;

(h) A secondary blowup of the Man alone looking at the Girl and Thomas.

SEARCH FOR TEXT

I have described these photographs as forming a narrative array, a "textualization" or "entexting" of what would otherwise be a random group of photographs. Indeed, much of the film can be seen as an account of the artist's effort to textualize a puzzling experience. In this instance, the text is narrative, though other types—lyric, exposition, description, to name only three—are possible. Narration is both the readiest and the most dramatic way of explaining an otherwise incomprehensible group of events.[13] Though photographers, like painters, generally concentrate on single pictures that say "everything," Thomas likes to work with sequences. The fact that Thomas narrativizes the park sequence recalls Antonioni's other exploration of the process of making visual narrative, *L'amorosa menzogna*. Thomas's work also resembles that of making a narrative movie in that it is a kind of storyboard. Thomas's efforts obviously relate in some important way to Antonioni's own labors as a maker of feature films.[14]

Thomas reconstructs the crime in several stages. In the first, he tries to understand what happened simply by connecting photos (a) and (b). But he notes something strange in the Girl's expression in (b), and so (stage two) he makes the secondary blowup of her face (c). Thus (c) functions like a close-up insert in montage; it does not signal the next narrative moment, but (like the close-up on the spy's missing finger in *The Thirty-Nine Steps* or the poisoned cup in *Notorious*) it calls attention to a detail crucial to the plot. Thomas scans (b) for the reason for the Girl's consternation. He traces her eye-line toward the copse; not finding anything there, he shrugs his shoulders as if to dismiss the matter. But (stage three) he cannot resist trying again. A magnifying glass helps him find a clue in (b), which he marks with a white grease pencil. He blows it up into (d), which contains two suspicious blobs, one above the assassin's face and the gun in his fist. Thomas's moving gaze is communicated by two pans along the studio wall—left to right, then back and left to right again. The repeated movement of the camera is an important signal of Thomas's struggle to textualize (another is counting off the photos on his fingers). The second pan also entails a forward track by the movie camera to convey Thomas's own movement toward the pho-

Frame 103

tos. But Antonioni's camera, like Thomas's, goes too close: the gun hand is cut off by the lower edge of the frame, and without it it is impossible to perceive a face. Indeed, Thomas has not understood the blobs: he stands back and rubs his face perplexedly.

Stage four: baffled, Thomas prints all the negatives he has. He hangs four of these, (e) through (h), to the right of those already hung. They are not in the correct story sequence: (e) clearly took place after (f).

Stage five: still baffled, Thomas tries to phone the Girl but discovers that she has given him a false number. He goes back and contemplates the enigmatic blobs in (d). He sees something and runs to the darkroom. There he prints a blowup (i) of a small area of (d): it shows a hand holding a gun. Now we understand why the movie camera close-up had missed the gun in stage three; it was so that Thomas could make the discovery at this later stage. He returns to his narrative array and replaces (e)—clearly out of sequence—with (i), not because (i) temporally follows (d) and precedes (f), but because it is an improved version of the telling montage insert that (d) tried to be. (In a reversal of the close-up on (b) of stage three, (i) deletes the face. But that does not matter: Thomas is excited about the fact of the assassination attempt, not the identity of the would-be assassin.) Standing back, Thomas contemplates his constructed story, and Antonioni's camera now presents it for us to see, too, not in a slow, halting left-to-right pan in

Frame 104

emulation of Thomas's inquiry procedure but by straight cuts from one image to another in the sequence to which Thomas has assigned them. It is very much as if Thomas were asserting to himself (and to anyone who cared to look on): "This is what happened out there in the park. The pictures tell the story." And in their immediacy the straight cuts suggest a flashback to the scene itself. Like Antonioni, Thomas is an artist who prefers images to words (notwithstanding Ron's captions to the contrary).[15]

Stage six: after the distraction provided by the brief orgy, Thomas returns to (1). He examines the base of the tree and confirms the presence of the corpse by an examination of the same area in (k). Only now does he grasp the full story.

The artist discovers the facts by creating a narrative text. But these facts occur in what we know to be a fiction, hence an illusion. Thomas's disappointment, at the end of the film, reminds us that it is he and not "history" that conjures up this particular illusion. As a fashion photographer, Thomas is already something of a prestidigitator, a master of illusion, as we learn by looking at the props in his studio and at the otherwise unmotivated piece of business in which he mystifies the teenage girls by making a coin appear and disappear behind his fingers. Nor is it an accident that he feels kinship with the student mimes: Thomas, like them, masquerades to practice his art—he dons tatty clothes so that he can pass as a bum in a doss house, and he recognizes and appreciates the mimes' art of reducing the world to absurdity by filling real spaces with imaginary objects. Behind them all, of course, is the master illusionist Antonioni, who practices an art that can make an imaginary tennis racket resound against an imaginary ball—and can whisk even the hero into thin air.[16]

The tennis game seems like a commentary on the inevitability of illusion in art. Thomas says nothing, and the expression on his face is open to a variety of interpretations. I see in it concern about his own sanity but also rueful resignation about the limits of art's power to interpret. The conclusions that the artist reaches, however concrete his materials, may be mere will-of-the-wisps, of no greater substance than the mimes' imaginary tennis rackets and ball, which are the materials of *their* art. And the illusion exists only because the artist allows it to, because he gives it permission, so to speak. Under such circumstances, is it a wonder that the artist becomes so concerned about the possibilities of madness?

In an interview during the making of *Blow-Up*, Antonioni said, "I'm really questioning the nature of reality. This is an essential point to remember about the visual aspects of the film since one of its chief themes is 'to see or not to see properly the true value of things.'"[17] (*Value* here surely means "import" or "quality," not "worth" or "price.") The chief inspiration for the story was a technical fact: the more one enlarges a photo, the more obtrusive the grain becomes, until it begins to interfere with the very contours of the objects depicted. Indeed, if one goes too far, the contours seem to disappear in a general atomic welter. The image literally comes apart before one's very eyes. That, of course, is the effect that action painters like Bill desire and achieve by flinging paint at canvas. Hence the importance of Patricia's association of the blowups with her husband's paintings. Scale is everything: the more one enlarges images under a microscope, the less stable they are. Sufficiently enlarged, even the photograph of a rock shows only an amorphous group of particles. Only the effort of the perceiver can hold things together: Bill says that it is "only later," after the painting is finished, that he finds something to "hang on to." "Only later," that is, after the creative hand and eye have done their work. Coherence is always man-made: the universe offers us nothing but chaos. We make what sense of it we can. Again, Antonioni's vision is bleak, but at least it is one that tells us honestly what the artist is up against.

THOMAS'S CHARACTER

More than Antonioni's other protagonists, Thomas is a person without a history. And by ordinary standards he seems less sympathetic than any character since, say, Momina of *Le amiche*. Some critics have felt literally repelled by him. But that misses the point. Thomas is first and foremost an artist, and the film justifies the ruthlessness he uses to get his pictures on esthetic if not on moral grounds. (David Hemmings plays the role beautifully, flashing his eyes in eaglelike vigilance.) And, as has been pointed out, Thomas's love of beauty in itself makes him a figure of some dignity. His interest in nature and art is pure and direct. His reaction to the beautiful light in the park is to leap instinctively in "agile, youthfully awkward-graceful self-delighting high spirits."[18] His taste is swift and sure: attracted by Bill's latest canvas, he immediately offers to buy it. Even his method of working is not as callous as it may seem if it is looked at from an esthetic point of view. The photographic seduction of Verushka may seem manipulative, but it simply reflects his understanding of what inspires her to give her best performance. He is not dominating her for the mere sake of domination: rather, his approach to his art is equal in its passionate intensity to the sexual act. If, as a substitute for that act, he ends panting on his knees above her with his camera as if detumescent, it is not necessarily some mod perversion but Antonioni's way of showing the intense absorption that art exacts and how it can replace other strong passions like sex. As for his treatment of the models, the "birds," who can deny that his cruelty has its effect, enhancing the chic posturing, the elaborate harlequinade of black and white stripes? Thomas knows what he is doing, and he works hard and attentively, though he has not slept all night. By fashion standards, his compositions are excellent, whatever the price that he and the models pay. And most critics agree that his "orgy" is less evidence of depravity than of childlike amorality. Thomas is no better but also no worse than his times.

RETURN TO DEPTH

In *Blow-Up*, the camera turns away from the flat abstract visual style of the tetralogy and renews its preoccupation with effects of depth. Antonioni said:

I worked a lot in *Il deserto rosso* with the zoom lens to try and get two-dimensional effects, to diminish the distances between people and objects, make them seem flattened against each other. This time, I'm trying to do something quite different. I've tried to lengthen the perspective, to give the impression of space between people and things.[19]

Why? Because the whole film turns on the problem of how to capture in a two-dimensional medium that which is out there in reality, that is, in depth. Unlike the hallucination of poor Roberto Michel, Thomas's art is not literally holographic: he clearly understands its limits. And so does his creator: Antonioni is only doing what Thomas might have done if he had had time and the proper equipment (a wide-angle lens on his Nikon that would better grasp the effects of depth—or even a stereoscopic camera). Clearly, with added depth perception, it would have been easier for Thomas to distinguish the outline of the killer from other blotches in the vicinity. (This is a skill practiced by archaeologists and above all by aerial intelligence officers, whose task is to disentangle the forms of guns, tanks, and trucks from the camouflage stripes and colors with which the enemy tries to conceal them. Like Thomas, they compare photographs of a suspicious area taken from different angles and distances to secure a perspective that will enable them to interpret two-dimensional images.) There are telephoto shots in *Blow-Up*, but they are limited to local effects, for example, pushing Thomas and Verushka onto the same plane in the photo seduction sequence or intensifying the sense of crowding among the ugly new skyscrapers of London. But wide-angle camera work predominates in the crucial scenes, emphasizing the fact of intervening space and so its thematic and diegetic importance.

In editing, *Blow-Up* resembles even less the long-take films of the fifties. Right from the beginning, in the interchange between the mimes and the bums leaving the doss house, shots tend to cut from one stationary setup to another, some-times, as in the sequence with Verushka, in imitation of the snapping of Thomas's still camera. Pans and tilts are brief and modest but for that reason all the more telling; in the sequences in Thomas's studio, each short movement reveals an extraordinary new composition of models and props. Antonioni seems expressly to avoid tracking the characters (for instance, when Thomas pays his visits to his neighbor's studio). When tracking does occur, the emphasis is clear, as when the camera roars off in the Rolls Royce leaving the teenyboppers gasping on the curb at all that wealth and speed, or when it runs with Thomas along the catwalk of his studio to test some new hunch about the blowups, or when it joins him as he looks for the owner of the antique store on his first visit. The camera's reticence really pays off in the park scene. Because it has remained so quiet, it becomes especially eloquent when it does begin to move. Thomas, on the prowl for good shots, scans the landscape. He startles a covey of pigeons, and Antonioni's camera sweeps up gracefully to capture their scattering. Once up in the clearing with Thomas, it makes a very special slow pan—about twenty degrees—first to the right, then back again, to show how he is measuring the couple's behavior for the story it might tell. (Ironically, of course, the movement anticipates the same kind of scan-ning that he does later in his studio to make sense of the blowups.) In the last sequence, its earlier reticence makes its sudden collaboration with the looping trajectory of the imaginary tennis ball all the eerier, setting us up for Thomas's final disappearance from the screen.

The voyeuristic illusionism of the photographer's profession, hence of the movie itself, is already illustrated in the opening titles. A gyrating model can be seen through spaces cut out of pasteboard and held up against the lens that spell the letters B-L-O-W-U-P. The effect of depth is enhanced in many shots by screening or filtering the characters behind an array of objects—colored feath-ers, glass panels, spotlights, lighting umbrellas, tripods, architectural beams and poles in Thomas's studio. The smoked glass panels are particularly intriguing: often we cannot tell at what depth, that is, through how many panels, we see models at one end or Thomas at the other. Similarly, both Thomas and the crotch-ety old clerk in the antique shop are screened by classical busts, figurines, furni-ture, wrought iron grillwork, and other artifacts. In both sequences, art and its tools are shown as a kind of necessary debris: the clutter is distracting but none-theless essential. The messy uncertainty of human feelings is similarly reflected in the mazes of Bill's apartment; its inner windows, slats, lattices, mirrors, pan-els, dividers underline Thomas's perplexity about the relationship between Bill and his wife. One is reminded of the films of Joseph von Sternberg, except that Sternberg's screen decor seems purely ornamental, whereas Antonioni's func-tions thematically and evocatively of the surface of the mod world. Where the heroines of his films of the tetralogy stood vulnerably against flat unprotective walls, Thomas is typically trapped between layered screens (of his own making) as he pores over the inexhaustible puzzles of visual reality.

Frame 105

Frame 106

The only editing transition is the straight cut, its crispness often exaggerated by jarring changes in composition. In brief sequences, Antonioni experiments with the jump cut. The sequence with Verushka brilliantly communicates the modern technique of fashion posing, which turns the model into a kind of staccato ballerina. Our understanding of the continuity of her movement is ensured by the soundtrack: a phonograph plays cool jazz. But to remind us that the end product

Frame 107

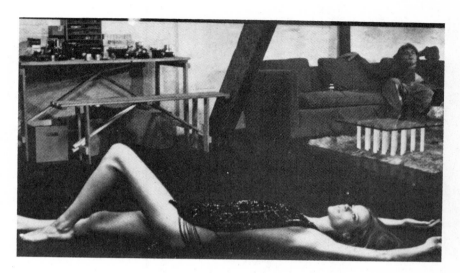

Frame 108

is, after all, a still photograph, the editor cuts brusquely and jerkily. The slow
dance movements are periodically interrupted; the frozen interval shows us what
the finished photograph will look like. The cutting rhythm speeds up as Thomas
approaches his climax. In the first, voyeuristic stage, he keeps Verushka at a
certain distance; in the second, more active stage, he closes in on her, his movements now matching hers as he calls to her, "Give it to me." Antonioni's camera
makes wide, fast movements across their bodies as if it were itself in a state of
sexual excitement. At the critical moment—Thomas shouts "Yes!"—the camera
zooms in on her as she lies on her back. Afterwards, she lies exhausted, "satisfied," framed by a phallic brace holding up Thomas's ceiling.

A fascinating and characteristic bit of editing at the very beginning of the film
also deserves notice. After the titles, the first images are of the mimes cavorting
in downtown London. Suddenly, we cut to the bums leaving the doss house. In
the first shot, a mime stares offscreen with such fixity that we expect an eye-line
match to the something at which she is staring. Instead, what we see is Thomas
talking with bums at the exit gate of the doss house. Since they are not nearby and
since there is no other story relation between the mime and the bums, the effect is
a kind of discourse framing: her glance makes her a speechless chorus or commentator on the spectacle of a rich photographer disguising himself to get some
pictures and, more generally, on the events in the film as a whole. Physically, she
cannot possibly see him; she is not a realistic but a spiritual onlooker. The match
anticipates and explains the whole nonrealistic and ironic function of the sequence of the mimes at the end.

The colors of *Blow-Up* are at the opposite end of the spectrum from the hot
colors of *Il deserto rosso*. Chosen as carefully as for a page in *Vogue*, blues, pur-
ples, and greens are used to express "cool" London, not only in the bravura

sequence of the models but throughout the film. The subdued color scheme reminds one of the subdued gray tones of the British sequence of *I vinti.* Black and white appear more frequently than usual in a color film, not only to suggest "coolness" but to underline and justify the fact that Thomas works in black and white.

The sound track continues to function noncommentatively: contemporary jazz (Herbie Hancock) and rock (the Yardbirds) are used as environmental audibles, on records (the suitable background for models' work, Thomas's way of calming the Girl) and live (in the frenetic rock club sequence). Among the natural sounds, the most noteworthy is the rustling trees. Again, as in *L'eclisse,* they evoke both the realism of a place and its mystery. At the crucial moment of discovery, the trees become audible again in Thomas's studio, making the shot subjective in the classical cinematic sense, since it recalls both Thomas's and our own memories of the park. With his usual restraint, Antonioni resists the temptation to introduce a musical comment to mark the moment when the gun and the gunman in the copse are discovered.

Blow-Up is a happy instance of a director's making a congenial match with foreign writer, actors, and production people. Antonioni said that from the thematic point of view the events could as easily have occurred in another Western European capital or in New York, but one wonders if the resultant film would have been quite so successful. Given his own affinity for the English scene and that special combination of high civilization and decadence that London shares with Rome, it is hard to imagine a better city. The choice of Southern California for *Zabriskie Point* was to prove less fortunate.

8

Zabriskie Point and *Chung Kuo Cina*

"America is a mysterious country." —ANTONIONI

Zabriskie Point (1969) opens on a meeting of students debating how to attack the establishment most effectively. Black Panther elements argue immediate violence; white students urge moderation. Mark (Mark Frechette), a loner, says that he is ready to die for the cause but not out of boredom and leaves the room. Then begins an extensive crosscut sequence[1] between the stories of Daria (Daria Halprin) and Mark. At the skyscraper headquarters of Sunnydunes Enterprises, Daria attracts the real estate tycoon Allen (Rod Taylor), who hires her as a secretary. Cut to Mark at the police station requesting permission to see his friend Morty, who has just been arrested in a demonstration. He irritates the policeman and is arrested himself. Mark buys a gun under the pretext that he has to defend his sister against potential black rapists (the gun store owner tells him that if anyone dies in the backyard, the corpse should be dragged inside, since the law permits killing in self-defense). Meanwhile, back at Sunnydunes, the board of directors is watching a television commercial promoting desert vacation homes. Allen tries to reach Daria, who is to take a business trip with him to Phoenix, but she has already left in her ancient Buick. On campus, a police lieutenant demands that students occupying the library come out; four blacks emerge amid tear gas and lie on the ground. A fifth follows "fooling around as if he's trying to put his shirt into his pants." A policeman shouts, "He's got a gun," and another shoots him dead. Mark, seeing everything, reacts "immediately and instinctively." He grabs at the pistol that he has hidden in his boot; a shot rings out, and the policeman falls. Mark escapes, calls Morty from a drugstore, and, passing a small airport, is prompted to steal a private airplane, the Lilly 7. Meanwhile, Daria calls Allen from a bar in a small town in the desert. She has stopped there to look up a friend who has taken a group of juvenile delinquent boys out of the city to "detraumatize" them. Far from helping Daria, the boys—who look to be about eight or ten—ask her for a "piece of ass." Stunned, she flees as they try to grab her.

Out on the road, Daria's 1954 Buick meets Mark's newly acquired Lilly 7, and it is love at first sight. He buzzes her as she stops for water; later, when she finds the plane out of gas on a dry lake bed, they drive off together to find some. But on

159

the way they stop at Zabriskie Point, slide down a hill, and make love. They are joined (in fantasy) by numerous members of Joe Chaikin's Open Theater, in what the Italian version of the scenario calls "a natural, primordial, and also slightly ironic promiscuity."[2] Returning to the road, Daria is stopped and eyed narrowly by a highway patrolman, presumably with lust in his heart. Hiding behind an outdoor toilet, Mark is about to shoot when Daria interposes her body. The policeman leaves. She questions Mark about the university shooting, and he admits that, though he would like to have shot the policeman, somebody else did it first. They paint the airplane to resemble a prehistoric bird and cover it with slogans ("Suck Bucks," "She-He-It," and so on). Daria asks him why he wants to take the plane back; he says he likes risks. He flies off, and another sequence intercuts between Daria's car on the way to Phoenix and the Lilly 7 on the way back to Los Angeles. The police are waiting for him there: three patrol cars surround the plane, and a policeman kills Mark with a single shot. Daria hears the news over the radio, pauses as if to return, but then drives on to Phoenix. Arriving at Allen's luxurious desert home, she walks through the glass and fieldstone architectural maze, crying bitter tears and refreshing herself by standing under a small fountain. Allen is busy closing a big deal upstairs. He meets Daria, forlorn and dripping wet in a corner of the house, and tells her to go downstairs to change. Instead, she returns to her car and drives away. At a short distance, she stops and looks back at the house. The house explodes, but silently; the image is presumably to be read as Daria's first fleeting impulse of destruction. Then she gets out of the car and stands and stares malevolently at the house. Again, it explodes, not once but thirteen times and with a great roar. This time the explosions seem to represent not her mere impulse but deliberate and focused intention. First the exploding house is shown from various angles and distances. Then the camera closes in on an exploding refrigerator, whose contents spill out and float across the blue—a box of Kellogg's Special K, a loaf of Wonder Bread, a chicken, a lobster. A bookcase also bursts, and books and magazines go floating by. The baleful gaze of Daria seems to want to destroy not only the things that so obsess America but all the written scraps of its ideology. Satisfied, she returns to her car and drives off into the sunset.

Zabriskie Point was derided by most American critics and rejected by the American public. For its day, it was the most expensive failure ever made ($891,918 return on an investment of about $7,000,000), and it figured in a list of the fifty worst films of all time.[3] Today, it is the object of a cult revival, perhaps on grounds of nostalgia or of curiosity among the younger generation, who wonder what the rebellious sixties were all about. It certainly has an element of documentary value. Antonioni was one of the few major directors to take a serious look at campus unrest in America. What went wrong? It would be comforting to find a single cause—say, the terrible performances by Frechette and Halprin. But beyond that, and despite its beautiful surface, the film is flawed in many respects. Problems derive from subtle—and some not so subtle—misconceptions and misperceptions of the American scene. These would not have been so crucial if *Zabriskie Point* did not

Frame 109

pretend to be about America (in a way that *Blow-Up* does not pretend to be about England). Though Antonioni denies this intention,[4] the film is hard to read except as a portrayal of the American scene, as a defense of revolutionary youth, and as an attack on a materialism that finds its ripest head in Southern California. Despite certain marvelously exact details, there are many mistakes in Antonioni's reconstruction of Sunbelt people and preoccupations. Nor can his vision pass as parodic stylization:[5] Antonioni, after all, is no Stanley Kubrick. One is hard put to find anything more than the romanticization of the life and early death of a boy who is neither convincingly hippy nor convincingly revolutionary and whose lonerism is not particularly American. Not even exciting cinematography, elegant composition, and breathtaking color can make him interesting.

One says this fully conscious of how easy it is to be trapped by one's cultural bias. *Blow-Up* was less favorably received in England than elsewhere, and there are Italians who prefer Antonioni's international films to his home products. For an American, the cultural mistakes of *Zabriskie Point* seem so pervasive as to disable the film. They range from major premises to small but glaring details. Item: the Black Panthers movement had little to do with the student movement (Antonioni told *Rolling Stone* magazine, "I include them in the general category of students"). Item: the interesting shots of the dizzying array of billboards along Los Angeles streets are taken from Mark's point of view. But what native would ever actually look at them? (Mark, unlike Lidia, is no critic of architecture.) Item: the Santa Monica cops may be brutal, but they certainly know the difference between a professor and a clerk. Item: it is unlikely that Allen would chat with his friend about the number of billionaires that California has produced or that his friend, presumably another tycoon, would drop him at his office and drive off in Allen's car. Item: the legend on the painted airplane surely should read "Bucks Suck" rather than "Suck Bucks." And so on: many such molehills make a mountain.

And it is not only the minute sort of cultural mistake that mars the film. Its very structure is compromised.

CHARACTERS AND ACTORS

Consider the main characters. A young man from a rich family has dropped out. Now he operates a forklift in a meat-packing plant. Though he is interested in revolution (or at least in rebellion), he walks out of meetings because "the students only talk about violence, while the police do it." An old hand, played by Frank Bardacke, an actual member of the Free Speech Movement, is justifiably indignant at Mark's lonerism; someone mutters prophetically, "That guy's going to get himself killed." Mark buys a gun with the express intention of killing a policeman; when somebody else does it, he runs off and on a whim steals an airplane. Why? "I needed to get off the ground." He joyrides through the desert and makes love to a girl who wants him to abandon the plane and drive off with her. But he insists on taking the plane back, ostensibly to thank the owner but really because he "likes to take risks." Given the gun-happy attitude of the police in Antonioni's Los Angeles, he cannot help knowing what his fate is likely to be.

All of this makes Mark a special case, neither a run-of-the-mill hippy nor a run-of-the-mill revolutionary, both of whom move in groups and are not necessarily suicidal. But the film's structure tacitly suggests that the character is recognizable as a type whose details can be filled in by a knowledgeable audience. Further, a surface-of-the-world style does not sort well with special cases, especially when the nuances of the foreign culture have not been mastered. Capturing the surfaces of American hippy life—fascinating as it may be to foreign visitors—does not guarantee that the analysis of that life is in any way profound. Antonioni knows Italian and European culture so intimately that the appearances he chooses are precise and genuinely reconstitutive. When he does not know the culture, his style is jeopardized; only when it accepts the mystery of the culture— as The Passenger accepts the mystery of black Africa—does it seem to reach safe ground again.

Mark comes off as rather shallow and dull, despite the cute lines that are supposed to make him charming: about having been expelled from college for stealing hardcover books (presumably paperbacks would have been all right); about using the dean's credit card to make long-distance calls; about smuggling forbidden objects like women, dogs, and bicycles into the dorm; about programming the computer to require engineers to take art courses. Whoever wrote those lines did the director no great service. Edward Bond's achievement in Blow-Up seems all the more impressive by comparison. What is vexing is that nothing else about Mark— either character or actor (what's the difference?)—suggests the least iota of wit.

Hiring a nonactor literally off the street might have worked in Italy, to whose sounds and sights Antonioni's ears and eyes are exquisitely tuned. (One remembers the splendid performance as Ugo by the nonprofessional de Pra in *Il deserto rosso*.) But whatever authenticity of appearance Antonioni gained by recruiting Frechette was vitiated by the spiritlessness of his performance and his inability to deliver his lines. A director who lets his actors find their own way in a difficult script relies on hidden reserves in their training, on instinct and second sense. Antonioni could manage with professionals like Hemmings or even Cochrane but not with the inexperienced and untalented Frechette. De Sica or Bresson might have, but not Antonioni. Indeed, Robert Bresson's words ironically describe the case of Mark Frechette: "Their [amateur actors'] way of being the people of your film is by being themselves, by remaining what they are. (*Even in contradiction with what you had imagined.*)"[6] Another of Bresson's keen observations is apposite here: the voice of the untrained actor, he writes, "gives us his intimate character and his philosophy better than his physical aspect."[7] But Antonioni did not introduce Mark Frechette's "philosophy" (whatever it might have been) into the composition of the dialogue. Further, Mark's voice is hopelessly weak, just as Daria's accent is all wrong for the part. Their physical aspects are wrong, too: they are too attractive, they look too much like movie stars without having the training or talent that even the minor stars possess. When everyone else in the film is a professional, the resulting effect is uneven (Rod Taylor's presence makes Daria's performance worse by comparison). As Stanley Kauffman observed, "It is not so much that [Antonioni] has cast badly, it is more that he seems to have lost faith in the processes of art, has relied on the fact of youth to supply the truth of youth."[8]

It may be paradoxical but it seems to be true that the more a director wants to evoke the surface of the world, the more dependent he is on professionals, especially professional actors. Antonioni relies so much on the confrontation of character with world that he needs especially gifted performers, of the caliber of Vitti, Moreau, Mastroianni, Delon, Nicholson, and Schneider. Since actions and dialogue are minimized, a great deal of the meaning of a performance depends on the actor's sheer presence on the screen. Especially since Antonioni's direction is somewhat less than fully explicit, the actors need to give off the right vibrations, to be the surface that represents the complex depth he seeks to sketch. They need to be not only highly skilled but also highly intuitive.

The character of Daria is no less problematic than that of Mark. It does not seem plausible that she should be interested even in working for Allen, let alone in accompanying him to his desert home. What is going on between them anyway? Have they already made love? Or is he inviting her out there to seduce her (to use an absurdly outmoded word)? Surely she cannot think that all he wants from her is her secretarial services. Her appearance and manner make it difficult to believe that she would be attracted to Allen. Nor is indiscriminate promiscuity with Establishment types consistent with her earth child personality. The relationship simply does not ring true.

Even less plausible is her lightning conversion to the anticapitalist cause at the film's end. Till then she has expressed no interest in politics. Of course, the point is probably that even the peaceful flower child will be driven to violence by the frustrations and crudity of capitalist repression. But Halprin is particularly inept at conveying the seething emotions that would justify such an outburst.

THE THEMATIC

It was not surprising that viewers and critics should see the film as an attack on capitalist America and as a paean to rebellious students. The contrasts are too striking not to prompt a reading in which police violence justifiably provokes a violent response by the victims, aided, ironically, by guns bought from racist dealers who think they will be used against blacks. Not only are the police and big business found culpable, but so are the media—advertisers and sensationalist television and radio news broadcasters. And waiting for you at every vista are overweight tourists with their mobile homes, double knit bermudas, and funny sun hats.

But Antonioni's disclaimer of political intent did mean something; clearly two other themes inform the film. One is the theme of youth as savior.[9] Daria tries to get Mark to play a "death game" in Zabriskie Valley. Antonioni's point, for Joseph Morgenstern, was that "the American way of life is actually death, and the only vestige of life in this continental wasteland is alienated American youth."[10] The trouble is that the film finds youth glorious per se, independent of what it does or says (both rebels and hippies come off as better than anyone else). What is important is not that they are revolutionary but simply that they are young. They are even cute. As John Simon observes with some justice, "Antonioni seems to take the superiority of the young over their elders for granted."[11] Merely by being young, they solve all kinds of problems, for example that of "sick eros": "He has remarked that in making *Zabriskie Point* he learned that eroticism is not the disease of our era after all."[12] Certainly, that liberation led to some extraordinary imagery. The love-in at Zabriskie Point, whatever its value at the conceptual or symbolic level, is undeniably attractive as it evokes the erotic resemblance between tawny youth and the golden tones of the arid and sinuous landscape. In a way, the scene is a fulfillment of Giuliana's fantasy in *Il deserto rosso*. The group sex portrayed is not at all titillating: the organic resemblance of sexual rhythms to the rhythms of the scenery is visually persuasive, whatever one may think of Antonioni's notion of what hippies fantasize about.

The other basic theme is the familiar one of escape. Mark has many of the attitudes of other Antonioni heroes—most notably Corrado Zeller, David Locke, and T. in *Technically Sweet*. He is a man obsessed by the need to take mysterious and dangerous risks involving flight to still another place in the hope that salvation awaits him there. Mark's "I needed to get off the ground" is simply another version of Corrado's "I have to be abroad to feel all right." But where the earlier hero only fantasizes about escape, the later one actually attempts it.

Frame 110

Frame 111

Since this is not a biography, I do not find it important to know what needs Mark's youthful escape represented for Antonioni's own psyche. But a failure of the magnitude of *Zabriskie Point* must be considered in as broad a perspective as possible. Here, the wisest words may be those of Stanley Kauffmann, a long-time fan, who sees Antonioni's plight as one familiar to the artist still governed by Romanticism's imperative subjectivism. Since the Romantic artist's "life and internal experience . . . become more and more circumscribedly his subject matter," he is led to early burnout and repetitiveness, a "quick depletion of resources." Still, he must work, he must "live a *life* in art." Perhaps, Kauffmann speculates, that was Antonioni's state of mind in 1969:

At the moment, let us say, he feels drained of inner resources. This feeling of attrition is emphasized by contrast with some people around him who are not drained and who, artists or not, have vitality and address. They are the radical, dissident young of the world. They make him envious. Not so much to be young again, or to be as virile as he was at twenty-one—those envies apply to anyone. He is mainly envious of their surety and moral energy. He is experienced enough in politics to doubt salvation through politics; he is acute enough morally to see the dubiousness of youthful moral absolutism; nevertheless, he is envious of their *beings*. And, possibly, he tells himself that what he needs is to shift from a generally pessimistic view—which has been the fundamental view of most serious artists in the last century and a half—to a participatory and expectant view, at least as a motor device. His first move is to *Blow-up*, in which the protagonist and the ambience are young but the center of which is mature, a view down the perspective of some years. With *Zabriskie Point*, the exponents *and* the center are intended to be young.

But, Kauffmann goes on,

For a man of his philosophical temperament—I say this carefully—politics seemed to have become increasingly superficial, at least as a subject in art. Now his use of the rhetoric of revolution seems an escape, an emollient for a fever of frustration, a way of *seeming* to come face to face with root troubles in men, something that only the best political philosophers can do through politics and for which political activists can't afford the subtlety, even when they have it at their disposal. . . . For Antonioni, the political gesture of this film may not be much more than a kind of personal therapy.[13]

The vital word in this appraisal, I think, is *escape*. As we have seen, the thematic of escape is virtually obsessive in Antonioni's later films. Surely Mark's most characteristic movement—and the only one that can possibly explain the film—is escape, not rebellion. What if he had in fact succeeded in killing the policeman? Would it not seem that he did it to provide himself with a concrete need to escape, to validate his lonerism?

For the first time (excepting perhaps in *Il grido*) the signpost at the end of the road reads "Death." Mark surely must sense this at some level. Much of *Zabriskie Point* takes place in Death Valley, a desolate place, like that in which David Locke makes his fateful decision. There is in this film, as in the script for *Technically Sweet*, a kind of toying with death before the fact. But death represents the finality that even escape cannot achieve, and in that sense *Zabriskie Point* clearly bears the seeds that will ripen into *The Passenger*.

Even if you disagree with Stanley Kauffmann, it is not hard to believe that Antonioni's basic mistake was to ignore his previous practice of avoiding explicitly political themes. He is clearly a minimal—not an engagé—artist. He seems to work best when politics float about the edges of his work, rather than occupying the center. Even though Mark is a loner (one critic finds the major theme of the film "individuality at bay"),[14] his isolation, like Daria's reaction to his death, smacks too much of politics to permit Antonioni his usual and apparently necessary degree of detachment.

THE TECHNICAL BEAUTY OF
ZABRISKIE POINT

Despite the story, the themes, and the acting, Antonioni's vision of America is quite beautiful: especially memorable are the "orange-in" of the student meeting; the billboards of downtown Los Angeles flattened by the telephoto lens, especially the one showing two farmers doing in a pig; and the contours of Death Valley. The detailing of the exploding house is magnificent in composition, if not in conception or meaning. Critics who needed something to praise in a film by a respected director marveled at the sheer beauty of the photography. John Simon, not an easy man to please, admired the shot of Allen at his desk, the shot of Daria among the cactuses as she mourns Mark's death, the shot of the trash can labeled No Oil, Please—which reminded him of Morandi, one of Antonioni's favorite painters—and the Edward Hopper–like shot of the small desert bar, a typically American "ultimate cranny of loneliness."[15]

But with characteristic integrity Antonioni rejected backhanded compliments that treated *Zabriskie Point* not as a fiction film but as a travelogue. He said (of the color, but the point could be extended to the whole visual appearance of the film): "You cannot argue that a film is bad but that the color is good or vice versa. The image is a fact, the colors *are* the story."[16] That is honestly said and all too true, and it is one of the risks that the visually gifted filmmaker runs. Narrative so dominates one's experience of a fiction film as to control one's final reaction to it. Indeed, the more physically beautiful a weakly plotted and acted film is, the more pretentious it strikes us. One almost wishes that the film had been suspended in

Frame 112

Frame 113

mid production and that the footage had come down to us unedited, like that of Eisenstein's Mexican film, so that each of us could have figured out how to put it together. The next best thing would be to watch the film without the sound track.

Speaking of Eisenstein, it is interesting to note that the final sequence of the exploding desert mansion very much resembles a device that Eisenstein used several times. The effect is striking because, as Gordon Gow notes,[17] its reliance on montage represents a great departure from Antonioni's usual style. One is reminded of the recurring plate-breaking sequence in *The Battleship Potemkin* or of the horse and carriage repeatedly sliding off the bridge in *October*. Rarely used, the device of repeating a shot becomes a convention, much like italics in type, to suggest general emotional intensification.

Zabriskie Point is clearly a troubled movie. One can sense the conflict with MGM, which, after all, epitomizes precisely the kind of power that director, writers, and characters were reacting against. (Antonioni even complained about the way the studio threw money at the production.) It was to be five years before he would finish his three-picture contract with MGM, and much was to happen in the meantime.

CHUNG KUO CINA (1972): Documentary Revisited

The third film that Antonioni made for MGM, *The Passenger,* was not completed until 1975. In the intervening five years, he shot only one film, a documentary on China. When the Chinese decided to solicit a Western film about their country, they compiled a list of the world's leading filmmakers, and from that list they chose Antonioni. It would be interesting to know their reasons. It seems unlikely that they had seen *Gente del Po* or *N.U.;* perhaps they felt that the director of *Zabriskie Point* was revolutionary enough to honor their cause. At any rate, Antonioni received the official invitation. He accepted it without reservations and did not undertake his task lightly: in the introduction to the published screenplay,[18] he writes of the need to avoid the "temptation of China," contrasting his juvenile fantasies about the place (visual, not political) with the reality that he found. As could be expected, his hosts had already formed their own ideas about what he should shoot, and he describes vividly three days of tough negotiations about his itinerary. Though acknowledging that much of his footage was controlled by the Chinese, he observes philosophically that he probably would not have gotten closer to the truth if he had had a free hand. What the authorities permitted him to see "was propaganda, but it was not a lie . . . The 'representations' are evidently the image that the Chinese want to give of themselves, and it is not an image radically different from the reality of the country."[19]

Despite his disclaimers, Antonioni clearly attempted to draw as comprehensive a picture of China as a "mere tourist" could in so short a time. He shot thirty

Frame 114

thousand meters of film in twenty-two days in Peking and vicinity, in a mountain village in the Linhsien district of Honan, in a valley of the Yangtze, in Suchow, in Nanking, and in Shanghai. He filmed factory workers, farmers, market people, river people, soldiers, schoolchildren, acrobats, and, everywhere, indiscriminately, pedestrians, by the tens and hundreds and thousands. He shot a cesarean birth in which the only anesthetic was acupuncture. He tried to shoot a funeral but was told it was too private a matter, so he had to content himself with shots of the grave digging.

The organizing principle of the film? North to south perhaps. Or inland capital to chief seaport. Or the present amid memories of the past. Or the activities of life—working, eating, resting, talking, being entertained, taking physical exercise. Or the ages of man. Antonioni manages to braid these themes into a seamless three and one-half hour package—his longest film. The prevailing mood? Mostly joy, the joy of song and dance and mass exercise—old style (Tai Chi) and new (Mao's own calisthenic regimen) side by side, impromptu, in the streets, and in empty lots.

Inevitably for this kind of exploratory documentary, the dialogue is of a directly instructional kind. The voice-over speaks regularly, but sparely, in the manner of the early documentaries. It translates conversation, songs, banners, and wall slogans. And it explains images: for instance, a visit is paid to the apartment of a couple who work in a factory. As we see the couple unpacking groceries, we are told that their rent is fixed, as everywhere in China, at five percent of salary. But there is no unnecessary redundancy between image and voice: indeed, the image track seems sometimes to be quite independent. For instance, as we hear the housewife's soft voice and the clatter of her sewing machine, the camera explores the bedroom—the bed, a lamp, a white bust of Mao, the little red book. Such sequences, though they are not frequent, evoke some of the old Antonionian raptness at the minor mysteries of life, quite independent of the explicit task of the film: to give an account of a country whose exotic culture and politics have suddenly become accessible. More often, interpretations are made and historical explanations are offered. The voice tells us that the acupuncture needles do not really hurt, that Buddhist temples have been closed or turned into factories or museums, that a woman hobbling along had her feet bound when she was an infant. Occasionally, the visual image seems chosen only to exemplify a generalization: we hear that Peking is an austere city and that its populace is homogeneous, and we see a crowd, all of whose members wear blue uniformlike clothing.[20]

Much of the explanation is historical. The voice tells us about the twelve men who met in a little room in 1921 to plot the Revolution (all except Mao soon dead or declared traitors); the Great Wall, more useful in peace than in war because it stops the winds of the steppes and thus helps agriculture; the vast network of canals and locks needed to irrigate the fields of China and the enormous effort that was required to build them; the grandiose temples and pavilions that the ancient regime built in the Forbidden City; even, amusingly, Marco Polo's discovery of Chinese pasta ("They thought of everything: even fettucini"). Value judgments are few, but they are pointed and apt: that the society looks "poor but not miserable, without luxury but also without hunger"; that the Chinese discuss things passionately but tend to be repetitive and monotonous; that urbanization is discouraged, though building on the outskirts of cities continues to flourish; that the Cultural Revolution places political fidelity ahead of professional competence. The frankest comments are reserved for Antonioni's own experiences, especially for his frustration at not being allowed to photograph what he wished. At one point, he became so upset by the restrictions that he literally threw himself out of a moving car and, against the wishes of his guide, managed to photograph an impromptu "capitalist" black market in which country people got together to buy and sell little trinkets. On other occasions, he successfully hid his camera and photographed scenes that had not been approved in advance by the authorities. His most wistful and philosophical comment concerns the shy curiosity of the people in the tiny mountain village in Hunan that he visited: he recognizes that it is he and his crew who are the strange ones in this environment, with their round eyes, thick hair, long and bony noses, faded skin, extravagant gestures, and awkward-looking clothes.

The camera work in the film bears more relation to the circumstances of shooting than to Antonioni's usual style. He wanted to convey the sense of being a tourist in China. That need, along with the constraint of traveling in government

Frame 115

Frame 116

cars, resulted in the many tracking shots that sweep along streets following bicyclists, trucks laden with people, rickshaws, hand-pushed or towed wagons of many kinds, young people marching, and hordes of pedestrians. The camera gives us a sense of surprised discovery, not so much of objects and environments as of people: their faces and their behavior at the exercises in which "they move rhythmically, as following a music which no one else can hear." The close-ups on faces are inquiring, as if Antonioni hoped to pry some secret from skin and eyes and hair. But what the camera saw was serenity, placidity, at most curiosity. The voice-over says (as if it had learned by hard experience): "Emotions and miseries are almost invisible in China, circumscribed by modesty and reserve." And the faces, especially of young people, always show vigor and strength. The film teems with physical activity, mass athletics, exercise for the joy of it. Though they use little or no equipment, the Chinese exude fitness. In retrospect we see how heavily Antonioni's delicate art of fictional portraiture depends on context: the faces of Sandro and Claudia, Giovanni and Lidia, Piero and Vittoria, even at their most impassive, are made somewhat legible by the story in which they participate. But these Chinese faces are genuinely enigmatic: it is as if the whole film reluctantly concludes that the Orient is as inscrutable as *The New Yorker* jokingly maintains.

On a few occasions, the conditions of shooting seem to have been open and tranquil enough to allow Antonioni to compose a shot, and the results are reminiscent of the style of his feature films. The camera makes something of the many visitors to the Great Wall. There is a nice shot of a boy carrying water through a narrow street in the village of Ta Zei Tuan and a haunting composition of an immobile old man in a china shop (not unlike the old man in the antique shop in *Blow-Up*). One is tempted to call it an Antonionian *temps mort*. What is evoked, perhaps, is the "other" story, the story of the old China, almost forgotten or, if

Frame 117

remembered, remembered only by the elderly. The immobile man seems to be one more monument, silent, pagodalike, a mere shadow of his former self. For an Italian, the relics of past glories must seem particularly poignant.

The film goes back and forth between geographic and ideological depths and over absolute surfaces. Again, the telephoto lens is employed to flatten crowds into a single plane. The zoom lens is also often used, in an expressive movement of inquiry, as if to capture the detail that perhaps will explain things. But it seems always to fail. It even seems to sense that failure is inevitable. One taciturn face pulled out of the crowd will show no more than any other.

But Antonioni remains faithful to his credo, announcing in the introduction, "I still believe, after so many years in the cinema, that images have meanings." That remark was made in response to the know-nothing attitude of certain Italian Maoists who, he had reason to believe, had never been to China. Antonioni invited them with polite irony to go there. He quoted a radical reviewer, who had written of his film, "Enough of documentaries: long live the Chinese Republic." To which Antonioni replied, "Is it still possible to shoot a documentary?" The film itself shows that the answer is yes, but it is still worth quoting his sensible and vigorous words:

I do not know what I am supposed to think when I read in a review that "socialism is not something which you can see" and that "once we understand that the revolution is a mental and material and moral but not necessarily visible thing, it cannot be made into a documentary by Antonioni, or by Ivens, or into a feature film by Godard." The author of this review, a usually serious and committed writer, looked closely at the film, recorded a large number of particulars, recognized that it is an "honest monologue," and then concluded "Enough with film documentaries and long live the Chinese Republic." As if there were a cause-and-effect relationship between the death of the documentary and the long life of the Chinese Republic. But to understand the intentions of this review, one must draw a conclusion that I refute, namely that all forms of cinema are empty of meaning and that for "the most bourgeois and positivisitic of the arts" it is impossible to do better. If the film of Antonioni is wrong, the fault belongs to Antonioni, not to the faceless fantasm that is "cinema," the abstract conception of the cinema.[21]

From the point of view of distribution, *Chung Kuo Cina* has had a sad fate. It was the most ravaged foreign victim of the Chinese Cultural Revolution. In 1973, the regime officially condemned it and accused Antonioni of maligning the country. Indeed, Chinese officials seemed to single him out as a leading culprit in what they took to be a widespread foreign conspiracy against China. One finds little in the film to warrant the violence of their condemnation. There may be unintended slights that neither we nor Antonioni—not being experts on China—could easily understand. The best discussion of the question is in an amusing essay by Umberto Eco entitled, "De Interpretatione, or the Difficulty of Being Marco Polo," written after Eco consulted with a Chinese film critic at the Venice Film Festival. Eco reminds us that Antonioni is not only a Western artist but one "particularly inclined to plumb the depths of existential problems and to emphasize the representation of personal relationships rather than abstract dialectical problems and the class struggle" and that he does so "by stressing the inessential, the secondary episode charged with multiple meanings and subtle ambiguities."[22] It is not surprising that Chinese ideologues would fail to understand the motives behind such treatment of the daily life of ordinary people, reading into it notes of deprecation that the artist never intended. For instance, where Antonioni wants to celebrate Chinese austerity and enforced frugality in what to us are near utopian terms, the Chinese read a damning of their economic achievement with faint praise:

where[as] the Chinese see a suddenly acquired collective "fortune," the film commentary speaks . . . about a serene and just "poverty." Where[as] the film means "simplicity" for "poverty," the Chinese viewer reads "miseria" and failure. When his Chinese escorts told Antonioni, with pride, that a refinery had been built from nothing, using scavenged material, the film emphasizes the miracle of "this humble factory, made with discarded materials"—and western taste for the ingeniousness of *bricolage,* to which we currently attribute esthetic value, is at play . . . But the Chinese see in it an insistence on an 'inferior' industry, just at the historical moment in which they are successfully closing their industrial gap.

In short, "Antonioni's film presents a tender, docile picture. For us, gentleness is opposed to neurotic competition, but for the Chinese that docility decodes as resignation." Similarly, "Antonioni explores with realistic gusto the faces of the old and of children . . . [but] Chinese revolutionary art is not realistic, it is symbolic, and [it] presents, in posters as in film, an 'ideal type' that goes beyond ethnic characteristics."[23] That ideal type is a strong man or woman in splendid physical condition carrying a gun. Pictures of old people and children, no matter how healthy and well-fed, do not project the model of militancy that was official in China in 1972. Their reaction to Antonioni's film resembles one we might have to a communist film called *America* that showed only skid row and ghetto types.

Eco also points out some interesting formal aspects of the cross-cultural misunderstanding. To Chinese eyes, Antonioni's sharply angled and tilted shot of the Nanking bridge might seem "distorted and unstable, because a culture which prizes frontal representation and symmetrical distance shots cannot accept the language of western cinema which, to suggest impressiveness, foreshortens and frames from below, prizing dissymmetry and tension over balance." As for the sequence in Tien An Men Square, the largest square in the world, the shot may seem to the Chinese "the denunciation of swarming mass disorder, while for Antonioni such a shot is the picture of life, and an ordered shot would be the picture of death, or would evoke the Nuremberg stadium [in *Triumph of the Will*]." The meaning of straight cut editing seems to have been misunderstood: "Antonioni shows the vestiges of feudal superstition, [then cuts to] students returning to work in the fields, spades slung over their shoulders, and the post-'68 viewer thinks that that is justice: the Chinese critic sees another logic (today, too, students work hard in the fields as they did in the past) and becomes indignant." Even the lovely pastel colors that to Western eyes so beautifully capture the soft and delicate haze of the Chinese atmosphere became cause for complaint. They were "denounced . . . as unbearably pale and cold, and rightly so, if you compare a film like *Red Detachment of Women,* where extremely bright colors acquire a precise linguistic value and directly symbolize ideological positions."[24]

Chung Kuo Cina was shown on RAI, Italian state television, and in America on the ABC television network. Since then, few people have seen it. RAI has the rights and has not elected to release the film commercially. (The only copy I was able to see was Antonioni's own.) But the story may have a happy ending. On November 18, 1980, the Chinese publicly apologized to Antonioni on the occasion of the beginning of an Italian film on Marco Polo. Antonioni was satisfied, and there was talk of his making another film about China. Let us hope that RAI will now muster its courage and rerelease the full three and one-half hour version on a worldwide basis to theaters as well as to television.

The Passenger
and *Il mistero di Oberwald*

The Passenger (or *Profession: Reporter,* as it was called in Europe) was the last film that Antonioni made under his three-film contract with MGM. It was not his screenplay, and it was based not on one of his own sketches but on the story "Fatal Exit" by Mark Peploe. Still, Antonioni found Peploe's story highly congenial to his temperament and expressive desires.

It resembles the ill-fated screenplay *Technically Sweet* (published in Italian as *Tecnicamente dolce*),[1] abandoned after two years of preproduction literally on the eve of shooting in the jungles of Brazil. Antonioni had written the treatment in 1966 and later wrote the screenplay in collaboration with Peploe, Niccolò Tucci, and Tonino Guerra. Antonioni feels that *Technically Sweet* might well have been his masterpiece. The Italian edition of the screenplay contains stills of the locations that he had chosen in Sardinia and along the Amazon. Jack Nicholson and Maria Schneider had agreed to star in the film, and Antonioni had solved some enormous logistical problems (for instance, how to light the primordial darkness of the deep jungle). Then Carlo Ponti, the producer, "suddenly and inexplicably" called the film off.[2] Antonioni had planned to shoot it with color-mixing television cameras, with techniques similar to those he used later in *Il mistero di Oberwald*. The title was taken from a remark by J. Robert Oppenheimer that he had worked on the atomic bomb because of the "technically sweet" theoretical problems that it posed.

Antonioni has observed that a film not actually shot does not exist, that scenarios have no autonomy, that they are dead pages. This is particularly true for a director who does so much composing in the act of shooting. Still, *Technically Sweet* is worth studying not only in its own right, but because it shows why Antonioni was attracted to the story that became *The Passenger*. *Technically Sweet,* like *The Passenger,* contains some interesting innnovations in narrative structure, particularly in the handling of time. It is built on a system of crosscutting between a Now story, of T.'s meeting with a Girl and her anthropologist boyfriend S. on Sardinia, and flashforwards to a Later story, of his adventures on the Amazon with S. after their plane crashes. (I try to preserve the discourse-time relation between these two series of events in my paraphrase.)

The story opens on a street in Rome. A newspaper vendor quarrels with a customer. T. stands in front of a gun shop and meditates the meaning of good marksmanship. Back at home, he tries to send an insulting telegram to his boss, but the telephone operator will not accept it because of the profanity. At the airport in Sardinia, he sees the Girl and is picked up in a jeep by his friend A. Cut to the first Amazon sequence: a light plane containing the pilot, S., and T. flies low over the jungle. Cut back to Sardinia, a shooting reserve overlooking the sea: while skeet shooting with a millionaire land developer, T. is enraged at the sight of a boat fishing with dynamite. He fires at it. One figure on the boat remains standing: it is S., the developer's twenty-three-year-old son, out on the boat to irritate his father. T. makes friends with S. even as he has an affair with the Girl, who is S.'s mistress and remains so during her affair with T. (Neither S. nor the Girl suffers from jealousy; as in *Blow-Up* and *Zabriskie Point,* the casual sexual attitudes of youth are implicitly praised.)

Over the Amazon, the plane's motor falters, and the pilot warns T. and S. to don parachutes. Back in Sardinia: T. meets the Girl, who has just bought a knife (she does not know why: the aimless, oracular quality of the dialogue resembles the dialogue between David and the Girl in *The Passenger*). They begin to make love. Flashforward to the jungle: the plane crashes, the pilot is killed, but T. and S. survive; T. is angry at his plight but tells S. that it is his own fault; besides, no one is waiting for him. There follows, interspersed with the Sardinian story, an account of the adventures of T. and S. in the jungle: hunting an armadillo without success, cutting open a plant for the fresh water inside, eating bits of jaguar meat, fighting off ants, getting caught in rapids and a waterfall, and so on.

In Sardinia, between bouts of lovemaking, T. gives S. shooting lessons; for T., marksmanship is a way of life, a "moral exercise, a spiritual fact which puts him in limpid and direct rapport with things."[3] "You must get to the point where you don't know any longer if you are the target, the marksman, or the bullet." In fact, the goal is ultimately to shoot without a gun. T. wanders about the Sardinian village (some of the description is reminiscent of the Spanish town of Osuna, where Locke meets his fate in *The Passenger*). T. has dinner with S. and the Girl, and they behave as if nothing were happening. Later, the three sail to an islet off the coast. On the way, they notice a periscope sticking up out of the water. The Girl is outraged at the invasion of privacy, and T. characteristically points his gun at it. As they approach, it disappears. Explosions can be heard in the distance; S. senses that naval exercises are taking place, and they leave hastily. On the islet, they reach the home of S.'s friends, a scientist and his wife (the latter exhibits "typically neurotic gestures and expressions"). The husband has been out recording the sounds of mullet. Inside, a strange accident occurs: the wires of the fish tank have crossed with those of the record player, and the fish have been electrocuted. Two others are staying there, a twenty-nine-year-old woman and the scientist's male assistant. The latter starts flirting brazenly with the Girl, and she seems to encourage him. The discussion turns on spying, then the scientist plays his tapes of fish sounds. Flashforward to the jungle: S. and T. sit at their fire, and

Frame 118

T. speaks a line that appears as an epigraph on the title page: "There is a theory that man lives in a state of instability, which through the years becomes more and more stable, until he achieves equilibrium, which is death."

Sardinia: desiring to be alone, T. goes into the scientist's park. He meets a young intruder, whom he threatens to shoot; then he returns to the house. A discussion is in progress about whom one would kill if he or she had a chance. The Girl says that she would kill herself, "because I don't want to repeat myself." When asked whom he would kill, T. says that he has just killed someone; then denies it. Actually, he offered the prowler his gun, but the startled man only ran off. In private, the Girl tells T. about her mother, who has cancer. He says he must leave in a day or two to go back to work. Jungle: the two men hack their way through spiderwebs. They hear a jet airliner above them; S. climbs to the top of a tree, but the plane is gone. Cut to the airliner: lunch is being served, and the stewardess casually points out that they are passing over the virgin forest of the Amazon. Sardinia: T.'s voice-over wonders whether he should join S., and then notes: "Those idiots think they've hurt me by ruining my apartment." Cut to his apartment in Rome: T. and A. are looking stunned at the ruin left by vandals (presumably political enemies).[4] The loss of all his possessions seems not unwelcome to him. "It's better that way," he tells the Girl; "I have changed skins, like the snakes."

Jungle: convinced that they will not get out alive, T. asks what happened back at the scientist's house when S. and the Girl quarreled. S. tells him, in voice-over against a flashback of the actual scene, that the scientist's wife wants to have a baby, but the scientist is impotent. The Girl offers to help; she visits the couple's room while they lie naked in bed; she takes off her clothes as the couple start making love, becoming the object of the husband's fascinated gaze (one is reminded of the scene of voyeurism in *Blow-Up*). The Girl becomes troubled by what is happening, but the husband's glance tells her to come closer so he can touch her. But once he does so, she hurries from the bedroom to the living room, where she attacks S. (Why is it his fault?) The day after, the Girl tells S. that she wants to end their relationship. Sardinia: at her mother's wish, the Girl calls the *New York Times* to see if there is a cure for cancer; a tough-talking reporter hangs up in disgust. That afternoon, the Girl leaves with her mother, telling T. that he no longer needs her, "because in the fire at his apartment he has lost everything that is no longer useful to him."

The Sardinian story ends there, and the final scenes take place in the jungle. By chance, T. and S. discover a notch in a tree that only a knife could have made. They hear rustling and realize that they are in grave danger.[5] Suddenly an arrow thuds into a nearby tree trunk. Nothing else is visible. They begin to run. S., the younger, gets farther and farther ahead and finally disappears. T. realizes that he is finished; "his eyes, filled with tears of rage, [are] fixed on a wild orchid just nearby." The camera joins S. He hears a shout and a gunshot, but "not a muscle in his face moves." He runs until he, too, falls, near a hole full of vermin, which begin to crawl over his hand.

The last scene is brilliantly conceived, in the best tradition of Antonioni's strong finales. The camera cuts to a vast savanna, which begins at the edge of the jungle. The grass is neatly trimmed, and wide asphalt roads stretch to the horizon. A group of children, between eight and ten years old, have organized a game, "or more than a game, a sport exercise." Led by a fourteen-year-old, with whom they communicate by wireless telephones, they have constructed an ingenious net trap at the edge of the jungle. There is an opening, and once an animal enters the opening, the trap is sprung, and the net closes. They all look off to the forest: "Something [is] crawling slowly on the grass. They still cannot tell what kind of animal it is. Everybody is silent, waiting . . . The animal, however, stops. It cannot go any farther. It is exhausted. It has dragged itself along the ground by its nails. With difficulty we see that it is S. . . . he drags himself forward . . . he sees a drawn rope before him . . . a familiar object . . . The trap sprung, the opening closes. The children smile with satisfaction. They follow his movement with cold curiosity. They have recognized in this being a man, but this only increases their interest . . . The man does not have the strength to open his mouth and call for help. He holds out his hand and waits. But the children do not move . . . They watch his agony with much attention, as a lesson in natural history. It is one sight they have never seen, the death of a man . . . Supine, [S.] looks at the sky, which becomes bluer and bluer and then becomes rose. The rose gets concentrated into a spot, which takes the form of a house: the red house [in which S. lived in Sardinia], and on the threshold [there is] a figure, whom he recognizes as the Girl."

Many characters in Antonioni's earlier films yearn to escape to exotic places. Antonioni recently admitted the autobiographical implications of this ongoing theme: "I felt a sort of obscure dissatisfaction, the need . . . to get out of the historical context in which I live and in which the characters also live, that is, civic and civilized, to enter a different context, like the jungle or the desert, where one could at least imagine a freer and more personal life."[6] In *Technically Sweet* and *The Passenger*, the heroes do in fact make their escape, only to find, looming beyond that remote wasteland, the ultimate haven—death itself. The connection suggests moral or psychoanalytic meditations that I will not venture. Suffice it to say that for these men, both of whom feel they have nothing more to lose, escape has a more profound connotation than it does for Antonioni's earlier characters. T.'s metaphoric "change of skin" will become all too literal for David Locke and lead to consequences as inevitable as the fates of the heroes of Greek tragedy.

Another theme carried over from earlier films is the precariousness of civilization. But whereas *La notte* and *Il deserto rosso* touch upon the environmental impact of industrial society and the prospect of technological annihilation, *Technically Sweet* is preoccupied with more explicitly ecological issues: the destruction of fish with dynamite, the pollution of the Mediterranean with oil from vessels, and so on. But there is an interesting and possibly unresolved irony. T.'s answer to these assaults on the environment is a form of the theory of the survival of the fittest. There is nothing wrong, he argues, with hunting game and even with enjoying the kill if it is done one on one (T. would be an ardent member of the

American gun lobby). In a deleted sequence, he speaks such lines as the following: "Look how [the pigeon] comes down, with what elegance. Its flight is a massacre of insects, yet it is something very harmonious. . . . Now I'll shoot it, and that is natural in the animal reign to which we belong: slay and make love, kill and couple [a pun in the Italian: *accopparsi e accoppiarsi*]. I follow the law of nature, like the pigeons, the fish, the insects, the law of the strongest. So, now I shoot."[7] In the jungle, these words shall echo all too ironically in T.'s ears; a vivid stage direction describes the scene: "Filthy as [T. and S.] are, with clothes that have now taken on the color of the vegetation which engulfs them, they are no more than two organisms in a struggle with other organisms." In another stage direction, they are described as being as helpless and vulnerable as "larvae." Outside its own environment, even the most highly evolved species cannot compete with the native organisms.

As we have seen, the theme of violence that emerged in *Zabriskie Point* persists in *Technically Sweet*. But unlike Mark, T. has very much suppressed—perhaps he would say sublimated—his compulsion. Shooting at targets, at skeets (like shooting with a camera!) represents a respectable out for the civilized man. T. turns it into one of the fine arts, into a kind of yoga or spiritual practice. (In *The Passenger,* the question becomes even more theoretical; the hero is only fortuitously a trafficker in arms.) In the absence of a finished film, it is hard to know whether Antonioni intended irony or not. T. barely resists his impulse to shoot fishermen, periscopes, airplanes, and the like. (For what it is worth, Antonioni has said, "I am violent by nature. A doctor told me so when I was a boy. And I must give vent to this violence one way or another." He has also said, "I think that arms which are used by the oppressed against the oppressors are most civil instruments.")[8]

T. and David Locke share the frustration of the mere bystander. Both are journalists, men ever constrained to be mere witnesses, to report what others do, and never to do anything themselves.[9] For those who have strong views, this is a particularly unpleasant stance, since it involves them in passive complicity with the status quo. Part of the rationale of escape is surely that the exotic place will force them to take real action. In both instances, of course, it proves all too powerful a stimulus, one that overwhelms them.

It is easy to see Jack Nicholson in the part of T., a character not so different from David Locke. Antonioni has praised Nicholson's acting ability and the expressiveness of his "cold, North European" face. Maria Schneider also seems a good choice for the Girl. But in that role she would have resembled the heroine of *Last Tango in Paris* more than the character she plays in *The Passenger*. The Girl in *Technically Sweet* is not the comforting and even idealistic personage of the 1975 film. As we have seen, she is sexually unreliable, and she does not really provide T. with the kind of support that Locke gets from her counterpart. On the contrary, she breaks off with him, as with S., without any real explanation. Except for amatory moments, her dialogue is restricted to expressions of vague self-pity: "Everything I buy quickly becomes useless." "I feel bad, I'm too happy." "Everything I do is wrong." "I . . . have so many years ahead of me" (and then she is described as looking discouraged at the "chasm" of the years). "I'm an orphan. (Pause) That's not true, but it is as if I were." And so on. She has none of the healthy animal spirits of Daria or the slightly ironic buoyancy of the heroine of *The Passenger.* Like the scientist's neurotic wife, she seems to be a holdover from the films of the sixties. One wonders why S.'s dying vision is of her. Antonioni says about her, "She is an unrealized creature, with all the preoccupations, caprices, and insecurities of girls of that type."[10]

But S. is totally different. Antonioni describes him as "cold" and "secure." S. exudes such poise and self-confidence that ultimately T. finds himself more attracted to S. than to the Girl. Not sexually: rather, this seems to be the closest that Antonioni will come to portraying a deep and genuine friendship between men. "T. is amazed by the boy's calm, the security that impresses him as totally other than superficial. That boy, you see, makes him think."[11] And what does S. see in T.? Aside from the guidance that T. provides in learning to shoot, T. "mystifies him a bit, but . . . that pleases him!" As for indoctrinating S. into the yoga of marksmanship, "S. cannot follow him down that path. And perhaps his instinctive refusal has a weight in their relationship. At any rate, it is one of the reasons why T. nurtures a certain admiration for the boy. He does not want to be like him, but if he were, many of his problems would be resolved."[12]

No camera indications are given in the scenario of *Technically Sweet,* so we must speculate on the cinematic form that the film would have taken. As we have seen, Antonioni was clearly in a mood to experiment with narrative structure. "I had thought of a series of flashbacks that would give a sense of the lives of the two protagonists . . . but not so extensively. Then it occurred to me that the film 'was' the story of these two . . . With a series of flashforwards to the jungle, I began little by little to anticipate the destiny of these characters."[13] What seems particularly interesting in the temporal structure presented in the published screenplay is, as Aldo Tassone, its editor, has noted, that neither the present nor the future strand serves the other, not for the sake of suspense, explanation, analogy, or anything else. In their distinct autonomy and apparent randomness, the two temporal blocks comment on each other with delicate irony.

With Carlo Ponti's decision to terminate *Technically Sweet,* cinema may have lost one of its more interesting and innovative films.

THE PASSENGER:
"A Kind of Detachment"

David Locke (Jack Nicholson) is a British television reporter trying to make a documentary on a rebellion in a Central African country (Chad). He pulls into a village and, though ostensibly ignored by the inhabitants, is directed to a guide who will lead him to the rebel encampment. But the guide bolts when he sees a caravan of government troops. Utterly frustrated, Locke makes his way back to town on foot, leaving his Land Rover stuck in the sand. At his hotel, he discovers that a traveler with whom he has struck up an acquaintance, a man named Robertson (Chuck Mulvehill), has died suddenly of a heart attack. Locke bears a strong resemblance to Robertson, and in a matter of minutes Locke decides to assume the dead man's identity. All that he knows about Robertson comes from an appointment book and an airplane ticket: Robertson was planning to go to London, Munich, Barcelona, and the small Spanish town of Osuna.

In London, Locke's wife—now his presumed widow—Rachel (Jenny Runacre)· watches a television program in Locke's memory. Meanwhile, Locke, disguised by a mustache and dark glasses, enters his home (we can hear the television program from behind the door) and retrieves some papers. Cut to the Munich airport, where Locke rents an Avis car. Jokingly but prophetically, he says he will keep the car "the rest of my life." He discovers a leather envelope in a baggage locker (the key was among Robertson's effects); it contains illustrations of various military weapons. In his rented car, he follows a wedding carriage to a beautiful baroque church,[14] where he watches the ceremony. Afterward, in the church, he is approached by two men, Achebe (Ambroise Bia), a Chadian rebel leader, and his German contact. They express surprise that he did not recognize them at the airport, but they agree to the gun deal and give him a large sum of money.

In London, Rachel visits the studio of Knight (Ian Hendry), Locke's associate, who is trying to assemble a portrait of Locke by compiling selections from his programs. Rachel seems unenthusiastic about the footage on the moviola; she tells Knight that Locke lacked idealism and even integrity in dealing with reactionary leaders. We cut to a Barcelona restaurant: a Chadian diplomat and some thugs abduct (and presumably assassinate) Achebe. Locke arrives in Barcelona, where he is supposed to meet Achebe (under the code name "Daisy") in a covered garden, the Umbraculo, but Achebe does not show up. Back in London, at her lover's apartment, Rachel is preoccupied with Locke's death: she has some kind of premonition about him. Meanwhile, Knight has gone to Barcelona to ask Robertson about Locke's last moments. Locke sees him on the Ramblas and beats a quick retreat, first to a shoeshine parlor, then to a strange building that turns out to be Gaudí's Palacio Güell. Inside, he sees the Girl (Maria Schneider) reading in the same posture as when he first saw her on a bench in Bloomsbury. She is a student of architecture. He goes to Avis to rent another car and is stunned to learn that Knight has left a message for Robertson. He rushes to another Gaudí building, the apartment house La Pedrera, hoping to find the Girl. He meets her on its weird roof, where he explains that he wants to avoid someone who is looking for him and asks her to retrieve his baggage from his hotel. She agrees, then packs her own bag and leaves with him. On the road, she asks what he is running away from; he tells her to look behind her: the road, the past, stretches out behind them. They enjoy an idyllic trip down the coast.

Meanwhile, Rachel has received Locke's effects; the passport photo is Robertson's, not her husband's, and she realizes that Locke is alive. Since Knight has not found Robertson, she inquires about him at the Chadian consulate; the Chadian diplomat is, of course, very interested and orders his men to follow Rachel, convinced that she will lead them to the gunrunner. Rachel realizes that she made a mistake by confiding in the diplomat and that she has placed Locke in jeopardy. She flies to Spain and contacts the Spanish police. In Almeria, Locke and the Girl check into a hotel, but Locke sees Rachel making a call in a telephone booth. He rushes off with the Girl, jumps into the car, and drives wildly off into the country-side. After escaping a roadblock, they have to abandon the car because the oil pan is damaged. Locke wants to give up the whole escapade and go to Tangier, but the Girl urges him to keep his appointment in Osuna: "Robertson made these ap-pointments," she says. To which Locke responds, "Robertson is dead." "But you're not," she answers. He agrees to stay but sends her off in a bus. He arrives at the Hotel de la Gloria only to discover that "his wife" has preceded him: it is the Girl. Stretched out on the bed, he tells her a depressing story about a man who was blind until he was forty and then recovered his sight; no one had told him how ugly the world was, and after three years he killed himself. Then he says that she had better leave. She goes outside, and we can see her in the wide street in front of the hotel. The camera begins a long slow track towards the window. Locke's face goes off camera as the camera moves inexorably forward. Soon all of him that is visible is his feet, which he turns away from the window. As the camera con-tinues forward, a black Citroën pulls up, and two Chadian agents get out; one moves toward the hotel, and the other moves toward the Girl, as if to flirt with her; she will have none of him. Muffled sounds can be heard over—"something

Frame 119

falling, a chair, scraping metal, probably a gun." But by now the camera has passed through the window (between the bars!), and the sounds from the room are first muffled, then covered by sounds from the street—"a passing truck, a radio, some shouts." A driver-training car putters about. Then a police car appears; Rachel, Knight, and two policemen run to the hotel entrance. Finally, having made a complete loop, the camera moves along the outside of the hotel and focuses through the barred window on the body of Locke lying face up on the bed. A policeman asks Rachel if she recognizes him; she says she never knew him. He asks the Girl if she knows him, and she says yes. The film ends with a tranquil shot of the Hotel de la Gloria at dusk, in "another of those Antonioni 'still lifes,' mysteriously reverberant with the sense of something momentous and ineffable which has taken place and left its residue."[15]

THE DOPPELGÄNGER AND DEATH

The philosophical and psychological preoccupations of The Passenger differ from those of Antonioni's two other MGM films. Instead of the relation between the individual and visual reality or between the individual and capitalist society, The Passenger, in Antonioni's words, is about "the relation . . . of the individual with himself."[16] The film bases its meditation on selfhood on a motif familiar to students of Romantic literature: the doppelgänger, the double or counterpart. Thus, Antonioni's film fits into the tradition of works by E. T. A. Hoffmann, Edgar Allan Poe, Oscar Wilde, and Guy de Maupassant. Particularly interesting parallels can be found with Luigi Pirandello's Il fu Mattia Pascal (The Late Mattia Pascal) and Hanns Ewers' famous silent film The Student of Prague.[17]

Like Romantic heroes who sell their shadows to the devil or change their identity in other bizarre ways, Locke lives to regret his decision. Ironically, he himself acknowledges the impossibility of escaping one's fate even before his strange opportunity arises:

LOCKE: It's we who remain the same. We translate every situation, every experience, into the same old codes. We condition ourselves.
ROBERTSON: We're creatures of habit. That's what you mean.
LOCKE: Something like that. However hard you try, it stays so difficult to get away from your old habits.

Otto Rank explains doppelgängerism in these terms: "The 'basic idea' is supposed to be that a person's past inescapably clings to him and that it becomes his fate as soon as he tries to get rid of it."[18] As much as David tries to shake his past, especially his wife, who does not love him and who ultimately denies even that she knows him, fate makes her follow and unwittingly betray him.

But the principal "bad habit" (to use his own phrase) that Locke cannot shake

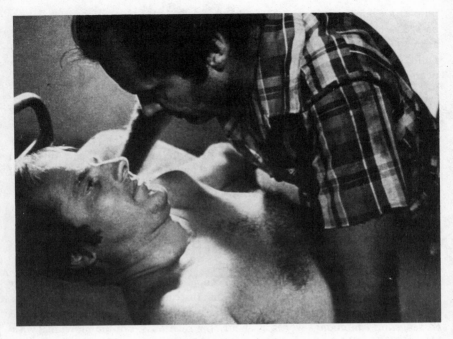

Frame 120

is his world-wariness and sense of futility, which find vivid expression in the parable of the blind man. It is not difficult to understand Antonioni's attraction to Mark Peploe's story. We have already noted the Faustian bargain in *Blow-Up*. In an interview about *The Passenger*, he asked rhetorically, "Who hasn't contemplated, once in his life, changing his skin?"[19] Nor is the double a new preoccupation: *L'avventura*, as we saw, turns on the notion that one person can "stand in" for another. The scenes in which Claudia puts on Anna's blouse and Patrizia's wig have counterparts in *The Passenger* in the startling shots of a bare-chested Locke dragging a bare-chested Robertson, almost in an embrace, to his room. But there are important differences: physical resemblance is obviously more crucial to the plot of *The Passenger*. To underline the resemblance, Antonioni accentuates the parallelism of the two deaths by adding commentative music of an indigenous cast—the African flute, the Spanish guitar—and by the motif of the open French windows. Further, while Claudia is the unwitting inheritor of Anna's problem (namely Sandro), Locke consciously assumes Robertson's situation. It is precisely the mystery of the existence of the other that attracts him. In his case, the doubler picks the doublee, rather than vice versa. Of course, that leaves him utterly subject to the vicissitudes of Robertson's fate—as is appropriate to a philosophical tale. Also unlike *L'avventura*, in which the interchangeability of lives is

Frame 121

presented as a social phenomenon, *The Passenger* explores the nature of identity as an existential problem. It does not critique a superficial society in which roles can be put on like new clothes but, rather, demonstrates the impossibility of genuinely changing identity. Of course, Locke could have taken the money and run to Tangier, but then he would have betrayed his original intention, the projected fantasy—the voyeuristic excitement, if you will—of immersing himself in the intimate details of another man's life. The encouragement that he receives from the Girl to live up to Robertson's appointments is merely a reminder of what he himself had decided in the hotel room in Chad.

The parallel with *Technically Sweet* is also evident. Not that T. tries to assume S.'s identity, but he certainly admires S.'s approach to life enough to drop everything and follow him off to the jungle. And like T., Locke bears the professional burden of bystanderhood, of being a passive witness to events: so "one can understand that he could be driven to taking over someone else's identity if the occasion presented itself" and not only that person's identity "but also his role, his political role."[20]

The theme of the double is tied inextricably to the theme of death. Robertson knows that his weak heart will finish him off sooner rather than later. He is not afraid of dying. Admiring the landscape, he waxes poetic: "So still. A kind of waiting." For him, death is a natural occurrence, something that takes place in nature, something for which one waits. Locke absorbs this lesson when he as-

Frame 122

sumes Robertson's identity. But even before that, his face seems to show the mark of death. Nicholson wonderfully communicates the degree to which the character is ruled by Freudian *morbido,* or death instinct, in a way of speaking and moving that is slightly too deliberate, even forced, as if with each gesture the man barely resists the impulse to lie down and let accumulated waves of defeat roll over him, to cry to heaven, as he does kicking the tires of his marooned Land Rover: "All right, I don't care." At the same time, death for Locke, as for Robertson, becomes a philosophical, not a psychological, matter. He is not particularly neurotic, not suicidal in the ordinary sense. Rather, he is world-weary, like a Romantic hero. Locke has seen enough of the world. Even the opportunities of another life shared with the likes of Maria Schneider cannot alter his basic melancholy. So he decides that nothing will and accepts his fate. For him, death is liberation. Hence the muffling of his violent end. Hence, too, the preparations throughout the film: renting a car "for the rest of his life";[21] divesting himself of useless pretenses like the false mustache; "flying" with his outspread arms in the cable car over Barcelona Bay;[22] asking directions of an old man seated under a huge white cross (clearly a "station" of the cross). Whatever lightness of attitude survives his melancholy is the product, we feel, of his acceptance of death. Nicholson's performance delicately mixes the two moods.

Locke is very much a man in transit, hence the appropriateness of the film's American title. He, not the Girl, is the passenger, as when we say that someone has "passed." And Avis is the up-to-date facilitator of that more profound passage. (As in "Il provino" and *Blow-Up* Antonioni makes a little joke with the capital letter "*A*." It stands not only for Antonioni but also for the Author behind it all, "paring his fingernails," as Joyce would say.) Still, it is not insignificant that his rented car breaks down and that Locke has to be carried by taxi to his last stop, the Hotel de la Gloria. One other interesting detail suggests Locke's unconscious preparation for his passing. He is asked twice to admire the landscape, first by Robertson on the veranda of their desert hotel, later by the Girl as they stand next to their broken-down car. The first time he refuses: "I'm interested in men more than landscapes." But the second time, just as Robertson, sensing his approaching death, recognized the beauty of nature, Locke in a similar mood says simply "Yes" to the Girl's praise for the dry Andalusian countryside.

Antonioni is clearly more interested in conveying the sheer experience of an exchange of identity and the liberation of death than in accounting for aspects of the character's background that provoke his need for such experience. Exposition is no more important in this than in his previous films. The tire-kicking scene is symptomatic, but it does not argue that Locke's misery issues from this particular assignment. Like Brando's cry "Fucking God" in the opening scene of *Last Tango in Paris,* it functions as a sign of far deeper despair than what any single event can provoke. Still, it "tells us all we need to know about the character at this point in his life."[23] Antonioni is so little concerned with motivation that he muffles the sound track of the television program in Locke's memory, during which colleagues discuss his character in revealing detail (for example, one says, "Locke wanted to be involved but didn't know how"). What he was like as a person seems almost incidental to his fate.

Antonioni departs radically from the more melodramatic strain in the doppelgänger tradition. Death is presented not as a morbid state, not as the shocking consequence of violence, but as a natural function, as the state of tranquil equilibrium described by T. in *Technically Sweet.* The whole of the long slow penultimate shot out of the hotel room connotes that state; it is implicit in the very technique, the camera-steadying devices—gyroscopic stabilizers, huge cranes, and the like. Antonioni needed all that technology to ensure the smoothness of Locke's passing. Whose perception is the tracking shot supposed to convey? Is it Locke's? I think not. He has turned away from the window, first psychologically, when he asks the Girl what is happening outside as if he cannot bear rousing himself to see with his own eyes (he is already the blind man he has described), then physically, as he rolls over onto his left side and faces the door. So the point of view must be the camera's own. But to what end? If it were merely a question of rounding out the story, even on a tranquil note, so elaborate a shot would hardly be necessary. ᴛhe shot insists on an enormous degree of visual continuity, on an unbroken glide through time and space. Is it too fanciful to suggest that its function is to bear Locke's soul out of the room? Certainly there is a great sense of quiet release into the outdoors. Once the soul is let loose, the camera rejoins the world of the survivors, not only the relatives and associates of the dead man, but bystanders, chil-

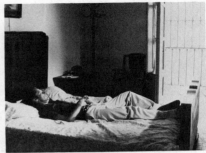

Frame 123

Frame 124

Frame 125

dren, those who are just learning to drive. It does so in a continuous movement as if to emphasize the unity of the universe. Soul is not religious or mystical; it has nothing to do with questions of afterlife. It suggests rather the biologism of *Technically Sweet,* which sees death as a transformation into other elements, ultimately into energy. Antonioni's view is comforting but unsentimental. It resembles the serenity of certain syntheses of science and religious tradition, like that of Alan Watts: "An enduring organism is simply one that is consistent with its environment. Its climate and its food agree with it; its pattern assimilates them, eliminating what does not agree, and this consistent motion, this transformation of food and air into the pattern of the organism, is what we call its existence. There is no mysterious necessity for this to continue or discontinue."[24] And, "death is the goal of life. Nonbeing fulfills being; it does not negate being, just as space does not negate what is solid. Each is the condition for the reality of the other."[25] Locke's death has very much this quality. It is more exemplary than tragic.[26]

Frame 126

QUESTIONING THE CODES:
The Passenger as
Self-Conscious Narrative

In *Citizen Kane,* the editor-in-chief complains that the film clips of "News on the March" that the staff have assembled do not add up to a convincing account of the life of Charles Foster Kane. Knight has the same problem assembling a portrait of David Locke from the footage at his disposal. We see three examples of Locke's work: an interview with a reactionary African ruler who assures him that the rebels have been defeated, a clandestine sequence showing the execution of a rebel leader (actual footage that Antonioni acquired from some undisclosed source), and an interview with a witch doctor who reverses roles with Locke, turning the camera on him as he says, "*Now* we can have a real interview."

Critics were quick to note that Locke's footage "queries the relationship between 'documentation' and political commitment." The shots of the execution, for instance, substitute for the real issues sensationalist "human interest," "the voyeurist newsreel . . . display[ing] no analytic or moral responsibility of any kind."[27] And in the interview with the witch doctor, Locke's voice and manner hint at the underlying condescension of the colonialist attitude, an attitude that leaves him at a loss for a response when the witch doctor turns the camera on him. The interview with the African ruler is even more revealing of the duplicity of media rendition of visual events. As a purveyor of television news, Locke accepts without demur the dubious answers that his questions receive. There is a clear difference between the facts as they reproduced by Locke's video camera and by Antonioni's film camera. In the video shot, the African ruler appears to be master of the situation: his disarmingly bespectacled, scholarly face dominates the screen in close-up, and his calm measured voice exudes a studied confidence ("There is no fighting anymore . . . a couple of hundred guns in the hands of some common bandits . . . There is no opposition; we are a unified nation"). But the real picture (corresponding to Rachel's memory of the scene), which is registered by the authorial camera, is quite different. The camera makes a 360–degree pan, suggesting that this is the full view and that Locke's video shot was only a small and misleading selection. Antonioni's shot begins with the face of Rachel, the critical onlooker, who remarks just before this flashback begins that David "wasn't any different" from the run-of-the-mill reporters who callously serve the system. The camera proceeds to show Locke kneeling in front of the African leader (though his head turns back questioningly toward Rachel). The pan continues, first picking up the leader, who says that peace has been restored; then we see soldiers, policemen, and servants, whose numbers belie this claim. Finally, the camera returns to Rachel's ironic face, thereby closing the loop and implying that now the full story has been told. It is the same kind of turnaround that the witch doctor performs.

The view, of course, is Rachel's, and we know that she had other (though unspecified) reasons for being dissatisfied with her husband. But Locke is no mere sellout: he did ask the African leader a touchy question about treatment of foreign nationals (though he was not very forceful in following up on it). A degree of servility was probably necessary if he wished to get the interview at all. Locke's participation may have been culpable, but it was understandably pragmatic. Besides, in his conversation with Robertson, he is conscious of his own colonialist attitudes: he says, "Even the way we talk to these people, the way we treat them, it's mistaken." Who knows? Perhaps Locke was the kind of man who felt that it is better to show what one can of the world's plight, even in the sensationalist television network terms forced on him, than it is to show nothing at all, just as it is better to make a pseudothriller for MGM than it is to make no film at all. And Locke finally does have the courage to opt out, though in a bizarre way.

The Passenger, of course, goes beyond an inquiry into television news reporting. It ponders the very means by which stories are told through visual media. On the face of it, *The Passenger* resembles *Zabriskie Point* in using a narrative design familiar to the movies since Griffith, that of parallel crosscutting. First we see Locke in the baroque church in Munich, then Rachel and Knight in the television

Frame 127   Frame 128

Frame 129

editing room in London, then the rebel leader Achebe being abducted in Barcelona, then Locke unsuccessfully searching for "Daisy" in the Umbraculo, then the television studio for more of Locke's unedited footage, and so on. The form is familiar, and it generates some traditional suspense, raising the question, Will Rachel be able to reach David before the Chadian assassins do? The question is urged by a not unconventional chase sequence, in which Rachel and the police pursue Locke's convertible across southern Spain from Almeria to Osuna. It is clear that Rachel's motive in seeking him is less to get him back than to warn him of the imminent peril. Indeed, in the hotel restaurant, he receives that message, relayed through the police and the Girl. But so single-mindedly bent is he on escaping the past that he fails to hear the new and genuine note of urgency in his wife's communication, or if he does hear it, his own death urge prevents him from listening carefully.

Thus, *The Passenger* differs from *L'avventura,* with which it has been compared, by adhering to the exigencies of suspense, at least nominally, whereas *L'avventura* simply loses interest in the search for the missing person. It also differs from *Blow-Up,* which ends inconclusively both about the murder and about Thomas's fate. Still, *The Passenger* is not a thriller: the possibilities of suspense are undercut by the inevitability and tranquility of Locke's death. Thrillers depend on a sense that there is something to be saved—a fair maiden, the secret position of the fleet, the plans, everything that Hitchcock means by "the Macguffin." Here, the cause—guns for rebels—is forgotten. Not only is the hero not saved, but the question of his salvation seems in some ways to be a red herring.

In exchange for suspense, *The Passenger* offers some narrative experiments. Though it does not exalt juggling with time—or "anachrony"[28]—into a structural principle, as does *Technically Sweet,* it makes effective use of flashbacks at certain interesting moments. The most spectacular is the early sequence in which Locke recalls his conversation with Robertson as he is forging his passport. The flashback enables Antonioni to show the men together and hence their striking resemblance in face and frame, thereby establishing the plausibility of the exchange of identity to come. That exchange is marked at the appropriate moment by a simple change of clothing: Locke trades his own plaid shirt for Robertson's solid blue jacketlike one (see Frame 121 above). The flashback dramatically enhances a scene that must proceed in silence. Locke's bizarre opportunity depends on Robertson's past, but we must be convinced of both the plausibility and the magic of the exchange of identity. The flashback format emphasizes the frailty and relativity of life: here one moment, gone the next, though reconstitutible in memory. It makes the circumstances of Locke's own approaching death more ironic and poignant. The effect would have been much flatter if the meeting between the two men had taken place in its "proper" place in the discourse, before Locke set out to look for the rebels. Both mysteries—that of the opening desert scene and that of his discovery of Robertson's body—would have been compromised.

Antonioni heightens the impact of the flashback in an unusual way. Instead of a straight cut or dissolve to the past, he uses a single sustained camera movement, a pan from the seated Locke, intent on his forgery, around the room and out onto the veranda, where we see him conversing with Robertson. A narrative discontinuity is conveyed by a cinematic continuity.[29] The pan argues not only that the camera can take us back in time but that it can do so as smoothly and as summarily as narrative can, that the few seconds of discourse time it entails can summarize a much longer period of story time—the day or so that has elapsed since Locke and Robertson had their drink and chat together. Thus it is less a flashback than a glideback. This novel effect raises some interesting questions about the meaning of time and its reality, questions appropriate to the theme of death as passage. The smoothness of the transition is particularly interesting as a precursor of the long tracking shot that ends the film. Just as the camera in the later shot can be said to move the memory of Locke to the outdoors, the flashback pan moves the memory of Robertson (in Locke's mind) to a similar place. Death is spatialized and smoothed as a movement out of a room, a confined space, through a window. Time, too, is spatialized and so (in a way) rendered powerless; the perceptions and the mind are set, rather, to eternity. This is not the kind of death that one expects to see in a thriller. But then *The Passenger* is not an ordinary thriller.

There is another interesting aspect of the same sequence: the visual flashback is apparently anticipated by an overlapping auditory flashback. First, we see Locke's passport containing his photograph; then, after a swish-pan, we see Robertson's, containing his. The next shot shows Locke's profile (though half his head is out of frame, as if the identity switch had already begun). During this shot we hear Locke in voice-over saying, "Come in." Another voice-over—it proves to be Robertson's—answers, "Sorry to barge in." Cut to an extreme close-up of Locke's passport, his hand, and a razor blade, with which he removes his own photograph. During this action, Locke says in voice-over, "Oh yes; come in. I saw you on the plane." Cut to another extreme close-up of Locke's face intent on his work: Robertson says in voice-over, "My name's Robertson." Here again, Antonioni plays with a convention and undercuts it. We assume from past movie experience that these voice-overs are in the head of the character who is remembering, that they are the auditory counterparts of visual mindscreen effects and a device for introducing the flashback material. So accustomed are we to this convention that a more literal explanation does not occur to us. So in the next shot we are surprised to see Locke's Uher tape recorder running. The dialogue has not been in Locke's mind at all—it is not in voice-over but comes from a perfectly natural source. (The original scenario obviated the surprise by beginning the scene with a shot of Locke turning the tape recorder on and locating the spot: we hear him in voice-over saying, "Wild track. Testing, one, two, three, four. Rhubarb, rhubarb, rhubarb." Antonioni dispensed with this explanatory stuff, presumably in the interest of sustaining the general mystery of the *doppelgänglich* situation.) The naturalism of the tape recorder makes us all the less prepared for the panning flashback that occurs just at this moment. Locke's face in profile looks up as if he were reliving the conversation; the camera pans left as Robertson's voice on the recorder says, "I'm here on business"; the camera moves to the window as Robertson's voice says, "I've been in so many places the last few years. It doesn't make any difference any more." We assume that we are still in Locke's point of view, that he is looking reflectively out the window. But no, for Robertson emerges in a blue shirt, followed by Locke in a plaid shirt. The flashback ends in a similar way: inside the room, Locke walks off frame left to get drinks, leaving the camera on Robertson, whose eyes follow him to the left. Then the camera leaves him and pans right until it finds Locke, in the present moment again, at the table, preparing the passports and listening to Robertson's voice on the tape recorder. The apparent discrepancy, of movement right rather than left, turns out to signal the glideback to the present. The camera is moving through time as well as through space. This transformation of the meaning of camera movements calls into question the nature of space, time, and, for that matter, mortality.

A second flashback in the film is quite different in conception but no less remarkable in effect. It goes from a shot of Locke in the Munich church to Locke "back then" burning leaves in his own front yard in London. It is marked conventionally, by a straight cut, but its meaning is more obscure. Locke is observing the wedding—then suddenly he is burning leaves with gusto, what seems to be a destructive smile playing on his lips. (In the scenario, not just leaves but other "old things" are burned—cartons, clothes, even a chair.) The flashback seems to function as Locke's commentary on marriage in general and on his own marriage in particular. In the next shot, Rachel rushes outdoors in her slip, puzzled by Locke's behavior. Then, to make the effect all the odder, the film cuts to a shot of Rachel standing fully dressed, looking out the window at the yard, where neither fire nor Locke are to be seen. We infer that the present story moment has been resumed and that, whether by accident or by telepathy, Rachel in London has recalled an old incident at precisely the moment when it crosses Locke's mind in Munich. She has no reason as yet to believe that he is still alive.

THE WANDERING CAMERA
AND THE MISLEADING CUT

As in Antonioni's previous films, many camera movements in *The Passenger* wander from the subject at hand. But the reason now seems to be different. In an earlier film like *Il deserto rosso,* the wandering was generally associated with a character's point of view, becoming typically a mark of his or her distraction. In contrast, in *The Passenger,* and from the outset, the camera seems to wander on its own, in an objective, not a subjective, manner. In an interview in 1975, Antonioni said, "I no longer want to employ the subjective camera, in other words the camera that represents the viewpoint of the character."[30]

At the plot level, the effect is not distraction but spatial disorientation, both for the character and for the audience. In the desert, for example, a shot will typically start with a broad pan from left to right. The camera seems to be looking for something. The effect is strangely tense, as if the camera itself did not know what to expect. Locke is often picked up accidentally and contingently, as if diegesis (or at least this diegesis) were not the camera's real responsibility. And it is just as likely to leave him again in mid shot as it moves on. True, Locke himself is looking for something, for a meeting with the rebels. But the camera seems to be conducting its own inquiry, one not quite at the service of the character.[31] It remains aloof, alert to independent inquiry, even to the possibilities of a completely different story. What is the story, it asks, of the enigmatic dromedary and rider at the beginning of the film or of the driver-training car at the end? What is the story of the passengers in the cars racing back and forth on the highway, which it momentarily follows instead of staying with Locke and the Girl in the hotel restaurant?

Even the central event of the film, Locke's donning of Robertson's blue shirt, takes place offscreen. Locke, smoking a cigarette, has been pondering Robertson's corpse: he takes the cigarette out of his mouth and looks up. The camera wants to see, too: it tilts up the wire to view the ceiling fan whirling about. Then it moves left and down to Locke, who is already dressed in the blue shirt: the act takes place almost gratuitously, offscreen. The camera avoids drama, as a Greek tragedy avoids the show of violence. *Temps mort* has won out over *temps vivant*.

Why? Antonioni tells a story that perhaps sheds some light on his camera's wandering.[32]

One morning last November I was flying over Soviet Central Asia. I was looking down at the vast desert bounded on the east by the Aral Sea, whitish and inert, and thinking about *The Kite,* the film that I hope to make in those parts in spring: a story, a world that was never mine, and for that very reason pleasing to me. And thus it was, while preoccupied with this story and watching it fix itself docilely to the landscape below, I felt my mind wandering to other, faroff thoughts. It's always like that. Every time I'm ready to begin a film, another one comes to mind.

Antonioni is so fascinated by the diversity of the world that he has to guard himself against distraction, against allowing his camera to be led away from its present purposes. He pulls it back to the main subject, but reluctantly, as if it were loath to leave the trace of stories that might have been. Pascal Bonitzer finds in this attitude a "fascination with chance, and, on the screen, the effects of chance, erratic traces, unclear trajectories, vague gestures, which are inscribed, as by a lapse, a falling asleep of the camera, on the lens, the film, the screen, the retina. Few cineastes have . . . been so sensitive to the *inertia* of filmmaking."[33]

One might speculate that, by exchanging identities with Robertson, the fictional Locke satisfies the real Antonioni's desire to "see what the next story is like," a satisfaction that the camera cannot permit itself. It is as if the story had more courage than the discourse. Antonioni does not allow himself to go all the way, as Buñuel did in *The Phantom of Liberty,* literally dumping the first story for an intruding second one, the second one for a third, and so forth. But perhaps the amazing penultimate shot of *The Passenger* bears, in addition to its other meanings, the suggestion that the camera is liberating itself—of this story, Locke's story—to go off in search of others.[34]

Even where Locke remains in the frame, the camera, as Martin Walsh notes, "pushes him to the edge . . . discovers him 'accidentally' (as at the [Munich] airport), relegates him to the rear of a composition (Nicholson on the phone, in the rear, while foreground is dominated by a waiter filling beermugs with engrossing efficiency . . .)."[35] Walsh feels that "the choice of camera position, its axis of orientation toward the events it records, is [often] deliberately 'inadequate,' as far as direct, transparent communication of the plot is concerned," for example, when Achebe and the German aide are abducted by loyalist thugs behind a charming Spanish fountain that partially conceals what is going on.

The editing of the film is often no less perplexing than the camera movements. There are several examples of an odd match that Noël Burch has called "retroactive" or "retrospective": "Something in shot B or some other subsequent shot might *retrospectively* reveal that the transition actually belongs in an altogether different temporal or spatial category, or perhaps even both."[36] Typically, in the desert sequence, the context sets us up for an eye-line match with something from Locke's point of view, since he is the stranger trying to find his way. He looks offscreen, and we expect to see the object of his gaze in the next shot. But the next shot, after wandering about, picks him up in a completely unexpected position within the frame, showing us that we were mistaken to assume that we would continue to see things through his eyes. For instance, shot A begins looking over Locke's shoulder through the windshield; shot B cuts to a long pan right across the desert, which our conventional movie sense tells us imitates the movement of his eyes scanning the horizon. But suddenly, still in shot B, the back of his Land Rover appears from screen left, and we see it barrel into the center of the frame in a cloud of sand.

The confusion can also entail a question of scale. In the sequence in which Locke meets his guide, the first shot effects a mismatch of the kind that Noël Burch discovered in *La notte,* in which "the 'real' dimensions (and, hence, distances) of whatever is visible on the empty screen are impossible to determine until the appearance of a human figure makes the scale obvious."[37] The camera scans a broken desert horizon. How far away is it? Are we seeing small hills close up or mountains far away? Suddenly, at the extreme right of the frame we see a bit of roof thatch under which the guide appears in a medium-close shot. We are jolted: we assumed that, if anyone were to appear, it would be at a distance appropriate to Locke's point of view, that is, relatively far off. But here is the object of his search under our very noses, and we now see that the hills, whose distance had been indeterminate, are much closer, and hence much smaller, than we had thought. One source of our confusion is that the guide lives on higher ground. We follow his glance and are surprised to see the tiny figure of Locke standing far below on the desert floor. There follows a shot of Locke looking up curiously, then a shot of the guide looking back. This seems to establish reliable eye-line matches at last, much to our perceptual relief. We expect, by conventional rhythms, that the next shot, another pan of the desert, will resume Locke's point of view. Wrong again, for at the end of the pan Locke is discovered once more at a completely arbitrary middle distance accompanied by the guide: laden with equipment, they are struggling up still another mountain.[38]

The strategy of the camera shots is constantly to undermine any sense that Locke's point of view is central and constantly adhered to. Antonioni plays on the absence of landmarks in the desert. It is only the natives who can find you; you can never find them. Everything comes out of the desert: one is a fool to think that one can find anything in it.

The various kinds of confusion created by the camera's wandering and the surprise editing correspond to deliberate confusions in the story. Locke's (and our) perceptual bewilderment confirms his disorientation, in a land without visible boundaries, where he does not speak the language, where dark-skinned men snap their fingers contemptuously at him for cigarettes and make no effort to respond to his questions. But we do not experience a traditional identification with the hero. Just as Locke himself suffers from a kind of detachment from the world, the camera keeps us detached from him. The question then becomes less one of sympathy or empathy than of meditation—a rare mood in a commercial film that is ostensibly a thriller.

A quite separate issue, of course, is the sheer beauty of the barren scenery, depicted in something of the spirit of a photographer like Ansel Adams. The camera achieves the same impossible task that it had taken upon itself in *L'avventura* and *Il deserto rosso:* it manages to make the landscape at once functional to plot and the characters' moods and "irrelevantly" beautiful, worthy of esthetic contemplation in its own right. It remains a positive visual force, not ironic to the story events, just disinterested in them.

It is an exaggeration, I think, to argue (as Martin Walsh does in an important article)[39] that the whole point of *The Passenger* is to undermine cinema's basic conventions. Walsh makes much of a line addressed by Locke to Robertson that ostensibly expresses Locke's world-weariness: "We translate every experience into the same old codes." We have seen how that line informs the theme of changing identity. No matter what sorts of excitement an adopted life can give him, Locke discovers that he will render them banal by his detached and passive attitude. That is one of the bad habits that stay with him. But, Walsh points out, the "old codes" may also refer to the conventional cinematic codes with which Antonioni toys: "the narrative codes at points are placed *against* the meanings we infer." He reminds us that the semiotician Peter Wollen was one of the coauthors of the scenario, so that the word *codes* surely bears its modern semiotic sense: "even as it tells its story," writes Walsh, the film "simultaneously engages in an ideologically self-aware examination of cinematic articulation."

Walsh's line of argument is interesting, but it should not be taken too far: *The Passenger* is not a "metafilm" in the vein of Michael Snow or even Godard. The illusion of story and character is still strong.[40] But it is obvious that it is much concerned with the reality of images and the ethics of image making, with the

Frame 130   *Frame 131*

nature of the strange "truth" that we derive from visual records. Not only the task of reconstructing the personality behind the footage but the very meaning of that—or of any—footage becomes a central issue in this film.

The Passenger is an unqualified success. Indeed, it is probably the best film of Antonioni's third period. Like *Blow-Up,* its thematic is serious enough to support the technical splendors of Antonioni's craft. Unlike *Zabriskie Point,* it is superbly acted: despite the *bizarreries* of the plot, the characters seem very genuine, and the action of the film is convincing (with an occasional exception, like the rough-house scene in which Achebe is beaten up by the African ruler's hooligans).

What is perhaps most impressive is the smooth internationalism of the film. Antonioni's evocation of the desert hamlet seems flawless documentary, and the quick-cut transitions to European cities are no less convincing. With few exceptions, there is nothing touristic about the views of the locations, particularly in Africa and Spain. The Ramblas of Barcelona, the hotels and restaurants of the southern coast, the town of Osuna—all were excellently chosen to illustrate the stages of Locke's passing. Spain of all countries provides a convincing relay of stations of the cross.

Each place has its own kind of light and color. Like Locke, we are over-whelmed by the glaring intensity of the Sahara's hues and the scorching blue of its sky. The muted grays and browns of London come as a relief; Locke's springy gait as he walks through Bloomsbury and Dawson Place reflects not only his change of identity but the relief provided by the climate; he is like a man renewed by the coming of autumn after a particularly hot summer. The transition is re-versed in Spain, as Locke moves from the cool urbanity of Barcelona to the hot dustiness of the southern countryside. But that is as it should be—he must return to the desert to meet the fate of his double. After the pyrotechnics of *Zabriskie Point, The Passenger* is visually a more sober film, but its very sobriety reflects its greater thematic maturity.

Frame 132

The same is true of the sound. It is a relief to hear Antonioni return to the spare dialogue of the tetralogy. (There is too much talk in *Zabriskie Point*—perhaps a mark of Antonioni's uncertain grasp of the characters.) In the first desert sequence, Locke's lines can be counted on the fingers of one hand. His reticence, of course, results from his difficulty in communicating with the natives. The sole verbal exposition is a single line, which he shouts as he whacks the tires of his stalled vehicle with a shovel: "All right, I don't care." Antonioni uses that one piece of behavior to motivate Locke's momentous decision; it epiphanizes the long series of frustrations and compromises of Locke's life; it is the straw that breaks the camel's back. The direction and acting are so good that the line needs little expository corroboration later in the film—mostly his admission to the Girl that he has "run out of everything," wife, house, adopted child, successful job. Though his discussions with the Girl are marked by extreme honesty, the phrase *run out of* is not totally unequivocal. Strictly speaking, he has relinquished—run out *on*—his old self, because, for unstated reasons, it no longer satisfies him. Antonioni asks us to take the decision on pure faith. But then he has always asked us to accept his characters on faith. We know even less about the early doings of Claudia or Vittoria or Thomas. His characters come to us already fully formed, already totally in their situation. That is why the dialogue can afford to be so spare, so oracular.

The recording of nondialogue sound is also unusually effective in this film, especially in the desert sequence. Two sounds particularly evoke the heat and desolation of the scene—the buzzing of flies and the constant high-pitched whipping of the wind. And the sounds of the streets and public places in England, Germany, and Spain are no less convincing.

For the first time since *L'avventura,* Antonioni introduces a bit of commentative music, serene and romantic Spanish melodies played on a solo guitar (a critic guesses the compositions to be by Tárrega and Llobet).[41] But the music is first established noncommentatively in the restaurant on the Costa del Sol where Locke and the Girl stop for lunch. On that occasion, the source of the music seems to be just offscreen, perhaps from a guitarist playing dinner music. The same sort of music is repeated over the final shot of the Hotel de la Gloria after Locke's death, where it takes on great poignancy. Along with the gentle sunset, the music insists on the serenity of the scene. Antonioni was clearly trying to downplay the sensationalism or shock effect of Locke's murder. Silence would sound too mysterious or ominous if extended to the aftermath of Locke's passing, and it would detract from the sense that he wished to convey of the world simply going about its business. Locke's death must not strike us as tragic or even alarming. In this most philosophical of Antonioni's films, death must seem as much a state of mind as of the body. For all intents and purposes, Locke has been dying throughout the movie. The process is gradual, as gradual as the penultimate seven-minute tracking shot. And the music celebrates his passing, gently and lyrically and with only the slightest trace of melancholy.

IL MISTERO DI OBERWALD (1980): A Melodramatic Turn

Another five years passed in which Antonioni made no films, again not for lack of projects. During the interval, he published many treatments and stories, collected now in the volume *Quel bowling sul Tevere.* Ideas came prolifically to him, and even if he could not make them into films, he decided to share them with the public.

In 1980, he shot *Il mistero di Oberwald* (The Mystery of Oberwald) under the auspices of RAI. The film was mounted as a vehicle for Monica Vitti, now reigning queen among Italian actresses (not, ironically, for her work in Antonioni's films of the sixties but for a long series of light comedies that she made since then). It is her first appearance in an Antonioni film since *Il deserto rosso.* She and Antonioni originally thought of Cocteau's *La voix humaine* but decided that it would be "in bad taste" to try to improve on Rossellini's version (in his multipart film *Amore,* 1947). Having Cocteau in hand, they decided to make instead a version of *L'aigle à deux têtes* (The Eagle with Two Heads).[42] A loquacious costume drama set in nineteenth-century Austria is obviously far removed from Antonioni's usual concerns, and he confessed that Cocteau was not one of his favorites ("clever, fanciful, but limited"). His interest in making the film seems to have had a lot to do with the opportunity to shoot in video and thus to complete the experiments in manipulation of color that he had long meditated. Further, he had not made a film in five years. The film business being what it is, his decision to participate in such a project seems to reflect the stoic pragmatism that he has expressed in recent interviews. One does what one can. "Why that choice?" he asked. "It was not a choice, it was a chance."[43] (*Caso*—translated here as "chance"—can also mean "case," "fate," and "opportunity.") He quipped, "The 'mystery' is perhaps why I made the film." He approached Cocteau's play with "detached respect," a desire to render it faithfully but to subdue some of its effects. (In an interview, Monica Vitti expressed the same need: "to make a temperate melodrama.") Most of the dialogue is translated directly from Cocteau's French, though pruned to make it *asciugato* ("dry"), to use his exact word. A strange fate for Cocteau! And despite the damping down, much of the plot is preserved, including a denouement that Antonioni called "as romantic as one could imagine." To his own surprise, he found it a relief "to escape from the difficulty of moral and esthetic commitment, from the obsessive desire to express oneself. It was like recovering a forgotten childhood."[44]

A summary of the elaborate plot will demonstrate how far the play removed Antonioni from his usual concerns. For ten years, a widowed queen (Vitti) mourns the death of her royal husband, Frederic, stabbed at twenty-five by an

Frame 133

assassin. Always veiled, she lives a virgin life devoted to his memory. One stormy night, she arrives at her castle of Kranz in Oberwald, accompanied by Edith (Elisabetta Pozzi), ostensibly her *lectrice* but really a spy for the archduchess, her mother-in-law, who, with the Count of Föhn (Paolo Bonacelli), the chief of police, is the real power in the kingdom. Exulting in the storm, the queen dismisses Edith and prepares to dine before a full-length portrait of the king. A panel behind the portrait opens, and a young revolutionary, Sebastian (Franco Branciaroli), staggers out and collapses at her feet. The effect is hallucinatory, for Sebastian could be her late husband's double. While interrogating him, the queen hears Edith at the door. Concealing Sebastian, she learns from Edith that a young terrorist has gotten onto the grounds despite intensive pursuit by the police. She guesses that Föhn has actually given the terrorist freedom to assassinate her so that he can become regent. Ironically, she is actually happy that Sebastian has come to kill her, because she has wanted to die for many years, and she was only awaiting a fate as violent as that which befell the king. She sequesters Sebastian, to give him ample opportunity to kill her. She keeps a poisoned capsule with which to commit suicide, but, she tells Sebastian, death at the hands of a political assassin would be much more suitable. Sebastian grasps his knife to stab her but faints from loss of blood. The next day she passes him off as her new reader, though Edith knows from the bloodstains on the carpet who he really is. Föhn arrives, and Sebastian overhears him plotting against the queen. Sebastian decides to side with her. In a flowery meadow, they exchange vows of love. He urges her to seize power by replacing Föhn with the loyal Duke of Willenstein (Luigi Diberti). When she is victorious, she need only sound the cannon, and he will come to her. As the queen goes out riding in the woods, Föhn summons Sebastian for a talk. He proposes that Sebastian help persuade the queen to turn her power over to the archduchess, in exchange for which Föhn will guarantee his right to remain in the capital as her reader. If not, Föhn will have him arrested and executed, for his men surround the castle. The count gives him an hour to think it over. The queen returns and tells Sebastian that she loves him so much that she no longer needs the capsule of poison, which she has left in her room. She says jokingly that she will take it only when she is old and he no longer loves her. With a strange gravity, he urges her to march on the capital. The queen orders Willenstein to arrest Föhn and his men. As Willenstein exits, Sebastian comes in; his face is pale. He has swallowed the poison, he says, to avoid embarrassing her at the trial that would follow upon his arrest. The queen is livid: she accuses him of betraying her and denies that she loves him. At first incredulous, he comes to believe her and suspects that she left the capsule in her room to trick him into suicide. Disdainfully, she strikes him with her whip and descends to the courtyard, where her soldiers await her. With difficulty Sebastian extracts a pistol from a cabinet and makes his way downstairs. When she sees him, all the hardness disappears from her face; she smiles as he levels the pistol at her. He shoots. She staggers and says, "Pardon me. I had to madden you; otherwise you would not have killed me." She falls, crawls toward him, and tries to grasp his hand, but she cannot; her hand remains only inches from his (in a close-up) as they both die.

Frame 134

Such a plot, with its stormy night, poison capsule, and murder-suicide, results in a film that must surprise fans of Antonioni and make them feel that he lent himself to the task more as an employee of RAI than as one of cinema's great *auteurs*. This is how he reports his role: "Confronted with this material, I tried to sustain a distanced respect, without losing my identity as a director. I hope that a few echoes of that identity can be heard here and there."[45] Unfortunately, the echoes are few, and, to these ears at least, they are all too weak. True to its source, *Oberwald* is very much a filmed stage production, not unlike some done by the American Film Theater. Perhaps it resembles the Antonioni–Vitti stage collaborations at the Teatro Eliseo in Rome in 1957 (which included a production of Van Druten's *I Am a Camera*). The action occurs in a strict dramatic unity of time—

two days, clearly indicated as such, within the confines of a single space (the location was a palazzo in the Piedmont). There are, of course, outdoor shots: of the lovers on a hillside, of the queen galloping through the woods on a beautiful white horse, and, most interesting from a documentary point of view, of soldiers and domestic staff at their tasks speaking the German dialect of their region. But these do not sort well, either photographically or narratively, with the histrionic events taking place in the castle, which seem to belong to another kind of movie. Part of the problem lies in the transfer of the television image from tape to film; in the outdoor shots, telltale television lines can be clearly perceived. And the color differs strikingly from that of the indoor sequences. The result is not quite grand opera, in the style, say, of Visconti's *Senso*, but it is not unfair to call it closet opera. For Antonioni himself, it is *melodramma*—the Italian word does not bear the literary stigma that its English cognate possesses. The thick commentative music, taken from Richard Strauss and Arnold Schoenberg, underlines the characters' emotions, pronouncements, and actions in ways that are predictable. The scenes consist chiefly of dialogue, at times of monologue. As in the conventional proscenium play, the speeches usually recount what is happening elsewhere or what happened before the film began. And the setup normally includes only two people at a time, who speak to each other; the plot is basically told, rather than shown. Indeed, the film seems to contain more dialogue than all the other Antonioni films combined. A good part is taken up with the stories that the queen and Sebastian tell each other about their own—and each other's—lives. The rest is mostly verbal plotting and counterplotting between them and the other side. Virtually every theme—restlessness, memory, love, politics, idealism—is expressed not in images but in words. Not only is there a lot of talk, but much of it is in Cocteau's flamboyant style: "Do you know why I love the storm so much? Because it confounds etiquette. The archduchess is etiquette. I am the storm." Or: "We were one idea confronting another. And now what are we? A woman and a man, arm on arm. Two equal persons." It is hard to keep a production "dry" that contains lines like that. Many lines seem to exist solely for stock theatrical purposes, for instance, the expository encounter between secondary characters in the first scene, which recounts the history of the present situation, or the queen's grand entrance, when she rebukes Edith for wanting to close the windows against the storm: "Close the windows, draw the drapes, shut yourself up, hide yourself, deprive yourself of this stupendous spectacle. But why? This is my weather, Edith. The storm has its caprices. And I have mine."

The theatrical grandeur does not sort well with the realistic details that Antonioni has introduced, especially the bits of documentary. The acting tends to make the film more theatrical than cinematic. From beginning to end, it is a vehicle for Vitti. Her first entrance occurs many minutes into the film, after the suspense has been fueled by the conversation between Edith and the Duke of Willenstein. It is almost as if, as in the theater, the action is delayed so that the diva can make a more dramatic entrance. The props play their part: "A lamp and a ripple of candle flames caused by the wind accompany her entrance." Vitti herself

Frame 135

is thoroughly regal and as beautiful as ever, more convincingly thirty-five than
her actual forty-seven. But we could not be further from the cinematic style that
treated actors as elements in a visual composition. Here the sets and props are as
verisimilar and subservient to the characters and plot as in the most conventional
film. Still, though more histrionic than any other of Antonioni's films, *Il mistero
di Oberwald* is not histrionic enough to achieve what Cocteau's plot requires. The
film is too subdued, too restrained. Cocteau's queen is more deeply passionate,
and her assassin dies a more painful and noisier death. Cocteau's peculiar irony is
missing. His play stresses the queen's determination to let destiny decide her
fate; she has kept, she says, the poison capsule only "*par caprice.*" But she cannot
make destiny do her bidding: she must still resort to a form of suicide by lying to
provoke the assassination: "*Dix ans que je triche. Dix ans que tout ce qui m'arrive
me vient de moi et que c'est moi qui décide.*"[46] Yet still it is she who must decide.

Frame 136

Nothing has changed at all. By deleting such lines, Antonioni muffles the ironies that make of this play, as they do other Cocteau plays, something more than mere melodrama. Especially the final irony is missed: in the stage play, the hero falls the full length of the royal staircase, which comes to symbolize the vast distance of political reality that separates the lovers in death as it has in life. In *Oberwald*, Antonioni's decision to show the lovers dying so close together that their fingers fail to touch only by inches seemed more risible than pathetic (at least to the Berkeley audience with whom I saw it).

But Antonioni has lost none of his compositional gift. Often the placement of a face in the frame is as precise and delicate as in a canvas by Titian. The castle and the baroque furnishings are appropriately lavish, even if nothing prompts the eye to linger on them for their own sake as instances of the imponderable surfaces of life. The montage is traditional, with many close-up shot-countershot sequences. There are no *temps mort* effects despite a sustained interest in the architecture of the castle. Of course, it is unfair to expect that kind of effect in this kind of film. Given the requirements of this kind of film for seamless shooting and editing, Antonioni has done an acceptable, even elegant job. He integrates the backgrounds in imaginative if traditional ways. For example, as events reach their climax, the queen, having provoked Sebastian into a renewed desire to kill her, passes beneath old master paintings that admirably reflect and comment on her situation. But the dominant principle is to use setting as verisimilar plot support. It is beautiful, but not Antonionian in the sense that the film world has come to understand that word.

Frame 137

THE NEW TECHNOLOGY

Antonioni has said that *Oberwald* served as a pretext: the "popular fable" provided him with a simple narrative, with uncomplicated characters and straightforward action, to ensure that the audience would have sufficient leisure to appreciate the new television color effects.[47] It is not clear why that should be necessary, since his first venture into color in *Il deserto rosso,* the subtlest of movies, was so artistically successful. If all that he meant was that he wanted to reach a large audience, it seems sad that he felt he should have to at this stage of his career.

The means by which magnetic tape is transferred to film entails a technical discussion beyond my competence. Suffice it to say that Antonioni finds television production most satisfying, especially when it comes to color composition and visual mixing in general. The chief advantage, he feels, is its greater degree and immediacy of control over the registration of images. Obviously, it must be very exhilarating for a director interested in engineering and science to utilize technical advances to satisfy artistic needs. The technique of multiple cameras controlled by a central console at which he can mix colors and angles and distances provides Antonioni with what he has always wanted: a means of seeing exactly what is being shot in the very process of shooting. If he does not like what he sees, he can shoot it again, without having to wait for the laboratory to develop the rushes. Nor is television production the plaything of the weather, as film is. Antonioni is excited by the prospect of being able to revise the film as it is being shot, of inventing it on the spot. In conventional filmmaking, he says, before shooting a sequence, one first tries to envision it as a theoretical problem in need of a precise and often complicated solution: a tracking shot here, a pan there, a transition from long shot to close-up, and so on. But when one works with television, various images are delivered in a simultaneous visual reading. The director can choreograph and blend the efforts of his cameramen, with whom he communicates by microphone, to obtain a synthesis that would otherwise be unimaginable. There is also a considerable speedup in production time: *Oberwald* was shot in sixty-four days.

The proof, of course, is in the pudding—not in its mixing but in its eating. For all Antonioni's enthusiasm, it is difficult to see the film's being very popular either with his fans or with the mass audience.[48] Certainly the color, as interesting as the process may be, will not stimulate the popular imagination; indeed, some of the effects are so subtle that many people will not notice them. A defender of Antonioni might respond that he was looking for more subliminal effects anyway, and they do occur. The colors change sometimes imperceptibly and in ways that we are unused to, and doubtless it will take a while to appreciate them properly. The trouble is that this is a field in which the public has been overstimulated for years. Television colors are neither as strong nor as varied as what is offered by Technicolor, Eastmancolor, Deluxe, and other processes. (I am not saying that this is necessarily bad; I am simply talking about potential mass audience responses.) Further, they are familiar *as* television colors, and so they set up certain unwanted associations—one knows that lavender only too well from tedious nights spent in front of the tube. Certain other undesirable artifacts also arise. For example, the outlines of moving objects tend to smear, especially against a light background. A ghost moves ahead of the image itself, which is etched for a split second as the image races to catch up. Within the area of color blending, it is true that *Oberwald* does things that have never before been seen on the screen: landscape and buildings convincingly brighten with the arriving morning, or blood from a decapitated chicken darkens from red to black before our very eyes. These effects are less flamboyant than a verbal account suggests. And other color changes are so subtle that one is not sure exactly what has happened. For instance, on a blank wall of the castle, a faint pattern begins to appear and then changes: from a glacier to a mountain landscape to an abstract design. In several shots of the large sepia photograph of the dead king, it is less that we see a color change than it is that we sense it; something odd is happening, especially in the moments just before Sebastian enters from behind the portrait and collapses on the floor. Antonioni explained that the image of the king was minutely enhanced: all that happened was that the dark tones became a little stronger, and the landscape in the photo was colored faintly. Similarly, to call attention to the dueling pistol at the moment when Sebastian grasps it to end the queen's life, the brown background darkens slightly so that the outline can stand out more intensely against it. Doubtless other subtle changes occur elsewhere in the film that a concerted search could identify. But audiences used to bravura color effects may well feel frustrated, especially if they are led to expect something unusual.

Since these effects are so subtle, it is a shame that Antonioni did not attach them to material worthy of his usual subtlety. Settling for simple heroes and villains can only banalize the use of colors to characterize them, no matter how clever the process itself is. The film uses uncharacteristic symbolism, representing a thought or moral trait with a single color. Since Föhn is evil, and lavender suggests evil, he is colored lavender. One remembers with nostalgia the lurid reds of Giuliana's Walpurgisnacht on Ravenna's docks or the post-coital rose of Corrado's hotel room.

The technology of color is one thing, its filmic use is another. Progress in the former does not necessarily lead to progress in the latter. It is hard to prefer the Count of Föhn's lavender cloud to the nuanced effects of *Il deserto rosso* or *Blow-Up.* The mere coloring of faces, no matter how ingeniously done, must look slightly absurd if not accompanied by similar expressionist effects in other details—makeup, lighting, music, and so on. There must be coherence among such effects, as in Brecht, or in Fassbinder's fascinating *Berlin Alexanderplatz.* In *Oberwald* there is none. Everything about Föhn except the color of his face is highly realistic. The color seems to introduce an element of moral judgment that the ironic Cocteau could not have wanted. After all these years, it is strange to find Antonioni expressing moralisms with such direct symbolism. Föhn's face reminds us of Andy Warhol's version of Nixon's television face, whose strange hue—however justified by Watergate revelations—could have been achieved independently by any viewer fiddling with the knobs on his color television set.

Still, there is no reason not to believe that video technology and its transference to film will improve and that Antonioni may feel more confident in the future about the public's capacity to understand and appreciate the subtle uses of color that he is famous for. Indeed, he expresses a desire to use video to add color to L'avventura—not by reshooting the film but by recording it on videotape and electronically superimposing colors on the images. He confesses great curiosity about the outcome.

Color effects are not the only ones in Oberwald that television techniques make possible. They also facilitate trick visual effects. Willenstein remembers seeing the queen without her veil once, so the image literally appears on the wall next to him; Edith's true feelings appear on a nastier surrogate face standing next to her outwardly visible one; the queen keeps vigil over Sebastian's recovery, but at a certain point she vanishes from the chair. These visionary manifestations come as narrative surprises, because the film is realistic in other respects, but in themselves they are not unfamiliar; the effects are like those produced by well-known processes of superimposition, cutting, and so on. Whatever they contribute to the plot of the film depends on one's enthusiasm for ghosts and disappearances. Antonioni's audience, after all, is not quite that of Méliès. In a recent interview, Antonioni spoke of a cinema "freed from the limits of realism, a cinema which is the consequence of our different attitude toward a world which in recent years has completely changed its appearance . . . We need to seek other truths, even through cinema, truths which everyday reality no longer gives us. I am convinced that the fantastic world of which my film has disclosed a mere glimmer is at our door and that that door will open itself if we do not ourselves open it."[49] However that may be, a film generation raised on Star Wars and microcinematographic documentaries and NASA films may not be overwhelmed by either the fictional world or the technology of Il mistero di Oberwald.

10

Identificazione di una donna

Identificazione di una donna (1982) marks a return to the contemporary Italian scene.[1] It recounts the story of a filmmaker living in Rome, Niccolò Farra (Tomas Milian). The name recalls that of Niccolò Ferrari, who directed *Uomini in più* (1955), which Antonioni produced. Niccolò is searching for a woman or, as he contends, two women—one fictional and one real. The fictional one will release him from his esthetic doldrums and enable him to make his next film, while the real one will replace the wife he has divorced. He argues that they must be different women, but clearly his muse and his love partner are more closely related than he is willing to admit.

Niccolò fails on both accounts. He meets two women, but neither proves satisfactory, for different reasons. The first, Maria Vittoria Luppis, Mavi for short (Daniela Silverio), is a Roman aristocrat: beautiful, exciting, mysterious. Indeed, all too mysterious: she finally vanishes without a word of explanation. He meets her on the telephone, by accident. His sister is a gynecologist, and, visiting her office one day, he answers the phone because her receptionist is out. It seems not to be accidental that Mavi is consulting a gynecologist: her life turns a great deal on sex, and the medical risks run by the promiscuous constitute one of many hazards that, according to the film, complicate modern life. Niccolò and Mavi's own sexual encounters are shown in explicit detail. The relationship falls under a cloud almost immediately. Niccolò is threatened by the "*gorilla*" of some person who secretly loves Mavi and who is rich enough to employ one. The unpleasant thug calls him late at night, stakes out his apartment, and offers him "advice" over an ice-cream sundae. Mavi cannot identify the secret lover, and Niccolò becomes obsessed with finding out who it is. He asks her to introduce him to her circle of aristocratic friends. At a party, he makes inquiries but fails to identify the secret admirer and feels himself becoming the object of cold and intense scrutiny. He also observes that he is by no means Mavi's sole lover; she seems to be involved with a number of people, both men and women. Niccolò tries to remain cool about these discoveries, but his dissatisfaction is evident. Yet Mavi continues to fascinate him.

213

Frame 138

His involvement with her hinders his work. He covers the wall above his desk with female faces, but he is unable to pick one for his film; all he can do is listen to his telephone-answering machine. A producer leaves a message offering him a script; he is excited until he learns that the script is called "Voices from Beyond, or, Just Think! I Exist" and that it includes a list of persons who have communicated with the beyond. Like Sandro, who has already sold out, and Giovanni, who is about to, Niccolò has his share of temptations: but, we gather, he is strong enough to resist them. He vehemently denies that women have put him in a crisis, arguing with his friend Mario (Marcel Bozzufi), the most sympathetic person in the movie, that Mavi and his unfound heroine are strictly separate beings. The friend remains skeptical. Irritated beyond endurance by the thug who tails him, Niccolò roars off in the middle of the night, loses the thug, and fetches Mavi for a weekend in the countryside. They get lost in the fog and quarrel. She leaves the car but quickly returns. At the farmhouse, there is another confrontation: "You don't love me," she says, sounding a bit like Susan Kane. "You just need me." He confesses he has never been able to say he loved anybody and compliments her for her "lucidity." Cut to rapturous lovemaking. Then cut quickly to Mavi's apartment in town: she has mysteriously vacated, and Niccolò relinquishes his key to the new occupants, two women.

Frame 139

Niccolò continues his search without success. Mavi's mother and sister refuse to help, and he realizes that she has left of her own volition and does not want to see him. He calls an old girlfriend, then meets a stage actress, Ida (Christine Boisson). Ida is fresh, frank, and, though young, level-headed and warm. She is immediately attracted to Niccolò, who reciprocates, though clearly without the intensity of his feeling for Mavi. Sensible woman that she is, Ida realizes that her relationship with Niccolò will not progress until he confronts Mavi. She helps him find her through a copy of *Time,* in which Mavi appears as one of its European "women of the year." Through *Time*'s Rome editor, Niccolò learns that she is living in an apartment building in Trastevere. The residents of its three flats deny knowing her, but, suspicious of their answers, he returns to the building and hides on the staircase. Mavi appears at the door of a woman who lives in the building, and we understand that the woman is her lover. She turns around and looks up (see Frame 144 below). But it is not clear whether she sees Niccolò in the shadows on the landing (the screenplay says that she does not see him but that the suspicion that he is there leaves her breathless). Later, at the window of the woman's apartment, she watches him leave the building; it is obvious that she is moved, but she turns away without acknowledging his presence. In response to her lover's question about whether she will leave her, too, she says no.

Niccolò takes Ida for a brief holiday to Venice; in a rowboat on the outer lagoon, he asks her to marry him, and she agrees. When they return to the hotel, Ida is called to the telephone. She receives a message that she has been waiting for—she is pregnant by her previous boyfriend. With mixed emotions, she returns to Niccolò and tells him the news. He reacts negatively:[2] he sneers and asks her to repeat her avowal of love for him. She does so, but the affair is clearly over. However, it is not clear who terminated it. Repeating *"Tu sei il mio amore"* ("You are my love"), Ida compares the elation Niccolò inspires in her to a celebration, to a cocaine high, to "all sorts of things." But the one thing he is not, she adds, is her *ordine,* her self-coherence, her sense of the order of things, the system by which she governs her life. Ida is a strong and plucky woman, and presumably she does not want Niccolò if he does not want her. She asserts her close affinity with the child's father and adds, as if concluding the affair with an observation of what Niccolò doubtless has in mind, "But you don't want to act as the father of another man's child." She is not asking him but telling him, and he does not resist her interpretation of his attitude.

In the final sequence, Niccolò returns alone to his apartment. He sits at the window, looking at the sun through his dark glasses. Then, in a fantasy sequence, in voice-over, responding to his little nephew, whose questions in voice-over have suggested the project, he outlines the plot of his next film—a science fiction tale about a voyage to the sun. Antonioni has said that it may be better to escape to other worlds, for life has become too intricate on earth.

THEMES, REVISITED AND NEW

In *Identificazione di una donna,* Antonioni returns to some of his preoccupations of the early sixties.[3] Perhaps the most obvious theme is the deterioration of the quality of life in Italy. Rome, the screenplay tells us, is "noisy and vulgar." Certainly, Niccolò's daily existence is marked by discomforts ranging from simple irritation to downright threat, though the thug is careful to make a distinction: he is not menacing Niccolò, he says; he is merely giving him some *consiglio*—some "advice." The point is that such harassment is not suspenseful, as it would be in a Hollywood melodrama of the fifties, but simply annoying in a low-keyed way. It has become part and parcel of the general vexatiousness of urban life. When Niccolò finally complains to the police about the gorilla, he is politely ridiculed; it is happening to everybody, they say, including themselves.

Ironically, the very technology that was supposed to make life easier and safer proves to be irritating and even hazardous. As the film opens, Niccolò, an absent-minded fellow who often misplaces things, sets off the burglar alarm that his ex-wife installed because he cannot find the release key. (It is easier to get rid of a neurotic wife than it is to get rid of her alarm system.) His neighbor quickly arrives at the door, brandishing a gun. The telephone-answering machine contains no messages except the inane proposal for "Voices from Beyond" and painful reminders from his nephew that Niccolò has failed to deliver on a long-overdue promise of postage stamps. Another new gadget, a cordless telephone receiver, jangles at midnight: a threat from the gorilla. These elaborate refinements on communication do little more than intensify one's vulnerability to what is "out there." One cannot help responding to the gadgets as if they were as important as the human beings who activate them, or perhaps more so. Niccolò has taken to shouting back at the ringing phone, "*Arrivo*"—"I'm coming."

Yet Niccolò (doubtless speaking for Antonioni) would not consciously blame science for these annoyances. He is very much a fan: he reads the science page of the *International Herald Tribune* and dreams of solar exploration. Science is not to blame for the uses to which its achievements are put. The cordless telephone does not ask to convey threats, just as the industrial plant in *Il deserto rosso* did not ask to exacerbate a woman's neurosis.

The sense of *disagio* or discomfort is not limited to people like Niccolò. It also floats in the air that the aristocrats breathe. They, too, can be approached on the stairs with a devastating piece of news. Their privacy and safety are no more sure than the ordinary person's. In some of the most effective moments of the film, *i nobili* show with their eyes alone their mistrust and suspicion of others. They are constantly staring at one another, and they stare especially hard at interlopers. Niccolò is moved by the spectacle to comment wryly that times have changed: it used to be the poor who left Italy in droves; now it is the aristocracy. All the material luxury in the world cannot put an uneasy conscience to rest or allay fears of the Red Brigade or of being implicated in business and political scandals, secret Swiss bank accounts, sexual intrigues, or whatever. The aristocracy's traditional interest in culture is gone and with it its willingness to mix with the other classes. The difference between the party scene at the hotel in Taormina in *L'avventura* and the party at the private villa in this film is very striking. In the earlier film, the glances were mostly flirtatious; here, they are accusing and suspicious, as if these eyes were measuring the space that others would occupy in the last lifeboat off the sinking ship. Even history disapproves: in one shot, a classical Roman bust looks down disdainfully on an old fogey who is trying to place Niccolò. And there is precious little generosity or noblesse oblige. Mavi's mother does nothing to help Niccolò's sister recover her position at the hospital (she has been fired, apparently at his rival's instigation), even though it would be little enough for a woman of her mother's status to do. And nothing could be colder than the shoulders turned toward Niccolò when he makes inquiries about Mavi's whereabouts. This coldness is perhaps put on to conceal paranoia and incipient hysteria—at least if Mavi's behavior is any guide. Though she claims that she has broken off ties with her class, her attitudes belie her words. The wind blowing open a French door terrifies her. She sees the gorilla everywhere, in every parked car. Niccolò has to reassure her that "people have all kinds of motives for being out on the streets at night" and that "we only call them bandits because we're suspicious." In response to her anxiety, Niccolò drives wildly through the fog as if to elude a nonexistent pursuer. That sends her into a panic; she jumps out of the car and rushes off

Frame 140

into the fog. Getting out to search for her, Niccolò flags down an expensive car, only to hear a wild account from its occupant, a perfectly respectable-looking man, about hearing shots, cries, church bells, an ambulance siren. No help there: even the passerby is likely to prove crazy. Or is he? "*Hanno sparato,*" he says. "There were shots"—or, in a stricter translation, "They were shooting," these "they" being the dangerous ones out there who are itching to get "us." (The title of one of Antonioni's treatments of the fifties was *Stanotte hanno sparato,* There Was Shooting Tonight.) It is, of course, Antonioni's way to leave the situation ambiguous—things are equally bad, whether the man actually heard the noises or only imagined them. Of course, it is also Antonioni's way (as it is not Costa-Gavras's or Francesco Rosi's) to leave actual political issues unmentioned.

The sights and sounds of Rome have indeed become vulgar, even grotesque. After listening to the gorilla's "advice" in an ice-cream parlor, Niccolò has to vie for the phone with a loudmouth who is trying to use two pay phones at once.

Shopping streets look tawdry, and the shoppers are a motley, ill-dressed bunch. Friars press handbills into your hand. Squalid types wait for you at the foot of ancient stairs to propose drug deals.

Architecture and planning are worse than ever: the settings for intimate discussion make Vittoria's street corner in the EUR look like paradise. Mavi meets Niccolò in front of a mod clothing shop that is all hard surfaces—glass, plastic, ugly blue stripes, neon. You see too much of yourself and of everybody else.[4] Even the clothes are or seem to be made of plastic. Language, too, has turned vulgar, even in the best circles; all Mavi can think of to say when Niccolò tells her that his sister has been fired is *"Che inculatta"*—"What a shaft!" Then, remembering her own misery, she says she's "pissed" and turns away to cry. He looks for a spot where they can talk, and the best he can find is a narrow passageway covered with hideous reflective paint on both sides. (The screenplay gives the location as an *atrio* in the via Frattina.) Even this hideaway seems to be crowded with unwanted company. More actively than ever, the surfaces of the world conspire against intimacy. Facades are inimical, even hostile. The story that Mavi tells is about another uncomfortable meeting, with a man who appeared out of nowhere to announce that he is her father. This happened on a stairway that she was climbing to reach a party; the other guests pushed past them, and Niccolò himself was waiting on the landing just above. Everything happens in public; one cannot escape scrutiny; even aristocrats must resign themselves to being spied on, to the constant exhibition of their dirty linen in public.

The general tawdriness of the Mavi half of the film is reflected in the music, which is more plentiful than in any of Antonioni's films since the fifties. It is very "punk"—electronic, unsoothing, a constant source of nervous stimulation or irritation. Niccolò constantly plays it on his phonograph; it accompanies the sex scenes; it reaches a hoarse peak in the song that we hear in front of the clothing shop, sung in the ragged dead-end voice of the Italian rock singer Gianna Nannini. (In contrast, serene late-Romantic piano music accompanies Niccolò's separation from Mavi, then later from Ida. Music can only be beautiful in nostalgic moments, after an affair has ended.)

All in all, Antonioni's view of the quality of life in Rome today is summed up in Mario's words: "What kind of love story would make sense in this ruin (*sfacelo*), in this corruption?"

Sex, Unisex, Omnisex

Much of *Identificazione di una donna* concerns sex, which is more explicit than in any of Antonioni's other films. The clue to Mavi's character is sexuality, as is Niccolò's fascination with her. (Ida's sexuality is so "normal" or "old-fashioned" in comparison that it seems not to need graphic depiction.) Mavi, a trendsetter, seems to represent the attitudes of an entire generation. She dresses in a unisexual way (only once, at the party, does she wear a dress rather than pants). The mannishness of her appearance becomes even more pronounced after she leaves

Niccolò for her lesbian lover. But lesbianism does not really seem to be the main-spring of Mavi's character. There is no reason to believe that she stops being interested in men just because she claims that she will be faithful to her new lover. What is truer of her, I think, is that she has a restless need to experiment. There are hints at the party, for example, of arrangements for a ménage à trois. Many remarks that she makes to Niccolò suggest that she sees herself as a kind of sexual adventurer, one readied by sexual liberation[5] to take on anything that strikes her fancy.

Preparatory to their first lovemaking (which she briskly proposes), she discusses the etiology of her sexual attitudes. As an adolescent she attended a college in Wales, where she learned a lot about maritime lifesaving but was not permitted to have intercourse. There, presumably, she became habituated to masturbation—perhaps also to lesbianism. This information is supposed to explain some of Mavi's quaint customs, for example, her unwillingness to remove her panties until the very last moment. (As the treatment has it, *le mutandine, sempre con le mutandine*—"the panties, always with the panties.") Her attitude is far from embarrassed. She reveals it with the confidence of one instructed by her society that every person's sex is his or her own affair, not subject to moral or psychological evaluation. She is simply explaining her preferences, not excusing herself for having them.

Mavi and Niccolò's second round of lovemaking is the most revealing about her sexual attitudes. Its prelude is the scene in which the two stand in the shopping street. Having quickly forgotten her pain at discovering the identity of her real father, she notices a shopgirl in a store window putting a bathing suit on a male mannequin. The shopgirl caresses its crotch and smiles meaningfully at Mavi. Mavi tells Niccolò with evident pleasure and interest that she has seen the girl before, completely nude, making love with a man in a car. The glance between the two women is clearly complicit, and there are overtones of further possibilities. Cut to Niccolò's bed: Niccolò is giving Mavi a very elaborate pudendal massage through her panties. She coaches him, guiding his hands and fingers. There is no intercourse at all: his function is simply instrumental. At the moment of climax, she turns to the mirror to look at herself: *that* is the greatest turn-on. Her elaborate omnisexuality seems to be nothing but an extension of her intense narcissism. Niccolò is less her lover than her masseur, an elaborate extension of her own hands. The meaning of Mavi's guard over her panties is not prudery but the high esteem she places on their contents. This is the culture of narcissism taken to its furthest extreme. The attitude is spelled out by Mavi's erstwhile young lover, whom Niccolò meets at the swimming pool. Her remarks seem to articulate Mavi's feelings. When Niccolò asks what "her thing" is, she says, a bit tauntingly, "masturbation"—especially with help from someone else, above all a woman. Her reason has less to do with emotion than with pure sensation: it is simply "smoother" when a woman does it. Men get too ego-involved.[6] Another visual corroboration of Mavi's narcissism occurs a bit later in the film. The only thing hanging on her bedroom wall is a photo of herself in a bikini, with her hands on her groin. As she and Niccolò discuss how to escape from the gorilla, the camera tracks in so that the photo is the only thing we can see. She mutters *"Amore, amore"* as Niccolò proposes a romantic escape to the countryside, but it is obvious that the photograph represents the only true object of her *amore*.

(One could argue, however, that the narcissistic interpretation is contradicted by the couple's third and final sexual encounter, at the farmhouse in the country, because it is characterized by mutual joy and pleasure. They fondle each other and roll about under a sheet that billows magically. But the effect does not quite work. It is not only the mysterious source of the breeze that is troubling: it is difficult to relate the event itself to the rest of the movie. Is the idea that Mavi is beginning to give up her autoerotic preference under Niccolò's tutelage? Or is it rather that, knowing in her own mind that the affair is over, she can abandon herself to genuine mutual play? Or is it simply that Antonioni liked the imagery enough to disregard the narrative problem that it introduces?)

Amid all this sex, we might ask, plaintively, Whatever happened to Love? Antonioni answered the question forthrightly in an interview:

BACHMANN: So you think making a fuss about love is oldfashioned.

ANTONIONI: Let's say it's historical. It's part of other times, of past literature and of past art, past cinema, past theatre. . . . I admit to believing that 19th-century passion today arouses only smiles . . . Control becomes a habit. A way of life, maybe the only one. . . . [As a consequence,] there is love in the film, but it is a contemporary love, a love of today. A love for which a man who has two disappointments in a row doesn't tear his hair out, doesn't despair like one used to. He has a mature capacity for suffering, but he controls and in the end dominates it. He has learned to control his feelings and sentiments, especially within the framework of his craft which has taught him to hold back narrative flights of fancy.[7]

Niccolò decides to limit narrative flights of fancy to his work and to exclude them from his romantic life. That is very much the sense that we get as he sits at the window deep in a fantasy that he visualizes about interplanetary travel: desire has been sublimated into work, for better or for worse. But, at the same time, he is very much alone, and one wonders whether the old days were not somehow better, the days when community was still possible, when, as in Renoir's *Le crime de M. Lange*, a young man (with the warm support of an idealistic community) could forgive his sweetheart for being pregnant by the villain and live with her happily ever after.

The Artist's Search for Inspiration

So little is really made of the theme of the artist's inspiration that it is hard to take it quite seriously. Clearly, the film does not propose a genuine inquiry into the process of artistic creation. All that Niccolò does is to cut out pictures of women's faces and stick them on the wall above his desk. (The most notable is a picture of

Louise Brooks.) There is also that bit of desultory talk with Mario about his lack of progress, including an unpersuasive denial that he is confusing the women in his real life with the women in his professional fantasy life. Mario is right to doubt Niccolò's denial. Niccolò feels the desire to base a film on a female character whom he does not yet know. His two romantic experiences complicate things. As Antonioni says, "It's completely natural to take as model the woman with whom one is having an affair, if one loves and esteems her. At such a moment, one no longer knows if one seeks a woman for himself or for the film in one's head."[8]

Antonioni is obviously not interested in the rich probing of the artistic unconscious that characterizes Fellini's *8½* (a film that he admires very much). Guido Anselmi's fantasies clearly work to exploit cinema's ultimate visual capacities. *Identificazione* is a very different kind of movie, and too close a comparison would be unfair. Still, there are a couple of scenes in which the camera presents Niccolò's mental visualization of Mavi. In one, he telephones her in the middle of the night, but he does not respond to her anxious *pronto;* instead, he places the cordless receiver against the window (the curtain romantically waves in the evening breeze). It seems as if he were visually framing her in some kind of absented synecdoche. Perhaps he was calling into the dark for help from the muse. But all he gets is the anxious voice of an all too human lover. In another scene, a vision of Mavi materializes. As if on a wall of his apartment, there appears an image of her as she gets out of a bathtub. She remarks that her body shows signs of aging. In voice-over (since he does not appear in the shot), Niccolò reassures her that she is beautiful and that he loves her. It is not clear whether this scene really happened and is now being shown in flashback or whether it is a fantasy of the moment; perhaps it does not matter. The sequence seems oddly low-keyed, as if Antonioni does not really want to make too much of it. (It reminds one of the subtle materialization effects in *Il mistero di Oberwald*.) And it is hard to grasp its thematic import. It has nothing like the bravura articulation of other fantasy sequences—Giuliana's tale of the girl on the beach or the love-in at *Zabriskie Point*. We enter so little of Niccolò's consciousness in general that it is somewhat surprising to see his fantasy life suddenly displayed on the wall.

As for the science fiction project, it could relate to the escape theme of earlier films, but for the artist such escapes are relevant, since they can be captured and tamed for his or her work. The artist must be as free as a child: hence Niccolò's more than avuncular interest in his nephew's fantasy. He must be curious about how things are and why they look as they do. The sun appears in two sequences. The first, shot through a small telescope, is actually a direct (unmirrored) optic registration—apparently something of an innovation in celestial cinematography.[9] The second is a special effects fantasy sequence in which a spaceship approaches the sun for scientific inquiry. The ship looks a bit forlorn, more like a meteorite than Voyager II. The explanation that Niccolò offers is that the ship needs an extraterrestrial shell in order to withstand the tremendous heat of the sun. So some enormous cinder has been commandeered for the project. The sad truth may be that Antonioni's budget was too small for a more sensational effect.[10] In an interview, he expressed his admiration for *E. T.* and *Blade Runner* and a strong desire to make a science fiction film *à l'italien*.

Perhaps the most memorable image in the film is the one of Niccolò leaving his car and proceeding on foot because the fog is too thick. A mysterious flashing stoplight looms up out of the fog. It is obvious that he is not referring to local weather conditions when he says, "A stoplight—who knows what it means?" Life is uncertain, more uncertain than ever. Who knows what lies ahead? And, indeed, he immediately loses touch with Mavi, who runs off in a prelude to her final disappearance. The moment is reminiscent of the scene in *L'eclisse* when Vittoria and Piero cross the zebra stripes and of the scene in *La notte* when Lidia and Roberto have to stop in the car in a pouring rain in order to let a train pass. Only in this case, Niccolò, like Giuliana on the pier, remains alone, framed against the bewildering fog. And even when Mavi reappears (a mysterious tiny halo forming in the car as she lights a cigarette), she refuses to talk to him. He looks out the window, the camera pans across the fog, but nothing is distinguishable. What indeed lies ahead?

Yet this fine sequence fails to infuse the film with anything like the thematic tension of the earlier works. Antonioni clearly intended it to. The published treatment explains in an elaborate metaphor:

Here was the fog. It's not difficult to drive in the fog. Just don't lose sight of the white line in the middle of the road; move over only when you see another car coming toward you. In a relationship between a man and woman, there's also a white line, which at a certain moment divides into two: these two move parallel to each other for a while and then converge, only to diverge suddenly until finally they disappear. The fog remains.[11]

THE CHARACTERS

Niccolò, though not totally sympathetic, is believable enough as a character. His rejection of Ida seems petty, but then he never was really committed to her. And the denouement is problematic. The film implies that his decision to reject her is plausible, even necessarily so. It is natural, the film seems to say, that a man in his situation would not want a woman who is pregnant by another man, just as it is natural that a man blocked in his work might feel hypersexual (*L'avventura*) or that man who has "run out of everything" might accept and even welcome death (*The Passenger*). But the argument "I can't marry you because you're pregnant by another man" is not so easy to accept these days. Nothing has prepared us for this as the normal contemporary male reaction. (By *normal*, of course, I mean "culturally naturalized," a society's version of what constitutes usual behavior.) Indeed, if Niccolò were in a contemporary Hollywood film, his reaction might easily arouse the audience's contempt. Further, having Ida intuit Niccolò's rejection and articulate it—thus nominally rejecting him—weakens her characterization.

It is not totally believable that she should be so much in love with Niccolò and then suddenly reject him by asserting a mysterious, binding affinity with the father of her child.

Clearly, Niccolò's character has an anomalous streak. He says that his greatest desire is simply to be quiet with a woman, instead of always talking, always defining things. But once he has his way and is actually floating on the lagoon with the peaceful Ida, he is still not content. He shows a restlessness and uncertainty that reminds us of the heroes of the tetralogy. When the breakup with Ida occurs, we are not totally surprised. Indeed, at neither breakup do we see anything like grief in his face. In a "love of today," Antonioni argues, nobody goes to pieces; indeed, it is as if Niccolò were expecting it to end all along. His wariness itself argues his reluctance to make a commitment; thus, it, too, is a form of narcissism, that old Antonionian bugaboo. It is narcissistic to search for a woman who corresponds to the other voice in the dialogue that a man carries on with himself. It is simply another version of "being in the country" or "flying a glider." Niccolò wants to have it both ways: to be silent and yet to speak with a woman. He wants someone to read his thoughts, in short, to reduplicate him. This may be the necessary narcissism of the artist, but it is narcissism nonetheless, and one does not come away from the film feeling that Niccolò's attitude will help him to form a solid relationship with a woman. But, for all his protestations, there is reason to believe that he does not really want a solid relationship. A line in the treatment describes his feelings about Mavi when they are caught in the fog—but it could apply equally well to Ida when he is finally done with her: "Everything would be perfect if it were not for that girl who was walking in the fog without knowing where she was going."[12]

There is not a little machismo in Niccolò's character; it is visible as he roars through the streets of Rome and the fog in the countryside like a hot-rodder. Losing Mavi seems to be as much a blow to his vanity as it is anything else. When flowers continue to arrive from her secret admirer after she has left, he describes his feeling as "impotence," a kind of slap in the face from his mysterious rival. One wonders whether the jealousy he feels in discovering that she has left him for a lesbian relationship is not merely that of the bested male. Unlike Woody Allen in *Manhattan*, Niccolò seems constitutionally unable to express his feelings about the matter, let alone to sense any humor in it. And when Ida announces that she is pregnant, it is less the baby that bothers him than the fact that he is not the father. His reaction is immediate and visceral. Not for a moment does he stop to ask whether Ida's many redeeming qualities countervail her troublesome pregnancy.

Still, emotionally puzzled and artistically blocked as he is, Niccolò is an active spirit. He does not suffer from the weakness, ennui, and inhibition of Sandro, Giovanni, and Riccardo. He certainly does not share David Locke's death wish. From the artistic point of view, Niccolò's situation is quite reasonable. Antonioni says, "when one begins to think of a film, one starts always with a sort of chaos in the head ... Niccolò says that he has a feeling about female forms: that is already something: he feels the need to construct a film about a female character, though he does not yet know who."[13] And when the film ends, Antonioni feels confident that Niccolò has some film in hand—though clearly it is not the one he started with.

Niccolò really is a filmmaker, however stuck he is at the moment. He needs to see things: to visualize Mavi, even as he talks to her on the phone for the first time in his sister's office. Later, he needs to frame or "block" her against the window or wall of the apartment. He frames Ida, too, between thumb and index finger the first time she visits his studio. "Placing" somebody, in the literal visual sense, is essential to his scheme of things. Also, like many artists, he has a special affinity with children. The idea for the science fiction film comes from his small nephew, from the pictures of astronauts on the stamps that Niccolò gives him. Children and artists are interested in the tiniest objects in the visual field—he and his nephew both notice a curious bulge on the branch of a tree near his apartment. It has no particular meaning, it is just there, an interesting shape. Nor is it accidental that Niccolò gets enthusiastic about a science fiction film just as he breaks up with Ida. The search for a woman can cease. There are other exciting things in the universe.

Niccolò is as interesting from the social point of view as he is from the emotional and the artistic. He is no aristocrat; indeed, much of the uneasiness that he feels at the party can be read as reverse class consciousness. (He commits an interesting gaffe, mistaking someone's bracelet on a table for an ashtray.) Though he does not aspire to the class above him, he feels enough awe of it to exhibit discomfort in its presence. His situation is anomalous. He himself is a celebrity: people recognize him in the street and at the party, too. But that recognition does not make things better. Though he is attractive, his manner has a certain roughness, his voice a certain harshness. He is clearly out of place among these smooth people, yet it is obvious that they also fascinate him in some way—especially their exponent, Mavi. The real question of the film is why he is as obsessed as he is with her, why he is willing to put up with her erratic behavior.

According to the treatment, the intention was to show that Niccolò was fascinated by Mavi's ambiguity: "Niccolò watched her. Sometimes she seemed so ambiguous. 'I never know when you're telling the truth.' 'Is the truth important to you?' It was strange how this girl managed to show intelligence, stupidity, goodness, wickedness, in short all those qualities that usually make up character as if one alone were peculiar to her at a given moment. Only to contradict it the next."[14]

In an analysis of the story solicited by Antonioni himself (it was published with the screenplay), the critic Roberto Roversi describes Niccolò as a man less interested in making love than in "observing looking listening perceiving watching getting to the bottom of things collecting things."[15] But to be curious about changeable women is one thing, to fall in love with one is another. The basis of Mavi's fascination for Niccolò remains obscure. There is no discernible answer to the question that Niccolò writes in the steam on a window of his apartment (in the treatment only): "But why am I so attracted to this woman whom I cannot manage to respect?" It might have been well if the question had been asked in the film. At least it would have helped focus the issue a little more clearly. Whether

Milian was not quite up to the subtleties of the role or Antonioni did not provide him with sufficiently explanatory lines and action, the basis for Niccolò's absorption with Mavi remains unclear. In the larger context of the film, one might assume, for example, that it is Mavi's class (in the slang sense, too) that dazzles Niccolò, even as, intellectually, he wonders about her.

In other respects, Milian seems a good choice for the role. As an actor, his expressive range is limited, and he reflects pretty much all that happens to him. He projects a kind of rough sensitivity. As one critic puts it, "He's an actor without 'interiority' and without depth, whose presence on the screen is refractory to any psychological identification . . . unable to adopt the minimal posture, which is to try to identify, on his own, events as they present themselves to the character and simultaneously with him."[16]

The character of Mavi is more problematic. Indeed, she is the least well realized of the three protagonists. As we have already observed, she represents the eighties version of the *malattia dei sentimenti.* Now the principal symptom is narcissism; its physical manifestation is graphically evoked in the second love-making scene, which has already been described.

Antonioni himself expresses a view of Mavi's sexuality that is more sympathetic than that of the film itself. He sees it as her way of "contesting her [aristocratic] origins, trying to make a new life for herself without knowing what this new life may be," and he opposes her to Ida, "who has a sort of place in society and achieved more of an identity," through work rather than sex, so that the sex can come more naturally (pace Freud). Antonioni grants that the attempt to achieve self-realization through sex rather than work is the more neurotic, but work is not a viable option to the aristocracy. (Why not? we are prompted to ask.) Mavi, says Antonioni, "finds herself" in sex; "that's why the sexual scenes with her are so *osé,* so daring . . . Her sex activity is a liberating act. It is here she becomes herself."[17] But I wonder whether the film really works that way. One can hardly describe Mavi at the end, living as she does in questionable circumstances in Trastevere, as a liberated, self-fulfilled person. Either Antonioni's comment is ironic, or he has bought a rationalization that the character and her friends themselves might offer. It is hard to imagine that Mavi, having "solved" the problem of her identity through sex, will now go on to live a fulfilled life in which she will be able to include work as a meaningful activity.

The tie between class and sex is clear enough. Niccolò as masseur is very much the servant of Mavi's imperious sexual needs. And her "right" to so elaborate a sexual life seems guaranteed in some sense by her membership in the leisured class. Though she claims to have left her class and to be on Niccolò's "side," it is obvious that she is not: she enjoys the party, particularly its undercurrent of intrigue. She even defends the wastrel millionaires, explaining, zanily enough to raise Niccolò's eyebrows, that "you can't blame them when things go wrong . . . This society lacks a single unifying ideal . . . In Italy each party has its own." (As explanation for these off-the-wall remarks, the original treatment notes that "she has no sense of humor" and that she is "eccentric.") There is other evidence that she is deeply trapped in the devious snobbery of her class: in the way she rushes into her apartment to answer the telephone out of breath and looking guilty, in the way she offers to "swear" that something is or is not true, in the way she makes appointments with other men under Niccolò's very nose. Her mind moves as restlessly as her body. She gets over the trauma of meeting her father too soon. She is too frenetic to dwell long on sorrow—or on any other emotion, for that matter. It is obviously not accidental that she can move so quickly from the story of her father trauma to her gossip about the shopgirl making love in a car, which she recounts in a voice that mixes vindictive "shock" with a voyeurist's relish. In short, Mavi is unpredictable, chameleonlike, impossible to read, and, above all, totally incapable of engaging in quiet dialogue in a boat out on the open lagoon near Venice.

The Antonioni character of whom she most reminds us is Anna in *L'avventura*. Very little information is provided in the dialogue or action to account for her motives, and like Anna she disappears. True, she gives something like reasons in the quarrel in the farmhouse: "You'll ruin my life" and so on. When Niccolò reaffirms his love, she snarls, "Do you like the way I lead my life?" But when he gives up, murmuring, "Christ, how lucid you are" (one of the less fortunate lines in the screenplay), she runs to embrace him, and they make love. Like Anna, it is obvious that she derives some secondary gain from being enigmatic. But the effect does not work as well in this film as it did in *L'avventura*, perhaps because the enigma is diegetically resolved: we *do* see the last of her, ensconced in a new relationship. The film seems to say that this is what she wanted all along; at last she has found it. The problem is that there is no particular reason—the film has not provided any reasons—to believe that Mavi will persevere in this relationship either. So her character remains unresolved, not by design (as is Anna's) but faute de mieux.

Part of the problem with Mavi's characterization may lie with the actress who plays her. It is all very well to depict a character whose psyche is chaotic, incompletely formed, *inachevée*. But clearly the role must be played by someone who is herself clear about what she is doing. Unlike Lea Massari in *L'avventura*, Daniela Silverio seems to be confused about the character, and she does not manage to transform her confusion into Mavi's confusion. (An actress of the stature of Moreau or Vitti could perhaps have pulled the role off.) It is difficult to decide, for instance, whether Mavi's speculations about God and about society are supposed to sound addled or not. Further, though she is quite attractive, she does not strike one as particularly aristocratic. The actress who plays her sister is much more convincingly so.

Ida is another case entirely—healthy, down-to-earth, direct, sincere, in every way estimable, indeed to a fault: one cannot imagine why Niccolò would want to give her up. Antonioni has had the actress made up to emphasize her high forehead, which suggests both her intelligence and openness and a certain physical plainness—just enough to prevent her from attaining stardom. "The face is irregular but extremely expressive," says the treatment. (So much for glamor girl standards!) Boisson's face is so well chosen that one thinks of Eisenstein's theory

Frame 141

of facial typage. And the character's manner goes with her appearance: she smiles rarely, but when she does, it is a genuine beam, simple and sincere. She concentrates on people and things with intense and undivided attention, quite the opposite of the distracted and furtive Mavi. She holds her mouth open ever so slightly, a mark of innocence that mitigates the toughness in her body and manner. She radiates health and bears a simple and direct relation to nature. (Antonioni makes her fond of horses, shooting her as she canters about the fields of the estate adjacent to her house.) She is as calm as nature itself and flexible and easy to get along with. "She is always available," the treatment tells us. Her philosophy is to "take whatever comes along." Even though she is gregarious and likes people, she easily adjusts to Niccolò's love for solitude. And she is plucky when her principles are challenged. She proves her mettle in their final argument, at least up to the moment when she is made to express a preference for the father of her unborn child. Through tears that she barely restrains, she repeats her expression of love, even in response to Niccolò's angry taunt to "say it again."

Christine Boisson plays the role brilliantly. She makes great sense of the character, achieving something of the integrity that Monica Vitti brought to Claudia and Vittoria. Whatever difficulty Niccolò may have had, Antonioni certainly identified *this* woman correctly.

A RETURN TO CONVENTIONAL EXPOSITION

Unlike the films of the tetralogy, *Identificazione di una donna* makes efforts to account for the characters by going into their histories, especially those of Mavi and Ida. Mavi tells Niccolò about her school problems and, of course, about her relationship with her father. (In the treatment, she goes into even more detail.) And, at the swimming pool, her young blond friend tells him something of Mavi's sexual history. For her part, Ida volunteers information about her youth, when she worked for an itinerant clothing merchant, and she also talks about her relationship with her last boyfriend. Niccolò's sister wants to talk about his marital history, but he quickly squelches the discussion. What seems new here—and uncharacteristic of Antonioni's style—is a desire to provide verbal explanations for why characters are the way they are. We remember the disregard for etiology in the films of the sixties, how the personal past, if recollected at all, appeared only in the form of visible relics once experienced by the characters. But the relics were not commented upon, and they remained as mysterious and opaque as everything else in the films: the half-buried trolley track in the old quarter where the Pontanos once lived, the toys of Vittoria's and Piero's childhood, Giuliana's fantasy of the secret erotic beach and the strange boat. The refusal to use conventional exposition bespoke an absorption with the surface of the world for its own sake. But in *Identificazione di una donna* the world seems to have acquired a historical dimension. (*The Passenger,* too, goes into the protagonist's past, in the scenes of wife and home in London, the videotaping of the repressive African ruler, and so on.) It is not clear what Antonioni hopes to gain by this renewal of interest in exposition.

Formally, his new concern with the past as explanation finds its quintessential narrative shape in flashbacks, which are more frequent in this film than they are in any other. Unfortunately, they are also less smooth and less creative. In the first, Niccolò sits in his study jotting down notes for his film; he looks up distracted, smiles, and taps his pen on his pad. Music begins, and a brief dissolve carries us back to the scene in which he and Mavi met on the telephone in his sister's office. What we see in the flashback is interesting enough: Niccolò peers at X ray negatives as he tries to imagine from Mavi's voice what she looks like. But the transition markers themselves—the dissolve and the rush of music—seem old hat. Exposition is written all over them. They differ totally in spirit from Antonioni's dry, minimalist style of the sixties. The flashback continues with an extensive ellipsis forward; we cut to the first time they make love, in Niccolò's apartment. In bed, Mavi tells Niccolò about her experience at college, and we see representative scenes of how she lived in Wales—a flashback within a flashback. They resume their lovemaking, and then we return to the narrative present, again through a dissolve: Niccolò sits at his desk drawing a picture of the gorilla. At least, I think that that is the order of events. But the very fact that I am not totally clear is perhaps a mark of a technical problem.

A similar problem arises with the second flashback, in which Mavi recounts to Niccolò what happened when her father approached her on the staircase before the party. In the original sequence, the father is hidden behind the pillar around which the staircase winds: we only hear his voice asking Mavi to stop and speak to him. Niccolò discreetly continues up the stairway, the camera cutting to him higher up just outside the front door of the mansion. A woman passes him, and they exchange a few words. Then Mavi comes up looking distressed and asks Niccolò if they can leave. He agrees. Later in the film, a flashback occurs as Niccolò and Mavi stand in the shopping street: in response to the concern he expresses about her tears, she asks him if he remembers her being stopped on the stairs by a man. Quick dissolve: the man, whom we have never seen before, appears in medium close-up and volunteers the information that she is his daughter. By way of proof, he asks her to compare the shape of her hand with his. The transition is not totally clear. The man is speaking directly into the camera, his back against a blank white wall, which might be anywhere. (Actually, it is the pillar around which the stairway winds. But the camera is too close to reveal its cylindrical contour.) To make sense of the sequence, one has to recall the cut in the original sequence to characters moving up the stairway around the pillar. But this happens many minutes before. Struggling for context, one has recourse not to

Frame 142

visuals but to background auditory details like the piano music coming from the party above. The clarity of the flashback is undermined and for no identifiable diegetic or thematic reason.

The narrative status of a third sequence is even less clear, although that may be intentional. It, too, is marked by a dissolve, in this case from a wall in Niccolò's apartment that is covered with esoteric symbols to the image of Mavi, naked, stepping out of a bathtub, looking at her body, and seeking reassurance that she is not aging. Niccolò's voice is heard in voice-over—we do not see him. Presumably, the shot is from his point of view, the camera occupying the position of his eyes. Is this another flashback to something that actually happened? Is it Niccolò's fantasy of something that might happen? Or is it a generalization about the state of their relationship at this moment? The published screenplay indicates that the shot is a flashback, but our uncertainty when watching the film itself may lead us to ask whether there is enough context to make that reading inevitable. The events depicted could have been handled more simply by a dialogue report.

These flashbacks are not really motivated (if we compare them, say, with the powerful moment in *The Passenger* when Locke exchanges identities with Robertson). It is almost as if they were gratuitous, as if Antonioni simply had decided that he would like to try some flashbacks. But formal gratuitousness does not serve him as well as the gratuitousness of content of his films of the sixties. Then the *objets trouvés* provided perfect support for the sense of a fragmented world. But the use of arbitrary forms does not mesh with the verisimilitude evoked by the films of the eighties. Instead, they suggest a troubling artistic uncertainty. The same sense crops up occasionally in the dialogue: a few speeches seem to have little raison d'être. Niccolò calls Mavi, but he has nothing in particular to say. And then there seem to be one or two mistakes in the plot: Niccolò's sister asks him when she will meet Mavi. But there is reason to believe (and nothing is provided to counter it) that Mavi is already her patient. With whom could a woman be more intimate than her gynecologist? Does *meet* here mean "meet socially"? Or must we infer that Mavi never succeeded in getting an appointment with Niccolò's sister, and why?

The published screenplay shows that Antonioni remained uncharacteristically close to his original treatment, especially to the dialogue. The increased reliance on words suggests that his working methods may have changed. Many lines of dialogue are kept virtually intact. A few Italian critics have found the dialogue unnatural.[18] Antonioni's response was angry: "Some have reproved me for the 'banality' of the dialogue. But where have these people been? I have used an everyday parlance that anyone can hear in the street. The screenplays of certain films are laughable: they propose a language that does not exist on heaven or earth . . . And in any case words can never be separated from images when pronouncing judgment on a film."[19] It is difficult for a non-Italian to grasp the nuances that are involved, and in any case one could argue that the very awkwardness of the language may be one more sign of the "collective banality" that is so prominent a theme of the film.

But I am more concerned with the implications of Antonioni's close adherence to the written treatment for the style as a whole. One can only speculate, but it would seem that the more a director follows dialogue and indications of action written before shooting, the less open he will be to visual inspiration on the set. His state, by definition, has become something less than "virgin." Instead of using the scenario as a springboard for totally free visual creativity, he looks for visual corroborations of material that has already been conceptualized. For all the visual beauties of *Identificazione di una donna,* one cannot help feeling that it is controlled more by script directions than the earlier films were. This is not to say that it is stilted or that Antonioni has lost his spontaneity. Clearly, his production methods remain very different from Hitchcock's (whose scenario for *Frenzy,* it is said, was so tight that he did not have to leave his Rolls Royce during shooting at Covent Garden). Rather, it may be that to satisfy the random or aleatory promptings of his genius, Antonioni is relying less on the camera and more on his auditory memory (or a tape recorder). One can imagine him noting down lines in much the way that Niccolò does, at odd moments, interrupting the normal course of his life to record things that he or someone else says—fragments of documented audio reality, in their exact idiom—then introducing such lines verbatim into the film. There is nothing particularly surprising about this increased favoring of the verbal dimension. Antonioni has become an established figure in the world of Italian letters through frequent publication of treatments, stories, unshot screenplays, and the like. The word *autore*—like French *auteur*—can mean both writer and filmmaker.

What may be troubling the critics is less the accuracy of Antonioni's transcription of bits of current Roman speech than the way in which he splices them together. His films, particularly this one, often seem to join brief documentary speech records on a principle resembling the one that joins his visual images—in montage, that is, on a mosaic kind of juxtaposition that emphasizes contingency and gratuitousness at the possible risk of conventional coherence. In the tetralogy, this technique enhances the discontinuity between visible appearances and the deeper realities of troubled urban souls. The auditory track has a life of its own. By not corroborating the visuals, it helps to undermine them, make them ambiguous or at least difficult to read, "like life itself." In later films like *Blow-Up,* the principle of gratuitous juxtaposition helps to underscore the theme of the modern fragmentation of life. We have noted the brilliant non sequiturs in the exchange of utterances between Thomas and the painter's wife, for example. But the context of *Identificazione di una donna* seemed to promise something different. (At least it did to some disappointed critics.) The very figure of Niccolò suggests a coherence of viewpoint that, though new for Antonioni, is relatively traditional in fiction. The characters in the tetralogy do not stand above their world, do not critique it the way Niccolò does. They are too enmeshed in its problems to provide an objective perspective. The tetralogy offers the viewer precious little assistance in learning to read meanings out of its surfaces. Even in later films like *Blow-Up* and *The Passenger,* our identification with the protagonists (and the consequent diegetic coherence) is minimized by the subtleties of the problems they face. The viewer is still very much on his or her own, meditating on the hubris of a spaced-out fashion photographer or the change of life of a world-weary television journalist.

But even if we do not (as we should not) identify Niccolò with his creator, he is, as Antonioni says in an interview, "a director of a certain age; his métier has taught him to take life with a certain savoir-faire."[20] We cannot escape the sense that we are to see life through his critical eyes and hear it interpreted through his relatively articulate voice. That he articulates is what is new—or old-fashioned, depending on how you look at it. Not only is his situation not that extraordinary, but he is by no means averse to spelling out his views about it—and about a lot else besides. He may be frustrated, but everything that he says either relates directly to the plot or clearly comments on the world. He may be alienated from the life of Rome, but he is not alienated from coherent discourse about that life. He may not be a spokesman, but he is certainly a focalized or central consciousness (in James's sense of the word). Mavi's philosophizing about God and politics, the bizarre alliance between thugs and the aristocracy, the scenario "Voices from Beyond," and so forth are absurd precisely because he pronounces them so. The norm that he provides, unlike the norms established through the mute gaze of characters like Lidia and Vittoria, is chiefly articulated in words. It is not the camera that wanders the streets with Niccolò but the sound track that makes his opinions about the state of things audible. One longs for the eloquent silences of the films of the sixties. It is one thing to hear Mavi's inane remarks about the innocence of the aristocracy: we can write that off to the eccentricity of the character and the insensitivity of the times. But how are we to respond when our own monitor of values says, apropos, for instance, of Mavi's concern that the wet wood in a fireplace will not ignite, "Why so pessimistic? Don't you have any faith in nature? In Baku, in Russia, there is a temple dedicated to the god of fire where a flame always burns, fed from the bowels of the earth. In reality it is oil that burns. They're loaded with oil in those parts: lucky them"?[21]

The film is very talky by traditional Antonionian standards. Too many lines are spent establishing the believability of Niccolò's erotic charm. For instance, the initial dialogue with Ida is excessively cute:

IDA: Why did you come back to see the show?
NICCOLÒ: I didn't come to see the show, I came to watch them bake *rosette.*
IDA: Ah . . . I've heard that you're one of those rotten eggheads with whom it is impossible to discuss anything.
NICCOLÒ: But I'm not an egghead, neither rotten nor fresh.
IDA: Two people told me, it must be true.
NICCOLÒ: And I've heard nothing about you. Oh yes, someone told me that you're sexy.
IDA: Only that?
NICCOLÒ: Okay, lots of other things are being said that I haven't heard; I'll have to find out.
NICCOLÒ: Who are you sleeping with now?

IDA:	With a boy my age.
NICCOLÒ (*off*):	Ah. Your director?
IDA:	No. Do you go to bed with your actresses?
NICCOLÒ:	Rarely . . . I'm glad it's not your director.
IDA:	Why?
NICCOLÒ:	For two reasons. The second is that that guy has the kind of face that reminds me of Heine's line, "He's as sad as a day-old German corpse."
IDA:	And the first reason?
NICCOLÒ:	Guess.

Comparisons in a way are unfair, but one cannot help remembering the exquisite silence of the scene in *L'avventura* (analyzed in Chapter 6 above) when Sandro and Claudia first sense their mutual attraction.

A MORE TRADITIONALIST STYLE

Identificazione di una donna has all the familiar compositional brilliance of an Antonioni film. The framing is as elegant as ever. Proportions are marked off crisply by the horizontals and verticals of door frames and windows and other architectural details. Particularly memorable are scenes like the one that opens

Frame 143

the film: Niccolò is caught by the camera, as by his own alarm system, trying to sneak under the electronic surveillance beam. The drama of the shot is serio-comic, and the patch of light that switches on is placed in an oblique part of the frame as deftly as in an abstract painting. Other beautiful squares or oblongs or circles include the swinging doors of the ice cream parlor, with Niccolò's head just above them; the doorway to the elegant party, which is flanked by servants so calm they seem to grow out of the woodwork; Niccolò's own study window, where the place of honor is reserved for a photo of Louise Brooks, presumably the norm by which the women in the photos pinned to the adjacent bulletin board are measured (see Frame 138 above); the whole room at the second party, which catches the thick, static, and slightly comic opulence of the aristocracy in imagery reminiscent of Velázquez; the circular convex traffic mirror above Niccolò's head against a wall in the Gianicolo. Perhaps the most exquisite composition is helical, as Mavi looks up the stairwell of her Trastevere apartment.

Frame 144

Antonioni's camera is quieter than ever. There are few pans and fewer tracks, and all are strictly functional, serving as establishing shots or, with eye-line matches, following Niccolò's point of view. Sometimes the movements are subtle and profound, as in the sequence in the fog. The camera moves, but it finds nothing: the fog is no less murky for us than it is for Niccolò. The pan establishing the second party captures perfectly the awkwardness that goes with all that inbreeding. And so do the camera movements that orchestrate the chorus of suspicious looks directed at Niccolò as he moves through the rooms of the villa. Other pans are less fortunate, as when the camera moves "discreetly" away from the lovers' embrace in the farmhouse (shades of Hollywood in the forties); the discretion seems particularly ill advised given the explicitness of the love scenes elsewhere in the film.

Antonioni edited the film himself. He explained his reasons in an interview. After acknowledging his debt to Eraldo Da Roma, who edited most of the Italian films of the fifties and sixties, and to Franco (Kim) Arcalli, who edited *Zabriskie Point* and *The Passenger,* he says he has

discovered that the collaboration between editor and director . . . was limited to telling the editor what I wanted. The editor did it but, when I found myself in difficulty, would propose suggestions, ideas, sometimes ingenious ones—especially Kim, who was extraordinary. Kim has been dead two years. I haven't had much confidence in other editors. So I've tried to do it myself, because it seemed to me that I knew quite well what I wanted, having shot with a certain montage in mind. I always have the montage in mind when I shoot. Practically, at least a priori, the montage is only a consequence of the shot. Obviously, it sometimes happens that once one has the material in hand, one has another idea, and that also becomes a creative phase. But if you want the film to have its own unity and personality, these ideas can only be those of the director . . . So I like to be seated at the moviola, to have the film in my hands directly, without the mediation of the editor. It's a physical job, even "epidermic" in a sense.[22]

(Editing video, of course, is much more complicated, and he needed the help of technicians on *Il mistero di Oberwald.*)

The editing of *Identificazione* is by and large well done, in the familiar elliptical style. The cuts are crisp and work well with the narrative structure and characterization. For instance, there is a quick cut from Mavi refusing to speak to Niccolò in the car to a long shot of the two approaching the farmhouse. She is now full of curiosity about the Roman ruins underneath. The ellipsis underscores the erratic changeableness of her moods and establishes a subliminal basis for her disappearance a few sequences later. As ever, the editing avoids all explanatory clichés.

There are more dissolves than usual. Mostly associated with flashbacks, they help, as we have seen, to make the film seem more traditional.[23] But in compensation there are some interesting, novel matches in which color is used to represent longer time changes. A particularly subtle one registers nightfall at the farmhouse. Another is the clever bit in which the passage of time between Niccolò's two visits to Mavi's Trastevere apartment is marked by showing his car, after only a beat, entering the frame from which it has exited. The change of color and lighting indicates that night has fallen as the car parks in exactly the same spot (underneath an Italian Communist Party placard). The subtle effects remind one of *Il mistero di Oberwald,* and it is good to know that Antonioni does not need television technology to create them. There are occasional *temps morts,* but they are no longer the strongly marked feature that they were in the sixties, since they usually serve simple narrative functions, as when the camera lingers on the car that Mavi feared might contain her mysterious suitor's gorilla. The camera holds briefly on an interesting architectural feature or two, caryatids that support a roof or a baroque detail on the corner of a building in Trastevere. In a few spots, unfortunately, the lingering seems to be unmotivated and even to destroy the dramatic effect, for example, at the end of the sequence in which Niccolò sees the gorilla in an angled traffic mirror and confronts him while a group of religious novices looks on. The hold on the two actors gives the impression that they have awkwardly run out of words. In general, continuing the trend of *The Passenger,* the shots are quite short.

Whether these new effects work depends on how much you like the film. A French critic is quite enthusiastic:

Such a subject, as modern for its time as *L'avventura* was for its, but based on a profound change in mentality, clothing, and social system, could not be represented in the manner of 1960 . . . The deep-focus shots, the long takes encompassing the whole of the immobile universe in which the men and women of the sixties wander in solitude, expectation, and desperation can no longer work. The change, dispersal, existential course, speed, and violence of acts and feelings are translated here into an extremely punctuated direction, into brief shots linked by ellipses, into camera movements that explore fragments of reality.[24]

This is a fair description of the Mavi half of the film, for the editing and camera work match her erratic behavior (would that Silvero's performance had been up to Antonioni's standards). But it does not do justice to other aspects of the film — for instance, the representation of the aristocracy at play, which captures the tedium as well as the pent-up aggression of these people in elegant tuxedos and evening gowns. Similarly, it does not account for much in the Ida half of the film, when a certain tranquillity falls over Niccolò's life. In a certain sense, the shooting and editing in the later part of the film seem less noticeable in themselves, more "invisible" in the classic Hollywood fashion, perfectly adequate to the narrative but not particularly Antonionian.

It is sad that Antonioni's budget did not permit him to end the film with the kind of finale that he wanted (and that it seems to need). For if the science fiction sequence had been realized with effects of the caliber of *2001, Star Wars,* or *Blade Runner,* one's feelings about Niccolò and his situation as an artist might be entirely different. (Image *The Passenger* without its expensive finale.) Antonioni is clearly a filmmaker whose work should not be constrained by budget, and we all suffer when his productions are not adequately financed.

As for the sound track: having pioneered the dry style cleansed of music, Antonioni seems to have decided to introduce it once again, and he does so with a vengeance. In the Mavi half of the film, it is electronic, synthetic, noisy, even slightly hysterical, as are the times. This works reasonably well when the source is clear (as when Niccolò, like Thomas, plays the latest hit on his phonograph) or when the setting suggests that there might be an earshot source (Gianna Nannini's hoarse cacophonic counterpoint to the turmoil in the shopping street could be coming from a stereo in a mod clothing shop). The mad music works less well when it sounds commentative. Then one wonders what has happened to the old subtlety. Niccolò is hanging photos of women's faces, *strum,* he looks up, *strum,* he goes to his bedroom to watch Mavi sleep, *strum, mysterious oriental-cum-science-fiction theme,* and so on. Why this combination of Latin American flute with electronic whatever? Do we really need this externalization of the artist lover's throes? And if so, what of the claims to the ordinariness of Niccolò's situation, to the pedestrianism of a "love of today"? Or is it that noisy electronic music *is* the pedestrian and silence the mystery? What perturbs more than anything else is the uncharacteristically heavy-handed pointing to how we are supposed to feel. At the culmination of Mavi and Niccolò's affair, in the farmhouse, sweet themes can be heard on piano and cello (though most of the encounter actually takes the form of a quarrel). These dissolve rather awkwardly into another kind of music, a tinny, happy hurdy-gurdy tune, suitable to a more cheerful *Il grido.* When Niccolò contemplates the stamps bearing astronauts' portraits or when he runs upstairs, after his love affairs are over, to peer through his telescope, there is a rush of science fiction music. The extraordinary view of the sun's flares is trivialized by electric guitar and drums playing "extraterrestrial" electronic chords (surely the most suitable sound for the awesomeness of space is intense and absolute silence). When Ida pays her first visit to Niccolò's apartment, we hear the equivalent of royal entry music, mock baroque chords on an electric harpsichord (or perhaps a synthesizer programmed to sound like a mandolin?).

The only really successful use of music (at least to my ears) occurs in the Ida half of the film. Then we hear gentle late-Romantic piano music (Grieg, Scriabin), which succeeds in evoking some of the nostalgia implicit in the situations of the two breakups. We first hear it in the sequence in which Mavi and Niccolò separate for good without saying goodbye. Perhaps the poignancy of the situation can surface precisely because there is no redundancy: since nothing is said, the music can speak. The same kind of music is played in the hotel in Venice as a commentary on Niccolò's second breakup. (As in *8 1/2,* it starts offscreen, but at a certain point a piano in the lobby becomes visible. The effect is a neat blending of physical and psychological reality.) But even here, one feels inclined to trade the bought nostalgia (since that is not really the point of the film) for something more striking and original—namely silence, like the silence of the coda of *L'eclisse.*

WHAT NEXT?

Identificazione di una donna is an interesting film but not a successful one. It pales in comparison with Antonioni's Italian films of the sixties. It has problems in narrative and theme and in its style and finish. It is not that Antonioni has re-gressed but (perhaps) that with *Blow-Up* and *The Passenger* he outgrew the Italian scene, so that a script with its roots in the sixties simply will not work for him today. Something of that seems to be acknowledged in a statement he made to the press about his next projected film, *The Crew* (*La ciurme*), to be shot in English off the coast of Florida:

With *Identificazione di una donna* I feel I have closed a certain period of my career, that of the intimate cinema, of the chamber cinema [*cinema camera*]. I need to go out into the open, to change. The public has changed, it has other sensibilities, other mechanisms of thought, other emotional requirements . . . I'll do something different, more violent . . . [*The Crew* contains a lot of violence.] A logical violence. The characters seem to behave like maniacs. But that is because madness is the only contemporary way to live and to survive. Violence and madness are the refusal to think according to the logic that has prevailed up to now, the refusal to accept the conventions and mechanisms handed down to us. On the yacht, the crew attacks the rich owner who is trying to save everything from the storm; this behavior seems counter to good sense, but the sailors have their reasons.[25]

Conclusion

As of this writing, Antonioni is seventy-two years old. He is a young and vigorous seventy-two, and he has now completed his fourteenth feature film. Like Cukor and Kurosawa and Huston, he will doubtless make more. It is impossible to predict their contents, so diverse are his interests and plans, but it seems certain that at the formal level he will remain in the vanguard of his craft. His fascination with and proficiency in science and technology have made him one of cinema's important technical innovators. He has experimented with deep-focus effects, control of color, electronic sound, stabilization of the image in long, hitherto unimaginable tracking shots, video color-mixing techniques, and so on. This experimentation never has the appearance of experimentation for its own sake but contributes directly and forcefully to his themes, plots, and characterization. Antonioni is the kind of artist who is inspired by the technical problems and opportunities of his medium: like a poet seized by a rhyme that he expands into a sonnet or like a sculptor who sees the outline of his next statue in a block of marble at the quarry, the prospect of new ways of filming sets Antonioni off on a creative train that ends in the total human experience of a film.

But along with his technical mastery, I think, history will see in the composition of his imagery Antonioni's greatest contribution to cinema. He is a member of that small and elite band of filmmakers, which includes Eisenstein, Dreyer, and Sternberg, who are blessed with the touch of the great painter or photographer; in the subtlety of his effects, he may be the most eminent. His way of placing characters and their situations in an architectural ambience is unique and constantly refreshing. I know of no director whose films so consistently tolerate, nay profit, from repeated viewings. (I refer, of course, to his mature films. Antonioni's apprenticeship was long and arduous, and his reputation cannot rest on the films of the fifties.) He is one of the few filmmakers whom we can discuss, without seeming absurd, in the context of Degas, Braque, Mondrian, and Morandi, of Weston, Man Ray, and Cartier-Bresson. His ties with serious twentieth-century art are clearer and more direct than any other commercial filmmaker's.

As for his literary powers, Antonioni has contributed as much to the development of modern narrative as have directors who come more readily to mind, such as Welles, Godard, and Resnais. He developed a *cinéma du regard* that measures favorably with its novelistic counterpart. We have seen him infuse a popular literary genre, the roman noir, with serious purpose: however much mystery and suspense are mere pretexts, *L'avventura, Blow-Up,* and *The Passenger* involve the mass audience in more serious questions than the usual trivialized violence — questions about the nature of identity, love, and death. The audience always gets more than it bargains for when it sees one of his films. Its perceptions are sharpened about many things, about how our surroundings really look, about how complex people are, about how unlikely it is—despite our tendency to privilege sight above the other senses—that we shall ever achieve coherent insight into another soul. For Antonioni is no more confident than was Proust about capturing and setting down personality. The more we look at Anna, Sandro, and Lidia, at Giuliana, Corrado, Thomas, and David Locke, the more opaque they seem. Yet that opacity is familiar. It reminds us of how often a dear face (that of a lover, offspring, dear friend) bears an expression that has no conceivable relation to all that we think we know about the person behind it. Antonioni has often been criticized for adopting negative attitudes about life. But his searching demonstration of how little we can know about others is, to me, salutary. Unexpectedly, and without the least moralism, he provides one more instance of art's capacity to instruct as well as to delight. We come away from his films with our eyes—as the Russian Formalists would say—"made strange." The world is defamiliarized, and we question, for a healthy moment, our stereotyped "power" to read the faces that we meet.

It is true that his range is limited. He is at his best with characters of a very particular sort—contemporary, intelligent, sensitive, well-off (though his documentaries and *Il grido* show that he is quite able to render people from other walks of life). Granted, he is not interested in the broad sweep of society; he is no Dickens or Griffith. But if in his intensity he is more like Proust than Joyce, more like El Greco than Goya, does that make him less valuable? The important thing in art is, surely, profundity, and within a certain range of sensibility no filmmaker has been more profound. To write him off as "too depressing" would be like writing Jean Renoir off as "too jovial." There is no more convincing portrait on film of the neurotic personality of our time than that of Giuliana. Yet there is nothing clinical about that study: it is truly an artist's vision of neurosis. The problems faced by characters like Sandro, Anna, Giovanni, Lidia, Piero, Thomas, and David make them less attractive, less easy to identify with than most characters whom we see on the screen. But, by the same token, they have more at stake. In that sense, Antonioni can be seen as a more serious artist than his peers.

In the best of his films, Antonioni's way of telling a story is one of the most sophisticated in cinema. Working with threads that seem tangential, elliptical, problematic, even irrelevant, little dialogue, and no explanatory music, he somehow weaves a hauntingly meaningful fabric.

Antonioni's themes have come and gone—the obsolescence of monogamy, eros as anodyne, *fredezza morale,* escape, distraction, the awesome beauty of science and technology, the vulgarization of life, and so on. However accurately these themes spoke to the issues of the day, they themselves mean less than the fact that the issues were, again, serious. Antonioni is a man of ideas, and he uses his films as an arena in which to engage them. Unlike directors who use other people's ideas or, at best, "work something up" for a film, his ideas are always there, in his head, available for whatever inspiration the location or the exigencies of shooting may provide. In his best films, this fingertip responsiveness endows his characters with an intellectual substance that exceeds the ordinary requirements of commercial cinema. Somehow, despite the paucity of information that we have about them, they seem more like us and people we know.

Antonioni's seriousness, however, is not tied to anything like an ideology. He is incapable of using his films to argue a political position. (When he tried, in *Zabriskie Point,* the result was disastrous.) He stays too close to the complexities of the individual to see politics except in its minutest implications for private life. The surfaces of the world come first, and they are too complex for the neat categories of ideology. His seriousness and his complexity will, I think, guarantee that his films will continue to be seen. Future audiences have to don historical spectacles if they are to understand the characters' situations, but the human relevance will not escape them. I think Antonioni's oeuvre will prove more durable than the entertainments of a Truffaut or the moral exercises of a Rohmer or the abstract schematics of a Godard. As long as there is a list of the ten best films, *L'avventura* will surely be on it. (We can hope that the judges will come to see the merits of *L'eclisse,* which at this distance in time seems to me even more striking.) Antonioni's contribution to the cinema rests not on a single film but on a rich oeuvre in which at least seven stand out—*Il grido, L'avventura, La notte, L'eclisse, Il deserto rosso, Blow-Up,* and *The Passenger.* These films must be seen and studied not only by future filmmakers but by anyone who pretends to cinematic literacy.

Notes

Introduction

1. 1980 television interview with Lino Miccichè (unpublished).
2. Roland Barthes, "Caro Antonioni," in *Catalogo della rassegna: Tutto Antonioni in 13 giorni,* ed. Vittorio Boarini (Bologna, 1980), p. 4. (Translations from Italian and French are mine unless I cite the translator's name.)
3. 1980 television interview with Lino Miccichè.
4. Antonioni is a reticent man, preferring to talk about his work rather than himself. There are few biographical sketches: the most comprehensive in English is Pierre Leprohon, *Michelangelo Antonioni: The Man and His Work,* trans. Scott Sullivan, 2d ed. (New York, 1969). Additional details can be found in Italian in Carlo Di Carlo, *Michelangelo Antonioni* (Rome, 1964), and Aldo Bernardini, *Michelangelo Antonioni da "Gente del Po" a "Blow-Up"* (Milan, 1967).

Chapter 1

1. My attempts to see the last three documentaries have been unsuccessful; I rely on the account of Philip Strick, *Antonioni* (London, 1963), p. 25:

Sette Canne, un vestito . . . was filmed at Torniviscosa, a village near Trieste. For a change, Antonioni showed more interest with the machinery than with the people, although the film did not sever itself completely (like Resnais' *Chant du styrène*) from the factory workers, or eulogise the cellulose plants to the exclusion of their controllers. It was put together with great precision and an almost impersonal style. . . . *La villa dei mostri,* the short which followed . . . dealt with sculptures designed by the proprietor of the Orsini villa at Bomarzo (near Viterbo), who used for the purpose stones fallen from a mountain. These statues were scattered in gay abandon about the villa gardens, with something of the incongruity, if not the phallicism, of the weird monoliths in Sweden's Vigeland Park. They portrayed monstrous anthropomorphic forms through which Antonioni wandered with his cameraman; the result was a film expressing much the same feeling towards the statues as was expressed towards the machines in *Sette canne*—an inference of their latent menace. The two films attracted some attention to Antonioni, and he was offered several subjects; he agreed to do a documentary on the cable-car which connects Cortina d'Ampezzo and Monte Faria, although the theme did not greatly appeal to him. He went to Cortina, set himself up on the roof of the cable-car and endeavoured to capture on film his impressions of the emptiness around him. But again he found his budget was reduced; sooner than waste time on something unsatisfactory, he returned to Rome. The documentary *La funi-*

via del Faloria was, as a result, a rather meagre collection of very bleak shots, Antonionian in little more than their sense of isolation.

2. A phrase used by the voice-over commentator: see the scenario in *Il primo Antonioni,* ed. Carlo Di Carlo (Bologna, 1973), p. 26.

3. According to Carlo Di Carlo, *Michelangelo Antonioni,* p. 123, it is actually Antonioni who wrote *Lo sceicco bianco* in 1948. He agreed to collaborate with Fellini and Pinelli but "insisted on a free and antitraditional rendition of the story." He did not prevail, and he yielded the story to Fellini, who finished the film, somewhat modified, in 1952.

4. Antonioni apparently disowned the film because of meddling on the part of the producer; see Bernardini, p. 29.

5. Lorenzo Cuccu, *La visione come problema: Forme e svolgimento del cinema di Antonioni* (Rome, 1973), p. 19. Antonioni produced but did not direct a short documentary, *Uomini in più* (Too Many People, 1955), which I have not seen, on the problems of immigration and overpopulation in Italy.

6. Paraphrased from Francesco Bolzoni, "Un ritratto di Antonioni," in Di Carlo, *Michelangelo Antonioni,* p. 158.

7. In addition, there are hints in this scene of that "contemplative suspension" (Cuccu, p. 89) of the camera on the landscape that will play such an important role in the later films.

8. Cuccu (pp. 23–24) attributes Antonioni's interest in the long take to his experience in France, where he was assistant director on Carné's *Les visiteurs du soir* in 1942. But, Cuccu argues, Antonioni was more interested in the camera styles of Renoir and Bresson than of Carné. To the influence of Carné he attributes only the decor of the Milanese suburbs and of Guido's *pensione.* Antonioni himself expressed his preference for Renoir and Bresson over Carné in an interview in *Cinéma 65* 100 (1965): 43.

9. Noël Burch, *Theory of Film Practice,* trans. Helen Lane (New York, 1973), pp. 76–77. Antonioni pointed out in the 1980 television interview with Miccichè that the absence of close-ups had a strictly technical reason: "To move the camera in every direction . . . I needed to use certain lenses which did not permit me to approach the character too closely, hence the close-up was excluded." Still, its loss was not felt, for "certain attitudes of the actor's body, certain of his ways of moving and walking and looking take the place of the close-up."

10. See the interesting book by Bruce Kawin, *Mindscreen* (Princeton, 1978), for a discussion of point of view in film.

11. Antonioni argues the point in the 1980 television interview with Miccichè: "It did not interest me at that time to analyze the relationship of the individual to society, something that was being done so well by directors like De Sica, Rossellini, etc.; but I was interested in seeing what had remained in those characters who had come out of the war and the postwar period feeling so searingly violent, what had remained of all those experiences within them." This remark also answers the question of whether *Cronaca di un amore* should be considered a neorealist film.

12. Bernardini, p. 30. Di Carlo describes the troubled history of the film: "Antonioni wanted to recount three crimes of youth without burdening the film with a priori meanings; the producers for their part, however, demanded that the film have an irrevocably moralistic and Catholic character. For Antonioni the layman, it was an unacceptable decision. After violent discussion, which lasted for months, a compromise was reached: to substitute for the [Italian] episode already scripted another by [Diego] Fabbri [the producer and founder of the production company Film-Costellazione] and to add a sort of preface made up of newspaper material on youth, a look at the so-called burned-out European youth" (*Il primo Antonioni,* ed. Carlo Di Carlo, pp. 123–24).

It would be a mistake to lay the blame for *I vinti* entirely on the producer's doorstep. The crudity of Antonioni's approach to the theme of troubled youth is evident not only in the film that he did shoot but also in one that he did not, namely *Stanotte hanno sparato* (There Was Shooting Last Night), a treatment proposed in 1949 and rejected by the Italian equivalent of the Hays Office as *sconsigliato*—not recommended (see *Cinema nuovo*, no. 9 [1953], pp. 246–48). Like *Cronaca di un amore*, the treatment is a curious permutation of film noir.

13. *I vinti* and *Amore in città* were among the first of what came to be a favorite Italian genre, the episode film, discussed by Peter Bondanella in *Italian Cinema from Neorealism to the Present* (New York, 1983). Later examples were *Boccaccio '70* and *I tre volti* (see Chapter 7). The genre was so popular that "some 50 such films appeared between 1961 and 1969, and almost every major director participated in such commercial ventures, sometimes with remarkable success" (Bondanella, p. 159).

14. For the banned version, see the English translation in Leprohon, pp. 109–25. Leprohon states that the original publication in Italian appeared in *Cinema*, July 25, 1954.

15. *Il primo Antonioni*, ed. Carlo Di Carlo, p. 18. Antonioni said that the film was made out of friendship and that its programmed message was the kind of cinema in which he did not believe (Bernardini, p. 54). His attitude toward the film is reflected in the following comment (quoted by Strick, *Antonioni*, p. 32):

Most of these people were happy that they had tried to kill themselves, and that they were now there talking about it in front of a camera; they were content to be making such easy money. They flirted with each other. They tried to make me believe they had wanted to die, that they had repeated their attempts several times, that all things considered they were unlucky not to have succeeded. Moreover, they were prepared to try again tomorrow if they found themselves in the same situation.

I am sure this isn't true. I am sure they didn't speak the truth, that they exaggerated from I don't know what form of vanity and masochism. From something not moral but psychological . . . Suicide is so enigmatic a gesture; it can be examined from multiple points of view—anatomical and physio-pathological, statistically, sociologically, and psychologically. It was not such a simple theme; one only has to scratch the surface and all sorts of difficulties come to light. Within the very constricted limits allowed me what could I do? I sought to arouse in the public an aversion to suicide by showing the spiritual desolation of these people. I aimed directly at the basic theme.

Apparently, when a theme was assigned to Antonioni, he felt relatively helpless and ended up making precisely the kind of message film that he so excoriated.

16. Some Italian critics argue that Clara's behavior is explained by her petit bourgeois background, but the point is either too muffled or too lightly sketched for the foreign audience to grasp.

17. The same scenarists wrote *Le amiche;* see note 20.

18. Antonioni originally cast Gina Lollobrigida in the role, reportedly because he felt that she really was a Clara. At the last minute, Lollobrigida backed out, claiming that the film was "incoherent, vulgar, banal, and inhuman" (Bernardini, pp. 30–31). However, Carlo Di Carlo reports that she felt that the character's life too closely resembled her own (*Michelangelo Antonioni*, p. 124). Antonioni then wanted to use Sophia Loren, who was eager to do it, but the producer insisted on Bosè.

19. I am indebted to Pio Baldelli's analysis of the film for my comparison of Pavese's novella with Antonioni's film: see Pio Baldelli, *Cinema dell'ambiguità: Bergman e Antonioni*, 2d ed. (Rome, 1971). See also Gian Piero Brunetta, "*Le amiche:* Pavese e Antonioni dal romanzo al film," in his *Forma e parole nel cinema* (Padua, 1970).

20. Antonioni said in a letter to Aldo Bernardini (cited in Bernardini, p. 119) that he supervised the screenplay, giving it independently to D'Amico and Cespedes, after which he "corrected it, cut it, and reworked it." But Pio Baldelli (p. 181) suggests that his impact on the screenplay was minimal.

21. Venanzo died tragically of hepatitis at the age of forty-six. He also shot Fellini's $8\frac{1}{2}$ and *Juliet of the Spirits,* as well as films by Rosi, Lizzani, and others.

Chapter 2

1. Antonioni was so frequently accused of being obsessed with suicide that he had to deny it publicly. The only actual suicides or attempted suicides in his films are those of Gianni in *La signora senza camelie,* Rosetta in *Le amiche* (where he was simply reproducing the events of Pavese's novella), and of the three women in *Tentato suicidio,* where the idea was assigned to him by the producers. Philip Strick recounts the circumstances, *Antonioni,* pp. 31–32, but proceeds to claim, extravagantly, that there are no fewer than fourteen suicides between *Cronaca* and *L'eclisse.* Strick's number includes the "spiritual" suicides (Clara in *Signora*), "civilisation-disease" suicides (Tommaso in *La notte,* the drunk in *L'eclisse*), political suicides, and murder-suicides for recognition (*I vinti*). Clearly, Strick stretches the notion of suicide so far that it has no useful meaning.
2. Michelangelo Antonioni, *Il grido,* ed. Elio Bartolini (Bologna, 1957), p. 32.
3. From "Colloquio con Michelangelo Antonioni," *Bianco e nero,* June 1958, as translated in Leprohon, p. 96.
4. Ian Cameron and Robin Wood, *Antonioni* (London, 1968), p. 70.
5. As quoted in "A Talk with Michelangelo Antonioni on His Work," *Film Culture,* no. 24 (Spring 1962), pp. 50–59 (trans. from "La malattia dei sentimenti: Colloquio con Michelangelo Antonioni," *Bianco e nero* 22, nos. 2–3 [February–March 1961]; no translator named).
6. Strick, *Antonioni,* p. 8.
7. Strick, *Antonioni,* p. 41.
8. Quoted in Di Carlo, *Michelangelo Antonioni,* p. 376.
9. As quoted in Leprohon, p. 59.
10. Cameron and Wood, p. 67.
11. John Russell Taylor, *Cinema Eye, Cinema Ear* (New York, 1964), p. 70.
12. Translated as "Reflections on the Film Actor," *Film Culture,* nos. 22–23 (1961), p. 66; no translator named. Some of the sentences already appear in "There Must Be a Reason for Every Film," *Films and Filming* 5, no. 9 (April 1959): 11.
13. André Labarthe, "Entretien avec Michelangelo Antonioni," *Cahiers du cinéma,* no. 112 (October 1960), translated in Leprohon, first English edition (1963), p. 95.
14. "Reflections on the Film Actor," p. 66.
15. Susan Sontag, "Film and Theatre," in *Film Theory and Criticism,* ed. G. Mast and M. Cohen (New York, 1974), p. 258.
16. See the Introduction to the published screenplay of *Il grido* by Elio Bartolini.
17. Leprohon, first English edition (1963), p. 56.

Chapter 3

1. Another misapprehension is that the films are needlessly depressing. But, as Geoffrey Nowell-Smith puts it:

Except for *La notte* . . . none of Antonioni's work is ever so arid, or so alienating, as a conventional analysis of his ideas might suggest. In each of his films there is a positive pole and a negative, and a tension between them. The abstraction, the 'ideology,' lies mostly at the negative pole. The concrete and actual evidence, the life of the film, is more often positive—and more often neglected by criticism (Geoffrey Nowell-Smith, "Shape Around a Black Point," *Sight and Sound* 33 [Winter 1963/64]: 17).

2. I heard the story from my friend Peter Selz, then curator of the Museum of Modern Art, who took Antonioni, at Antonioni's request, to Rothko's studio. Richard Gilman uses the remark as the title of one of the most perceptive early discussions of Antonioni to appear in America ("About Nothing—with Precision," *Theater Arts* 46, no. 7 [July 1962]: 10–12). Antonioni confirmed the story in conversation, adding that he later became friends with Rothko and even bought a painting from him, paying in advance. Unfortunately, Rothko died before he was able to meet his commitment.

3. Gilman, p. 11.

4. See Roland Barthes's *S/Z* (New York, 1970) for an account of the many ways in which traditional or *lisible* narrative reassures the reader.

5. Gilman, p. 11.

6. "A Talk with Michelangelo Antonioni on His Work," *Film Culture,* no. 24 (Spring 1962), p. 46.

7. "A Talk with Michelangelo Antonioni," p. 51.

8. And the psychoanalyst who thus quotes Freud goes on to say:

The movie makes a sweeping, it could almost be said an encompassing, statement about the erotic life of modern man. It is doomed from the start, the movie asseverates: doomed because the quest for the beloved is hopeless and because its hopelessness breeds disenchantment, cynicism, and self-hatred; doomed because sexual fulfillment is so often unsatisfactory and guilt-ridden; doomed because sex is used, wrongly, as solace for frustrations and defeats, as an anodyne for the soul-sickness which afflicts us because of our own compromises, weaknesses, and corruption, and as an outlet for angry, destructive feelings which besmirch it; doomed, finally, because despite all this the quest goes on and must go on, though joyless, sterile, and, after a time, devoid of any prospect of success. Eternal restlessness and frustration are the inescapable conditions of our erotic life (Simon O. Lesser, "*L'Avventura*: A Closer Look," *Yale Review* 54 [1964]: 45).

9. In his interview with Antonioni, Godard remarked, "There seem already to be traces of the neuroses which appear in *Il deserto rosso* in the character of Monica Vitti in *L'eclisse*." But Antonioni disagreed vigorously: "Oh no. The character of Vittoria in *L'eclisse* is the complete antithesis of that of Giuliana. In *L'eclisse,* Vittoria is a calm well-balanced girl who knows why she acts as she does" ("Jean-Luc Godard Interviews Michelangelo Antonioni," *Movie,* no. 12 [1965], p. 32).

10. *Il primo Antonioni,* ed. Carlo Di Carlo, p. 27.

11. The theme of escape is illuminated by Carlo Salinari, *Miti e coscienza del decadentismo italiano* (Milan, 1960). Salinari sees in escapism a central topos of the decadent movement in Italian literature.

12. Alberto Moravia observes somewhere that, though ennui—*noia*—seems to be the opposite of "fun," it is really quite similar from the psychological point of view. The latter, too, diverts or even distracts. Like other distractions, "fun" is really a kind of insufficiency or inadequateness or scarcity of reality.

13. Lesser, p. 44.

14. The best article I have seen on the psychiatric meaning of distraction in Antonioni's films is Piero Amerio's "Appunti per una psicologia dell'irrelevante," in Carlo Di Carlo, *Michelangelo Antonioni,* pp. 45–51. Amerio attributes the theme of distraction to "the irrelevant drive." Much of Sandro's behavior, he contends, is explainable as a "flight intended to block a less bearable state." Sandro busies himself with finding Anna so that he can get his mind off other problems, including Claudia. She in turn becomes the object of the irrelevant drive distracting him from the problem of his work. The state of mind is a kind of psychological "vagabondage."

15. Nowell-Smith, "Shape," p. 17.

16. Antonioni was interested as early as 1939 in making a film about the destruction of civilization. In an article called "Terra verde," he proposed a Technicolor production based on notes toward a novel published by Guido Piovene in the *Corrière della sera* in November 1937. Piovene envisioned a lost civilization on the east coast of Greenland, which flourished until the Gulf Stream deviated to the east, leaving the once flourishing land to the mercy of encroaching glaciers. Antonioni was particularly inspired by a passage in which a farmer, putting his horse out to graze one day, sees the grass change suddenly from green to silver and then back to green. This is not only the first sign of the coming of the glacier but the first sign of Antonioni's desire to control the color of natural objects, a desire that led him to have streets, woods, and hotel lobbies sprayed with paint for *Il deserto rosso* and to shoot *Il mistero di Oberwald* from a television console so that he could mix colors on the spot.

17. *The Screenplays of Michelangelo Antonioni* (New York, 1963), p. 230.

18. *The Screenplays of Michelangelo Antonioni*, p. 231.

19. Strick, *Antonioni*, p. 12. Dwight MacDonald was one of the reviewers who let a penchant for symbolism spoil his reading of *L'eclisse*. For instance, he found "pretentious" and "obvious" the shot of the two nuns walking below Piero's house as he tries to seduce Vittoria. But it is precisely because their presence is so common a sight in Rome's streets that they do *not* work as symbols of asceticism or sexual purity. In their silent and odd, antiquated shapes, they seem, rather, to be one more embodiment of that mystery of the quotidian that forms so much a part of the film. MacDonald is no less off base in arguing that the stockbrokers "stand for" Civilized Man and the African natives in Marta's photographs for Natural Man. Such readings reduce the film to mere allegory (Dwight MacDonald, *Dwight MacDonald on Movies* [Englewood Cliffs, N.J., 1969], p. 338).

Nowell-Smith was among the few who sensed the predominantly nonsymbolic or metonymic character of Antonioni's art:

> Contrary to what is often thought, Antonioni has a horror of obvious symbolic correspondences. It did not take him long to realise that his starting point for *L'Eclisse*, the actual solar eclipse, would provide in the finished film only a tedious and unnecessary metaphor—"the eclipse of the sentiments"—for what he really had to say. So he cut it out, and it survives only as an allusion in the title. Speculating here, I should also say that if it had been pointed out to him that the shots of the emptying water butt and the water running to drain in the final sequence of the same film would be taken conceptually as a straightforward symbol of Vittoria and Piero's affair running out, then he would probably have cut them out or altered them so as to minimise, if not eliminate, the association. The meaning of this final sequence, even in the cut version shown in London, is extraordinarily rich and complex, and is diminished rather than enhanced by this sort of interpretation. It depends, like much of the best lyric poetry, on a subtle interplay of subjective and objective, of fact and feeling; but it derives most of its imagery from the narrative structure of the earlier part of the film." ("Shape," p. 19)

The same point is made by Gavriel Moses in an excellent study of the opening sequence, *Eclipse: Opening Sequence* (New York, 1975). Moses sees Antonioni in the context of modernism and recognizes Antonioni's minimalist action, his relation to the nouveau roman, his use of the witness—which he calls *flaneur*—and the importance of figure-ground relationships in his films.

20. Roman Jakobson and Morris Halle, *Fundamentals of Language* (The Hague, 1956).

21. On several occasions, Antonioni was asked what the title *Red Desert* means. To Michèle Manceaux he answered: "It isn't meant to be symbolic. Titles of this sort have a kind of umbilical cord linking them to the work [a very good description of metonymy]. I don't really know why. It's more of an open title, and anyone can read into it whatever he likes" ("In the Red Desert," *Sight and Sound* 33 [Summer 1964]: 119). Antonioni has made

similar remarks about his films on other public occasions to questioners who pressed him for an interpretation. It is clear that he does not privilege his own interpretations, neither of titles nor of the films themselves, and that he intends the films to work as texts open to the viewer's own interpretation.

22. *The Screenplays of Michelangelo Antonioni,* p. x.

23. Michelangelo Antonioni, *Sei film* (Turin, 1964), p. xi. Antonioni also said (in an interview published in *Positif,* March 1962, as translated by Strick, *Antonioni,* p. 52):

The loneliness which separates us from others and brings on the eclipse of all feelings is what Vittoria in the film feels above all else, but it is not a dramatic crisis or a moral one, it's a choice. Under her layer of anxiety she is serene enough. She knows, so does Piero, that they will not be able to love as they would want to, that they will not know how to live with this love. So he plunges back into his search for money, and she accepts it. She is resigned, but eventually she is smiling: love isn't everything. And up to now eclipses haven't been final.

24. See my *Story and Discourse* (Ithaca, 1978), p. 54, for a descriptive diagram and, more generally, for the theory of narrative presupposed by the discussion here.

25. See Bernard Pingaud's important essay "Antonioni et le cinéma réel," *Preuves,* no. 117 (November 1960), pp. 63–66, reprinted in Carlo Di Carlo, *Michelangelo Antonioni,* pp. 214–20: "In Antonioni, the truly significant shots, instead of constituting hints in the chain of the action, insidiously bend them, deter them from their course, furnishing spectators with other motives of interest." (Antonioni confesses in interviews that he is often distracted as he writes a story by the *next* story or an alternative one.) Events " —like question marks in the margins—[show] that the past is not as clear as it seems, that it can be read differently." This causes a peculiar kind of articulation, a kind of intentional "misfiring": the plot moves along in short jerks, through small total fractures instead of the smooth "continuity" of traditional filmmaking. "The hinges of the story do not coincide with the beginnings and endings of the scenes."

For the theory of verisimilar irrelevance, see the classic essay by Roland Barthes, "L'effet de réel," *Communications,* no. 11 (1968); English translation, "The Realistic Effect," by Gerald Mead, *Film Reader* 3 (February 1978).

26. *The Screenplays of Michelangelo Antonioni,* p. 183.

27. Chatman, *Story and Discourse,* pp. 70–72.

28. Bosley Crowther said about one film that several reels must have gotten lost, and Dwight MacDonald complained that there were not enough reasons or causes provided and that "nothing happens."

29. Barthes, "Caro Antonioni," p. 4.

30. Nowell-Smith, "Shape," p. 16.

31. As quoted in Strick, *Antonioni,* p. 17.

32. Nowell-Smith, "Shape," pp. 19–20: "His camera here is the voice of a lyric poet who draws on real material but fuses it together in a purely imaginative way in order to envisage subjectively a purely imaginative possibility—that the light should have gone out on the love between Piero and Vittoria."

33. For the dialectic shifts between time and space, see Marie-Claire Ropars-Wuilleaumier, "L'espace et le temps dans l'univers d'Antonioni," *Etudes cinématographiques,* nos. 36–37 (1964), pp. 17–33.

Chapter 4

1. 1980 television interview with Miccichè.

2. Antonioni said in the interview with Godard (*Movie* 12 [1965]: 33) that he feels Corrado "takes advantage of her and of her state of mind."

3. Bruce Kawin, *Mindscreen* (Princeton, 1978), p. 10.

4. In *Corrière della sera,* December 28, 1975. Reprinted in *Quel bowling sul Tevere* (Turin, 1983), p. 140.

5. In "'Il mondo è un vecchio sbaglio' e un'altra storia mai scritta" ("'The World Is an Old Mistake' and Another Unwritten Story"), *Cinema nuovo,* no. 257 (February 1979), p. 5.

6. *Corrière della sera,* January 2, 1977, reprinted in *Quel bowling sul Tevere,* pp. 6–8, under the title "L'orizzonte degli eventi."

7. Cuccu, p. 33.

8. In *Cinema* 78 (1939), p. 205, as quoted by Aldo Bernardini.

9. 1980 television interview with Miccichè.

10. Nowell-Smith, "Shape," p. 20.

11. T. S. Eliot, "Hamlet and His Problems," *The Sacred Wood* (London, 1920). The critic John Russell Taylor recognized this effect very early on; see Taylor, p. 78.

12. MacDonald, p. 341.

13. For the technical sense of these words, see Chatman, *Story and Discourse,* pp. 19–20.

14. Chatman, *Story and Discourse,* pp. 151–2.

15. Failure to recognize the witness function regularly led to misinterpretations and hence false critiques of the films of the tetralogy. Even Nowell-Smith's otherwise correct reading of Lidia's walk in *La notte* asks, "Does she just want to be by herself for a bit? Or is she half hoping . . . for a sexual encounter that will in some way reassure her of her quality as a woman?" ("La notte," *Sight and Sound* 31 [Winter 1961–62]: 30). The questions are irrelevant, since Lidia walks in response more to the camera's need to *tell* than to the character's need to *be.*

16. *The Screenplays of Michelangelo Antonioni,* p. 105.

17. *L'avventura,* ed. Robert Hughes and David Denby (New York, 1969), p. 21.

18. *The Screenplays of Michelangelo Antonioni,* p. 119.

19. The lamentable state of film criticism in America is evidenced by Pauline Kael's frivolous comment on Antonioni's posterior views:

What are we to make of this camera fixation on her rear? . . . in *La Notte,* obviously we are supposed to be interested in Jeanne Moreau's thoughts and feelings while we look at her from the back, walking around the city. What kind of moviemaking, what kind of drama is this? Is the delicate movement of the derriere supposed to reveal her Angst, or merely her ennui? Are we to try to interpret the movement of her rear, or are we to try to interpret the spacial [*sic*] and atmospheric qualities of the city streets—and the only kind of interpretation we can draw from the settings is, for example, that the impersonal modern glass city reflects the impersonal life of modern man, that city people have lost their roots in the earth and all that sort of thing. It isn't much, is it? (*I Lost It at the Movies* [New York, 1966], p. 163)

20. The reaction shot is totally plot-oriented, deriving its meaning in a simple and direct way from the events that it frames. In *Psycho,* Marion Crane is taking a peaceful shower in a motel room; she suddenly looks up; her eyes widen enormously. Her mouth stretches and contorts, and her arms flail. The camera cuts to a shadowy figure outside the shower, registered from her point of view. We grasp the entire contents of Marion's consciousness at that instant. She is petrified with fear. The plot line is so compellingly simple that no other reading or ambiguity of interpretation is possible.

21. Guido Aristarco, "Cinema letterario," *Cinema nuovo* (January 1961), as translated in Leprohon, p. 162. Pasolini also speaks of a kind of "interior monologue without its conceptual and philosophic elements," which he dubs *free indirect subjective* in "The Cinema of Poetry" (in *Movies and Methods,* ed. Bill Nichols [Berkeley, 1976], p. 550).

22. Bernard Pingaud notes a paradox in the relation of modern films to modern novels, especially *romans du regard:* the novels utilize saying for seeing, whereas the films want to say what they are making seen; they want to compose "images that are no longer only the symbol—perfected, simplified, easy to read—of the thing, but the thing itself, in its weight and opacity" (in Carlo Di Carlo, *Michelangelo Antonioni,* pp. 214–220).

But Antonioni's vision is more like Flaubert's than like Robbe-Grillet's. He wants to describe "the flux of consciousness through the flux of time, in the cinematic equivalent of the Flaubertian narrative" (Marie-Claire Ropars-Wuilleaumier, "L'espace," p. 29). A meaning for the objects remains connected to their visual appearance. Further, there is nothing like the pure description characteristic of the Robbe-Grilletian text, which results from spelling out the abstract spatial properties of objects. No matter how far the camera glides down the Pirelli building in the opening of *La notte,* we never forget that it is a modernistic office building we are looking at. The effect is quite different from that created by the narrator's voice at the beginning of *La jalousie* with its precise geometric dissection: "Now the shadow of the column—the column which supports the southwest corner of the roof—divides the corresponding corner of the veranda into two equal parts." The question the camera suggests is not, What are the geometric properties of this object and its orientation in space? but, How does this shape—which I see is a modernistic building—relate to the fate of the characters who I know will soon appear?

Further, the stoppage of time characteristic of the nouveau roman only occurs in *L'eclisse* as a special apocalyptic effect, namely during the eclipse itself, that is, the moment when man is eclipsed by the things he has created. The eclipse is a visual representation of the catastrophe that occurs when time itself stops and with it all human emotions. The danger is that man, not content with natural eclipses, will create his own and obliterate himself. But a narrative can be stopped only if it has already been shown to be moving through time. Thus Antonioni appeals less to the spatial emphasis of the nouveau roman than to earlier conventions, honored by novelists who influenced him, like Fitzgerald and Vittorini. Antonioni does not want "to destroy human psychology but to reinvent a more complete and authentic expression of it: to reveal human beings through their emergence in the world, to define them in a spatial situation where only fragmentary and incomplete reflections of subjective experience occur" (Ropars-Wuilleaumier, "L'espace," p. 30).

23. Pasolini, "The Cinema of Poetry," p. 553.

24. In her otherwise sensitive article, Marie-Claire Ropars-Wuilleaumier confuses the issue when she says of *Il deserto rosso:* "It is by a traditional process—the alternation of fuzzy and clear images—that [Antonioni] tries to suggest the struggle between illness and Giuliana's effort to reintegrate the real: these subjective images remain static and make the psychology banal by no longer suggesting the exterior." And of the use of color to convey inner feelings, she says: "The work seems bathed in a uniform beauty which would be paralyzing if it did not suggest, in a very removed way, joy in the face of fear" (p. 31). I thought the same thing when I first saw *Il deserto rosso.* But then I came to realize the subtlety of a film in which the visual track often preserves the camera's strictly objective view, even as it communicates through the context of the narrative and Vitti's incredible performance a strong interest-point-of-view-identification with a character who sees the world with neurotic fuzziness. Thereby Antonioni conveys the idea that, to such people, the world is terrifying not in spite of but because of its very beauty.

25. Chatman, *Story and Discourse,* p. 207.

Chapter 5

1. *The Screenplays of Michelangelo Antonioni,* p. ix. Cf. "To me, the visual aspect of a film is very closely related to its thematic aspect—in the sense that an idea almost always

comes to me through images," Pierre Billard, "An Interview with Michelangelo Antonioni," in *Blow-Up*, ed. Sandra Wake (New York, 1971), p. 5

2. *The Screenplays of Michelangelo Antonioni*, pp. xvi–xvii.

3. This scene is remarkably like one in *Mrs. Dalloway* in which Clarissa, escaping from her party for a moment to a secluded little room, catches a glimpse through the window of the private life of an old lady who lives next door:

She parted the curtains; she looked. Oh but how surprising!—in the room opposite the old lady stared straight at her! She was going to bed. And the sky. It will be a solemn sky, she had thought, it will be a dusky sky, turning away its cheek in beauty. But there it was—ashen pale, raced over quickly by tapering vast clouds. It was new to her. The wind must have risen. She was going to bed, in the room opposite. It was fascinating to watch her, moving about, that old lady, crossing the room, coming to the window. Could she see her? It was fascinating, with people still laughing and shouting in the drawingroom, to watch that old woman, quite quietly, going to bed. She pulled the blind now. The clock began striking. (*Mrs. Dalloway* [New York, 1925], p. 283)

Both Virginia Woolf and Antonioni are clearly fascinated by the mysterious proximity of other lives. The motif recurs in *Identificazione di una donna:* the hero, Niccolò, watches his lover, Mavi, as she sleeps and asks himself in voice-over: "Who knows whether someone has ever seen me sleeping?"

4. See Di Carlo, *Michelangelo Antonioni*, pp. 131–33, for a shot list.

5. "Jean-Luc Godard Interviews Michelangelo Antonioni," p. 31.

6. Joseph Bennett, "The Essences of Being," *Hudson Review* 14 (1961): 432–36, identifies the various Sicilian locations of the film.

7. The relation to De Chirico is noted by Nowell-Smith ("Shape," p. 17) and by Cuccu, p. 23. Antonioni returns to the image of the bleak, white, new town in *The Passenger.*

8. Not only the atomic bomb but the shoddiness of imagination and workmanship and the thoughtlessness of planning promote man's eclipse. In *Technically Sweet,* the unmade film script written by Antonioni in 1966, published in Italian as *Tecnicamente dolce* (Turin, 1976), T., the hero, a disaffected journalist, articulates some of this foreboding. He attempts to stop a boatload of fishermen from callously destroying the ecology of a Sardinian preserve by fishing with dynamite. When congratulated by a local landlord for chasing them off, he acidly remarks, "Some people destroy one kind of thing, some another," alluding to the cheap, tacky houses (*di dubbio gusto*) that the landlord has constructed.

9. Rudolf Arnheim, *The Dynamics of Architectural Form* (Berkeley, 1977), pp. 22, 25.

10. Antonioni, *Sei film,* p. 420.

11. Rudolf Arnheim's technical explanation (*Dynamics,* p. 87) helps us understand why:

The center or focal point of a square is often explicitly marked by a fountain, obelisk, or monumental sculpture. Such an accent not only confirms the geometrical form of the symmetrical square, it also supplies a tangible site for the square's vectorial center. And while the centrally based field of forces helps actualize the square as an autonomous visual object, it also provides an architectural counterpart to the human occupant's presence. Antlike in relation to the dimensions of buildings and square, man could never assert the right of his presence by his own power. Only a crowd, such as the one filling St. Peter's Square on Easter Sunday, can possibly do that. But a crowd is a very particular manifestation of man; he gives symbolic expression to his special nature mainly by appearing as an individual. Singly, the human visitor must rely on being amplified by visual forces of architectural magnitude. Thus strengthened, he can perform his role as a well endowed partner in the encounter between man and the world he has built for himself.

12. *The Screenplays of Michelangelo Antonioni,* p. 342.

13. Arnheim, *Dynamics*, pp. 82–83.

14. Arnheim, *Dynamics*, p. 22.

Chapter 6

1. Pier Paolo Pasolini, *Dialogue en publique*, ed. G. Ferretti (Paris, 1980), p. 160.

2. J. T. Soby, *Giorgio De Chirico* (New York, 1955), p. 33.

3. Soby, p. 34.

4. Soby, p. 34. The original ending of *L'eclisse* is even more mysterious and apocalyptic than the filmed one. See *L'eclisse di Michelangelo Antonioni,* ed. John Francis Lane (Bologna, 1962).

5. *L'avventura,* ed. Robert Hughes and David Denby, pp. 82–84.

6. In the color films, however, the stasis may have had a more purely technical explanation: "I noticed too that certain camera movements did not have the required effect: for instance, a rapid panning shot is effective with bright red, but no use with dirty green, unless you are looking for an unusual effect. I think there is a *rapport* between camera movements and colour" ("Jean-Luc Godard Interviews Michelangelo Antonioni," p. 34).

7. Wilhelm Worringer, *Abstraction and Empathy: A Contribution to the Psychology of Style,* trans. Michael Bullock (New York, 1953). The German original, *Abstraktion und Einfühlung,* was published in 1908.

8. Worringer, p. 15.

9. Worringer, p. 16.

10. In *Cinema nuovo,* no. 157 (February 1979), p. 5. Another story has this title in *Quel bowling sul Tevere.*

11. "Jean-Luc Godard Interviews Michelangelo Antonioni," pp. 31–32.

12. "Jean-Luc Godard Interviews Michelangelo Antonioni," pp. 33–34.

13. The critic Manny Farber, who is also a painter, described the effect vividly in "White Elephant Art Versus Termite Art," *Film Culture,* no. 27 (Winter 1962–1963), p. 12: "a screen that is glassy, has a sliding motion, the feeling of people plastered against stripes." But he did not approve, complaining that the "pretentiously handsome image" of the nymphomaniac in *La notte* "compromises the harrowing effect of the scene." But that misses the point: the intention was not to harrow but precisely to contemplate the significance of a "glassy," smoothly sliding society that fosters compulsive sex, neurotic anxiety, and kindred ills.

14. Thomas Schmidt.

15. Worringer, p. 41.

16. "Jean-Luc Godard Interviews Michelangelo Antonioni," p. 34.

17. "Jean-Luc Godard Interviews Michelangelo Antonioni," p. 34. Cf. the Billard interview (*Blow-Up,* ed. Sandra Wake, p. 9): "From *Red Desert* on, I began using several cameras with different lenses, but always from the same angle. I did so because the story demanded shots of a reality that had become abstract, of a subject that had become colour, and those shots had to be obtained with a long-focus lens."

18. Rudolf Arnheim, *Art and Visual Perception* (Berkeley, 1969), p. 212.

19. Except very rarely, like the close-up of Claudia's hand on Sandro's head in the last sequence of *L'avventura.*

20. I use the term *diegesis* in the modern narratological sense of the "story" or content dimension of narrative, as opposed to its "discourse" or formal dimension. See Chatman, *Story and Discourse,* passim.

21. Pasolini, "The Cinema of Poetry," pp. 552–53.

22. Nowell-Smith, "Shape," p. 16.

23. The effect is much like that of the intensely described visual details in the *romans du regard,* especially of Robbe-Grillet.

24. Translation of "Colloquio con Michelangelo Antonioni," *Bianco e nero* (June 1958), in Leprohon, p. 96. See also Michele Mancini and others, "Conversazione con Michelangelo Antonioni," *Filmcritica*, no. 252 (1975), pp. 58-59: "The actors continue out of inertia into moments that seem 'dead.' In those moments, the actor often commits 'errors,' which however do contribute in some way to the scene. I feel that these are very sincere moments."

25. *L'eclisse*, ed. John Francis Lane (Bologna, 1962), p. 109.

26. Antonioni told me that an art gallery owner wants to do a show of stills of his best *temps mort* compositions. I certainly hope that he succeeds in his plan: this is an aspect of Antonioni's art that the public should be able to study at leisure.

For the last five years, Antonioni has been doing another kind of visual art—a combination of painting, collage, and still photography. He has had a highly successful show in Venice and at the Galleria Nazionale d'Arte Moderna in Rome. The show is called "Le montagne incantate" ("The Enchanted Mountains"). The art critic Pier Luigi Tazzi describes the works as "more or less defined profiles of mountains, with broad, luminous horizons, which the rising peaks do not so much obscure as exalt by virtue of their rich chromaticism—a counterpoint to the dense, full-bodied skies. In the films, the horizon line often suggests nostalgia, desire, or anguish, but here the horizon is ample, open, charged, and free . . ." The technique is very unusual: "He begins by using the process of painting and collage to make the pictures that will become the matrices of the finished work; next he crops, or 'frames,' the images; then he photographs the work, successively enlarging it to various scales before deciding on its final form."

27. This passage has been analyzed in detail by Karel Reisz and Gavin Millar, *The Technique of Film Editing* (New York, 1968), pp. 369-85.

28. The ambivalence is so well registered that it gave rise to a conflict in descriptions: the film book (*L'avventura*, ed. Robert Hughes and David Denby, p. 52) describes her expression as "resentful," but Antonioni, Bartolini, and Guerra had written in the scenario: "they find themselves staring into each other's eyes, almost embarrassed by their own behavior, yet unable to control it" (*L'avventura*, ed. Tommaso Chiaretti [Bologna, 1960], p. 135).

29. Antonioni published a half-whimsical, half-melancholy account of the circumstances of "Il bosco bianco" ("The White Woods") as a preface to the published screenplay of *Il deserto rosso* (ed. Carlo Di Carlo [Bologna, 1964], pp. 15-19).

30. "Jean-Luc Godard Interviews Michelangelo Antonioni," p. 34.

31. Strick, *Antonioni*, p. 7.

32. Michèle Manceaux, "In the Red Desert," *Sight and Sound* 33 (Summer 1964): 119.

33. For an introductory but useful and profusely illustrated introduction to the theory of color and its cinematic implications, see Lincoln F. Johnson, *Film: Space, Time, Light, and Sound* (New York, 1974), Chapter 6. Johnson also presents a long analysis of *Il deserto rosso* on pp. 153-64, with twenty-eight color reproductions.

34. Stanley Kauffmann, "The Artist Advances," *Renaissance of the Film*, ed. Julius Bellone (New York, 1970), p. 215.

35. Giuliana herself is concerned about the effects of colors on the spirit. She wants cool greens and blues in her shop so as not to "disturb the objects on sale"—even though she does not know what those objects will be.

36. One wonders why Penelope Houston ("The Landscape of the Desert," *Sight and Sound* 34 [Spring 1965]: 80) and Guido Fink ("La réalité acceptée," trans. François Debreczeni, *Etudes cinématographiques*, nos. 36-37 [1964], p. 92) felt that the change during the scene was "vulgar" or "in bad taste." The pink does not simplistically suggest a rosy future for the couple; it is rather the mark of the temporary lowering of tension in Giuliana's psyche that the sex affords.

37. On the score of color, too, critics reverted to simplistic symbolism, for example, Nicole Zand, "Un présent inadapté," *Etudes Cinématographiques,* nos. 36-37 (1964), p. 108: "Red marks each time what separates, what limits, what shuts one in. It is the symbol of a universe where everyone is imprisoned."

38. Andrew Sarris, *Confessions of a Cultist* (New York, 1971), p. 190.

39. "A Talk with Michelangelo Antonioni on His Work," p. 55.

Chapter 7

1. But there is a print of the film at the Centro Sperimentale di Cinematografia in Rome.

2. *Variety* confessed itself baffled about the director's intentions (*Filmfacts,* January 1, 1967, p. 304).

3. "Las babas del diablo," *Las armas secretas* (Buenos Aires, 1959): in J. Cortázar, "Blow-Up," *End of the Game and Other Stories,* trans. Paul Blackburn (New York, 1967), pp. 100-115.

4. Seymour Chatman, "The Rhetoric of Difficult Fiction: Cortázar's 'Blow-Up,'" *Poetics Today* 1 (1980): 23-66. Cf. two articles by Lanin Gyurko, "Truth and Deception in Cortázar's 'Las Babas del Diablo,'" *Romanic Review* 63 (1972): 204-217, and "Hallucination and Nightmare in Two Stories by Cortázar," *Modern Language Review* 67 (1972): 550-62. In the second, Gyurko notes (p. 550) that the configuration is common in Cortázar's fictional world: "the external life of the characters, most often a mundane or vapid existence, is constantly undermined by hallucination, nightmare, and obsessive delusions that for the solipsistic individuals become a monstrous reality. Often these fantasies are defensive reactions to fear, guilt, or anguish and serve to reduce anxiety through the projection of an afflicted state of mind upon an external object or presence."

Several studies of the relation between the film and the story have appeared, though none is very satisfactory, generally because of an inadequate interpretation of the story: see, for example, Henry Fernández, "*Blow-Up* From Cortázar to Antonioni: Study of an Adaptation," *Film Heritage* 4 (Winter 1968-1969): 26-30.

5. George Slover ("*Blow-Up*: Medium, Message, Mythos, and Make-Believe," *Massachusetts Review* 9 [1968]: 770) finds, in Thomas's joining the mimes in the tennis game, a "flight from his humanity . . . into a world created by his camera, a world insulated from the terrible anxieties of being human." This sounds very much like Roberto Michel's situation at the end of "Las babas del diablo."

6. Max Kozloff, "The Blow-Up," in *Focus on Blow-Up,* ed. Roy Huss (Englewood Cliffs, N.J., 1971), pp. 58-63, the best early review of the film. (Kozloff's review was first published in *Film Quarterly* 20, no. 3 (Spring 1967): 28-31.)

7. The dialogue of the film—written by the English playwright Edward Bond—is excellent, unlike that of *Zabriskie Point.*

8. "Moravia dialoga con Antonioni," in *Antonioni/Cortázar: Blow-Up,* ed. Daniel Mario Lopez and Alberto Eduard Ojam (Buenos Aires, 1968), p. 103 (Antonioni expressed himself in English, the better to paraphrase Hamlet); *Tecnicamente dolce* (Turin, 1976), p. xxviii.

9. I owe this discussion of *Blow-Up*'s Faustian implications to my friend Samuel R. Levin.

10. George Slover thinks Thomas "has not lost altogether a certain human common sensibility" (p. 755) and that his distraction is the result of conflict between the imperatives of his art and dim stirrings of civic duty. I doubt it. Thomas, like everyone else in Antonioni's London, was long gone in distraction before he witnessed the events in park.

11. Is it TOA or FOA? (The first possibility is the more intriguing, because the letters figure in Antonioni's name.) The sign illustrates an important point made by Roland Barthes in "Rhetoric of the Image," *Image/Music/Text,* ed. Stephen Heath (New York, 1977), p. 39: "In the cinema . . . traumatic images are bound up with an uncertainty (an anxiety) concerning the meaning of objects or attitudes. Hence in every society various techniques are developed intended to *fix* the floating chain of signifieds in such a way as to counter the terror of uncertain signs; the linguistic message is one of these techniques . . . The text helps to identify purely and simply the elements of the scene and the scene itself." The "terror" of the sign in the park is that it should be highly recognizable by virtue of its expensive prominence (only a rich company could afford that spot). Yet we will never know what the letters stand for or even what the first letter is.

12. Stills of events 4 and 7 appear on pp. 38 and 39 of Michelangelo Antonioni, *Blow-Up,* ed. Sandra Wake.

13. Recent theories of history argue that narration is not an artifact but rather the very means by which historical events are comprehended. See Louis O. Mink, "Narrative Form as Cognitive Instrument," in *The Writing of History: Literary Form and Historical Understanding,* ed. Robert H. Canary and Henry Kozicki (Madison, 1978), cited by Hayden White, "Value of Narrativity in the Representation of Reality," *Critical Inquiry* 7 (Autumn 1980): 8, and the interchange between Mink and White in *Critical Inquiry* 7 (Summer 1981): 777–83, 793–98.

14. Max Kozloff was the first reviewer to recognize in *Blow-Up* Antonioni's "skepticism about narrative as a cinematic vehicle of expression" ("The Blow-Up," in *Focus on Blow-Up,* p. 59). He also notes that "photography . . . is never so mechanistic as to assure one of what one is seeing. Or better, how one is to interpret it" (p. 61). See also John Freccero, "Blow-Up: From the Word to the Image," *Focus on Blow-Up,* pp. 116–28 (originally published in *Yale/Theatre* 3 [Fall 1970]: 15–24), who sees the film as " a highly self-conscious and self-reflexive meditation on its process" (p. 118). Marsha Kinder, "Antonioni in Transit," *Sight and Sound* 36 (Summer 1967): 132–37, feels that *Blow-Up* is a commentary on contemporary art, emphasizing as it does the transitory (photography itself values only the moment), the contextuality of things (the piece of the guitar), exploitation (models as "birds," the hypnotic trance of rock music), the fortuitous (the action painter never knows exactly where the paint will land), and confusion between the artist and his tools or artifact (Thomas did "see" the murder, his camera did not).

But the most theoretically interesting discussion of this aspect of *Blow-Up* is that with which Jurij Lotman, the Russian semiotician, ends his book *Semiotics of Cinema* (trans. Mark E. Suino [Ann Arbor, 1976], pp. 97–105). Lotman, too, sees the assemblage of the photos as the nucleus of the film; it represents to him the search to replace the context that was eliminated by the random photographic act. The original context suggested that the woman was angered by Thomas's presumption in taking pictures of her rendezvous. But in assembling the photos, Thomas begins to create a truer context to explain an agitation that strikes him as excessive. The important point for Lotman is that this makes the film a metasemiotic text, that is, one that is self-consciously concerned with the problem of interpreting signs as a problem: "Ordinarily both the historian and the criminologist see their task as the establishing of life from a document. Here a different task is formulated:

to *interpret* life with the aid of a document, since the audience has seen for itself that direct observation of life is no guarantee that profound mistakes will not occur. The 'obvious' fact is by no means so obvious. The director has convinced the audience that life must be deciphered. The deciphering is carried out in a manner which bears striking resemblance to structural-semiotic analysis" (p. 100). Lotman interprets Antonioni's appreciation of this fact as a major innovation not only in his own style but in modern cinema in general, a turn from the simple (Bazinian) confidence in the self-evidence of prowling documentary inquiry to a frank acceptance of the need (championed so ardently by Eisenstein) to interpret, to *assemble* reality. The reasons, Lotman argues, are ideological. Thomas cannot succeed by simply recording what he sees about him, because "he does not have an external viewpoint on events":

For a person who is not supported by a *construction of ideas* the only solid foundation becomes the world of everyday notions, faith in the real nature of every experience. This is how Antonioni explains the rise of 'the art of the fact' which has opposed 'the art of ideas' with considerable determination in cinematography of the last twenty years. But the world founded on unconditional reliance on empirical facts is being threatened. On the one hand . . . by science . . . and on the other [because] it can no longer find shelter in that feeling of social well-being which was the psychological underpinning of the era of positivism . . . [So this] is a world of clowns. The man who relied on bare facts found himself in a world of phantoms. In the beginning he did not see what was happening, and in the end he heard what was not happening. (p. 103)

It is essential not to equate Antonioni with his hero: structuralism teaches us that the "the describer is always outside the object being described, and is at least one logical degree above it" (p. 105). In this film, "cinema has begun to be aware of itself as a sign system and to consciously make use of this property. Semiotic analysis of accidental photographs makes it possible to establish the fact of a murder, but semiotic analysis of the world, in Antonioni's opinion, since it undermines unthinking belief in the unshakeability of 'facts,' opens the way to cinema-truth" (p. 104).

15. Interestingly enough, the movie camera does not restrict itself to a straightforward linear reproduction of the prints on the wall, nor does it simply match its frame lines with theirs. Rather, it closes in on the most relevant portions of the print, in its own montage insert program: for instance, we see (a), then not (b) but a close-up of (a) in which the Girl pulls the man along. Next it shows (b), then (c), but then it goes back to (b) and pans from the couple to the fence, where gun, hand, and face now stand out ever so slightly more clearly (did Antonioni enhance the images a bit to get the added clarity? Never mind: we feel that we, too, are beginning to fathom the mystery). Then we see blow-up (d), both face and gun in fist. Next Antonioni's camera moves in for a clear close-up of the gun in (i). Then (f), (g), and (h) follow in proper course, with a close-up repetition of a piece of (e) now inserted in its proper place—(g)—to intensify the drama. And to complete the story we are given two views that we have not seen before, though we remember them from the park scene itself—(j), the Girl running away, followed by its blow-up (k), and finally (l), the clearing after the Girl has disappeared. If our eyes are sharper than Thomas's, we can make out the outline of the Man's body at the base of the tree in (k). He does not see it, bragging to Ron on the phone that he saved the man's life.

16. Freccero (p. 120) argues that *Blow-Up* refutes Fellini's make-believe and proposes that "the only alternatives to the lie are the search or silence." But that ignores these very pointed illusions at the end.

17. *Blow-Up*, ed. Sandra Wake, p. 14.
18. Robert Garis, "Watching Antonioni," *Commentary* 43, no. 4 (April 1967), p. 88.
19. *Blow-Up*, ed. Sandra Wake, p. 16.

Chapter 8

1. Ernest Callenbach finds it "laboriously Griffithian," *Film Quarterly* 23 (Spring 1970): 36.
2. Michelangelo Antonioni, *Zabriskie Point* (Bologna, 1970), p. 67.
3. Harry Medved and Randy Dreyfuss, *The Fifty Worst Films of All Time* (New York, 1978), pp. 277–82. MGM's desperation to recoup its losses shows up in wonderful liner notes on the back of the sound track album. They are signed by Mike Curb, then president of the company, more recently lieutenant-governor of California: "If seeing is believing, then experiencing is being. 'Zabriskie Point' is not the kind of film one goes to see, for that implies a barrier between the film-maker and his audience. Instead, 'Zabriskie Point' exists as experience . . . The film and the music are not really meant to be understood, but to be lived. Let the music on this album happen to you, and you'll hear, understand, and experience what I mean." The irony is delectable: here is capitalism at its most arch (pun intended) trying to sell a product whose ideology it can only detest. In a delicious pass of rhetorical magic, it makes the ideology simply vanish. As wise Italians say, "*Dove l'oro parla, ogni lingua tace*" ("When gold speaks, every tongue is silent").
4. "Let's Talk About *Zabriskie Point*," *Esquire* 74 (August 1970), p. 69.
5. Charles Samuels, "Puppets: From *Z* to *Zabriskie Point*," *The American Scholar* 18 (Autumn 1970), p. 690: "If Antonioni had not tried to render America, even in shorthand, but had created a stylized equivalence for it, his film could not raise expectations that its second and third parts—even if better acted and written—are unable to satisfy."
6. Robert Bresson, *Notes on Cinematography* (New York, 1977), p. 41.
7. Bresson, p. 36.
8. Stanley Kauffmann, "*Zabriskie Point*," *The New Republic* 162 (March 14, 1970): 29.
9. In "Let's Talk About *Zabriskie Point*," Antonioni writes (p. 146): "If one is instinctively brought to make common cause with America's rebellious youth, perhaps it is because one is attracted by their natural animal vitality."
10. *Newsweek*, February 16, 1970, p. 87.
11. John Simon, *Movies into Film* (New York, 1971), p. 207.
12. Callenbach, p. 37.
13. Kauffmann, "*Zabriskie Point*," pp. 30–31.
14. Gordon Gow, "Michelangelo Antonioni's Film *Zabriskie Point*," *Films and Filming* 21 (1975): 33.
15. Simon, p. 209
16. "Let's Talk About *Zabriskie Point*," p. 146.
17. Gow, "Michelangelo Antonioni's Film," p. 36. Gow also compares the repetition with Agnès Varda's *Le bonheur*, "where the husband lifts up the dead body of his wife, and his action is repeated several times, as if the moment were going on and on in his mind, burning in, accentuating and prolonging his grief."
18. Michelangelo Antonioni, *Chung Kuo Cina* (Turin, 1974), p. xi.
19. As quoted in Umberto Eco's article "De Interpretatione, or the Difficulty of Being Marco Polo," trans. Christine Leefeldt, *Film Quarterly* 30 (Summer 1977): 8–12.
20. A more recent—and splendid—film on China, Murray Lerner's *From Mao to Mozart*, follows the adventures of the violinist Isaac Stern as he "makes friends with music." Taken together, the two films provide a stunning record of the changes that had taken place in China in the intervening years. For instance, in Antonioni's film, everyone wears blue Mao jackets and caps; in Lerner's film, the clothing is as variegated in colors and styles as the performances of Western music by gifted young Chinese interpreters.
21. *Chung Kuo Cina*, p. xi.
22. Eco, "De Interpretatione," p. 9.

23. Eco, "De Interpretatione," p. 10.

24. Eco, "De Interpretatione," p. 11. Because my own ideological orientation is semiotic but my knowledge of China minimal, I find Eco's analysis most useful but cannot vouch for its accuracy. Since this chapter was written, I have had the opportunity to show it to a film critic from Peking. He was most candid in his rejection of the hypothesis. In his view, the entire affair was political. It had, he said, nothing to do with Antonioni at all; Antonioni was only the nominal butt of an attack by the Gang of Four on Chou-en Lai: a case of defaming the host by discrediting the guest. But even if that was true, there must have been something in the substance and style of the film that made it so ripe a candidate for the maneuver.

Chapter 9

1. *Tecnicamente dolce* (Turin, 1976), with commentary by Aldo Tassone based on an interview with Antonioni.

2. *Tecnicamente dolce,* p. xxxv.

3. *Tecnicamente dolce,* p. xii.

4. This apparently was to have been an "as-if" shot, since T. tells the Girl a few scenes later that he has gotten a message (presumably from A.) that his apartment no longer exists.

5. In a deleted portion of the scenario, S. and T. witness a tribal rite in which a priest cuts gobbets of living flesh from a human victim and feeds them to others in the tribe.

6. Reported in Alberto Ongaro, "Antonioni: Nous en savons trop sur le soleil," *Ecran,* no. 36 (1975), p. 44.

7. The scientist, too, for all his interest in fish sounds, says with apparent satisfaction: "We are proceeding to an era in which killing will have become a natural fact."

8. *Tecnicamente dolce,* p. viii.

9. See Antonioni's discussion of this point in Ongaro, p. 44.

10. *Tecnicamente dolce,* p. ix.

11. *Tecnicamente dolce,* p. x.

12. *Tecnicamente dolce,* pp. xi-xii.

13. *Tecnicamente dolce,* p. xxvi.

14. Antonioni's preoccupation with architecture continues in full force. In addition to the baroque church, the camera examines desert houses in Africa, a new housing development in Bloomsbury, Gaudí buildings in Barcelona, a modern "planned village" in Spain that resembles the deserted town in *L'avventura,* a *posada* (described in the scenario as "very beautiful but overrestored"), and of course the "typical" hotel in Osuna. These buildings are not as clearly motivated as the buildings in earlier films. The meetings in the baroque church and the Gaudí buildings seem a bit strained: neither characters nor buildings comment on each other in a discoverably meaningful way.

15. William Pechter, "Antonioni '75," *Commentary* 60 (1975): 72.

16. *Tecnicamente dolce,* p. xxix.

17. For an interesting discussion of the genre, see Otto Rank, *The Double: A Psychoanalytic Study,* trans. Harry Tucker (Chapel Hill, 1971). Ewers's film is about a man who sells his shadow to a Mephistophelian old man. Perhaps it is not a coincidence that the only time Locke's shadow noticeably appears in the film is just as he picks up Robertson's blue shirt to assume his identity.

18. Rank, p. 6.

19. Aldo Tassone, *"Profession: Reporter,"* *Image et son* 297 (June 1975): 107.

20. Antonioni, quoted by Ongaro, p. 44.

21. The Avis girl asks him if he is going on a holiday. He replies, "Sort of." And when he says that he will need the car for the rest of his life, she asks him why he doesn't just

buy one. Actually, he ends up doing just that—the purchase can perhaps be seen as a rejection of the idea that he can "rent" Robertson's life instead.

22. A very rich gesture that occurs several times in the film, for example, as Locke waits for "Daisy" on the bench in the Umbraculo, but most importantly when it is performed by the Girl as she looks backwards from Locke's convertible speeding down the road: it is a sign of how deeply she understands and empathizes with him.

23. Richard Roud, "The Passenger," *Sight and Sound* 44 (1975): 134.

24. Alan Watts, *Psychotherapy East and West* (New York, 1975), p. 23.

25. Watts, p. 114.

26. But this rich shot has other meanings, too. See p. 195.

27. Martin Walsh, "*The Passenger:* Antonioni's Narrative Design," *Jump Cut* 8 (August–September 1975): 9, the best article on the film.

28. *Anachrony* is Gérard Genette's term for any disparity between the time order of the events of the story and the time order in which they are told by the discourse. Hence "prolepsis" (flashforward) and "analepsis" (flashback). See Gérard Genette, *Narrative Discourse,* trans. Jane Lewin (Ithaca, 1980).

29. The only similar shot I have seen occurs in Buñuel's *Diary of a Chambermaid.* The passage of a night is summarized by a slow pan from the bed in dead of night to the window, where the morning light is already streaming in.

30. Gideon Bachmann, "Antonioni After China: Art Versus Science," *Film Quarterly* 28 (Summer 1975): 28.

31. Furio Colombo, "Visual Structure in a Film by Antonioni," trans. Patrizio Rossi and Garrett Stewart, *Quarterly Journal of Film Studies* 2 (1977): 427, writes: "It seems that a documentary is being shot concurrently with the film as a kind of tentative commentary, affording 'more truth' than plot alone could contain. In this way the director reverses the game of his character, who wants to escape from documentaries and enter into the story of anyman, who wants a life picked up from the pile of every life." Colombo, who was the producer of the China documentary, also feels that *The Passenger* shows the influence of Antonioni's Chinese experience, "the trace of those immense Chinese silences into which Antonioni was peering and by which he was at the same time scrutinized" (p. 429).

Ted Perry, "Men and Landscapes: Antonioni's *The Passenger,*" *Film Comment* 11 (1975): 4, feels that because of the camera's self-assertiveness and autonomy "the area off-screen becomes dynamized. Through *The Passenger* the viewer is led to anticipate that something surely must exist off-screen which, when it finally appears, will restore the narrative focus of the film."

32. In "Un film da fare o da non fare" ("A Film That May or May Not Be Made"), *Quel bowling sul Tevere* (Turin, 1983), pp. 191–95.

33. Pascal Bonitzer, "Désir désert *(Profession: Reporter),*" *Cahiers du cinéma,* nos. 262–63 (1976), p. 98.

34. Colombo thinks so (p. 431): "a perfect and very slow tracking shot that consents to leave behind the zone of death, to explore the world . . ."

35. Walsh, pp. 8–9.

36. Burch, p. 12.

37. Burch, p. 28. The example he cites is of the masonry block whose size, and hence meaning, is unclear until a very small Lidia steps into frame to establish it as the facade of a building (see Frame 64 above). I was reminded of Burch's discussion by Ned Rifkin, *Antonioni's Visual Language* (Ann Arbor, 1982), p. 89. There is a useful discussion of the problem of scale in E. H. Gombrich, "Standards of Truth: The Arrested Image and the Moving Eye," *The Language of Images,* ed. W. J. T. Mitchell (Chicago, 1980), pp. 181–90.

38. It would be an interesting classroom exercise to re-edit these sequences in conventional Hollywood terms (shot-countershot, reversal angles, clearly marked matches, and so on). These would surely make the film the ordinary thriller that some people take it to be.

39. Walsh, pp. 8–9.

40. And, indeed, there are more traditional shots in this than in earlier films, for instance, inserts—close-ups on the Land Rover's wheels spinning in the sand and on Robertson's tickets and diary, as well as on pregnant objects, such as Robertson's gun.

41. Edward Stanton, "Antonioni's *The Passenger:* A Parabola of Light," *Literature/ Film Quarterly* 5 (Winter 1977): 63; film credits for musical consultation are given to Ivan Vandor.

42. Jean Cocteau, *Théâtre II* (Paris, 1948), pp. 298–415. Cocteau himself directed the play as a film, under the same title, in 1948.

43. Quotations and other material attributed here to Antonioni were gathered in an interview I had with him in November 1980 and from the RAI brochure that was distributed with the film.

44. RAI brochure, p. 3.

45. RAI brochure, p. 3.

46. Cocteau, p. 336.

47. According to remarks made by him in *Catalogo della rassegna: tutto Antonioni in 13 giorni,* ed. Vittorio Boarini (Bologna, 1980), pp. 15–16.

48. It is not clear, at this writing, when or whether the film will be released commercially in the United States.

49. *Catalogo della rassegna,* p. 16.

Chapter 10

1. Though it won the Thirty-fifth Anniversary Prize at the Cannes Festival, the film has yet to be released in the United States. The screenplay was published in Italy in 1983 by Einaudi, complete with Antonioni's original treatment. This chapter is intentionally long on description, on the assumption that the reader has not seen the film.

2. In the treatment, Niccolò's face is described as "brightening" (*se illuminà*) on first mention of the baby, but Milian's face does not show anything like that in the film.

3. Antonioni's earliest notes on the script date from 1966. Thus the screenplay is of roughly the same vintage as the tetralogy.

4. It remains possible, however, for discriminating individuals to find architectural comfort for their own personal needs. Niccolò has a glorious apartment, balcony, and views (in reality one of the villas owned by the American Academy of Rome in the Gianicolo section; a room in another Academy building was used for the aristocrats' party scene). Mavi's apartment is more modest, but it, too, has a certain character as a result of the older architecture. (The screenplay places it in the Piazza Navona.) The farmhouse to which Niccolò takes Mavi and the little gatehouse next to the estate that Ida rents are lovely rural buildings. It is as if only in personal life can one expect to escape the tawdriness of the general ambience.

5. Again, it is fascinating to observe the parallel interests but antithetical styles of Antonioni and Fellini. Where Fellini deals in *Città delle donne* (City of Women) with the women's liberation movement in typically carnivalesque fashion, Antonioni's approach is quieter and more serious, looking as it does for the impact of these new ideas on individuals whose private lives are fraught with all sorts of other personal problems. The narcissism of women, at least women of a certain class, clearly poses a problem for men who hanker after them. But, unlike Fellini, Antonioni makes no implicit appeal to women, offers no suggestion that they should take pity on poor males who cannot understand what all the fuss is about. Antonioni's vision of the sexual morass may be bleak, but it is not self-pitying.

6. Gianna Nannini's hit "America" is reported to praise the guitar as a symbol of self-satisfaction, of "masturbation as an act of liberation." She shouts to the female members of the audience that she likes it and asks them if they like it too (see the Dutch magazine,

Nieuwe Revue, February 25, 1982, p. 21). Obviously, these views make her voice the most timely one for this sequence.

7. Gideon Bachmann, "A Love of Today: An Interview with Michelangelo Antonioni," *Film Quarterly* 36 (Summer 1983): 1.

8. Serge Daney and Serge Toubiana, "La méthode de Michelangelo Antonioni," *Cahiers du cinéma,* no. 342 (December 1982), p. 7.

9. Daney and Toubiana, p. 62.

10. A very low budget had to be respected: Daney and Toubiana, pp. 5–6.

11. *Identificazione di una donna,* p. 30.

12. *Identificazione di una donna,* p. 31.

13. Daney and Toubiana, p. 7.

14. *Identificazione di una donna,* p. 21.

15. *Identificazione di una donna,* p. 7. Roversi's analysis appears in the screenplay under the title "I tre gabbiani," pp. 5–14.

16. Alain Bergala, "L'exercise et la répétition," *Cahiers du cinéma,* no. 342 (December 1982), p. 9.

17. Bachmann, "A Love of Today," p. 2.

18. See, for instance, Valerio Caprana, "L'impossibile gioco di Antonioni," *Mattino,* October 23, 1982, who speaks of *tante frasette letterarie* ("so many literary phrases") but who considers the work as a whole to be a masterpiece.

19. "Difende 'L'identificazione' poi Antonioni salpa in yacht," *Giornale,* October 28, 1982.

20. François Cuel and Bruno Villien, "Michelangelo Antonioni," *Cinématographe* 72 (November 1981): 3.

21. Not all of Niccolò's philosophizing sounds quite so pretentious. A delicate moment occurs when he comes into the bedroom to find Mavi asleep. He quietly covers her with the blanket and sits down in a chair to watch her, murmuring, "I wonder if anyone ever watched me while I was asleep?" Later, his observations to Ida about the "coherent lives" (and hence coherent love relationships) led by terrorists (compared, presumably, with the aimless rest of us) are quite interesting.

22. Cuel and Villien, p. 4.

23. "It is a film shot quite normally, without particular stylistic refinements except for those that are useful for the story." Thus Antonioni in an interview in *Corrière della sera,* August 5, 1982, quoted in Carlo Di Carlo, "Michelangelo Antonioni: Identificazione di un autore," *Inquadrature,* no. 3 (1982), p. 36.

24. Jacques Siclier, "Il ritorno del viaggatore," in *Identificazione di una donna,* ed. Aldo Tassone (Turin, 1983), p. 65.

25. Interview by Lietta Tornabuoni, "Antonioni sul mare della futura," *La stampa,* December 19, 1982, p. 3.

Filmography

Based on filmographies in Ian Cameron and Robin Wood, *Antonioni* (London, 1968); Carlo Di Carlo, ed., *Il primo Antonioni* (Bologna, 1973); Carlo Di Carlo, *Michelangelo Antonioni: Identificazione di un autore,* vol. 3 of *Inquadrature* (Ferrara, 1982); and the editions of published screenplays cited in the Selected Bibliography.

Assistant director

1942: **I DUE FOSCARI.** Directed by Enrico Fulchignoni.

1942: **LES VISITEURS DU SOIR.** Directed by Marcel Carné.

1958: **LA TEMPESTA.** Directed by A. Lattuada (second unit).

Director: documentaries

1943–47: **GENTE DEL PO**
Production: I.C.E.T. Photographed by Piero Portalupi. Music by Mario Labroca. Edited by C. A. Chiesa. 9 minutes. ["Partly lost in processing and partly destroyed by humidity when the negative was stored during the last years of the war, the final version was edited in 1947 from barely half the original footage." —Cameron and Wood]

1948: **N.U.—NETTEZZA URBANA**
Production: I.C.E.T. Photographed by Giovanni Ventimiglia. Music by Giovanni Fusco. Organization: Vieri Bigazzi. 9 minutes.

1948–49: **L'AMOROSA MENZOGNA**
Production: Filmus. Photographed by Renato del Frate. Music by Giovanni Fusco. Assistant director: Francesco Maselli. 10 minutes. With: Anna Vita, Sergio Raimondi, Annie O'Hara, Sandro Roberti.

1949: **SUPERSTIZIONE—NON CI CREDO!**
Production: I.C.E.T. Photographed by Giovanni Ventimiglia. Music by Giovanni Fusco. 9 minutes.

1949: **SETTE CANNE, UN VESTITO**
Production: I.C.E.T. Photographed by Giovanni Ventimiglia. Stock music. 10 minutes.

1950: **LA FUNIVIA DEL FALORIA**
Production: Teo Usuelli. Photographed by Goffredo Bellisario e Ghedina. Music by Teo Usuelli. 10 minutes.

1972: **CHUNG KUO CINA**
Production: RAI. Commentary by Andrea Barbato. Photographed by Luciano Tovoli in super sixteen millimeter color. Musical consultation by Luciano Berio. Sound by Giorgio Pallotta. Edited by Franco Arcalli. Assistant director: Enrica Rico. Shot in Peking, Nanking, Suchow, Shanghai, and the province of Hunan in May–June 1972. Shown on RAI television, Channel One, January 23, 1973.

Director: feature films

1950: **CRONACA DI UN AMORE**
Production: Villani Film (Franco Villani, Stefano Caretta). Screenplay by Antonioni, Daniele D'Anza, Silvio Giovaninetti, Francesco Maselli, and Piero Tellini from a story by Antonioni. Photographed by Enzo Serafin. Sets by Piero Filippone. Costumes for Lucia Bosè by Ferdinando Sarmi. Music by Giovanni Fusco (solo saxophone: Marcel Mule). Assistant director: Francesco Maselli. Director of production: Gino Rossi. Shot in and around Milan. First shown at the Biarritz Film Festival, October 1950. Premiere in Rome, November 25, 1950. 96 minutes. With: Lucia Bosè (Paola), Massimo Girotti (Guido), Ferdinando Sarmi (Enrico Fontana), Gino Rossi (detective), Marika Rowsky (model), Rosi Mirafiore (barmaid), Rubi D'Alma.

1952: **I VINTI**
Production: Film Costellazione, S.G.C. (Paris). Story and screenplay: Antonioni, Suso Cecchi D'Amico, Giorgio Bassani, Diego Fabbri, Turi Vasile, and Roger Nimier (French episode). Photographed by Enzo Serafin. Sets by Gianni Polidori. Music by Giovanni Fusco. Edited by Eraldo Da Roma. Assistant directors: Francesco Rosi, Alain Cuny. Director of production: Paolo Moffa. Shot in Rome, London, and Paris, 1952. First shown at the Venice Film Festival, September 4, 1953. 110 minutes. French episode with: Jean-Pierre Mocky (Pierre), Etchika Choureau (Simone), Henri Poirier, André Jacques, Annie Noel, Guy de Meulan. Italian episode with: Franco Interlenghi (Claudio), Anna-Maria Ferrero (Marina), Evi Maltagliati (Claudio's mother), Eduardo Cianelli (Claudio's father), Umberto Spadaro, Gastone Renzelli. British episode with: Peter Reynolds (Aubrey), Fay Compton (Mrs. Pinkerton), Patrick Barr (Kent Watton), Eileen Moore, Raymond Lovell, Derek Tansley, Jean Stuart, Tony Kilshaw, Fred Victor, Charles Irvin.

1953: **LA SIGNORA SENZA CAMELIE**
Production: ENIC (Domenico Forges Davanzati). Screenplay by Antonioni, Suso Cecchi D'Amico, Francesco Maselli, and P. M. Pasinetti from a story by Antonioni. Photographed by Enzo Serafin. Sets by Gianni Polidori. Music by Giovanni Fusco; played by Marcel Mule Saxophone Quintet. Assistant director: Francesco Maselli. Director of production: Vittorio Glori. Shot in Rome, Venice, and Milan, winter 1952–1953. Premiere in Rome, February 1953. 105 minutes. With: Lucia Bosè (Clara Manni), Andrea Cecchi (Gianni Franchi), Gino Cervi (Ercole), Ivan Desny (Nardo Rusconi), Alain Cuny (Lodi), Monica Clay (Simonetta), Anna Carena (Clara's mother), Enrico Glori (director), Laura Tiberti, Oscar Andriani, Elio Steiner, Nino Del Fabbro.

1953: **TENTATO SUICIDIO** (episode of *Amore in Città*)
Production: Faro Film. Story and screenplay by Antonioni, Cesare Zavattini, Aldo Buzzi, Luigi Chiarini, Luigi Malerba, Tullio Pinelli, and Vittorio Veltroni. Photographed by Gianni Di Venanzo. Sets by Gianni Polidori. Music by Mario Nascimbene. Edited by Eraldo Da Roma. Assistant director: Luigi Vanzi. Director of production: Marco Ferreri. Shot in Rome. Premiere in Rome, November 27, 1953. [*Amore in città* was the first film inquiry sponsored by the film magazine *Lo spettatore* run by Zavattini, Riccardo Ghione,

and Marco Ferreri.] 20 minutes. With: the people (nonprofessional actors) who took part in the events reported in the episode.

1955: LE AMICHE

Production: Trionfalcine (Giovanni Addessi). Screenplay by Antonioni, Suso Cecchi D'Amico, and Alba De Cespedes from the story "Tra Donne Sole" by Cesare Pavese. Photographed by Gianni Di Venanzo. Sets by Gianni Polidori. Costumes by the House of Fontana. Music by Giovanni Fusco; guitar played by Libero Tosoni; piano played by Armando Trovajoli. Edited by Eraldo Da Roma. Assistant director: Luigi Vanzi. Director of production: Pietro Notarianni. Shot in Turin. First shown at the Venice Film Festival, September 7, 1955. Premiere in Rome, November 18, 1955. 104 minutes. With: Eleanora Rossi Drago (Clelia), Valentina Cortese (Nene), Gabriele Ferzetti (Lorenzo), Franco Fabrizi (the architect, Cesare Pedoni), Ettore Manni (the architect's assistant, Carlo), Madeleine Fischer (Rosetta Savoni), Yvonne Furneaux (Momina De Stefani), Annamaria Pancani (Mariella), Maria Gambarelli (Clelia's employer), Luciano Volpato (Tony).

1957: IL GRIDO

Production: S.P.A. Cinematografica (Franco Cancellieri) in collaboration with Robert Alexander Productions, New York. Screenplay by Antonioni. Photographed by Gianni Di Venanzo. Sets by Franco Fontana. Costumes by Pia Marchesi. Music by Giovanni Fusco; piano played by Lya De Barberis. Edited by Eraldo Da Roma. Assistant director: Luigi Vanzi. Directors of production: Danilo Marciano, Ralph Pinto. Shot in the Po Valley, Winter 1956–1957. First shown at the Locarno Film Festival, July 14, 1957. Premiere in Rome, November 29, 1957. 116 minutes. With: Steve Cochran (Aldo), Alida Valli (Irma), Betsy Blair (Elvira), Dorian Gray (Virginia), Gabriella Pallotta (Edera), Lynn Shaw (Andreina), Mirna Girardi (Rosina), Gaetano Matteucci, Guerrino Campanili, Pina Boldrini.

1959: L'AVVENTURA

Production: Amato Penn for Cino del Duca, Produzioni Cinematografiche Europee (Rome), and Societé Cinématographique Lyre (Paris). Screenplay by Antonioni, Elio Bartolini, and Tonino Guerra from a story by Antonioni. Photographed by Aldo Scavarda. Sets by Piero Poletto. Costumes by Adriana Berselli. Music by Giovanni Fusco. Sound by Claudio Maielli. Edited by Eraldo Da Roma. Assistant directors: Franco Indovina, Gianni Arduini. Assistant to the director: Jack O'Connell. Director of production: Luciano Perugia. Organization: Angelo Corso. Shot in Rome and Sicily (the Isles of Lipari and Milazzo, Catania, Taormina), September 1959–January 1960. Premiere in Bologna, September 25, 1960. 145 minutes. With: Gabriele Ferzetti (Sandro), Monica Vitti (Claudia), Lea Massari (Anna), Dominique Blanchar (Giulia), Renzo Ricci (Anna's father), James Addams (Corrado), Dorothy De Poliolo (Gloria Perkins), Joe, fisherman from Panarea (old man on the island), Lelio Luttazzi (Raimondo), Giovanni Petrucci, Esmeralda Ruspoli (Patrizia), Professore Cucco (Ettore), Enrico Bologna, Franco Cimino, Giovanni Danesi, Rita Molè, Renato Piciroli, Angela Tommasi Di Lampedusa, Vincenzo Tranchina.

1960: LA NOTTE

Production: Emanuele Cassuto for Nepi-Film (Rome), Silva-Film (Rome), and Sofitedip (Paris). Screenplay by Antonioni, Ennio Flaiano, and Tonino Guerra from a story by Antonioni. Photographed by Gianni Di Venanzo. Sets by Piero Zuffi. Costumes by Biki. Music by Giorgio Gaslini; played by the Quartetto Giorgio Gaslini. Edited by Eraldo Da Roma. Assistant directors: Franco Indovina, Umberto Pelosso. Organization: Roberto Cocco. Director of production: Paolo Frascà. Shot in Milan, July–August 1960. Premiere in Milan, January 24, 1961. 122 minutes. With Marcello Mastroianni (Giovanni Pontano), Jeanne Moreau (Lidia Pontano), Monica Vitti (Valentina Gherardini), Bernhard Wicki (Tommaso), Maria Pia Luzi (patient), Rosy Mazzacurati (Resy), Guido A. Marsan (Fanti),

Gitt Magrini (Signora Gherardini), Vincenzo Corbella (Gherardini), Giorgio Negro (Roberto), Roberta Speroni (Berenice), Ugo Fortunati (Cesarino), Vittorio Bertolini, Valentino Bompiani, Salvatore Quasimodo, Giansiro Ferrata, Roberto Danesi, Ottiero Ottieri.

1962: L'ECLISSE
Production: Robert and Raymond Hakim for Interopa Film, Cineriz (Rome), Paris Film Production (Paris). Screenplay by Antonioni, Tonino Guerra, Elio Bartolini, and Ottiero Ottieri from a story by Antonioni and Guerra. Photographed by Gianni Di Venanzo. Sets by Piero Poletto. Music by Giovanni Fusco; "Eclisse Twist" sung by Mina. Edited by Eraldo Da Roma. Assistant directors: Franco Indovina, Gianni Arduini. Director of production: Danilo Marciano. Shot in Rome and Verona, Autumn 1961. First shown at the Cannes Film Festival, 1962. Premiere in Paris, August 1962. 125 minutes. With: Monica Vitti (Vittoria), Alain Delon (Piero), Lilla Brignone (Vittoria's mother), Francisco Rabal (Riccardo), Louis Seignier (Ercoli), Rossana Rory (Anita), Mirella Ricciardi (Marta), Cyrus Elias (the drunk).

1964: IL DESERTO ROSSO
Production: Antonio Cervi for Film Duemila, Cinematografica Federiz (Rome), Francoriz (Paris). Story and screenplay by Antonioni and Tonino Guerra. Photographed by Carlo Di Palma in Technicolor. Sets by Piero Poletto. Costumes by Gitt Magrini. Music by Giovanni Fusco; sung by Cecilia Fusco; electronic music by Vittorio Gelmetti. Edited by Eraldo Da Roma. Assistant directors: Giovanni Arduini, Flavio Nicolini. Director of production: Ugo Tucci. Shot in Ravenna and Sardinia, October–December 1963. First shown at the Venice Film Festival, 1964. 120 minutes. With: Monica Vitti (Giuliana), Richard Harris (Corrado Zeller), Carlo De Pra (Ugo), Xenia Valderi (Linda), Rita Renoir (Emilia), Aldo Grotti (Max), Giuliano Missirini (radio telescope operator), Lili Rheims (his wife), Valerio Bartoleschi (Giuliana's son), Emanuela Paola Carboni (girl in fable), Bruno Borghi, Beppe Conti, Giulio Cotignoli, Giovanni Lolli, Hiram Mino Madonia, Arturo Parmiani, Carla Ravasi, Ivo Cherpiani, Bruno Scipioni.

1965: PREFAZIONE (episode of *I Tre Volti*)
Production: Dino De Laurentiis. Story and screenplay by Antonioni. Photographed by Carlo Di Palma. Sets and costumes by Piero Tosi. Music by Piero Piccioni. Edited by Eraldo Da Roma. 25 minutes. With: Soraya, Ivano Davoli, Giorgio Sartarelli, Piero Tosi, Dino De Laurentiis, Alfredo De Laurentiis, Ralph Serpe.

1966: BLOW-UP
Production: Bridge Films (Carlo Ponti) for MGM. Executive producer: Pierre Rouve. Screenplay by Antonioni and Tonino Guerra from a short story by Julio Cortázar; English dialogue in collaboration with Edward Bond. Photography by Carlo Di Palma in Metrocolor. Sets by Assheton Gorton; photographic murals by John Cowan. Costumes by Jocelyn Rickards. Music by Herbert Hancock; "Stroll On" by the Yardbirds. Edited by Frank Clarke. Assistant director: Claude Watson. Director of production: Donald Toms. Shot in London and at the MGM studio in Borcham Wood. Premiere in New York, December 1966. 111 minutes. With: Vanessa Redgrave (Jane), David Hemmings (Thomas), Sarah Miles (Patricia), Peter Bowles (Ron), Verushka, Jill Kennington, Peggy Moffitt, Rosaleen Murray, Ann Norman, Melanie Hampshire (models), Jane Birkin, Gillian Hills (teenagers), Harry Hutchinson (antique dealer), John Castle (painter).

1969: ZABRISKIE POINT
Production: Carlo Ponti for MGM. Executive producer: Harrison Starr. Screenplay by Antonioni, Fred Gardner, Sam Shepard, Tonino Guerra, and Clare Peploe. Photography by Alfio Contini in Panavision and Metrocolor. Production designer: Dean Tavoularis. Set decorator: George Nelson. Special effects by Earl McCoy. Music by Pink Floyd; Kaleidoscope; "You've Got the Silver" by the Rolling Stones; "Sugarable" by the Youngbloods;

"Dark Star" by the Grateful Dead; "Dance of Death" by John Fahey; "I Wish I Was a Single Girl Again" by Roscoe Holcomb; "The Tennessee Waltz" by Patti Page. Editing assistant: Franco Arcalli. Sound mixing by Renato Caudieri. Assistant directors: Rina Macrelli and Robert Rubin. Production manager: Don Guest. 110 minutes. With: Mark Frechette (Mark), Daria Halprin (Daria), Rod Taylor (Lee Allen), Paul Fix (cafe owner), G. D. Spradlin (Lee Allen's associate), Bill Garaway (Morty), Kathleen Cleaver (Kathleen), and the Open Theatre of Joe Chaikin.

1975: **THE PASSENGER** (called *Profession: Reporter* in Europe)
Production: Carlo Ponti for MGM (in conjunction with Cinematografica Champion, Rome, Les Films Concordia, Paris, and CIPI Cinematografica, Madrid). Screenplay by Mark Peploe, Peter Wollen, and Antonioni based on a story by Mark Peploe. Photographed by Luciano Tovoli. Sets by Piero Poletto. Edited by Franco Arcalli and Antonioni. Costumes by Louise Stjensward. Production manager: Ennio Onorati. Assistant directors: Enrico Sannia, Claudio Taddei, Enrica Fico. Musical consultant: Ivan Vander. Shot in North Africa, London, Munich, Barcelona, and coastal Spain. 124 minutes. With: Jack Nicholson (David Locke), Maria Schneider (the Girl), Jenny Runacre (Rachel Locke), Ian Hendry (Knight), Stephen Berkoff (Stephen), Ambroise Bia (Achebe), Jose Maria Cafarel (hotel keeper), James Campbell (witch doctor), Manfred Spies (German), Jean Baptiste Tiemele (murderer), Angel Del Pozo (police inspector), Chuck Mulvehill (Robertson).

1980: **IL MISTERO DI OBERWALD**
Production: Sergio Benvenuti, Alessandro von Norman, Giancarlo Bernardoni for RAI. Screenplay by Antonioni and Tonino Guerra based on the play *L'Aigle à deux têtes* by Jean Cocteau. Photographed by Luciano Tovoli in video transferred to thirty-five millimeter film. Sets by Mischa Scandella. Costumes by Vittoria Guaita. Electronic editing by Antonioni and Francesco Grandoni. Consultation for color and electronic effects: Franco De Leonardis. Musical consultation: Guido Turchi, with selections from Richard Strauss, Arnold Schönberg, and Johannes Brahms. Sound: Gianfranco Desideri, Claudio Grandini, Fausto Ancillai, Sandro Peticca, Fiorenza Muller. 129 minutes. With: Monica Vitti (the Queen), Franco Branciaroli (Sebastian), Luigi Diberti (Willenstein), Elisabetta Pozzi (Edith de Berg), Amad Saha Alan (Tony), Paolo Bonacelli (Count of Föhn).

1982: **IDENTIFICAZIONE DI UNA DONNA**
Production: Giorgio Nocella and Antonio Macri for Iter Films and Gaumont S. A. Screenplay by Antonioni, Gerard Brach, and Tonino Guerra based on a treatment by Antonioni. Photographed by Carlo Di Palma. Sets by Andrea Crisanti. Edited by Antonioni. Music by John Foxx, with selections from Peter Bauman, Edoardo Bennato, Claudio Dantes, Hengel Gualdi, Steve Hillage, Mercenaries, Gianna Nannini, Orchestral Maneuvers in the Dark, Tangerine Dream, Alexander Scriabin, and Edvard Grieg. Shot in Rome and environs and in Wales. 128 minutes. With: Tomas Milian (Niccolò Farra), Christine Boisson (Ida), Daniela Silverio (Mavi), Marcel Bozzuffi (Mario), Lara Wendel (the girl in the swimming pool), Veronica Lazar (Carla Farra), Enrica Fico (Nadia), Sandra Monteleoni (Mavi's sister), Giampaolo Saccarola (the gorilla), Itaco Nardulli, Carlos Valles, Sergio Tardioli, Paola Dominguin, Arianna De Rosa, Pierfrancesco Aiello, Maria Stefani d'Amario.

Producer

1955: **UOMINI IN PIÙ.**
For the CIME (Intergovernmental Committee on European Migration), a documentary on overpopulation and emigration from Italy. Directed by Niccolò Ferrari.

Screenwriter

1942: **I DUE FOSCARI** in collaboration with G. Campanile Mancini, Mino Doletti, and Enrico Fulchignoni. Directed by Enrico Fulchignoni.

1942: **UN PILOTA RITORNA** in collaboration with Rosario Leone, Ugo Betti, Massimo Mida, and Gherardo Gherardi. Directed by Roberto Rossellini.

1947: **CACCIA TRAGICA** in collaboration with Giuseppe De Santis, Carlo Lizzani, Cesare Zavattini, Corrado Alvaro, Umberto Barbaro, and Tullio Pinelli. Directed by Giuseppe De Santis.

1952: **LO SCEICCO BIANCO** in collaboration with Federico Fellini and Tullio Pinelli. Directed by Federico Fellini.

Selected Bibliography

This bibliography is based on those of Ian Cameron and Robin Wood, *Antonioni* (London, 1968); Carlo Di Carlo, ed., *Michelangelo Antonioni* (Rome, 1964); the bibliography compiled by Enrico Pratesi and Andrea Vannini in Piero Mechini and Roberto Salvadori, eds., *Rossellini, Antonioni, Buñuel* (Padua, 1973); Carlo Di Carlo, "Michelangelo Antonioni: Identificazione di un autore," *Inquadrature,* no. 3 (1982); and items discovered in my own search. Although I have not been able to see all the articles, I list them for the English-speaking audience, especially titles that reflect Antonioni's own considerable contribution to film criticism and theory. In some cases I have not been able to secure complete bibliographical information. The sum of writings by and about Antonioni is unbelievably vast: by 1964, Di Carlo had counted 1,200 books and articles. I have tried to make a selection among the best of these entries insofar as I was able to find the material myself.

Writings by Antonioni

Screenplays

(See Filmography for names of coauthors. The order of these entries follows, by and large, the order of the dates of the films.)

Il primo Antonioni. Edited by Carlo Di Carlo. Bologna, 1973. [Includes *Gente del Po, N.U., L'amorosa menzogna, Superstizione, Cronaca di un amore.*]
Sei film. Torino, 1974. [Includes an important preface by Antonioni. The six films are *Le amiche, Il grido, L'avventura, La notte, L'eclisse,* and *Il deserto rosso.*]
The Screenplays of Michelangelo Antonioni. Translated by Roger Moore and Louis Brigante. New York, 1963. [Includes *Il grido, L'avventura, La notte,* and *L'eclisse.*]
Il grido. Edited by Elio Bartolini. Bologna, 1957.
L'avventura. Edited by Tommaso Chiaretti. Bologna, 1960; 2d ed., 1977.
L'avventura. Text reconstructed by David Denby; consulting editor, George Amberg; general editor, Robert Hughes. New York, 1969. [Also includes the 1961 *Bianco e nero* interview, "La malattia dei sentimenti," at the Centro Sperimentale and essays on the film by Tommaso Chiaretti, Pierre Billard, George Amberg, Dominique Fernandez, Penelope Houston, Bosley Crowther, John Simon, Dwight MacDonald, Joseph Bennett, and William Pechter.]
La nuit. Translated by Michèle Causse. Paris, 1961. [Includes essays by Bernard Pingaud and Jean Queval.]
L'eclisse. Edited by John Francis Lane. Bologna, 1962. [Includes a "Presentazione" by the editor, a note on "Le parole" by Antonio Guerra, and "Scoperta del cinema" by Ottiero Ottieri.]

Il deserto rosso. Edited by Carlo Di Carlo. Bologna, 1964; 2d ed., 1978. [Includes an impor-
tant essay by Antonioni, "Il bosco bianco," as well as one by the editor, "Il colore dei
sentimenti," and a diary of the production by Flavio Niccolini.]
Blow-Up. In Italian. Turin, 1967.
Blow-Up. Edited by Sandra Wake. New York, 1971. [Includes interviews with Antonioni by
Pierre Billard and Nadine Liber and Antonioni's essay "Reality and *Cinéma Vérité.*"]
Zabriskie Point. In Italian. Bologna, 1970. [With seventy-eight illustrations, many in
color. Contains an introduction by Alberto Moravia, a translation of Antonioni's de-
fense of the film in *Esquire,* and a selection of favorable reviews from America.]
Chung Kuo Cina. Edited by Lorenzo Cuccu. Turin, 1974. [Includes a defense of documen-
tary as a genre by Antonioni.]
The Passenger. With Mark Peploe and Peter Wollen. New York, 1975. [Many black-and-
white frame reproductions. Includes essays by Vincent Canby, Penelope Gilliatt, and
Richard F. Shepard.]
Profession: Reporter. Edited by Carlo Di Carlo. Bologna, 1975. [Differs from the English
version, *The Passenger,* at several points.]
Il mistero di Oberwald. Edited by Gianni Massironi. Turin, 1981. [Includes a statement by
Antonioni, "Quasi una confessione."]
Investigazione di una donna. Edited by Aldo Tassone. Turin, 1983. [Includes essays by
Tassone, Roberto Roversi, and Jacques Siclier.]

Unfilmed Screenplays and Treatments

Terra verde (1940). In *Bianco e nero* 4, no. 10 (October 1940): 57–69. [Inhabitants of a
North Atlantic island must flee their land when they realize that the Gulf Stream is
drifting to the east.]
Scale (Steps) (1950). In *Michelangelo Antonioni,* edited by Carlo Di Carlo (Rome, 1964),
pp. 131–33. [A documentary of vignettes about what happens to people on stairways.]
Uno dei nostri figli (One of Our Sons) (1952). In collaboration with Giorgio Bassani and
Suso Cecchi D'Amico. In *Il primo Antonioni,* edited by Carlo Di Carlo (Bologna, 1973),
pp. 175–84. [Intended as the Italian episode of *I vinti;* censorship prevented its filming.
Available in several sources but most easily accessible in the Di Carlo volume.]
Stanotte hanno sparato (There Was Shooting Tonight) (1953). In *Cinema nuovo,* no. 9
(1953), pp. 246–48.
Le allegre ragazze del '24 (The Light-hearted Girls of 1924) (1956). In *Cinema nuovo,* no.
85 (1956), pp. 362–64. [A comedy to have been shot in color.]
Ida e i porci (Ida and the Pigs) (1956). In collaboration with Ennio De Concini and Rudolfo
Sonego. [Unpublished.]
Makaroni (1958). In collaboration with Tonino Guerra. In *Cinema nuovo,* no. 163 (1963),
pp. 219–28; no. 164 (1963), pp. 299–308; no. 165 (1963), pp. 382–89. [An adaptation of
Ugo Pirro's novel *Le soldatesse* (The [Female] Soldiers). The novel was later filmed as
Le soldatesse by Valerio Zurlini.]
Tecnicamente dolce (Technically Sweet) (1976). Edited with an introduction by Aldo Tassone. Turin, 1976. [Contains many photographs of intended locations.]
Quel bowling sul Tevere (That Bowling Alley on the Tiber). Turin, 1983. [A collection of
thirty-three stories that were also treatments and notes for films never made published
over the years in Italian newspapers and journals. Some of the more important are the
title story, "Un film da fare o da non fare," "Il deserto dei soldi," "Il mondo è un
vecchio sbaglio," "Questo corpo di fango," "La ragazza, il delitto," and "Quattro
uomini in mare."]
In *Identificazione di un autore* (1982), Carlo Di Carlo attributes several other *soggetti* to
Antonioni that other directors developed into films: *Peccato che sia una canaglia* (1955,
directed by A. Blasetti), *La donna più bella del mondo* (1955, directed by R. Z. Leon-

ard), and *La diga sul Pacifico* (1957, directed by René Clement). He also reports that Antonioni collaborated with Visconti on two treatments that were never realized: *Furore* (1945) and *Il processo di Maria Tarkowska* (1945).

Other Writings, Essays, and Interviews

The writings listed here include Antonioni's discussions of the work of other filmmakers and of his own art, including his comments on specific films. The order is chronological; interviewers' names are included only if they appear in a byline. Antonioni is one of the most frequently interviewed of filmmakers. His comments are thoughtful, modest, and interesting and provide an important source of information about his work. The following represents a short selection only.

"Per un film sul fiume Po." *Cinema* (old series), no. 68 (April 1939), pp. 254–57.

"Omaggio a Clair." *Film rivista*, no. 13 (September 13, 1946), p. 4.

"Omaggio a Renoir." *Film rivista*, no. 18 (September 19, 1946), p. 6.

"Il problema del colore." *Bianco e nero* 9, no. 2 (1948): 78ff.

"Marcel Carné, parigino." *Bianco e nero* 9, no. 10 (1948): 17–47; reprinted in *Michelangelo Antonioni*, edited by Carlo Di Carlo (Rome, 1964), pp. 341–60.

"La terra trema." *Bianco e nero* 10, no. 7 (1949): 90–92.

"Miseria e poesia di Charlot." *Cosmopolita; settimanale di vita internazionale* (1944), pp. 22ff.; a shorter version appeared in *Film rivista*, no. 8 (May 1957).

"Suicidi in città." *Cinema nuovo*, no. 31 (1954), p. 156.

"There Must Be a Reason for Every Film." *Film and Filming* 5, no. 9 (April 1959): 11.

"Making a Film Is My Way of Life." *Film Culture*, no. 24 (Spring 1962), pp. 43–45. [Translated from "Fare un film è per me vivere," *Cinema nuovo*, no. 138 (March-April 1959).]

"Questions à Antonioni." *Positif*, no. 30 (1959), pp. 7–10.

Labarthe, André. "Entretien avec Michelangelo Antonioni." *Cahiers du cinéma*, no. 112 (October 1960), pp. 1–14.

Manceaux, Michèle. "An Interview with Antonioni." *Sight and Sound* 30 (Winter 1960/61): 4–11.

"Reflections on the Film Actor." *Film Culture*, nos. 22–23 (Summer 1961), pp. 66–67.

"Direction Noted." *New York Times*, February 18, 1962, sec. II, p. 9. [Comments on *La notte*.]

Alpert, Hollis. "A Talk with Antonioni." *Saturday Review of Literature* 45 (1962): 27, 65. [About *L'eclisse*.]

"A Talk with Michelangelo Antonioni on His Work." *Film Culture*, no. 24 (Spring 1962), pp. 45–61; translated from "La malattia dei sentimenti: Colloquio con Michelangelo Antonioni," *Bianco e nero* 22, nos. 2–3 (February-March 1961): 69–95. [Perhaps Antonioni's most important interview, with the students of the Centro Sperimentale di Cinematografia (Rome), March 1961.]

"Nevrosi, disperazione, e speranza." *Cinema nuovo*, no. 160 (1962), p. 445.

"Come 'vede' un regista." *La stampa*, June 6, 1963; reprinted in *Michelangelo Antonioni*, edited by Carlo Di Carlo (Rome, 1964), pp. 371–73.

"The Event and the Image." *Sight and Sound* 33 (1963/64): 14; translated from "Il 'fatto' e l'immagine," *Cinema nuovo*, no. 164 (1963), pp. 249–50.

"Reality and Cinéma Vérité." *Atlas* 9, no. 2 (February 1965): 122–23; translated by Heather Gordon-Horwood from "La realtà è il cinema-diretto," *Cinema nuovo*, no. 167 (January-February 1964), pp. 8–10.

Manceaux, Michèle. "In the Red Desert." *Sight and Sound* 33 (Summer 1964): 18–19.

"Deserto rosso." *Cahiers du cinéma*, no. 159 (October 1964), p. 14.

Baby, Yvonne. "Entretien avec Antonioni à propos du *Désert rouge.*" *Le monde,* October 28, 1964.
"Preface." In Michelangelo Antonioni, *Sei film* (Turin, 1964), pp. ix–xviii.
"Il colore sarà l'avvenire del cinema." *Cineforum* 4 (1964): 1024.
Godard, Jean-Luc. "Jean-Luc Godard Interviews Michelangelo Antonioni." *Movie,* no. 12 (Spring 1965), pp. 31–34; translated by Elizabeth Kingsley-Rowe from a tape-recorded discussion about *Il deserto rosso* at the Venice Film Festival.
Cinéma 65 100 (1965): 42–44. [Untitled response to a query about then-current French cinema.]
"Risposta all'inchiesta tra registi." *Sipario* 240 (1966): 8.
Reed, Rex. "Interview with Antonioni." *New York Times,* January 1, 1967, sec. II, p. 7. [Antonioni's letter to the editor in response to this article appears in the *New York Times* of January 15, 1967, sec. II, p. 17.]
"Antonioni—English Style." In Michelangelo Antonioni, *Blow-Up,* edited by Sandra Wake (New York, 1971), pp. 14–17; translated from "Antonioni à la mode anglaise," *Cahiers du cinéma,* no. 186 (January 1967), pp. 13–15.
Liber, Nadine. "Antonioni Talks About His Work." *Life,* January 27, 1967, pp. 66–67; reprinted in Michelangelo Antonioni, *Blow-Up,* edited by Sandra Wake (New York, 1971), pp. 18–20.
"L'arte deve tendere a communicare." *Cineforum* 7 (1967): 681.
"Moravia dialoga con Antonioni." In *Antonioni/Cortázar: Blow-Up,* edited by Daniel Mario Lopéz and Alberto Eduard Ojam (Buenos Aires, 1968), pp. 94–104.
Youngblood, Gene. "Antonioni." *Rolling Stone,* March 1, 1969, pp. 15–18.
Leprohon, Pierre. *Michelangelo Antonioni,* 2d ed. (London, 1969). [Includes a selection of pronouncements on the cinema by Antonioni.]
"Lettera testimonianza." *Cinema nuovo,* no. 200 (1969), p. 287.
"Licenziosità come ribellione (lettera aperta a Gian Luigi Polidaro)." *Cinema nuovo,* no. 202 (1969), pp. 414–15.
"Let's Talk About *Zabriskie Point.*" *Esquire* 74 (August 1970): 68–69, 145–48.
Samuels, Charles. "Interview with Antonioni." *Vogue* 155 (March 15, 1970): 96, 131–34.
Samuels, Charles. "An Interview with Antonioni." *Film Heritage* 5 (Spring 1970): 1–12.
Mancini, Michele, Alessandro Cappabianca, Ciriaco Tiso, and Jobst Grapow. "Conversazione con Michelangelo Antonioni." *Filmcritica* 26, no. 252 (1975): 58–63.
"Il 'reporter' che non avete visto." *Corrière della sera,* October 26, 1975.
Bachmann, Gideon. "Antonioni After China: Art Versus Science." *Film Quarterly* 28 (Summer 1975): 26–30.
"Michelangelo Antonioni Speaks Out." *American Cinematographer* 57 (February 1976): 158–59, 173.
Miccichè, Lino. "Antonioni visto da Antonioni." Interview for RAI television, 1980; unpublished typescript of thirteen pages.
Mori, Anna Maria. "Identificazione di una donna nei 'volgare' mondo di oggi." *La repubblica,* November 18, 1980.
"Dal colore dei sentimenti all nuova tecnica: Antonioni conversa con Carlo Di Carlo." In *Catalogo della rassegna: Tutto Antonioni in 13 giorni,* edited by Vittorio Boarini (Bologna, 1980), pp. 13–16. [A discussion of the opportunities for color mixing in video production apropos *Il mistero di Oberwald.*]
Cuel, François, and Bruno Villien. "Michelangelo Antonioni." *Cinématographe* 72 (November 1981): 2–7.
Daney, Serge, and Serge Toubiana. "La méthode de Michelangelo Antonioni." *Cahiers du cinéma,* no. 342 (December 1982), pp. 6–7, 61–65.
"Difende 'L'identificazione' poi Antonioni salpa in yacht." *Giornale,* October 28, 1982.
Tornabuoni, Lietta. "Antonioni sul mare della futura." *La stampa,* December 19, 1982, p. 3.
Bachmann, Gideon. "A Love of Today: An Interview with Michelangelo Antonioni." *Film Quarterly* 36 (Summer 1983): 1–4. [On *Identificazione di una donna.*]

Articles and Books About Antonioni

Amengual, Barthelemy. "Dimensions existentialistes de *La notte*." *Études cinématographiques*, nos. 36–37 (1964), pp. 47–65.

Amerio, Piero. "Antonioni: Appunti per una psicologia dell'irrelevant." In Carlo Di Carlo, *Michelangelo Antonioni* (Rome, 1964), pp. 45–66.

Andrew, J. Dudley. "The Stature of Objects in Antonioni's Films." *Tri-Quarterly* 11 (1968): 40–61.

Aprà, Adriano. "I tre volti." *Filmcritica*, no. 154 (1965), p. 136.

Arbasino, Alberto. "Alien Corn." *Atlas* 5, no. 1 (January 1963): 13–17.

Aristarco, Guido. "Cronache di una crisi e forme strutturale dell'anima." *Cinema nuovo*, no. 149 (1961), pp. 42–52. [On the literary roots of Antonioni's art in Flaubert, Proust, and Joyce.]

———. "L'evoluzione di Antonioni in *Zabriskie Point*." *Cinema nuovo*, no. 205 (1970), pp. 205–10.

———. "La donna nel deserto di Antonioni." *Cinema nuovo*, no. 173 (1965), pp. 12–15.

———. "*La notte* and *L'avventura*." *Film Culture*, no. 24 (Spring 1962), pp. 82–83.

———. "Un univers en voie de réification." *Études cinématographiques*, nos. 36–37 (1964), pp. 66–80.

Arnheim, Rudolf. *Art and Visual Perception*. Berkeley, 1969.

———. *The Dynamics of Architectural Form*. Berkeley, 1977.

Atwell, Lee. "The Passenger." *Film Quarterly* 28 (Summer 1975): 56–61.

Bachmann, Gideon. "Antonioni: The Creative Use of Reality." *London Times*, April 23, 1975, pp. 14–15.

———. "Antonioni Down Under." *Sight and Sound* 45 (Autumn 1976): 224. [Early work on *The Crew*.]

Baldelli, Pio. *Cinema dell'ambiguità; Bergman e Antonioni*. 2d ed. Rome, 1971.

Barthelme, Donald. "L'Lapse." *The New Yorker*, March 2, 1963, pp. 29–31. [A parody.]

Barthes, Roland. "Caro Antonioni." In *Catalogo della rassegna: Tutto Antonioni in 13 giorni*, edited by Vittorio Boarini (Bologna, 1980), pp. 3–4.

Bassani, Giorgio. "Michelangelo Antonioni e il diritto alla solitudine." *Cinema nuovo*, no. 186 (1967), pp. 88–90.

Baumbach, Jonathan. "From A to Antonioni: Hallucinations of a Movie Addict." In *Man and the Movies*, edited by W. R. Robinson (Baltimore, 1971), pp. 169–79.

Bennett, Joseph. "The Essences of Being." *Hudson Review* 14 (1961): 432–36. [On *L'avventura*.]

Benoit, Claude. "*Profession: Reporter*." *Jeune cinéma* 89 (1975): 35–38.

Bergala, Alain. "L'exercice et la répétition." *Cahiers du cinéma*, no. 342 (December 1982), pp. 8–11.

Bernardini, Aldo. *Michelangelo Antonioni da "Gente del Po" a "Blow-Up."* Milan, 1967. [Contains a valuable anthology of quotations from Antonioni's critical pronouncements, 1939–1965.]

Biasin, Gian-Paolo. *The Smile of the Gods: A Thematic Study of Cesare Pavese's Work*. Ithaca, N.Y., 1968.

"Blow-Up." *Film Facts* 9 (January 1967): 301–4.

Boarini, Vittorio, ed. *Catalogo della rassegna: Tutto Antonioni in 13 giorni*. Bologna, 1980. [Catalogue for a retrospective at the Cinema Tiffany, Bologna, January–February 1980.]

Bondanella, Peter. *Italian Cinema from Neorealism to the Present*. New York, 1983.

Bonitzer, Pascal. "Désir désert (*Profession: Reporter*)." *Cahiers du cinéma*, nos. 262–63 (1976), pp. 95–98.

Bonnot, Gerard. "La nuit d'Antonioni et l'agonie de l'amour courtois." *Les temps modernes* 16, no. 180 (April 1961): 1362–74. [On *La notte*.]

Borden, Diane M. "Antonioni and Architecture." *Mise-en-Scène* 2 (1980): 23–26.

Bresson, Robert. *Notes on Cinematography*. Translated by Jonathan Griffin. New York, 1977.

Brunetta, Giampiero. "*Le amiche:* Pavese e Antonioni dal romanzo al film." In G. Brunetta, *Forma e parole nel cinema* (Padua, 1970).

Bruno, Edoardo. "La Cina di Antonioni." *Filmcritica*, no. 231 (1973), pp. 12–13.

———. "Une réalité déshumanisée." *Études cinématographiques*, nos. 36–37 (1964), pp. 82–84.

Buffa, Michelangelo. "Lo sguardo/ripresa di '*Professione: Reporter.*'" *Filmcritica*, no. 252 (1975), pp. 77–78.

Burch, Noël. *Theory of Film Practice*. Translated by Helen Lane. New York, 1973.

Burks, John. "Fourteen Points to Zabriskie." *Rolling Stone*, March 7, 1970, pp. 36–39.

Butor, Michel. "Rencontre avec Antonioni." *Les lettres françaises*, no. 880 (June 1961), pp. 15–21.

Cadbury, William. *Film Criticism: A Counter Theory*. Ames, Iowa, 1982. [Contains an analysis of *L'avventura, La notte,* and *L'eclisse*.]

Callenbach, Ernest. "Zabriskie Point." *Film Quarterly* 23 (Spring 1970): 35–38.

Cameron, Ian, and Robin Wood. *Antonioni*. London, 1968.

Canby, Vincent. "Antonioni's Haunting Vision." *New York Times*, April 20, 1975, pp. D1, D15. [On *The Passenger*.]

Caprana, Valerio. "L'impossible gioco di Antonioni." *Mattino*, October 23, 1982.

Carpi, Fabio. *Michelangelo Antonioni*. Parma, 1958.

Cavani, Liliana. "*L'avventura, La notte,* e la critica." *Studium* 3 (1961): 195–98.

Chatman, Seymour. "The Rhetoric of Difficult Fiction: Cortázar's 'Blow-Up.'" *Poetics Today* 1 (1980): 23–66.

———. *Story and Discourse*. Ithaca, 1978.

Chiaretti, Tommaso. "Problemi stilistici in Antonioni." *Centrofilm*, nos. 36–37 (1965), pp. 21–49.

Cocteau, Jean. *L'aigle à deux têtes*. In Jean Cocteau, *Théâtre II* (Paris, 1948), pp. 298–415.

Cohen, Hubert I. "Re-sorting Things Out." *Cinema Journal* 10 (1971): 43–45. [On *Blow-Up*.]

Colombo, Furio. "Visual Structure in a Film by Antonioni." Translated by Patrizio Rossi and Garrett Stewart. *Quarterly Journal of Film Studies* 2 (1977): 427–32.

Corbucci, Gianfranco. "*Chung Kuo Cina.*" *Cinema nuovo*, no. 222 (1973), pp. 133–34.

Cortázar, Julio. "Blow-Up." In J. Cortázar, *End of the Game and Other Stories*, translated by Paul Blackburn (New York, 1967), pp. 100–115.

Cowie, Peter. *Antonioni, Bergman, Resnais*. New York, 1963.

Cremonini, Giorgio. "*I tre volti.*" *Cinema nuovo*, no. 175 (1965), pp. 204–5.

Cuccu, Lorenzo. *La visione come problema: Forme e svolgimento del cinema di Antonioni*. Rome, 1973.

Decaux, Emmanuel. "Le mystère d'Oberwald." *Cinèmatographe* 61 (October 1980): 61–62.

"Dibattito su *L'eclisse*." In *Michelangelo Antonioni*, edited by Carlo Di Carlo (Rome, 1964), pp. 87–118.

Di Carlo, Carlo, ed. *Michelangelo Antonioni*. Rome, 1964. [A collection of important essays on Antonioni and a 1,200-item bibliography up to 1963; some items are quoted at length. Di Carlo contributes a survey of Antonioni's career by way of introduction, pp. 8–41.]

Di Carlo, Carlo. "Michelangelo Antonioni: Identificazione di un autore; Gli anni della formazione e la critica su Antonioni." *Inquadrature: Quaderni di cinema*, no. 3 (1982), whole issue.

Dick, Bernard F. "*The Passenger* and Literary Existentialism." *Literature/Film Quarterly* 5 (1977): 66–74.

Di Giammatteo, Fernaldo, and Giorgio Tinazzi. *Michelangelo Antonioni*. Padua, 1961.

Eco, Umberto. "Antonioni 'impegnato.'" In *Michelangelo Antonioni,* edited by Carlo Di Carlo (Rome, 1964), pp. 67–71.

―――. "De Interpretatione, or the Difficulty of Being Marco Polo." Translated by Christine Leefeldt. *Film Quarterly* 30 (Summer 1977): 8–12. [On *Chung Kuo Cina.*]

Elkaim, Arlette. "*L'avventura.*" *Les temps modernes* 16, no. 178 (February 1961): 1038–43.

Ente Autonomo Espozione Universale di Roma (EUR). *Relazione sull' attività svolta nel decennio (1951–1961).* Rome, 1962. [Contains photographs of the EUR at the time *L'eclisse* was being shot.]

Farabet, René. "L'acteur, ce 'Cheval de Troie.'" *Études cinématographiques,* nos. 36–37 (1964), pp. 34–39.

Farber, Manny. "White Elephant Art Versus Termite Art." *Film Culture,* no. 27 (Winter 1962–1963), pp. 9–13. [On *L'avventura* and *La notte.*]

Fernández, Henry. "*Blow-Up* from Cortázar to Antonioni: Study of an Adaptation." *Film Heritage* 4 (Winter 1968–1969): 26–30.

Ferrara, Giuseppe. "Antonioni e la critica (bibliografia ragionato)." *Bianco e nero* 18, no. 9 (1957): 57–71. [An annotated bibliography.]

Ferrero, Adelio. "Da *L'avventura* a *L'eclisse:* 'La presenza' di Antonioni nel cinema italiano." *Cinestudio* 5 (1962): 1–17.

Ferrua, Pietro. "*Blow-Up* from Cortázar to Antonioni." *Literature/Film Quarterly* 4 (1976): 68–75.

Fink, Guido. "Antonioni et le film policier à l'envers." Translated by Jean Bastaire. *Études cinématographiques,* nos. 36–37 (1964), pp. 7–16.

―――. "*Il deserto rosso:* La réalité acceptée." Translated by François Debreczeni. *Études cinématographiques,* nos. 36–37 (1964), pp. 92–97.

―――. Giampaolo Bernagozzi, Gian Piero Brunetta, Leonardo Quaresima, and Giorgio De Vicenti. *Michelangelo Antonioni: Identificazione di un autore.* Parma, 1983. [Contains papers presented at a conference in Ferrara, December 1982.]

Garis, Robert. "Watching Antonioni." *Commentary* 43, no. 4 (April 1967): 86–89.

Giacomelli, A. M., and I. Saitta. *La crisi dell'uomo e della società nei film di Visconti ed Antonioni.* Alba, 1972.

Gilliat, Penelope. "About Reprieve." *The New Yorker,* April 14, 1975, pp. 112–19. [On *The Passenger.*]

Gilman, Richard. "About Nothing—with Precision." *Theater Arts* 46, no. 7 (July 1962): 10–12. [On *L'eclisse.*]

Gilson, René. "Michelangelo Antonioni, de *Gente del Po* à *Il grido.*" *Les temps modernes* 14, no. 158 (April 1959): 1662–72.

Gliserman, Marty. "*The Passenger:* An Individual in History." *Jump Cut* 8 (1975): 1–8.

Gombrich, E. H. "Standards of Truth: The Arrested Image and the Moving Eye." In *The Language of Images,* edited by W. J. T. Mitchell (Chicago, 1980), pp. 181–90.

Gow, Gordon. "Antonioni Men." *Films and Filming* 16, no. 9 (June 1970): 41–46.

―――. "Michelangelo Antonioni's Film *Zabriskie Point.*" *Films and Filming* 21, no. 10 (July 1975): 32–37.

Grande, Maurizio. "La condizione estetica tra lettura e semiosi (a proposito di *Professione: Reporter*)." *Filmcritica,* no. 252 (1975), pp. 68–73.

Gyurko, Lanin A. "Hallucination and Nightmare in Two Stories by Cortázar." *Modern Language Review* 67 (1972): 550–62.

―――. "Truth and Deception in Cortázar's 'Las Babas Del Diablo.'" *Romanic Review* 63 (1972): 204–17.

Handzo, Stephen. "Michelangelo in Disneyland." *Film Heritage* 6 (Fall 1970): 7–24.

Hernacki, Thomas. "Michelangelo Antonioni and the Imagery of Disintegration." *Film Heritage* 5 (Spring 1970): 12–21.

Hines, Kay. "Three Sequences from *Blow-Up:* A Shot Analysis." *Film* 5 (June 1967):

135–40. [Also in *Focus on Blow-Up*, edited by Roy Huss (Englewood Cliffs, N.J., 1971).]

Holland, Norman. "Not Having Antonioni." *Hudson Review* 16 (1963): 89–95.

Houston, Penelope. *"L'avventura." Sight and Sound* 30 (Winter 1960/61): 11–13.

———. "Keeping Up with the Antonionis." *Sight and Sound* 33 (Autumn 1964): 163–68.

———. "The Landscape of the Desert." *Sight and Sound* 34 (Spring 1965): 80–81, 103.

———. "Michelangelo Antonioni." In *Cinema: A Critical Dictionary*, ed. Richard Rond (New York, 1980), 1:83–95.

Huss, Roy, ed. *Focus on Blow-Up*. Englewood Cliffs, N.J., 1971. [Contains essays by Huss, Kauffmann, Kozloff, Freccero, and others; a plot outline; and a shot analysis.]

Huss, Roy, and Norman Silverstein. *The Film Experience*. New York, 1968. [Contains discussion of *Il deserto rosso*.]

Isaacs, Neil D. "The Triumph of Artifice: Antonioni's *Blow-Up* 1966." In *Modern European Filmmakers and the Art of Adaptation*, edited by A. Horton and J. Magretta (New York, 1981), pp. 130–44.

Jebb, Julian. "Intimations of Reality: Getting the Zabriskie Point." *Sight and Sound* 39 (Summer 1970): 124–26.

Johnson, Lincoln F. *Film: Space, Time, Light, and Sound*. New York, 1974. [Contains many frames in color from *Il deserto rosso*.]

Kael, Pauline. "The Beauty of Destruction." *The New Yorker*, February 21, 1970, pp. 95–99. [On *Zabriskie Point*.]

———. "Tourist in the City of Youth." In P. Kael, *Kiss Kiss Bang Bang* (New York, 1965), pp. 31–37. [On *Blow-Up*.]

Kauffmann, Stanley. "Antonioni." *The New Republic* 172 (April 19, 1975): 22, 34. [On *The Passenger*.]

———. "The Artist Advances." In *Renaissance of the Film*, edited by Julius Bellone (New York, 1970), pp. 211–17. [On *Il deserto rosso*.]

———. "A Year With *Blow-Up*: Some Notes." In *Film 1967–68*, edited by Richard Schickel and John Simon (New York, 1968), pp. 274–81.

———. *"Zabriskie Point." The New Republic* 162 (March 14, 1970): 20, 31.

Kawin, Bruce. *Mindscreen*. Princeton, N. J., 1978.

Kinder, Marsha. "Antonioni in Transit." *Sight and Sound* 36 (Summer 1967): 132–37. [On *Blow-Up*.]

———. *"Zabriskie Point." Sight and Sound* 38 (Winter 1968/69): 26–30.

Kinder, Marsha, and Beverle Houston. "Blow-Up." In M. Kinder and B. Houston, *Close-Up: A Critical Perspective on Film* (New York, 1972), pp. 255–62.

Knight, Arthur. *"Blow-Up." Film Heritage* 2 (1967): 3–5.

Kozloff, Max. "The Blow-Up." In *Focus on Blow-Up*, edited by Roy Huss (Englewood Cliffs, N.J., 1971), pp. 58–63; first published in *Film Quarterly* 20, no. 3 (Spring 1967): 28–31.

Lane, John Francis. "Antonioni Diary: A Day-to-Day Record of Work on *The Eclipse*." *Films and Filming* 8, no. 6 (March 1962): 11–12, 46.

Lawson, Sylvia. "Notes on Antonioni." *Sydney Cinema Journal* 2 (1966): 9–18.

Leprohon, Pierre. *Michelangelo Antonioni*. Translated by Scott Sullivan. 2d ed. New York, 1969.

Lesser, Simon O. *"L'Avventura: A Closer Look." Yale Review* 54 (1964): 41–50.

Lockerbie, Ian. "La difficulté d'être." *Études cinématographiques*, nos. 36–37. (1964), pp. 85–91. [On *L'eclisse*.]

Lotman, Jurij. "Problems of Semiotics." In J. Lotman, *Semiotics of Cinema*, translated by Mark E. Suino (Ann Arbor, 1976), pp. 97–105. [On *Blow-Up*.]

Lyons, Robert J. *Michelangelo Antonioni's Neo-Realism: A World View*. New York, 1976.

MacDonald, Dwight. *Dwight Macdonald on Movies*. Englewood Cliffs, N.J., 1969. [Contains essays on *L'eclisse* and *Il deserto rosso*.]

Macklin, Anthony. *"Zabriskie Point." Film Heritage* 3 (1970): 22–25.

Mancini, Michele. "Il corpo e la favola (Antonioni, Straub-Huillet)." *Filmcritica,* no. 252 (1975), pp. 84–88.

Martin, Marcel. "Antonioni: En souvenir de Conrad." *Écran,* no. 51 (1976), pp. 2–3. [On the Australian project anticipating *The Crew.*]

Mechini, Piero, and Roberto Salvadori, eds. *Rossellini, Antonioni, Buñuel.* Padua, 1973. [Contains articles on Antonioni by Adelio Ferrero and Giorgio Tinazzi and an excellent bibliography by Enrico Pratesi and Andrea Vannini of Italian books and articles on Antonioni published between 1964 and 1973.]

Meeker, Hubert. "*Blow-Up.*" *Film Heritage* 2 (1967): 7–15.

Micchichè, Lino. "Sur *Profession: Reporter.*" *Écran,* no. 36 (1975), pp. 46–48.

"Michelangelo Antonioni." *Camera/Stylo* 3 (1982): whole issue. [Contains articles by Bensard, Blum, Bollème, Cany, Collet, Crotta, Farges, Gauville, Helmskin, Hussenot, Joubert, Laigle, Lamoulen, Lauraus, Lockhart, Noquez, Sebbay, and Simsolo, plus French translations of Antonioni's introductions to the screenplays of *Il deserto rosso* and *Chung Kuo Cina.*]

"Michelangelo Antonioni." *Positif,* no. 30 (July 1959): whole issue. [Contains an interview with Antonioni and articles by Antonioni ("Une journée," a journal entry from Nice, 1942), Robert Benayoun, Jacques Demeure, Ado Kyrou, Louis Sequin, Roger Tailleur, P. -L. Thirard, and Glauco Viazza and P. -L. Thirard.]

Micheli, Sergio. "Il personaggio feminile nei film di Antonioni." *Bianco e nero* 28, no. 1 (1967): 1–9.

Il mistero di Oberwald. n.p., 1980. [RAI brochure. Contains articles by Antonioni ("Quasi una confessione") and Massimo Fichera and an interview with Monica Vitti.]

Moravia, Alberto. "E esplosa pure l'arte di Antonioni." In Michelangelo Antonioni, *Zabriskie Point* (Bologna, 1970), pp. 11–17.

———. "Un nuovo sensa della realtà." *L'espresso,* February 26, 1961.

Moses, Gavriel, *Eclipse: Opening Sequence.* New York, 1975.

Nowell-Smith, Geoffrey. "*La notte.*" *Sight and Sound* 31 (Winter 1961/62): 28–31.

———. "Shape Around a Black Point." *Sight and Sound* 33 (Winter 1963/64): 16–20. [On *L'avventura* and *L'eclisse.*]

Ongaro, Alberto. "Antonioni: Nous en savons trop sur le soleil." *Écran,* no. 36 (1975), pp. 42–45.

Paolucci, Anne. "The Italian Film: Antonioni, Fellini, Bolognini." *Massachusetts Review* 7 (1966): 560–62.

Pasolini, Pier Paolo. "The Cinema of Poetry." In *Movie and Methods,* edited by Bill Nichols (Berkeley, 1976), pp. 543–58.

———. *Dialogue en publique.* Edited by B. Ferretti. Paris, 1980.

Pechter, William. "Antonioni '75." *Commentary* 60 (1975): 69–72.

Perrin, Claude. "L'univers fragmenté de *L'avventura.*" *Études cinématographiques,* nos. 36–37 (1964), pp. 40–46.

Perry, Ted. "Men and Landscapes: Antonioni's *The Passenger.*" *Film Comment* 11 (1975): 2–6.

———. "A Contextual Study of Michelangelo Antonioni's Film *L'Eclisse.*" *Speech Monographs* 37 (1970): 79–92.

Pignotti, Lamberto. "Realismo e oggettività di Antonioni." In *Michelangelo Antonioni,* edited by Carlo Di Carlo (Rome, 1964), pp. 72–86.

Pingaud, Bernard. "Antonioni et le cinéma réel." *Preuves,* no. 117 (November 1960), pp. 63–66, reprinted in *Michelangelo Antonioni,* edited by Carlo Di Carlo (Rome, 1964), pp. 214–20.

Ranieri, Tino. *Michelangelo Antonioni.* Trieste, 1958.

Ranvaud, Don. "*Il Mistero di Oberwald.*" *Monthly Film Bulletin* 48 (September 1981): 180.

Reggiani, Stefano. "L'altro occhio della realtà." In *Professione: Reporter,* edited by Carlo Di Carlo (Bologna, 1975), pp. 11–25.

Reisz, Karel, and Gavin Millar. *The Technique of Film Editing.* New York, 1968.

Renzi, Renzo. "Cronache dell'angoscia in Michelangelo Antonioni." *Cinema nuovo,* no. 139 (1959), p. 214.

Rifkin, Ned. *Antonioni's Visual Language.* Ann Arbor, 1982.

Robinson, David. "The Shapes We Make." *London Times,* June 6, 1975, p. 12. [On *The Passenger.*]

Roemer, Michael. "The Surfaces of Reality." In *Perspectives on the Study of Film,* edited by John Katz (New York, 1971), pp. 98–109.

Ropars-Wuilleaumier, Marie-Claire. *L'écran de la mémoire.* Paris, 1970.

———. "L'espace et le temps dans l'univers d'Antonioni." *Études cinématographiques,* nos. 36–37 (1964), pp. 17–33.

Roud, Richard. "*The Passenger.*" *Sight and Sound* 44 (Summer 1975): 134–36.

———. "*The Red Desert.*" *Sight and Sound* 34 (Spring 1965): 76–80.

Salinari, Carlo. *Miti e coscienza del decadentismo italiano.* Milan, 1960.

Samuels, Charles Thomas. "The Blow-Up: Sorting Things Out." *American Scholar* 37 (1967–1968): 120–31.

———. "Puppets: From Z To Zabriskie Point." *American Scholar* 39 (1970): 678–91.

Sarris, Andrew. "An End to Antonioniennui." *The Village Voice,* April 14, 1975, pp. 75–76. [On *The Passenger.*]

———. *Confessions of a Cultist.* New York, 1961. [Contains essays on *Blow-Up* and *Il deserto rosso.*]

Sequin, Louis. "La fin de l'été avec Monica." *Positif,* no. 38 (1961), pp. 12–31. [On *L'avventura.*]

Simon, John. *Movies into Film.* New York, 1971. [Contains an essay on *Zabriskie Point.*]

Simon, John, and others. "Zabriskie: What's the Point?" *Film Heritage* 3 (1970): 26–40.

Slover, George. "*Blow-Up:* Medium, Message, Mythos, and Make-Believe." *Massachusetts Review* 9 (1968): 753–70.

Soby, J. T. *Giorgio de Chirico.* New York, 1955.

Sontag, Susan. "Film and Theatre." In *Film Theory and Criticism,* edited by Marshall Cohen and Gerald Mast (New York, 1974), pp. 249–67.

Spinazzola, Vittorio. "Michelangelo Antonioni regista." In V. Spinazzola, *Film 1961* (Milan, 1961), pp. 29–62.

Stanton, E. F. "Antonioni's *The Passenger:* A Parabola of Light." *Literature/Film Quarterly* 5 (Winter 1977): 57–67.

Stewart, Garrett. "Exhumed Identity: Antonioni's Passenger to Nowhere." *Sight and Sound* 45 (Winter 1975/76): 36–40.

Strick, Philip. "The Antonioni Report." *Sight and Sound* 43 (Winter 1973/74): 30–31. [On *The Passenger.*]

———. *Antonioni.* London, 1963.

Tailleur, Roger, and Paul-Louis Thirard. *Antonioni.* Paris, 1963.

Tassone, Aldo. "*Profession: Reporter.*" *Image et son* 297 (June 1975): 106–9.

Taylor, John Russell. *Cinema Eye, Cinema Ear.* New York, 1964.

Thirard, Paul-Louis. *Michelangelo Antonioni.* Lyons, 1960.

Tilliette, Xavier. "Cadrages sur Antonioni." *Études cinématographiques,* nos. 30–31 (1961), pp. 89–101. [On *La notte.*]

———. "Le mirage et le désert." *Études cinématographiques,* nos. 36–37 (1964), pp. 98–103.

Tinazzi, Giorgio. *Michelangelo Antonioni.* Florence, 1974.

Tiso, Ciriaco. "Prassi e procedimenti narrativi del film." *Filmcritica,* no. 252 (1975), pp. 64–67.

Tomasino, Renato. "Antonioni: Il meta-segno del cinema 'astratto.'" *Filmcritica,* no. 252 (1975), pp. 74–76.

Trebbi, Fernando. *Il testo e lo sguardo.* Bologna, 1976. [On *The Passenger.*]

Tyler, Parker. "Masterpieces by Antonioni and Bergman." In *Film Theory and Criticism,* edited by Marshall Cohen and Gerald Mast (New York, 1974), pp. 43–59. [On *Blow-Up.*]

Voglino, Bruno. *Michelangelo Antonioni.* Turin, 1959.

Volpi, Gianni. "Struttura, tecnica, e stile di *Cronaca di un amore,*" *Centrofilm,* nos. 36–37 (1965), pp. 50–54.

Walsh, Martin. "*The Passenger:* Antonioni's Narrative Design." *Jump Cut* 8 (August–September 1975): 8–13.

Wood, Robin. "*Zabriskie Point.*" *Movie* 18 (1970–1971): 21–23.

Worringer, Wilhelm. *Abstraction and Empathy.* Translated by Michael Bullock. New York, 1953. [Originally published in 1908 as *Abstraktion und Einfühlung.*]

Young, Colin. "*Red Desert.*" *Film Quarterly* 19 (Fall 1965): 51–54.

Zand, Nicole. "Un présent inadapté." *Études cinématographiques,* nos. 36–37 (1964), pp. 104–8. [On *Il deserto rosso.*]

Zorzi, Ludovico, and Lucio Armando. "Cinema: Antonioni e *L'avventura.*" In *Michelangelo Antonioni,* edited by Carlo Di Carlo (Rome, 1964), pp. 379–90.

Zucker, Paul. *Town and Square: From the Agora to the Village Green.* New York, 1959.

Index

Film characters discussed in this book appear in the Index under their first names.

Delon, Alain, 52, 163

De Pra, Carlo, 53, 163

Desert of Money, The (Antonioni), 85

Deserto dei soldi, Il (Antonioni), 85

Deserto rosso, Il (Antonioni), 3, 51, 53, 163, 243, 256; character development in, 43, 90–91, 113, 119–21, 250; cinematic form in, 8, 82, 153; color in, 131–35, 157, 210, 211; point of view in, 97–98, 196, 253; setting in, 16, 36–37, 99, 126–27, 137, 199; sexuality in, 59–60, 68, 164; title imagery of, 70, 73. *See also specific characters*

De Sica, Vittorio, 163, 246

Desny, Ian, 29

Detective, in *Cronaca di un amore,* 12, 74, 76

Diary of a Chambermaid (Buñuel), 262

Diary of a Country Priest (Bresson), 95

Diberti, Luigi, 204

Di Carlo, Carlo, 246, 247, 249

Di Palma, Carlo, 136

Drago, Eleonora Rossi, 33

Dreiser, Theodore, 95

Dreyer, Carl Theodor, 241

Dubliners (Joyce), 101–2

Duke of Willenstein, in *Il mistero di Oberwald,* 204, 212

Dumas, Alexandre, 29

Eclisse, L' (Antonioni), 2, 3, 28, 51, 243; character development in, 84–85, 253; cinematic form in, 81–82, 115, 117, 126, 158; imagery in, 11, 68, 70–73, 99, 223, 250–51; scenic background in, 5, 16–17, 106–12, 113, 219; thematic development in, 8, 52–53, 59–66, 96, 248, 255. *See also specific characters*

Eclipse, The. See *Eclisse, L'*

Eco, Umberto, 174–75, 261

Edera, in *Il grido,* 39

Edith de Berg, in *Il mistero di Oberwald,* 204, 212

8½ (Fellini), 2, 31, 222, 238, 248

Eisenstein, Sergei M., 95–96, 168, 227–28, 241, 259

Eliot, T. S., 47, 90

Elvira, in *Il grido,* 39

"Enchanted Mountains, The" (Antonioni), 255–56

Enrico Fontana, in *Cronaca di un amore,* 12, 15–19

E.T. (Spielberg), 223

Ettore Manni, in *La signora senza camelie,* 33

Ewers, Hanns, 185, 261

Fabbri, Diego, 246

Fabrizi, Franco, 33, 34, 36

Farber, Manny, 255

Farra, Niccolò. *See* Niccolò Farra

"Fatal Exit" (Peploe), 176, 186

Father of Anna, in *L'avventura,* 68–69, 102

Fausto, in *I vitelloni,* 34

Fellini, Federico, 2, 11, 245, 248; cinematic form and, 31, 44, 238; thematic development and, 34, 222, 259, 263

Ferrari, Niccolò, 213, 246

Ferreri, Marco, 26

Ferrero, Anna Maria, 23

Ferzetti, Gabriele, 34, 51, 55

Fink, Guido, 256

Fiore e la violenza, Il (Antonioni, Renoir, Reichenbach), 26

Fischer, Madeleine, 33

Fitzgerald, F. Scott, 253

Flaubert, Gustave, 253

Flower and the Violence, The. See *Fiore e la violenza, Il*

Francesca, Piero della, 115

Freccero, John, 258, 259

Frechette, Mark, 159, 160, 162–63

Frenzy (Hitchcock), 24, 232

Freud, Sigmund, 56, 249

From Mao to Mozart (Lerner), 260

Fu Mattia Pascal, Il (Pirandello), 185

Funicular of Mount Faloria, The (Antonioni), 5, 245

Funivia del Faloria, La (Antonioni), 5, 245

Furneaux, Yvonne, 33

Fusco, Giovanni, 23, 38, 50, 133

Gang of Four, 261

Gauthier, Marguerite, in *Camille,* 29

Genette, Gérard, 262

Gente del Po (Antonioni), 5–11, 24, 39, 40, 60–61, 101

Georges, in *I vinti,* 22

Compositor:	Innovative Media
Text:	10/12 Times Roman
Display:	Helvetica Bold Condensed
Printer:	Maple-Vail Book Mfg. Group
Binder:	Maple-Vail Book Mfg. Group